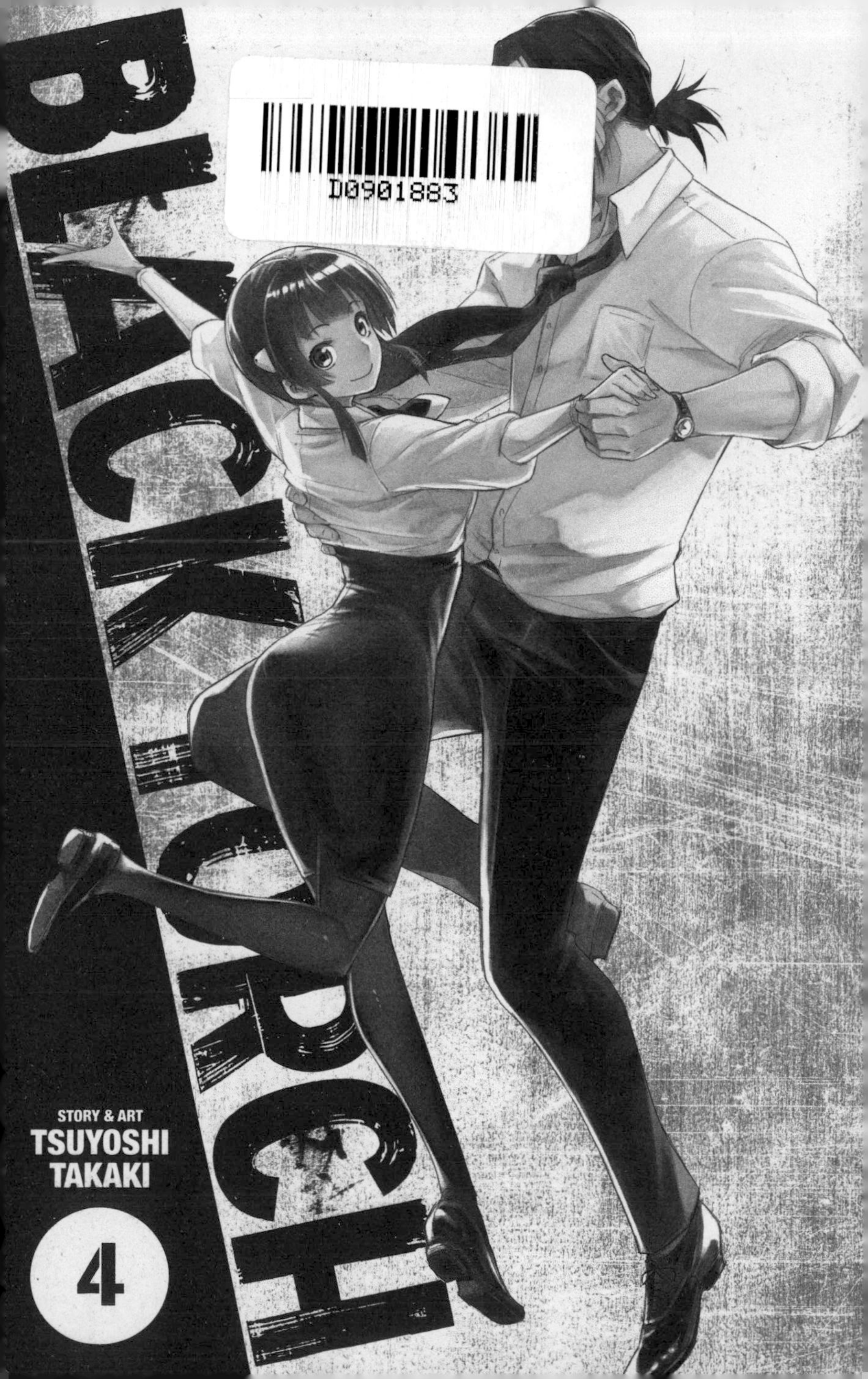
BLACK TORCH
STORY & ART
TSUYOSHI TAKAKI
4

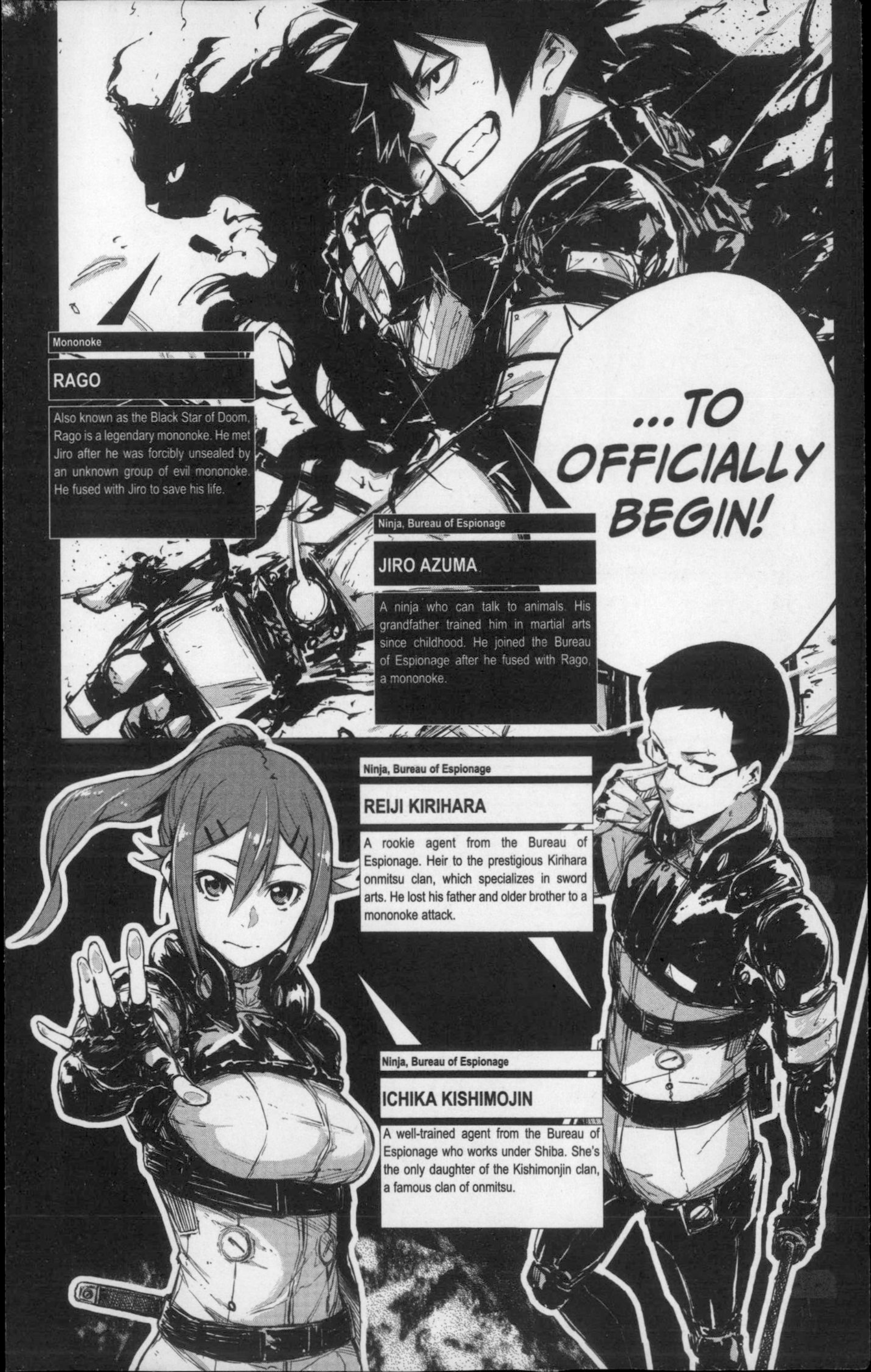
...TO OFFICIALLY BEGIN!
Ninja, Bureau of Espionage
JIRO AZUMA
A ninja who can talk to animals. His grandfather trained him in martial arts since childhood. He joined the Bureau of Espionage after he fused with Rago, a mononoke.
Mononoke
RAGO
Also known as the Black Star of Doom, Rago is a legendary mononoke. He met Jiro after he was forcibly unsealed by an unknown group of evil mononoke. He fused with Jiro to save his life.
Ninja, Bureau of Espionage
REIJI KIRIHARA
A rookie agent from the Bureau of Espionage. Heir to the prestigious Kirihara onmitsu clan, which specializes in sword arts. He lost his father and older brother to a mononoke attack.
Ninja, Bureau of Espionage
ICHIKA KISHIMOJIN
A well-trained agent from the Bureau of Espionage who works under Shiba. She's the only daughter of the Kishimonjin clan, a famous clan of onmitsu.

CHARACTER

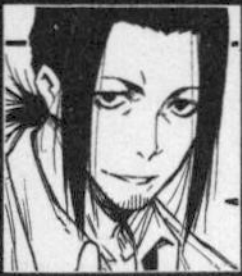

RYOSUKE SHIBA
Ninja, Bureau of Espionage

Chief of Special Operations Division 2 at the Bureau of Espionage, a secret national agency whose mission is the surveillance and disposal of Mononoke. Founder of a new squad, code named Black Torch.

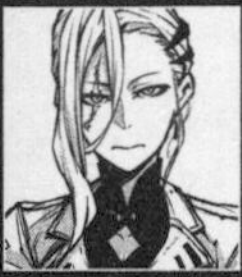

TOKO KUSUMI
Ninja, Bureau of Espionage

Shiba's co-worker and a coldly logical woman, she is Chief of Special Operations Division 1.

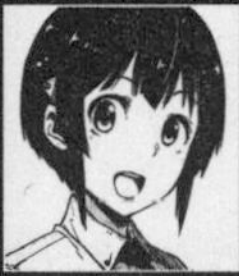

HANA USAMI
Ninja, Bureau of Espionage

One of Shiba's few subordinates, she is a backup member of Black Torch.

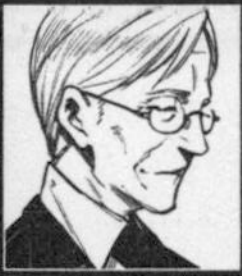

BANJURO TOKIEDA
Ninja, Bureau of Espionage

A capable lieutenant to Kusumi, he can do everything from chauffeur to participate in active battle.

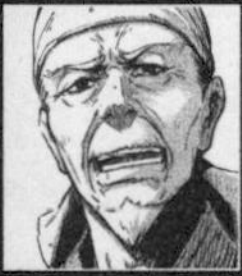

HANA USAMI
Former Ninja, Bureau of Espionage

Jiro's grandfather. Descendant of a long line of ninja, he is a former member of the Bureau of Espionage.

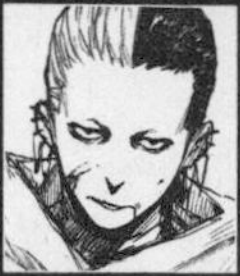

AMAGI

The mastermind behind the current mononoke attacks. Asked Rago to join him back in the Edo period, but Rago refused.

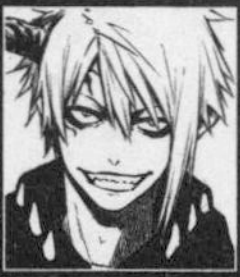

KOUGA

A mononoke. Young and hotheaded, he wants Rago to be his partner.

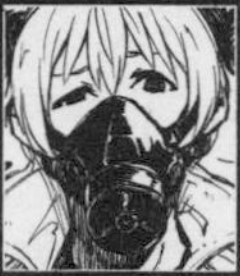

ROREN

A mononoke with the power of illusion. Ichika defeated him in battle by cutting off his horn.

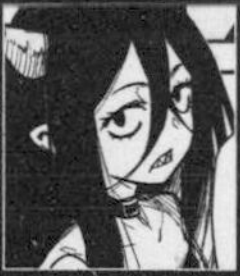

NARUKO

A mononoke capable of creating strong barriers. Will fall asleep wherever she's standing if she's tired.

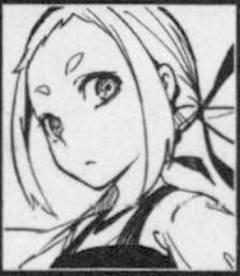

FUYO

A mononoke that looks like a little girl. An ally to humans, she helps Shiba out with various training activities.

STORY

Jiro Azuma, a descendant from a long line of ninja, meets Rago, a mononoke that looks like a small, black cat. After a series of mishaps, Jiro and Rago fuse together and, through an invitation from Ryosuke Shiba, join the secret organization called the Bureau of Espionage to become founding members of the Onmitsu squad called Black Torch.

During an anti-mononoke training session, Jiro and Rago are shown a vision of the Edo period. There they meet a mononoke named Amagi and learn he was the one who had Rago unsealed from his prison.

Days later, a string of mysterious murders is revealed to be the work of mononoke, and Black Torch is given the order to act. Sent alone into the haunted town, the three members of Black Torch quickly run across the mononoke responsible and the battle begins!

Ichika handily defeats the mononoke Roren, but Reiji is forced to fight the monster that his brother has become and is gravely wounded. Meanwhile, Jiro and Rago take out Kanawa, but in the process Rago becomes aware of a horrifying truth—in exchange for granting Jiro his powers, he has been unwittingly devouring Jiro's vital energy this entire time! Before Rago can tell this to Jiro, the two are confronted by Amagi himself. Jiro tries to fight, but is crushed in a single blow. In complete control, Amagi delivers an ultimatum to Rago—if he wants to save Jiro's life, he must swear his undying loyalty to Amagi!

CONTENTS 4

BLACK TORCH

#12 My Prerogative

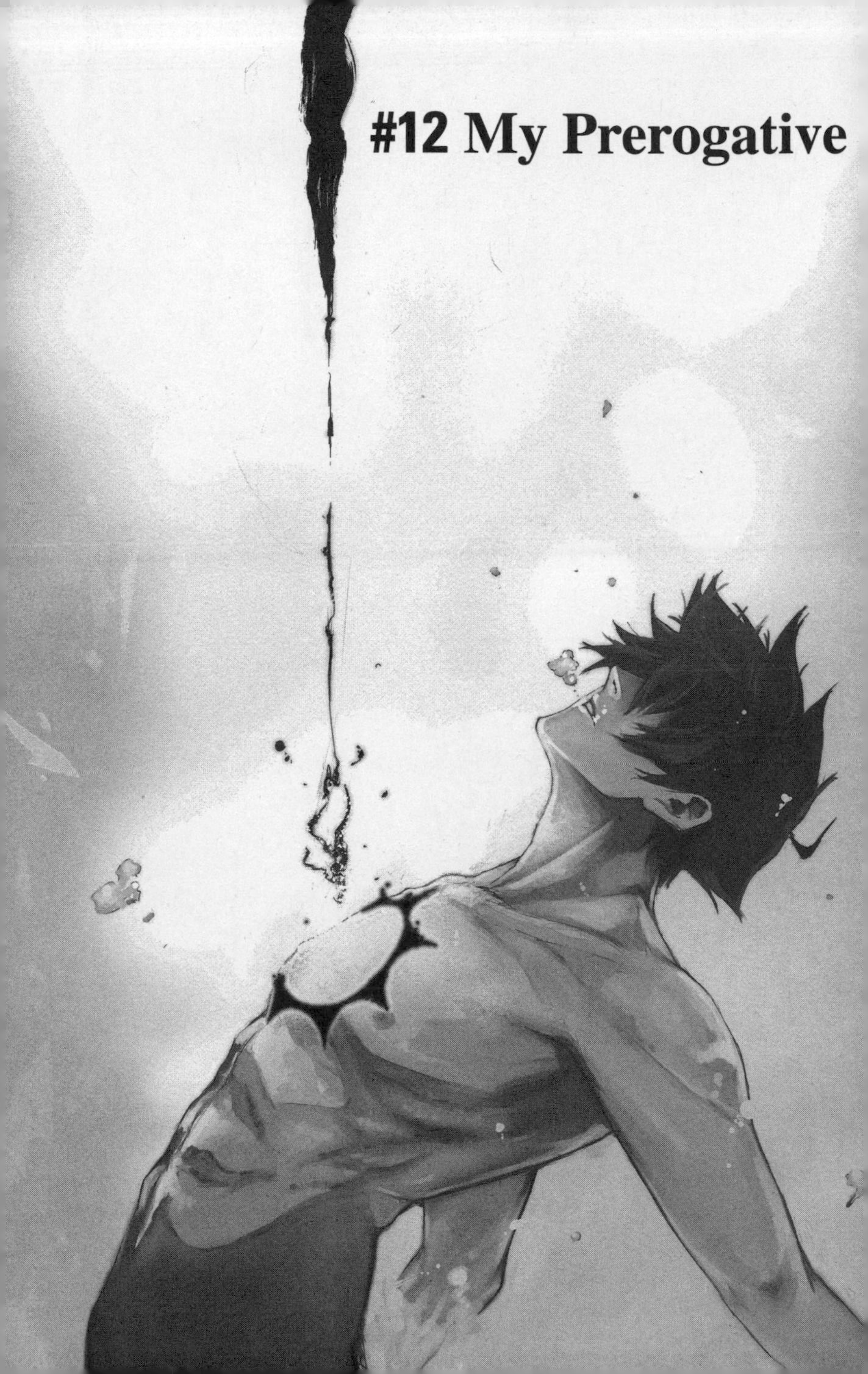

BLACK TORCH

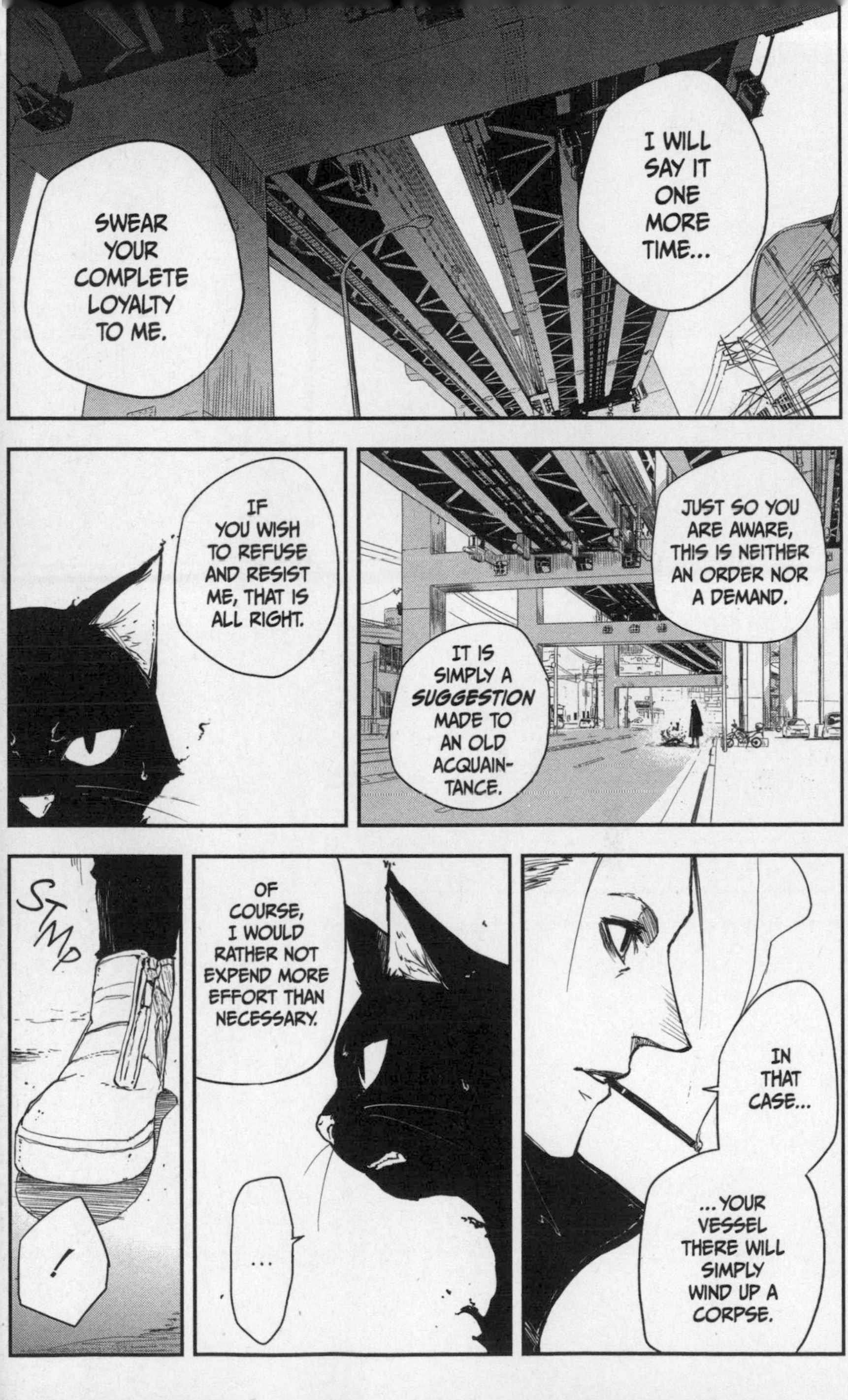
I WILL SAY IT ONE MORE TIME...
SWEAR YOUR COMPLETE LOYALTY TO ME.
JUST SO YOU ARE AWARE, THIS IS NEITHER AN ORDER NOR A DEMAND.
IT IS SIMPLY A *SUGGESTION* MADE TO AN OLD ACQUAIN-TANCE.
IF YOU WISH TO REFUSE AND RESIST ME, THAT IS ALL RIGHT.
IN THAT CASE...
...YOUR VESSEL THERE WILL SIMPLY WIND UP A CORPSE.
OF COURSE, I WOULD RATHER NOT EXPEND MORE EFFORT THAN NECESSARY.
...
STMP
!

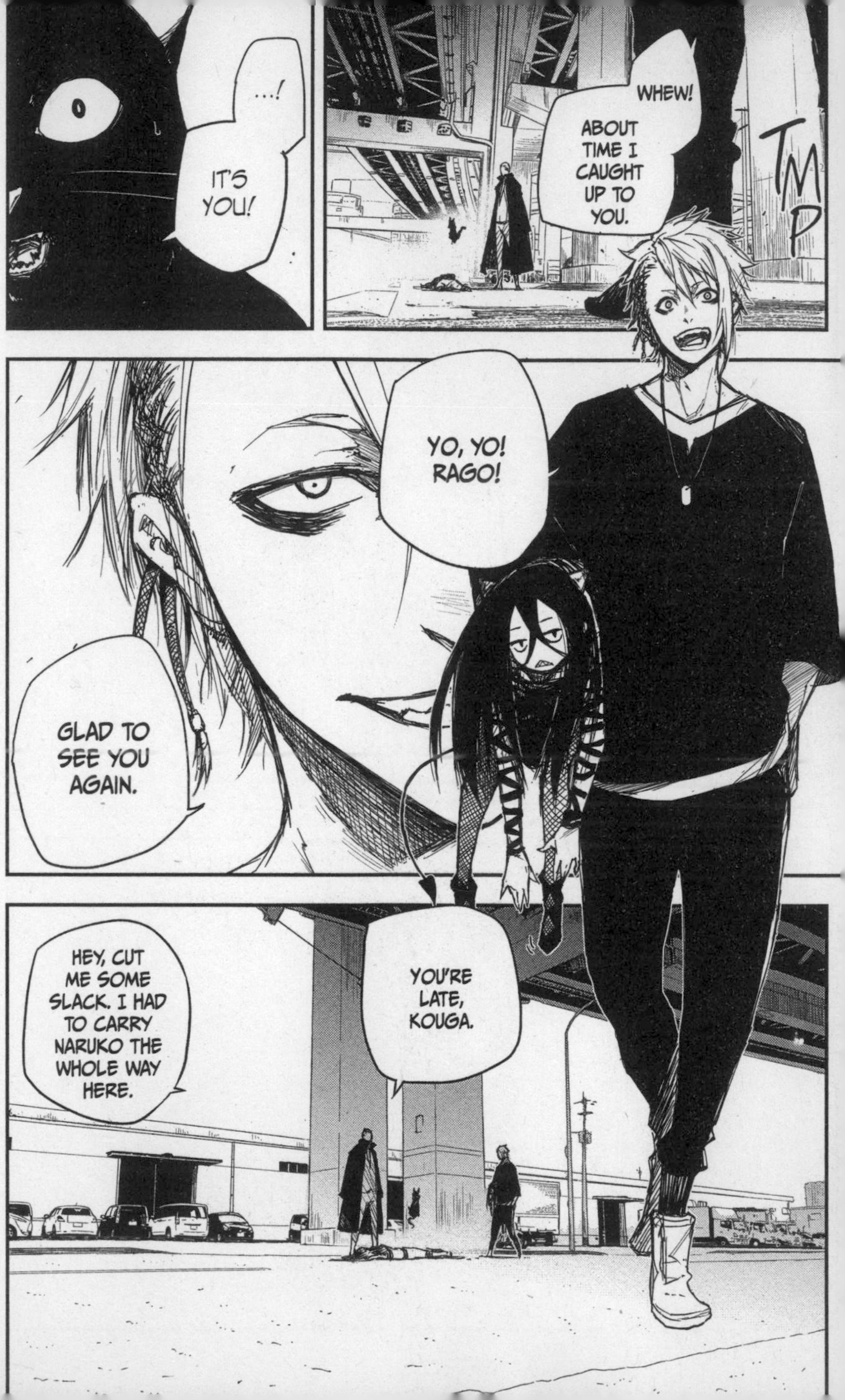
WHEW! ABOUT TIME I CAUGHT UP TO YOU.
TMP
...! IT'S YOU!
YO, YO! RAGO!
GLAD TO SEE YOU AGAIN.
YOU'RE LATE, KOUGA.
HEY, CUT ME SOME SLACK. I HAD TO CARRY NARUKO THE WHOLE WAY HERE.

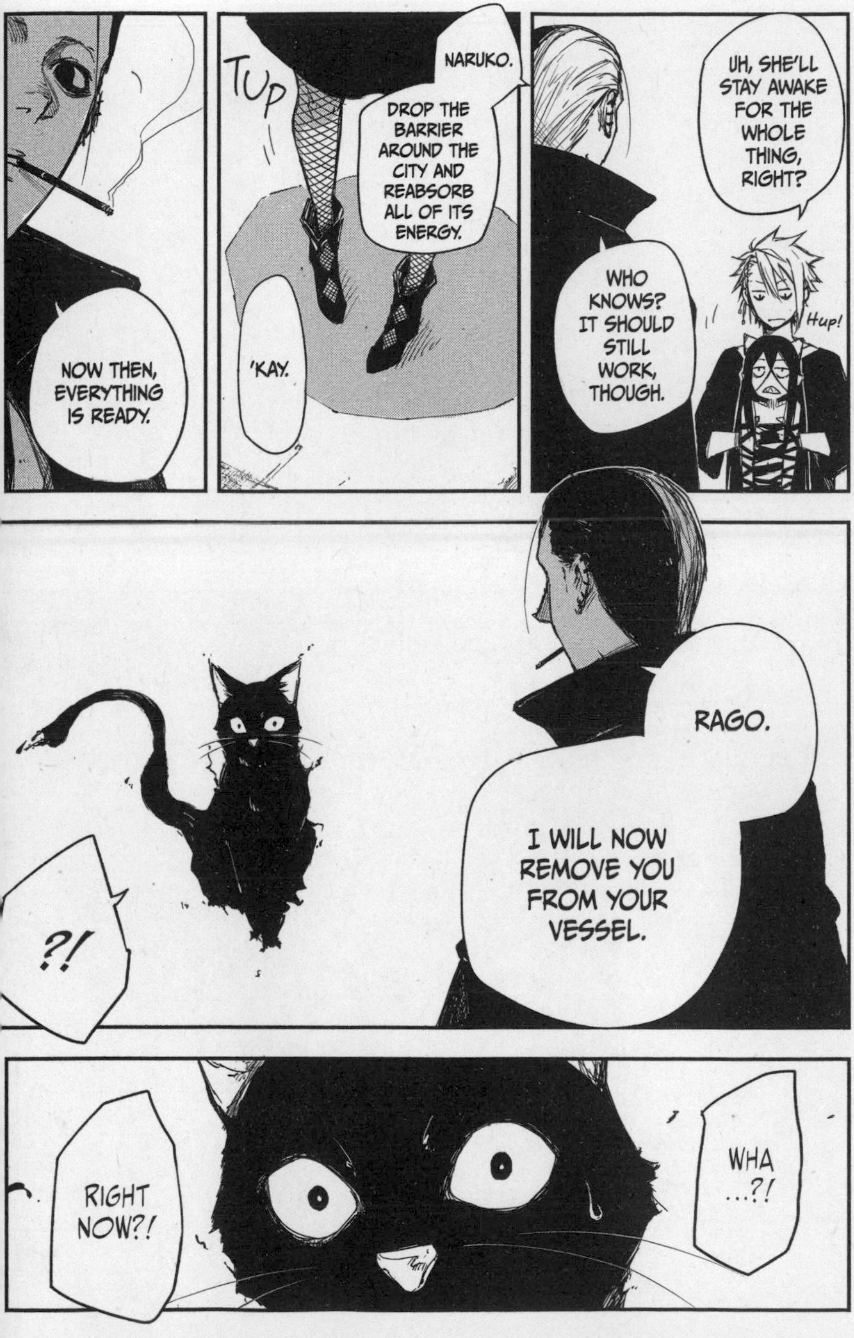
UH, SHE'LL STAY AWAKE FOR THE WHOLE THING, RIGHT?
WHO KNOWS? IT SHOULD STILL WORK, THOUGH.
Hup!
NARUKO.
DROP THE BARRIER AROUND THE CITY AND REABSORB ALL OF ITS ENERGY.
TUP
'KAY.
NOW THEN, EVERYTHING IS READY.
RAGO.
I WILL NOW REMOVE YOU FROM YOUR VESSEL.
?!
WHA...?!
RIGHT NOW?!

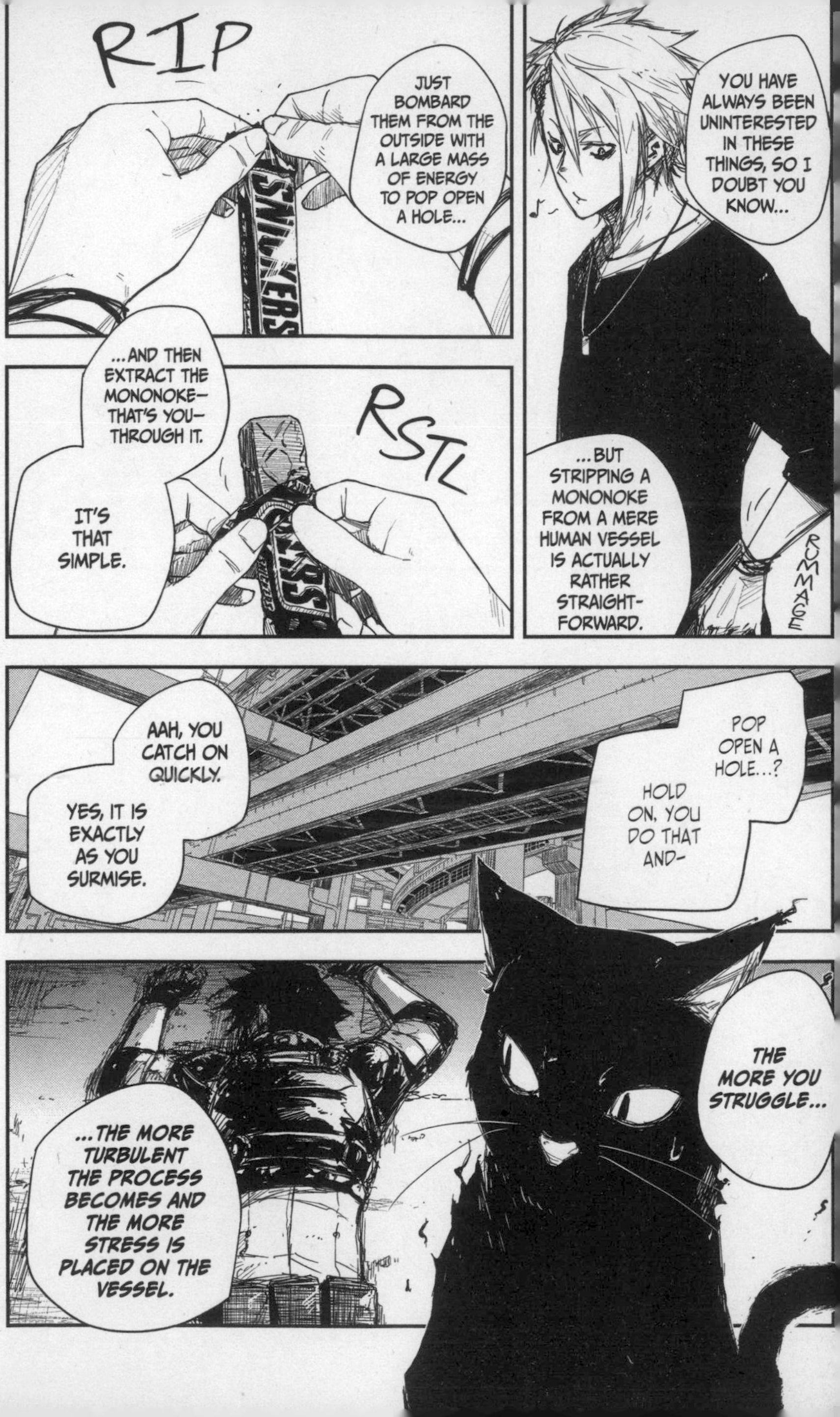
YOU HAVE ALWAYS BEEN UNINTERESTED IN THESE THINGS, SO I DOUBT YOU KNOW...
...BUT STRIPPING A MONONOKE FROM A MERE HUMAN VESSEL IS ACTUALLY RATHER STRAIGHT-FORWARD.
RUMMAGE
RIP
JUST BOMBARD THEM FROM THE OUTSIDE WITH A LARGE MASS OF ENERGY TO POP OPEN A HOLE...
...AND THEN EXTRACT THE MONONOKE—THAT'S YOU—THROUGH IT.
RSTL
IT'S THAT SIMPLE.
POP OPEN A HOLE...?
HOLD ON, YOU DO THAT AND-
AAH, YOU CATCH ON QUICKLY.
YES, IT IS EXACTLY AS YOU SURMISE.
THE MORE YOU STRUGGLE...
...THE MORE TURBULENT THE PROCESS BECOMES AND THE MORE STRESS IS PLACED ON THE VESSEL.

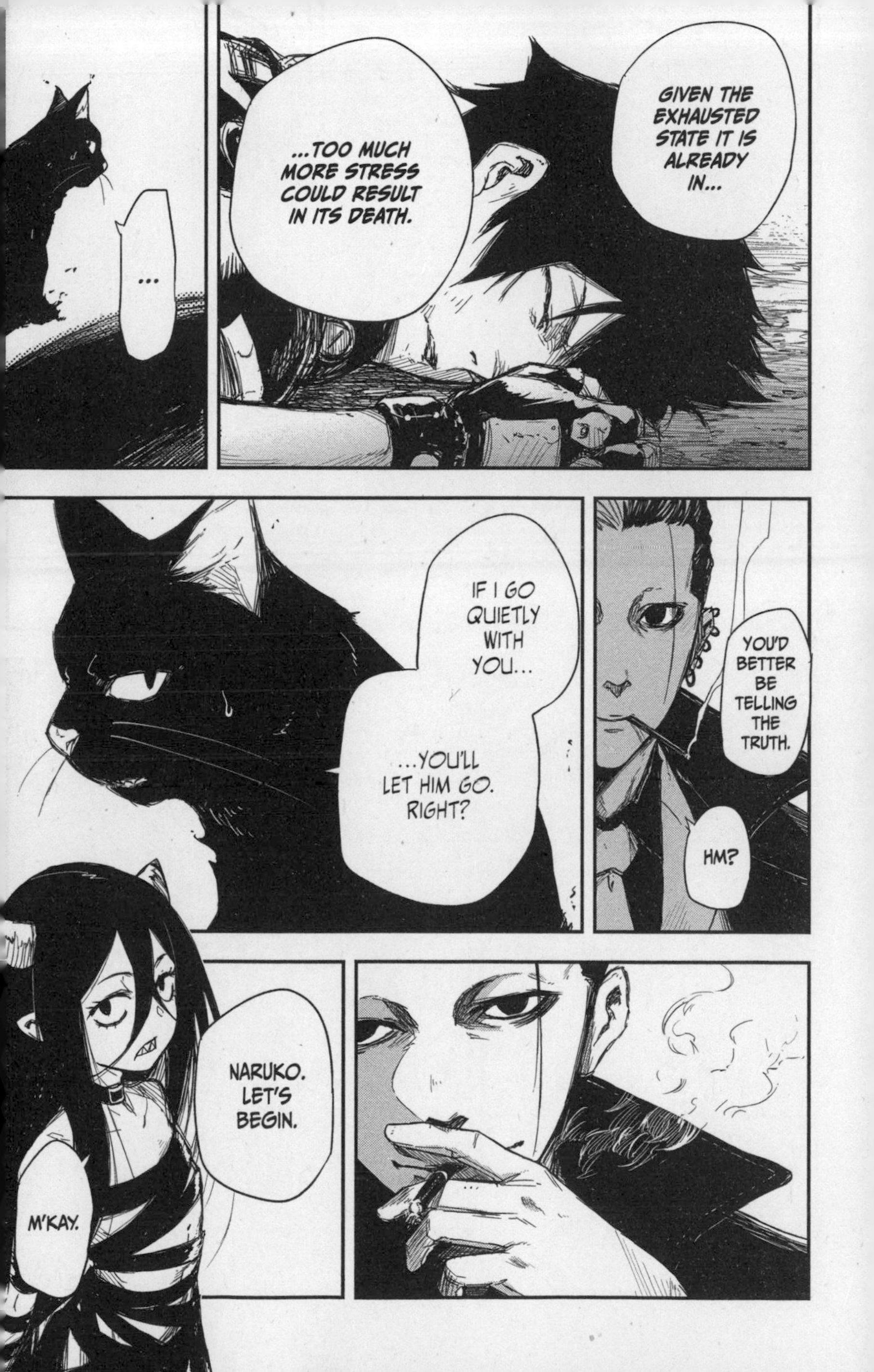
GIVEN THE EXHAUSTED STATE IT IS ALREADY IN...
...TOO MUCH MORE STRESS COULD RESULT IN ITS DEATH.
...
YOU'D BETTER BE TELLING THE TRUTH.
HM?
IF I GO QUIETLY WITH YOU...
...YOU'LL LET HIM GO. RIGHT?
...
NARUKO. LET'S BEGIN.
M'KAY.

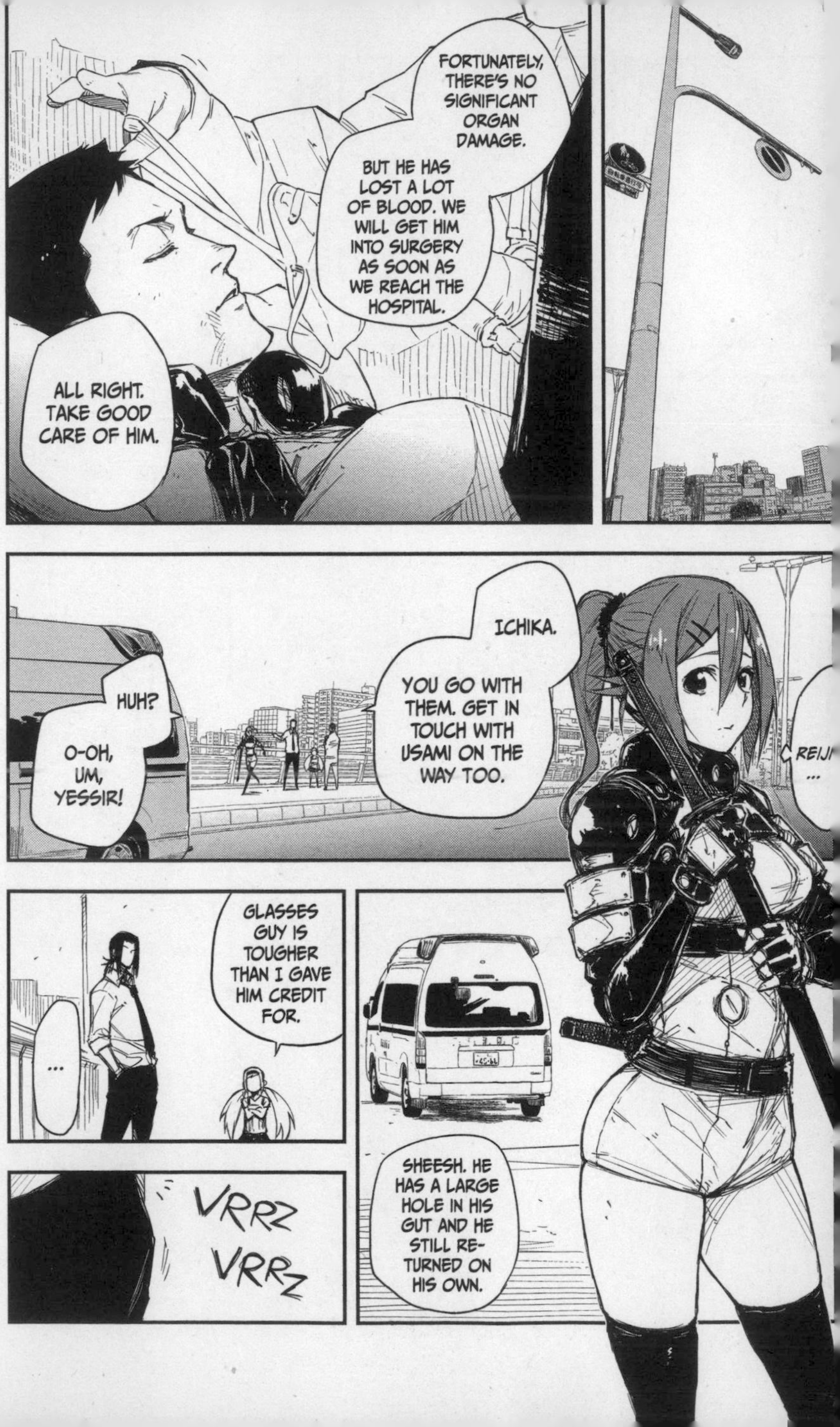
FORTUNATELY, THERE'S NO SIGNIFICANT ORGAN DAMAGE.
BUT HE HAS LOST A LOT OF BLOOD. WE WILL GET HIM INTO SURGERY AS SOON AS WE REACH THE HOSPITAL.
ALL RIGHT. TAKE GOOD CARE OF HIM.
ICHIKA.
YOU GO WITH THEM. GET IN TOUCH WITH USAMI ON THE WAY TOO.
HUH?
O-OH, UM, YESSIR!
REIJI ...
SHEESH. HE HAS A LARGE HOLE IN HIS GUT AND HE STILL RE-TURNED ON HIS OWN.
GLASSES GUY IS TOUGHER THAN I GAVE HIM CREDIT FOR.
...
VRRZ
VRRZ

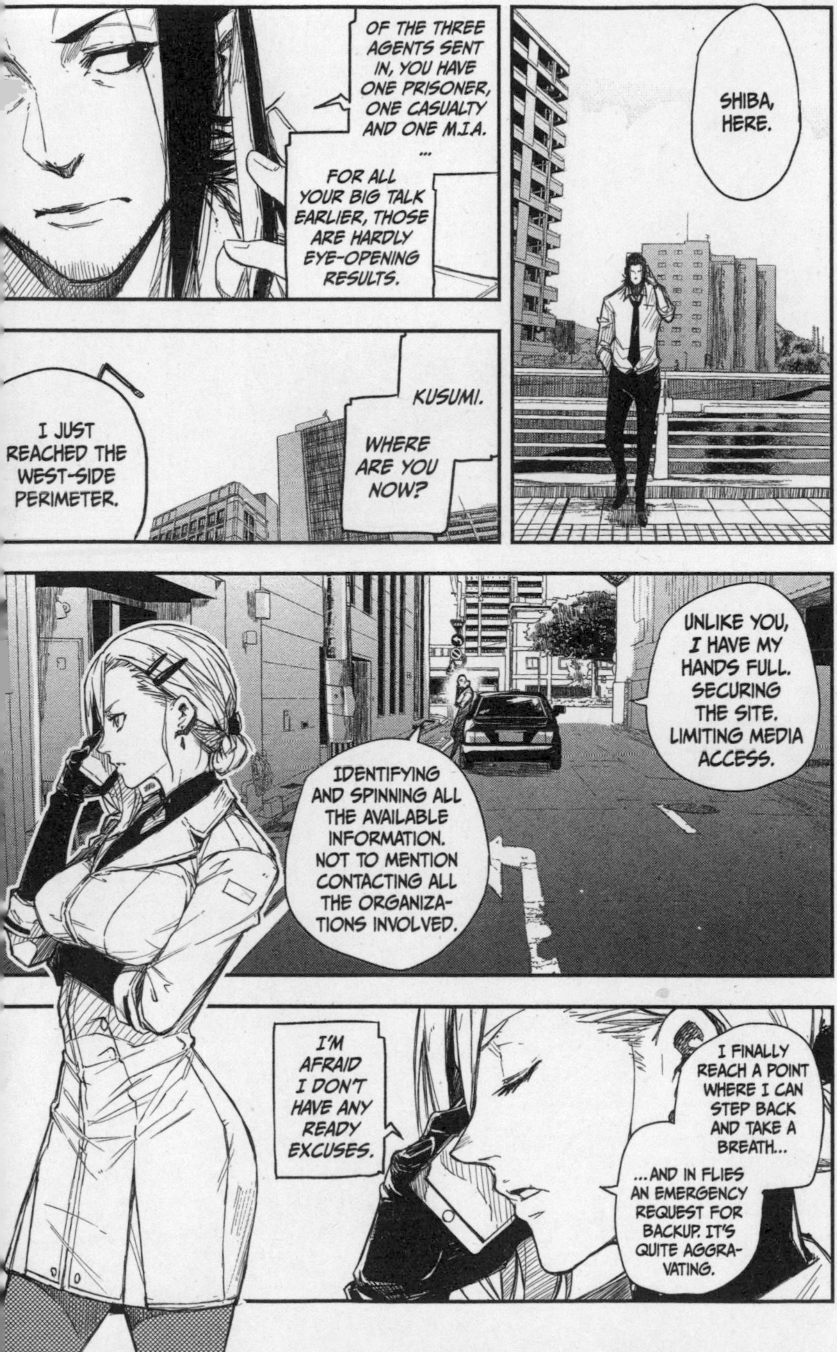
SHIBA, HERE.
OF THE THREE AGENTS SENT IN, YOU HAVE ONE PRISONER, ONE CASUALTY AND ONE M.I.A. ...
FOR ALL YOUR BIG TALK EARLIER, THOSE ARE HARDLY EYE-OPENING RESULTS.
KUSUMI.
WHERE ARE YOU NOW?
I JUST REACHED THE WEST-SIDE PERIMETER.
UNLIKE YOU, I HAVE MY HANDS FULL. SECURING THE SITE. LIMITING MEDIA ACCESS.
IDENTIFYING AND SPINNING ALL THE AVAILABLE INFORMATION. NOT TO MENTION CONTACTING ALL THE ORGANIZA-TIONS INVOLVED.
I FINALLY REACH A POINT WHERE I CAN STEP BACK AND TAKE A BREATH...
...AND IN FLIES AN EMERGENCY REQUEST FOR BACKUP. IT'S QUITE AGGRA-VATING.
I'M AFRAID I DON'T HAVE ANY READY EXCUSES.

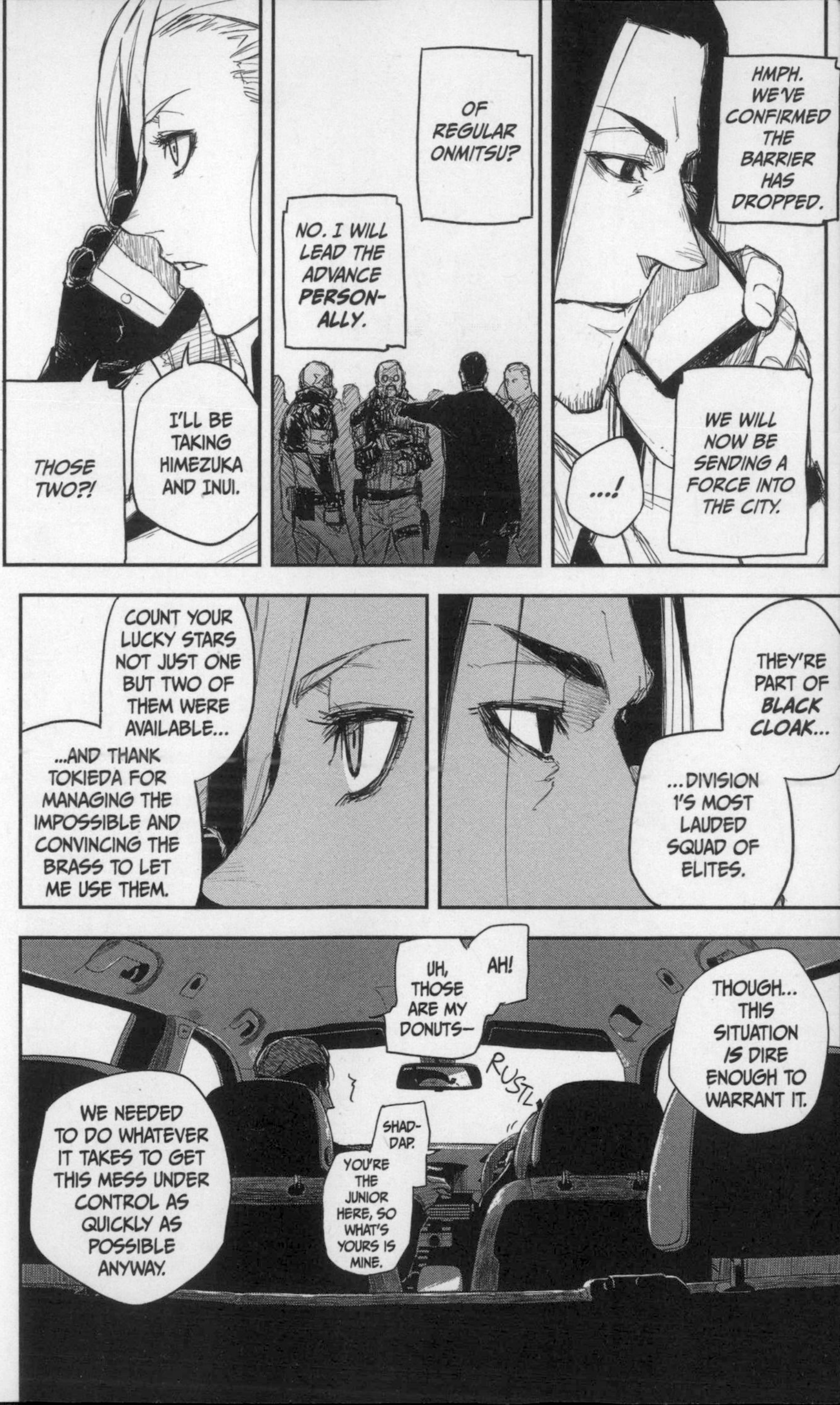
HMPH. WE'VE CONFIRMED THE BARRIER HAS DROPPED.
WE WILL NOW BE SENDING A FORCE INTO THE CITY.
...!
OF REGULAR ONMITSU?
NO. I WILL LEAD THE ADVANCE PERSON-ALLY.
I'LL BE TAKING HIMEZUKA AND INUI.
THOSE TWO?!
THEY'RE PART OF BLACK CLOAK...
...DIVISION 1'S MOST LAUDED SQUAD OF ELITES.
COUNT YOUR LUCKY STARS NOT JUST ONE BUT TWO OF THEM WERE AVAILABLE...
...AND THANK TOKIEDA FOR MANAGING THE IMPOSSIBLE AND CONVINCING THE BRASS TO LET ME USE THEM.
THOUGH... THIS SITUATION IS DIRE ENOUGH TO WARRANT IT.
AH!
UH, THOSE ARE MY DONUTS—
RUSTL
SHAD-DAP.
YOU'RE THE JUNIOR HERE, SO WHAT'S YOURS IS MINE.
WE NEEDED TO DO WHATEVER IT TAKES TO GET THIS MESS UNDER CONTROL AS QUICKLY AS POSSIBLE ANYWAY.

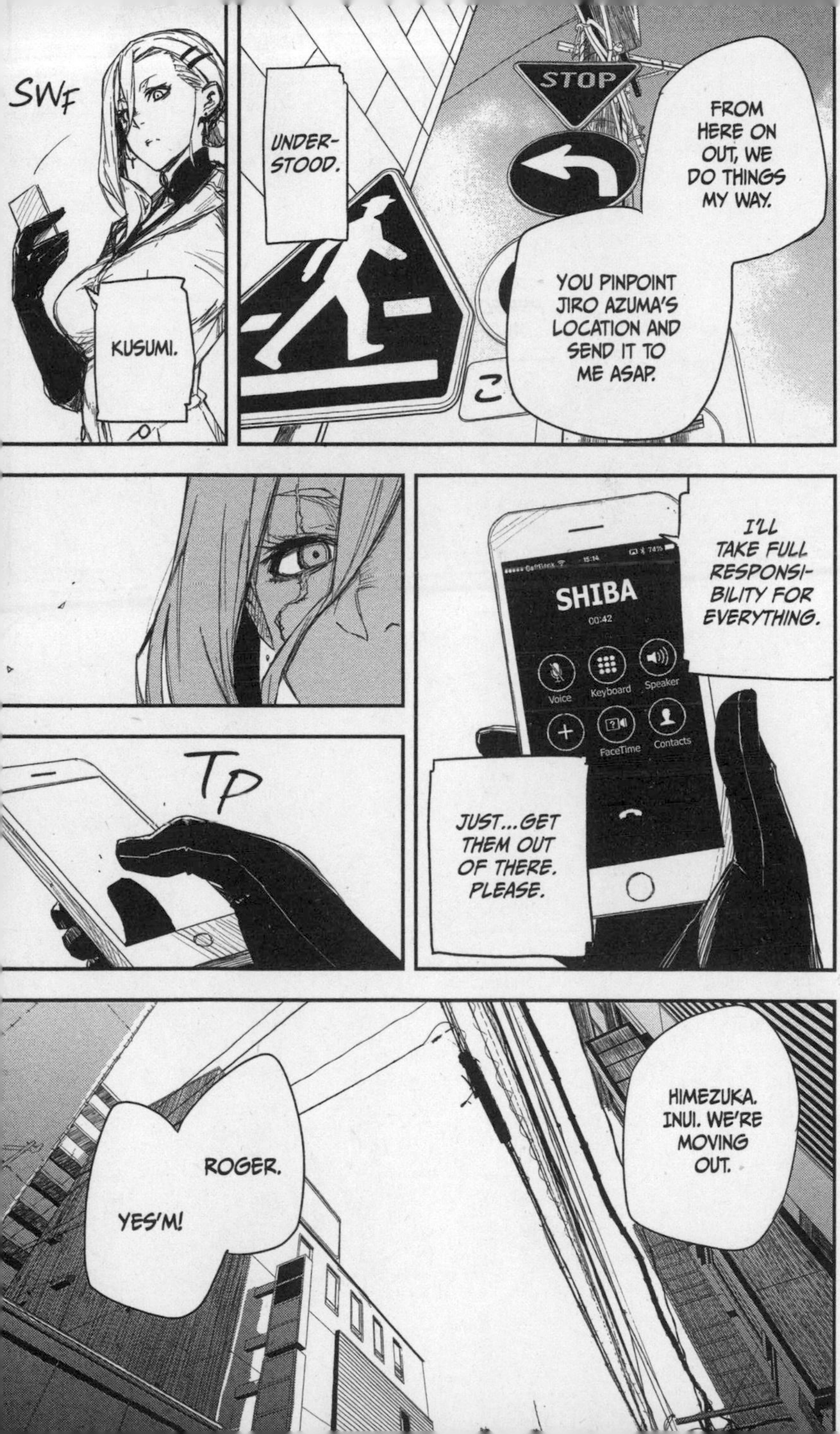
STOP
FROM HERE ON OUT, WE DO THINGS MY WAY.
YOU PINPOINT JIRO AZUMA'S LOCATION AND SEND IT TO ME ASAP.
UNDER-STOOD.
SWF
KUSUMI.
I'LL TAKE FULL RESPONSI-BILITY FOR EVERYTHING.
15:14
SHIBA
00:42
Voice
Keyboard
Speaker
FaceTime
Contacts
JUST...GET THEM OUT OF THERE. PLEASE.
TP
HIMEZUKA. INUI. WE'RE MOVING OUT.
ROGER.
YES'M!

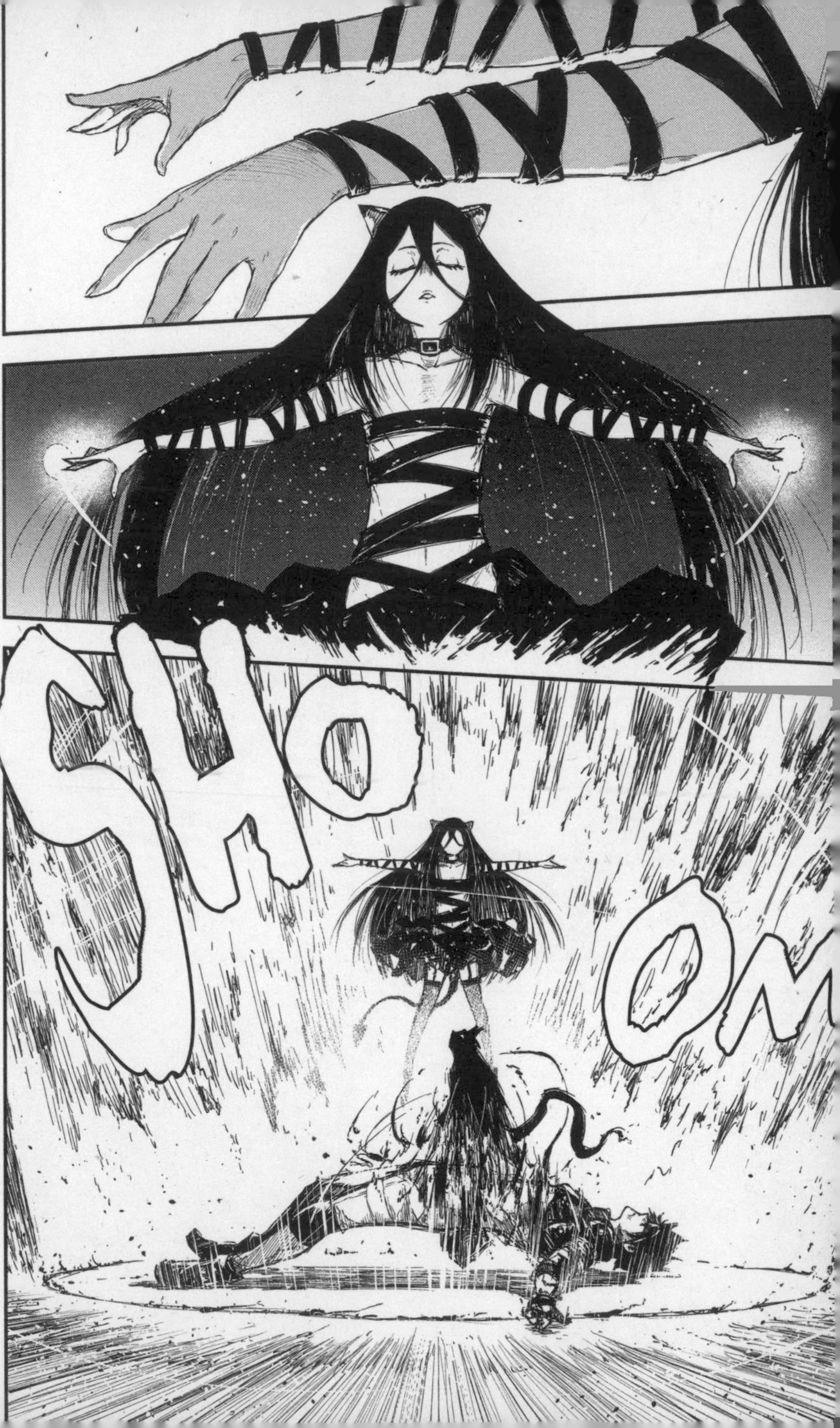
SHOOM

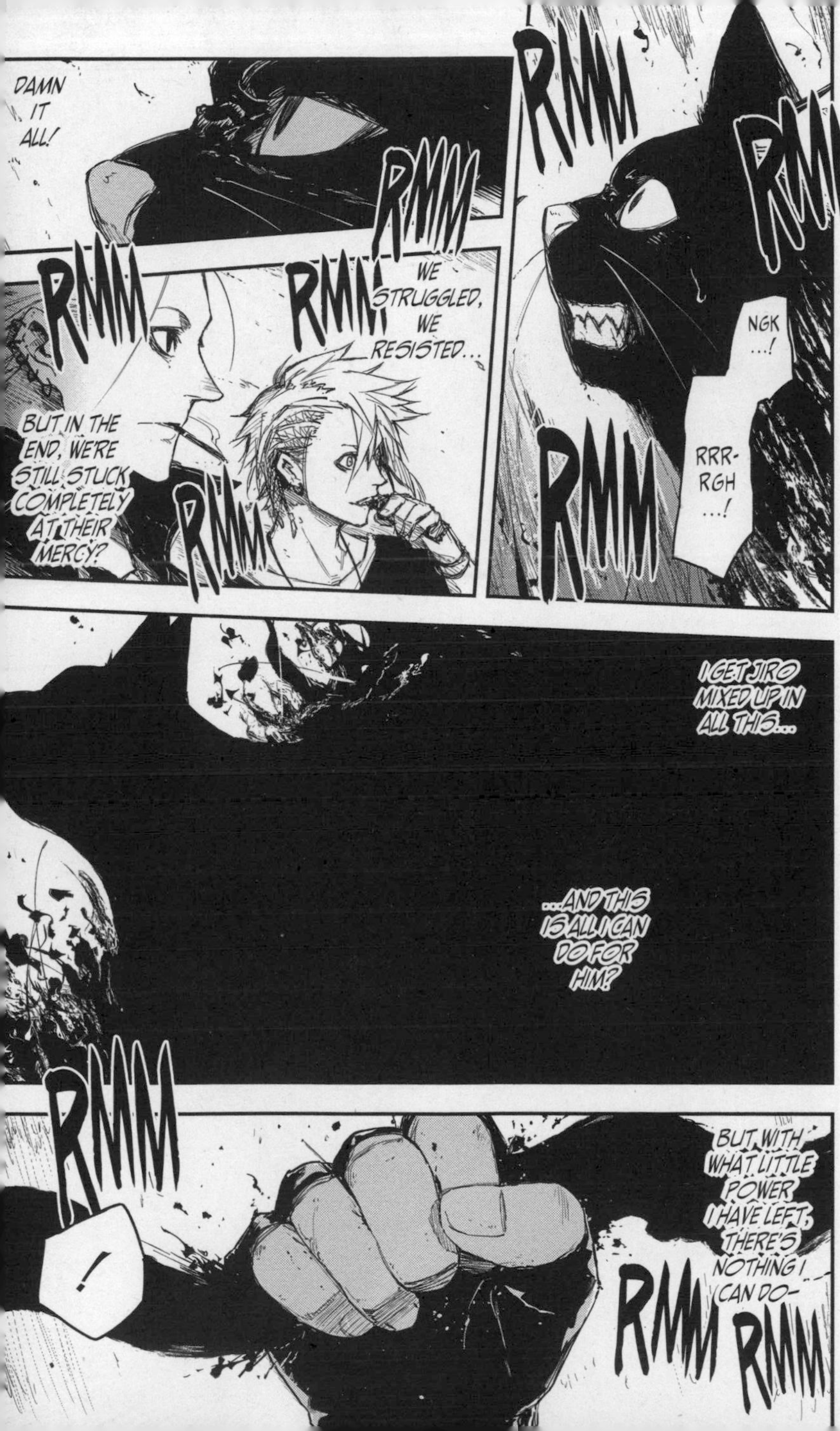
RMM
RMM
NGK ...!
RRR-RGH ...!
RMM
DAMN IT ALL!
RMM
WE STRUGGLED, WE RESISTED...
RMM
RMM
BUT IN THE END, WE'RE STILL STUCK COMPLETELY AT THEIR MERCY?
RMM
I GET JIRO MIXED UP IN ALL THIS...
...AND THIS IS ALL I CAN DO FOR HIM?
BUT WITH WHAT LITTLE POWER I HAVE LEFT, THERE'S NOTHING I CAN DO-
RMM
RMM
RMM
!

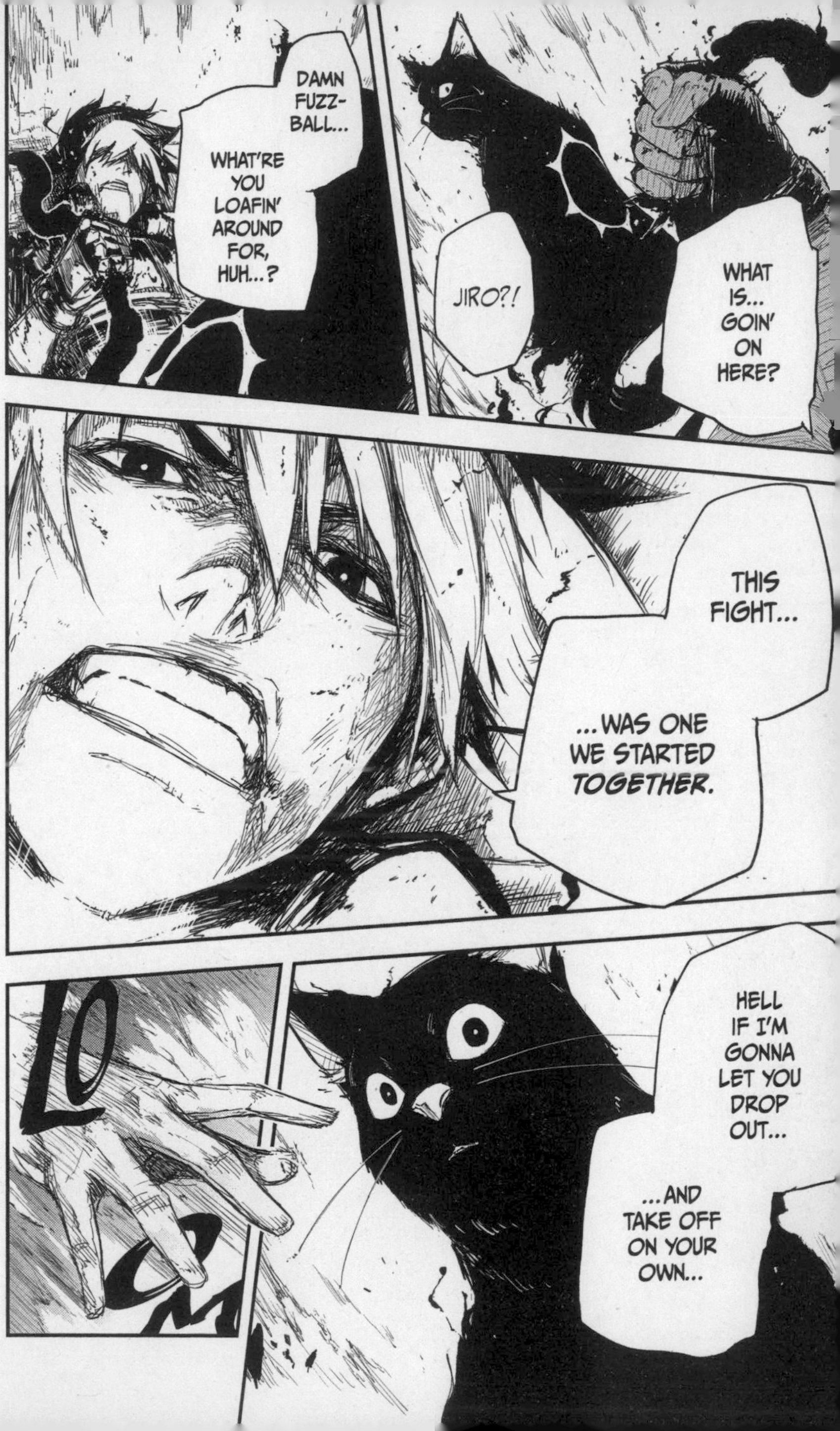
WHAT IS... GOIN' ON HERE?
JIRO?!
DAMN FUZZ-BALL...
WHAT'RE YOU LOAFIN' AROUND FOR, HUH...?
THIS FIGHT...
...WAS ONE WE STARTED *TOGETHER.*
HELL IF I'M GONNA LET YOU DROP OUT...
...AND TAKE OFF ON YOUR OWN...

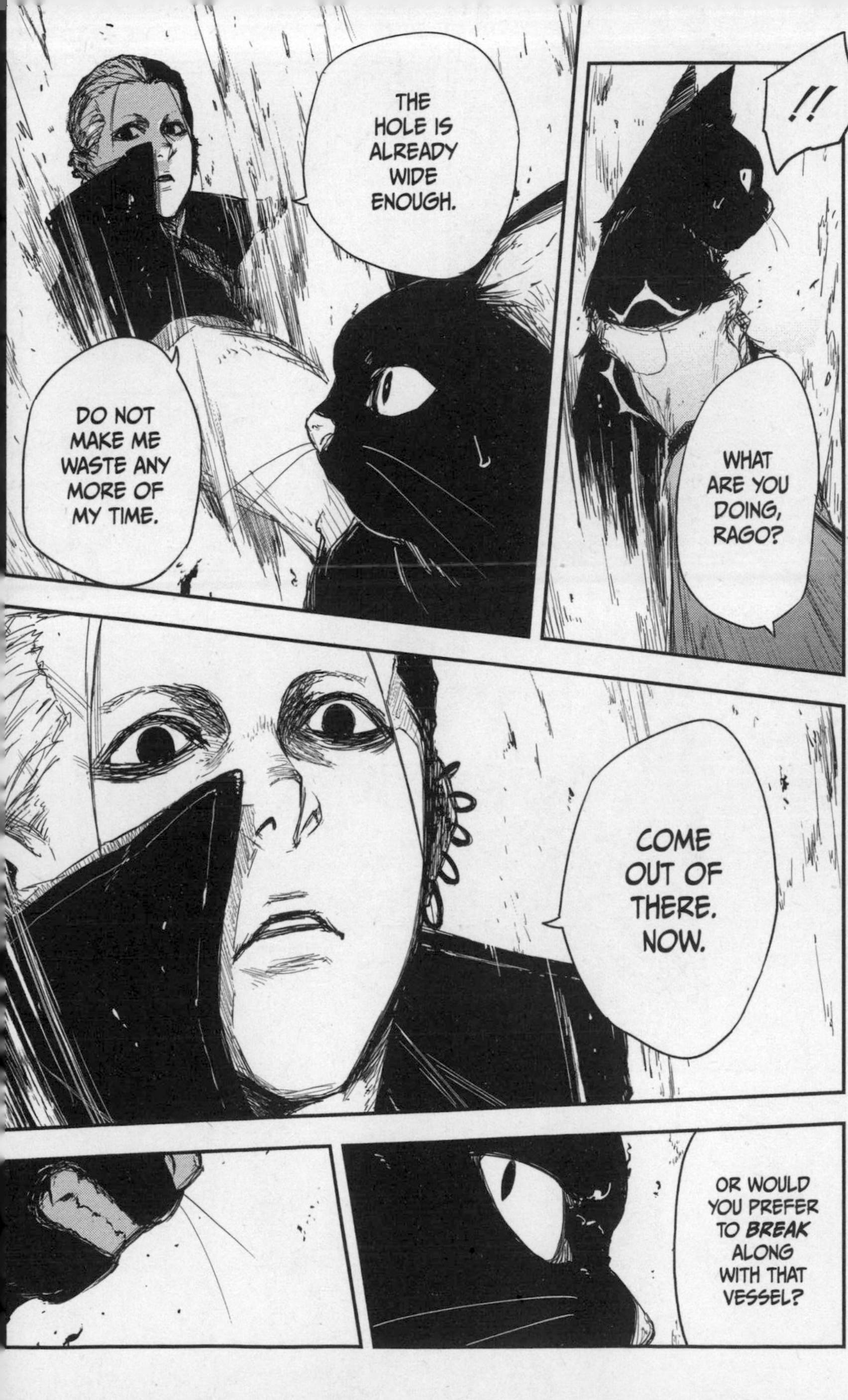
!!
WHAT ARE YOU DOING, RAGO?
THE HOLE IS ALREADY WIDE ENOUGH.
DO NOT MAKE ME WASTE ANY MORE OF MY TIME.
COME OUT OF THERE. NOW.
OR WOULD YOU PREFER TO *BREAK* ALONG WITH THAT VESSEL?

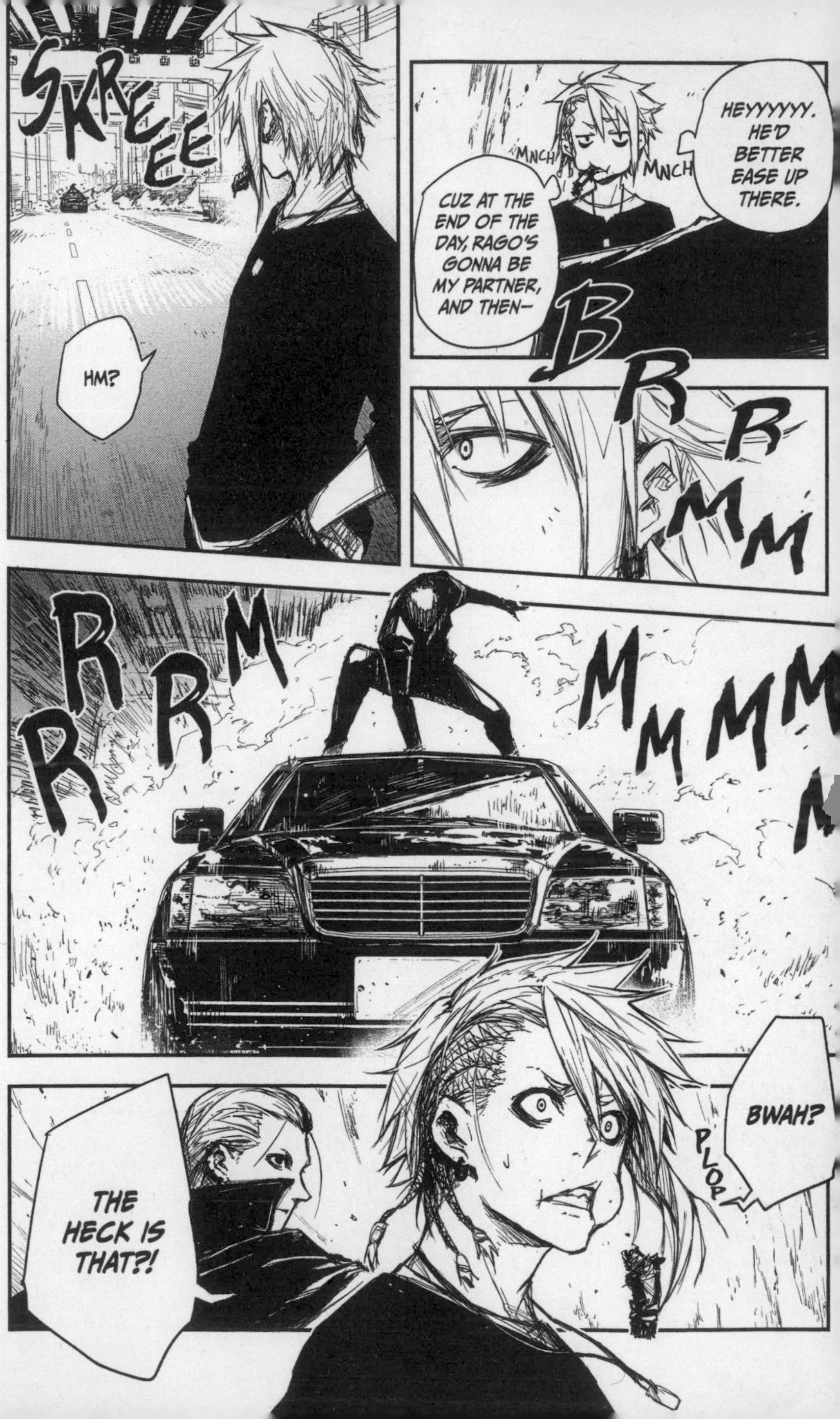
HEYYYYYY. HE'D BETTER EASE UP THERE.
MNCH
MNCH
CUZ AT THE END OF THE DAY, RAGO'S GONNA BE MY PARTNER, AND THEN—
BRRRMMM
SKREEE
HM?
MMMMMM
RRRM
BWAH?
PLOP
THE HECK IS THAT?!

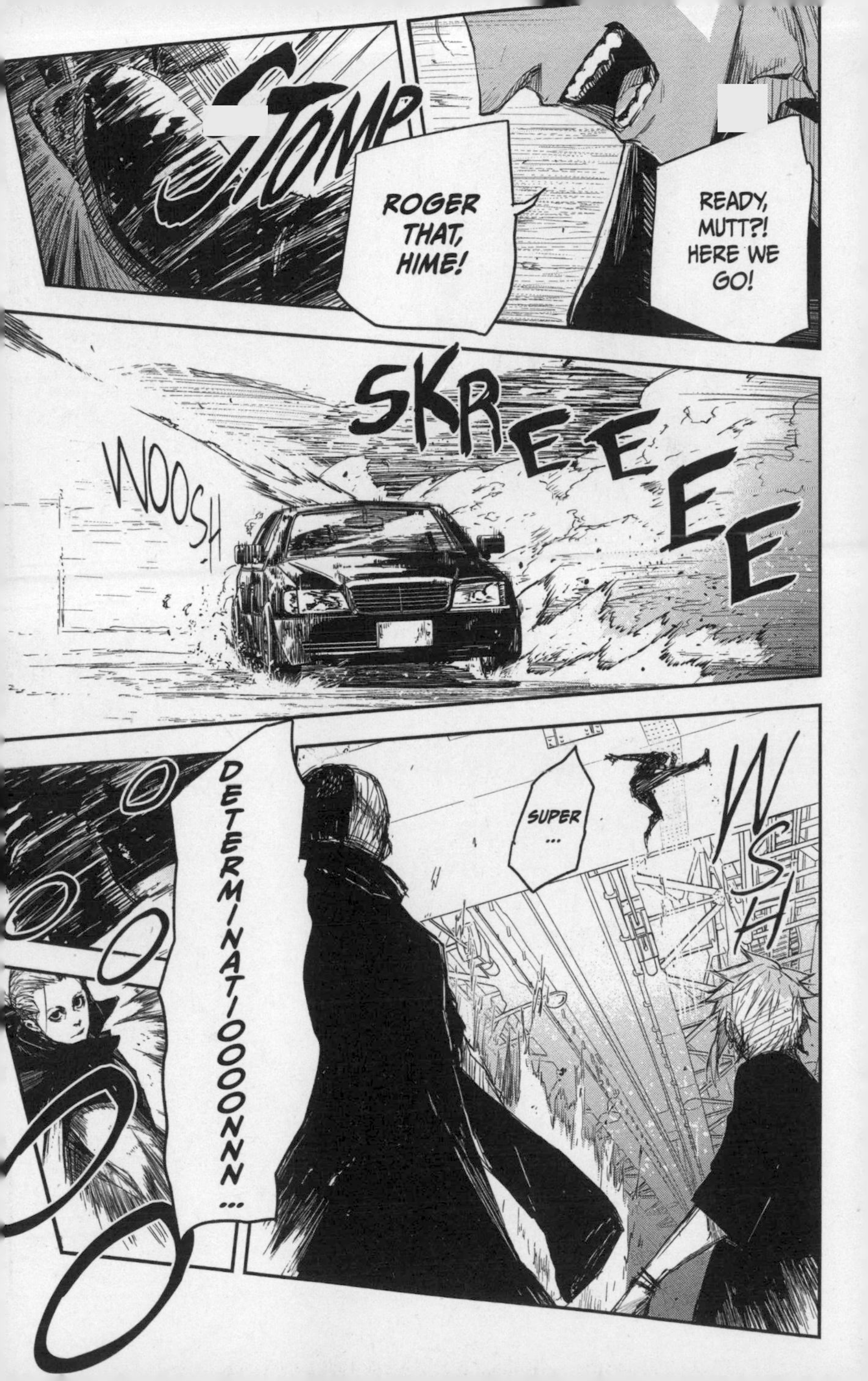
READY, MUTT?! HERE WE GO!
ROGER THAT, HIME!
STOMP
SKREEEEEE
WOOSH
WSH
SUPER ...
DETERMINATIOOOOONNN ...

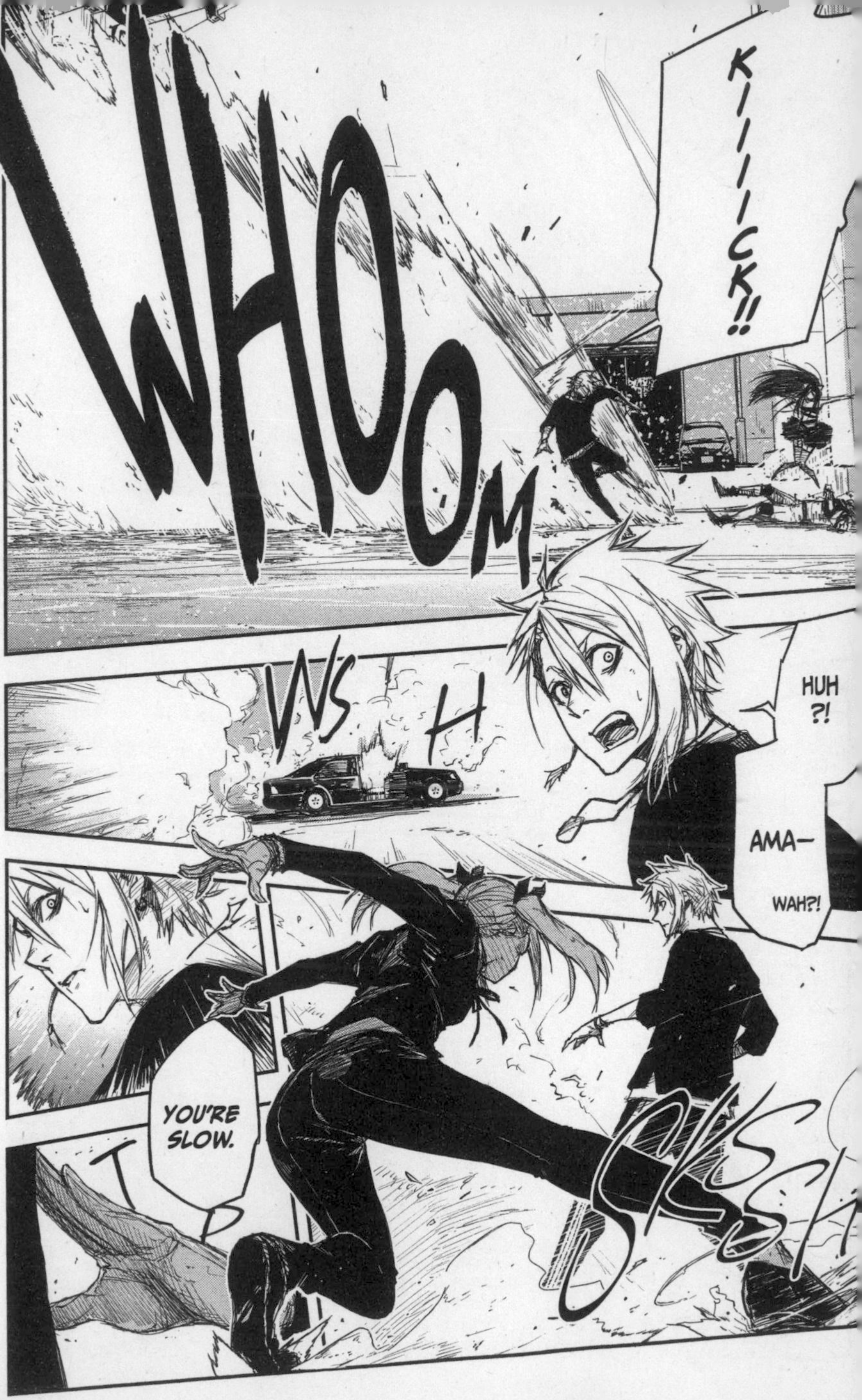
KIIIICK!!
WHOOM
HUH?!
WSH
AMA—
WAH?!
YOU'RE SLOW.
SKSH
TP

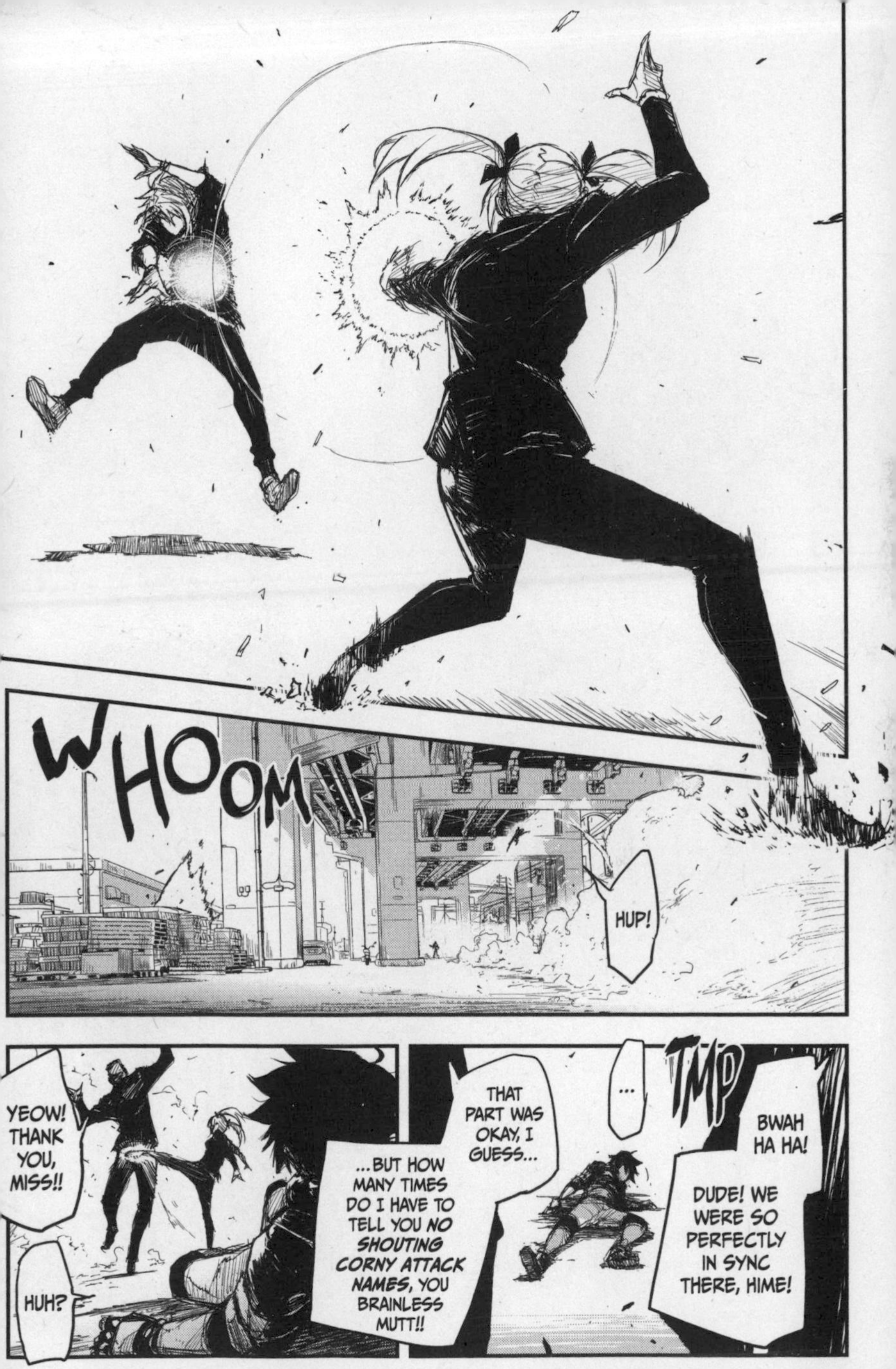
WHOOM
HUP!
TMP
...
BWAH HA HA!
DUDE! WE WERE SO PERFECTLY IN SYNC THERE, HIME!
THAT PART WAS OKAY, I GUESS...
...BUT HOW MANY TIMES DO I HAVE TO TELL YOU NO SHOUTING CORNY ATTACK NAMES, YOU BRAINLESS MUTT!!
YEOW! THANK YOU, MISS!!
HUH?

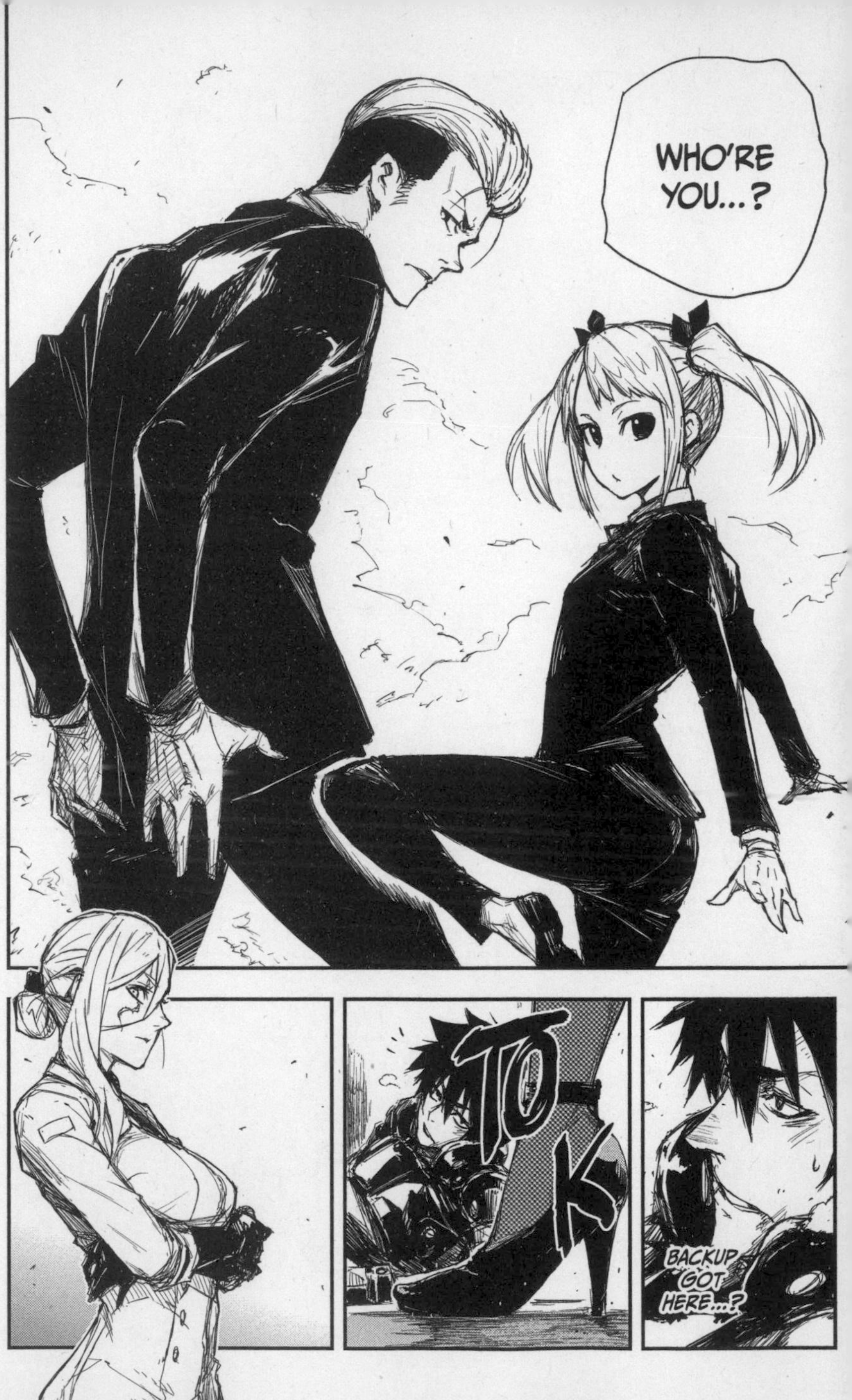
WHO'RE YOU...?
BACKUP GOT HERE...?
TOK

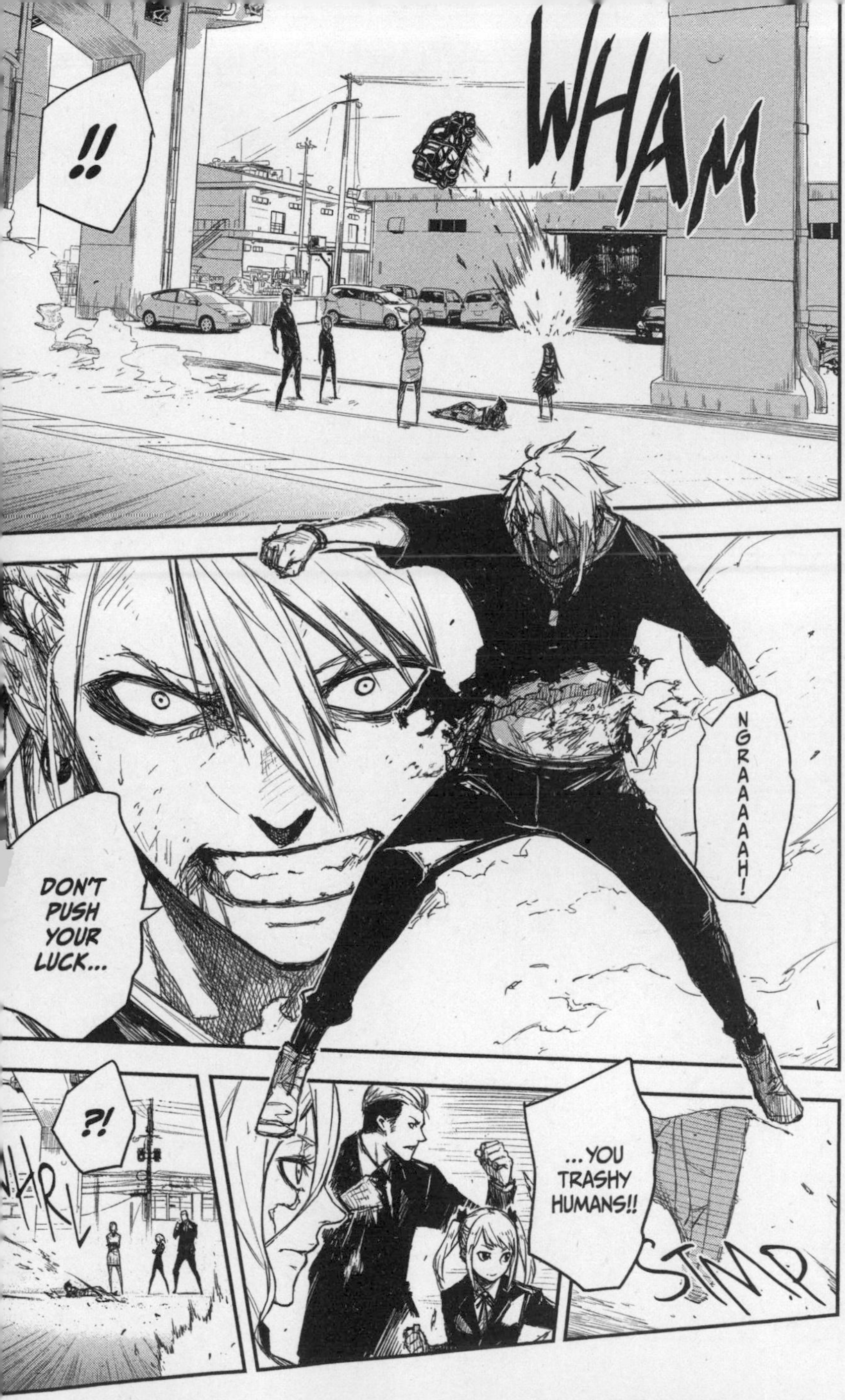
WHAM
!!
NGRAAAAAH!
DON'T PUSH YOUR LUCK...
...YOU TRASHY HUMANS!!
STMP
?!
WHRL

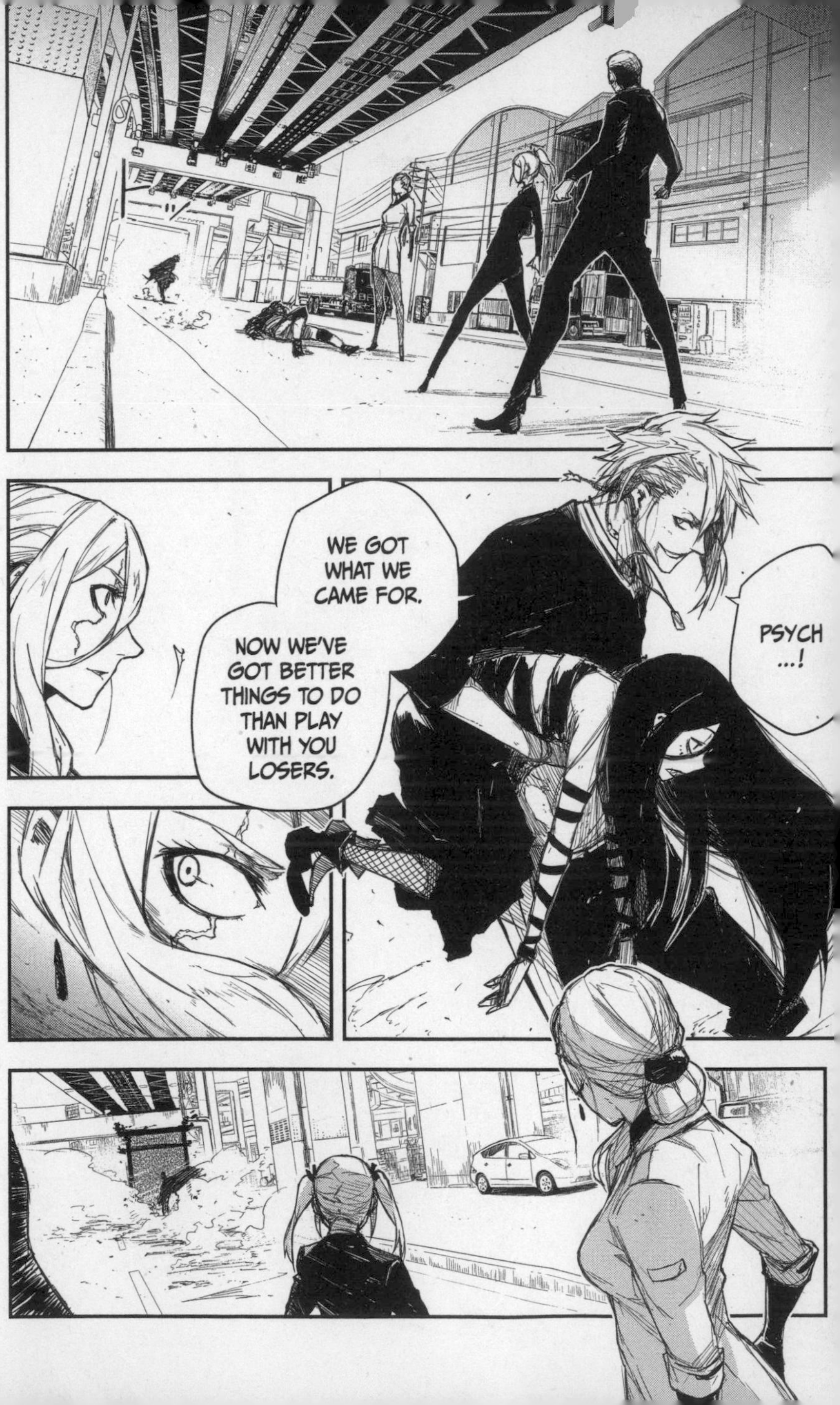
PSYCH ...!
WE GOT WHAT WE CAME FOR.
NOW WE'VE GOT BETTER THINGS TO DO THAN PLAY WITH YOU LOSERS.

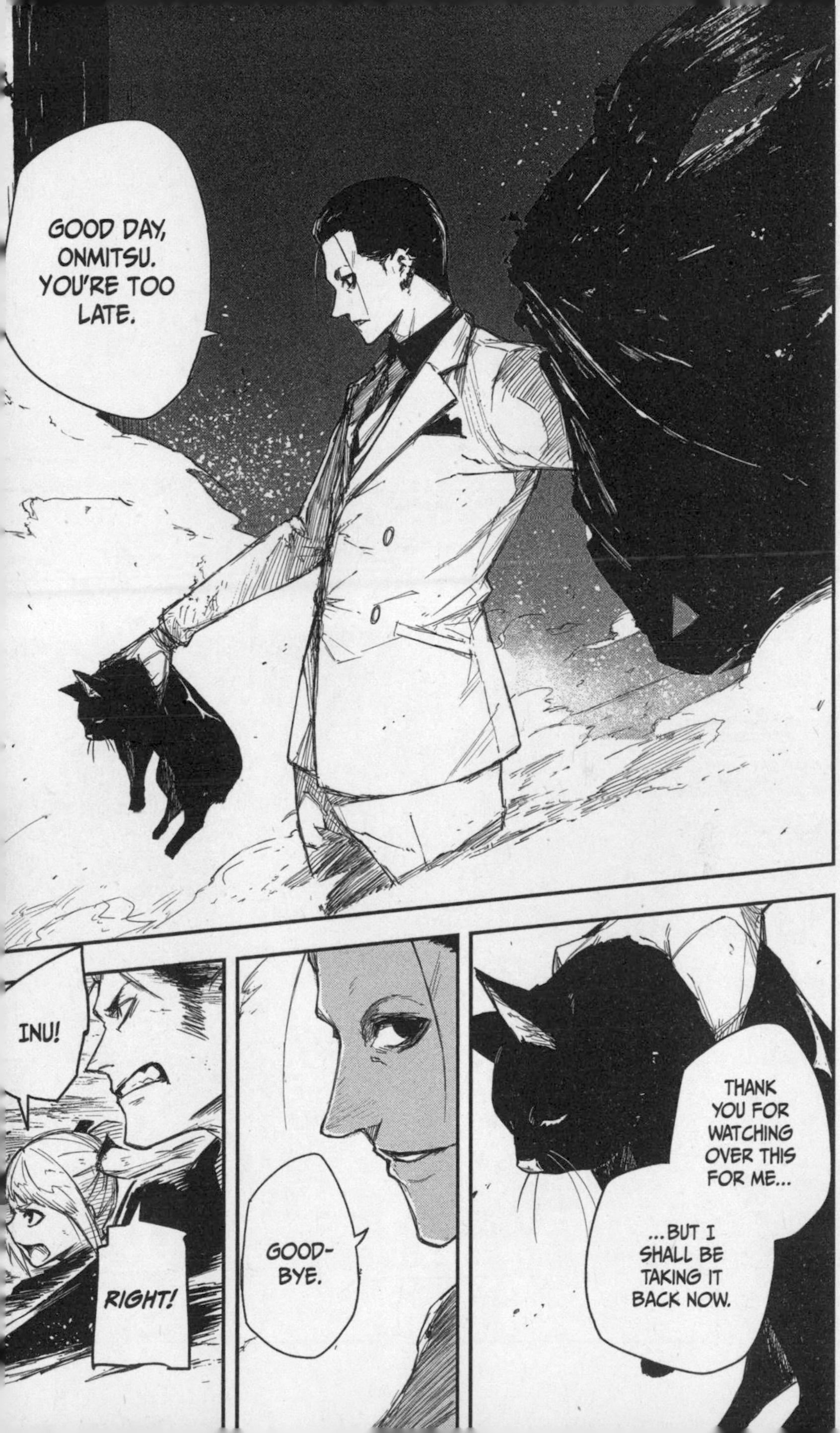
GOOD DAY, ONMITSU. YOU'RE TOO LATE.
THANK YOU FOR WATCHING OVER THIS FOR ME...
...BUT I SHALL BE TAKING IT BACK NOW.
GOOD-BYE.
INU!
RIGHT!

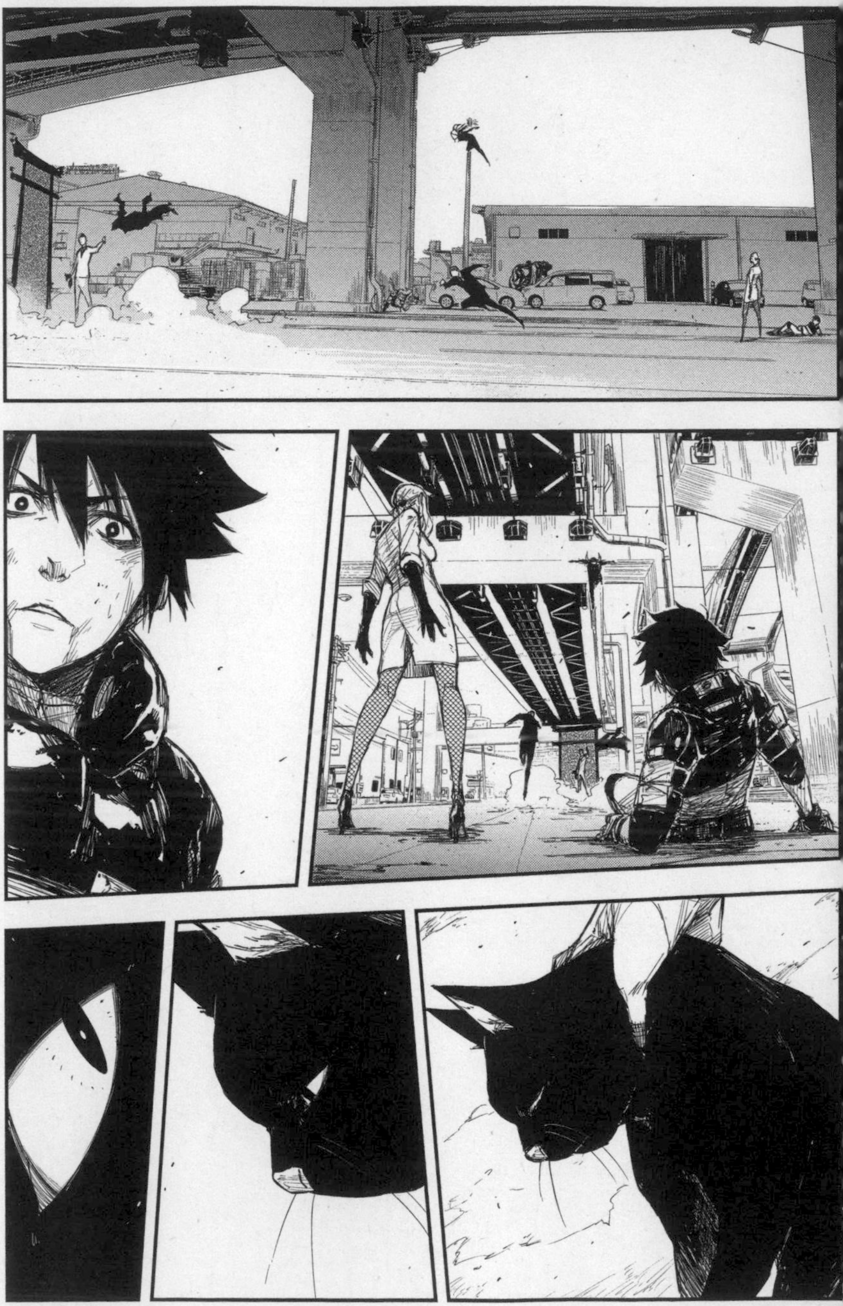

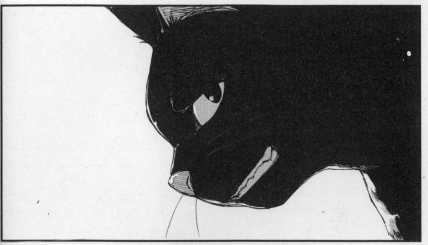

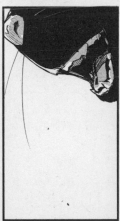

WUMP.

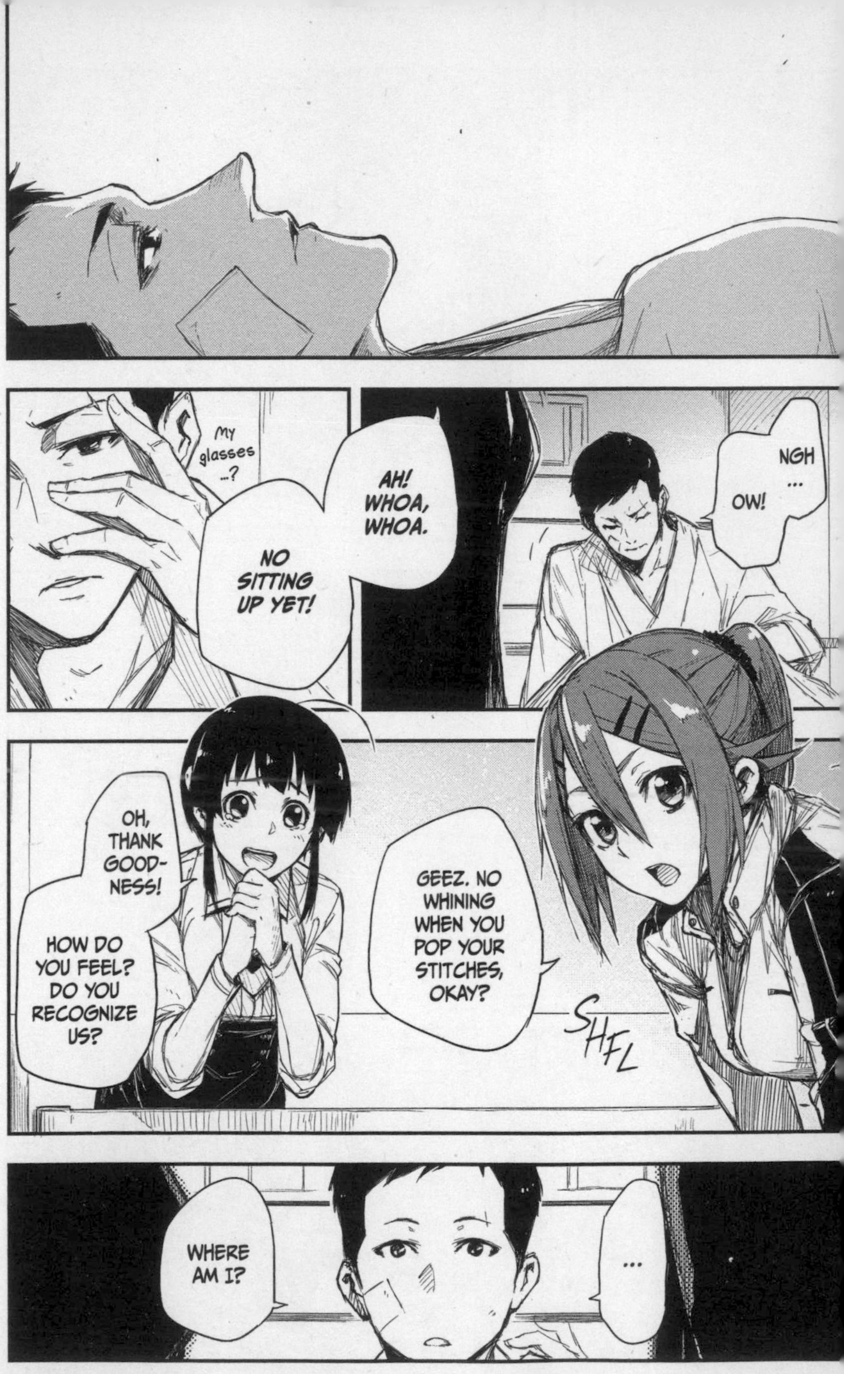
NGH ... OW!
AH! WHOA, WHOA.
NO SITTING UP YET!
My glasses ...?
GEEZ. NO WHINING WHEN YOU POP YOUR STITCHES, OKAY?
SHFL
OH, THANK GOOD-NESS!
HOW DO YOU FEEL? DO YOU RECOGNIZE US?
...
WHERE AM I?

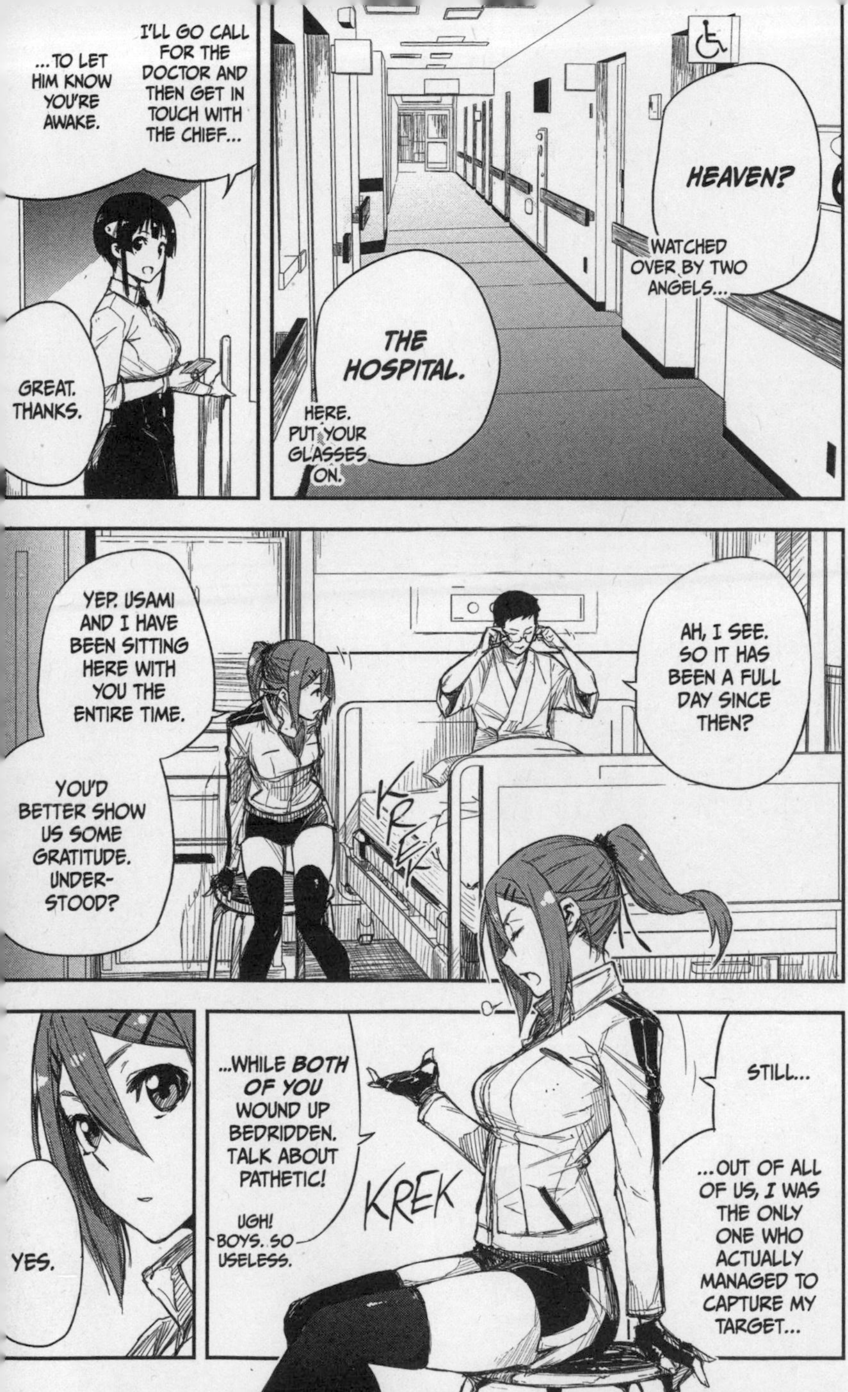
HEAVEN?
WATCHED OVER BY TWO ANGELS...
THE HOSPITAL.
HERE. PUT YOUR GLASSES ON.
I'LL GO CALL FOR THE DOCTOR AND THEN GET IN TOUCH WITH THE CHIEF...
...TO LET HIM KNOW YOU'RE AWAKE.
GREAT. THANKS.
AH, I SEE. SO IT HAS BEEN A FULL DAY SINCE THEN?
YEP. USAMI AND I HAVE BEEN SITTING HERE WITH YOU THE ENTIRE TIME.
YOU'D BETTER SHOW US SOME GRATITUDE. UNDER-STOOD?
STILL...
...OUT OF ALL OF US, I WAS THE ONLY ONE WHO ACTUALLY MANAGED TO CAPTURE MY TARGET...
...WHILE *BOTH OF YOU* WOUND UP BEDRIDDEN. TALK ABOUT PATHETIC!
KREK
UGH! BOYS. SO USELESS.
YES.

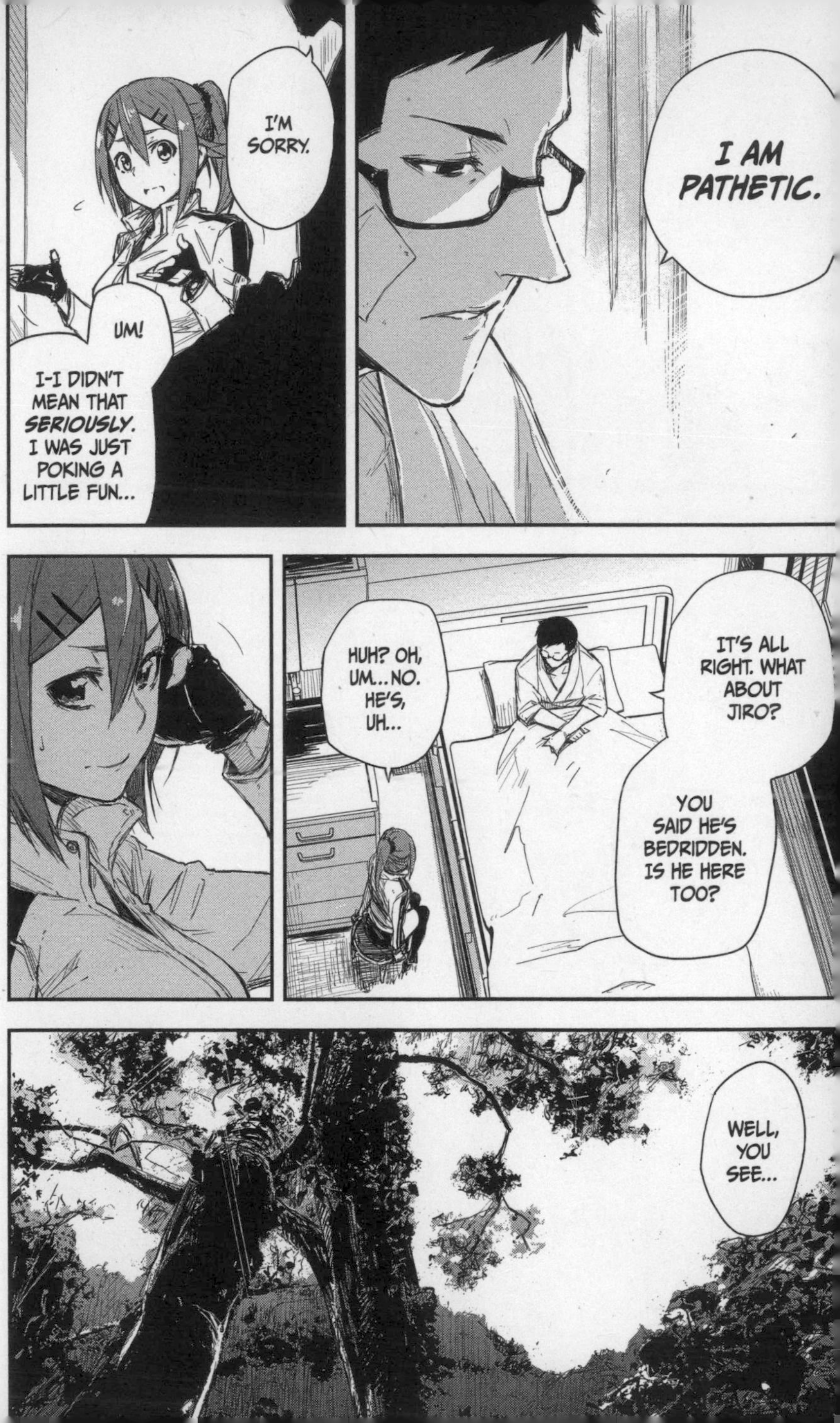
I AM PATHETIC.
I'M SORRY.
UM!
I-I DIDN'T MEAN THAT *SERIOUSLY*. I WAS JUST POKING A LITTLE FUN...
IT'S ALL RIGHT. WHAT ABOUT JIRO?
YOU SAID HE'S BEDRIDDEN. IS HE HERE TOO?
HUH? OH, UM...NO. HE'S, UH...
WELL, YOU SEE...

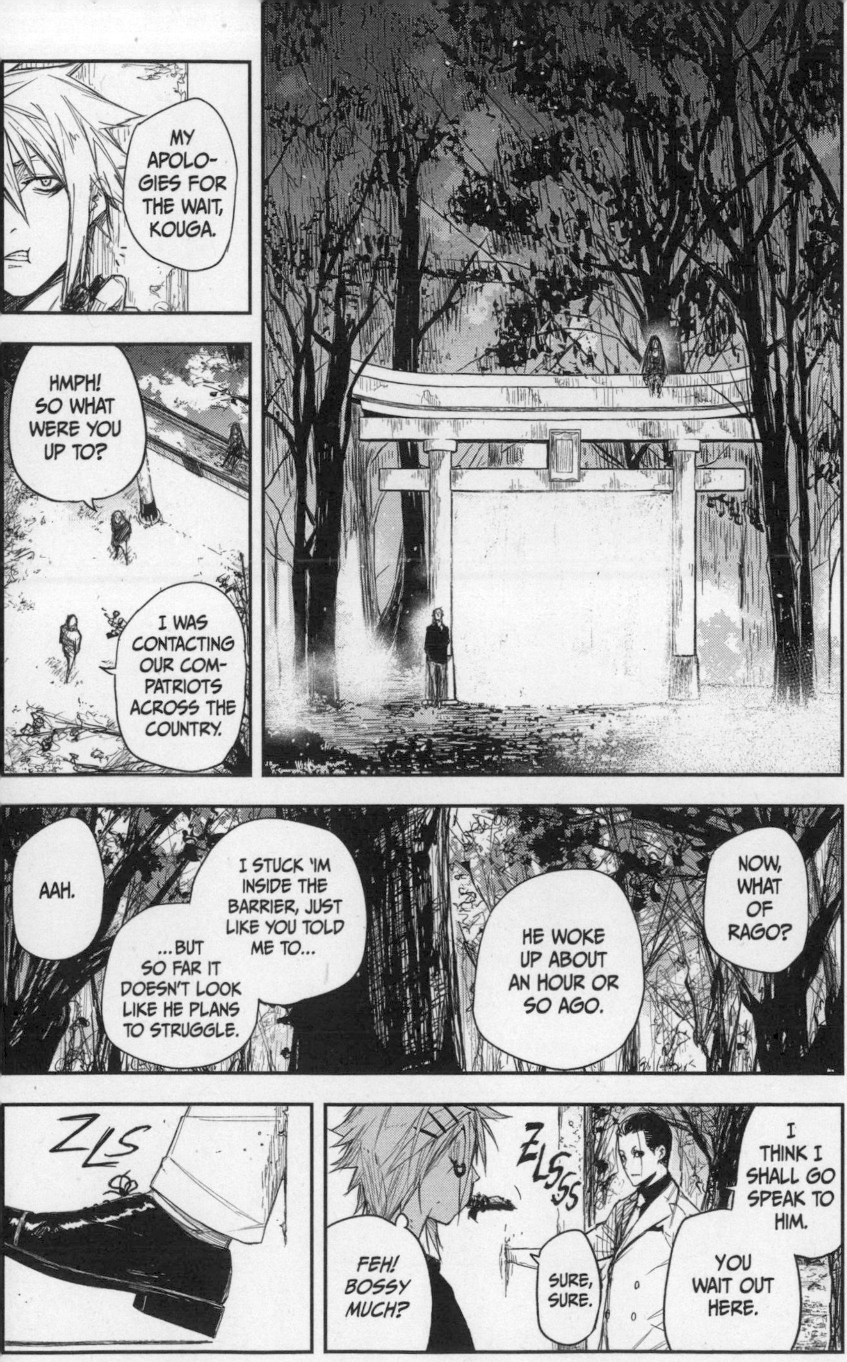
MY APOLOGIES FOR THE WAIT, KOUGA.
HMPH! SO WHAT WERE YOU UP TO?
I WAS CONTACTING OUR COMPATRIOTS ACROSS THE COUNTRY.
NOW, WHAT OF RAGO?
HE WOKE UP ABOUT AN HOUR OR SO AGO.
AAH.
I STUCK 'IM INSIDE THE BARRIER, JUST LIKE YOU TOLD ME TO...
...BUT SO FAR IT DOESN'T LOOK LIKE HE PLANS TO STRUGGLE.
I THINK I SHALL GO SPEAK TO HIM.
YOU WAIT OUT HERE.
SURE, SURE.
ZLSSS
FEH! BOSSY MUCH?
ZLS

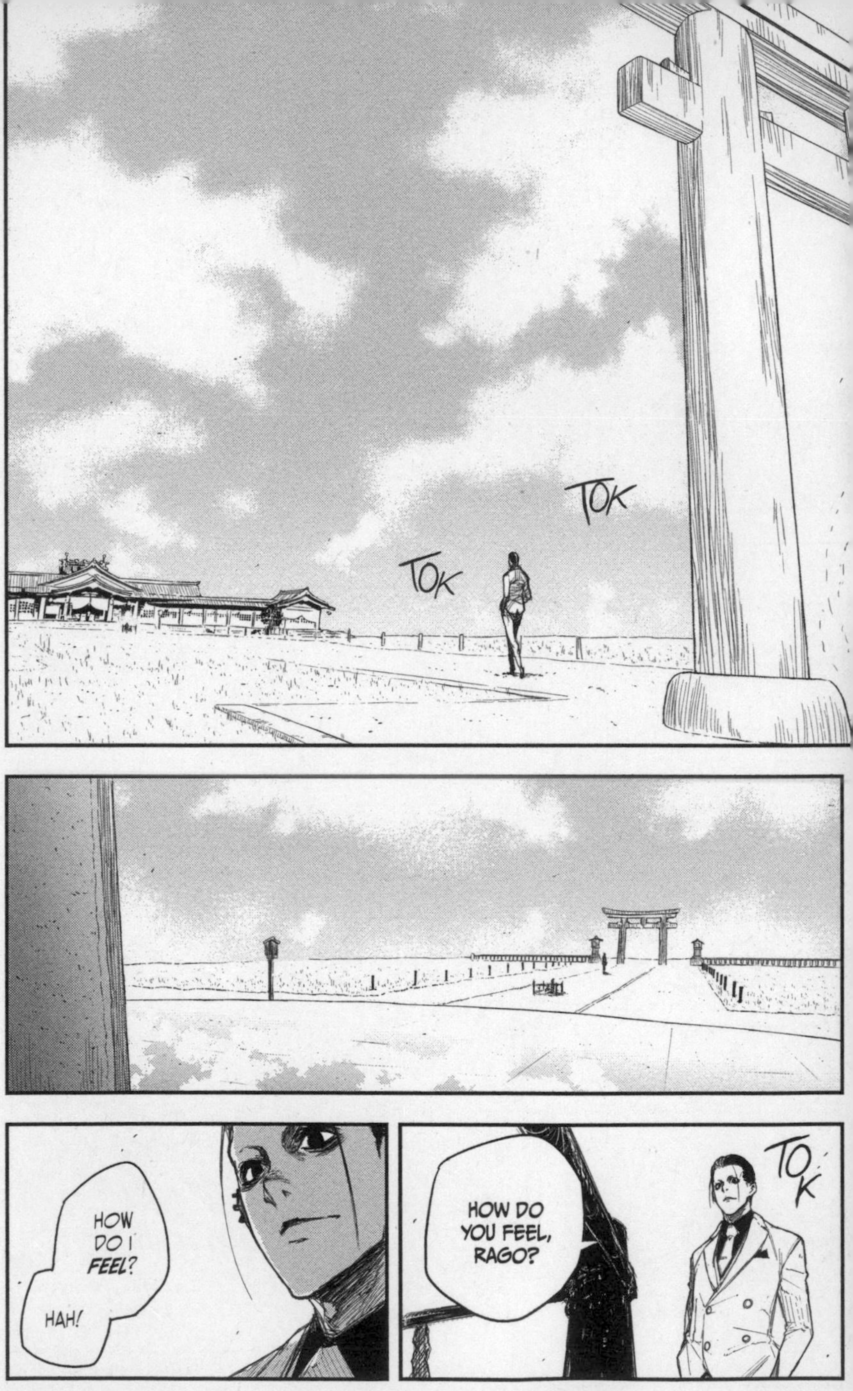
TOK
TOK
TOK
HOW DO YOU FEEL, RAGO?
HOW DO I FEEL?
HAH!

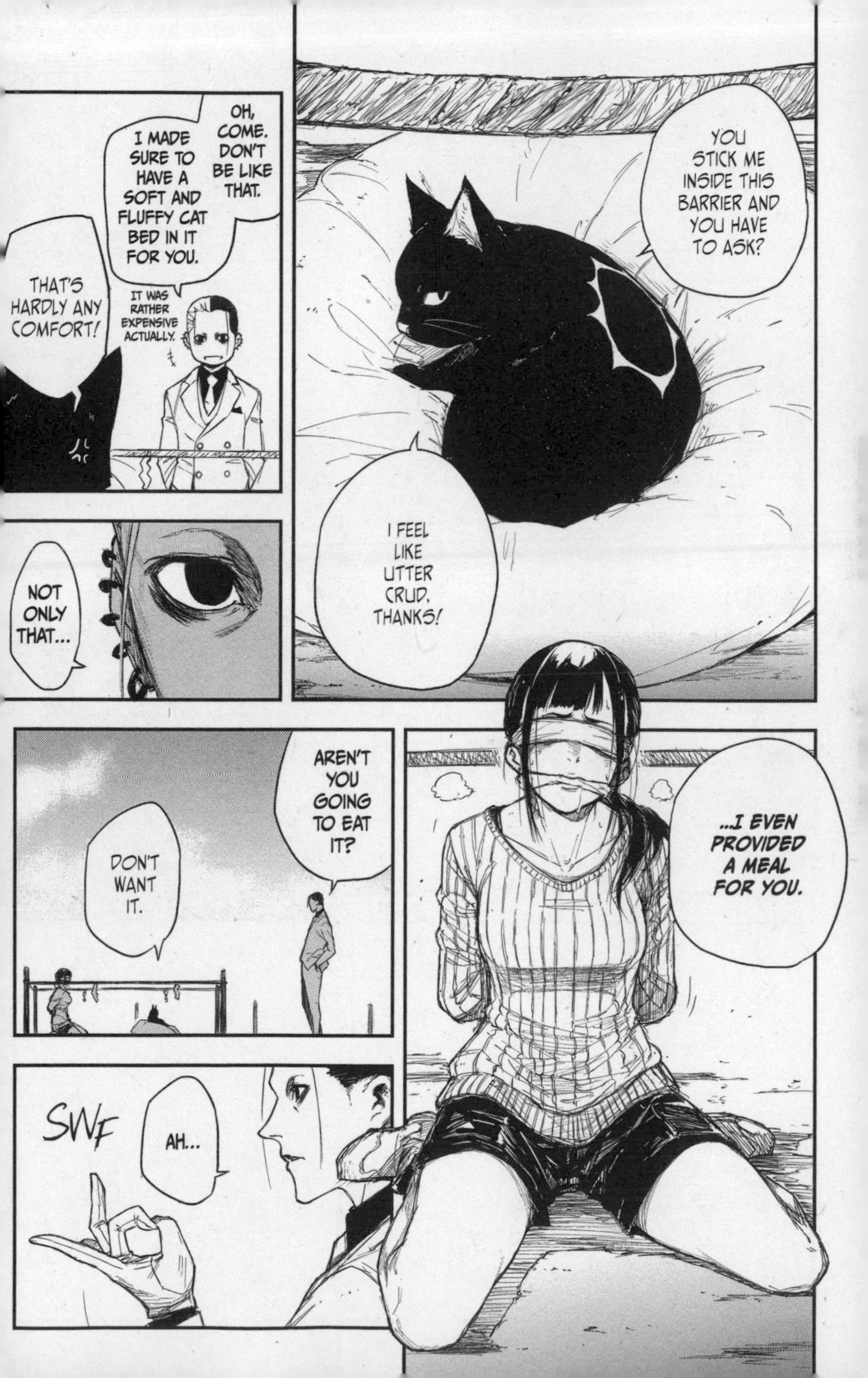
YOU STICK ME INSIDE THIS BARRIER AND YOU HAVE TO ASK?
I FEEL LIKE UTTER CRUD, THANKS!
OH, COME. DON'T BE LIKE THAT.
I MADE SURE TO HAVE A SOFT AND FLUFFY CAT BED IN IT FOR YOU.
THAT'S HARDLY ANY COMFORT!
IT WAS RATHER EXPENSIVE ACTUALLY.
NOT ONLY THAT...
...I EVEN PROVIDED A MEAL FOR YOU.
AREN'T YOU GOING TO EAT IT?
DON'T WANT IT.
AH...
SWF

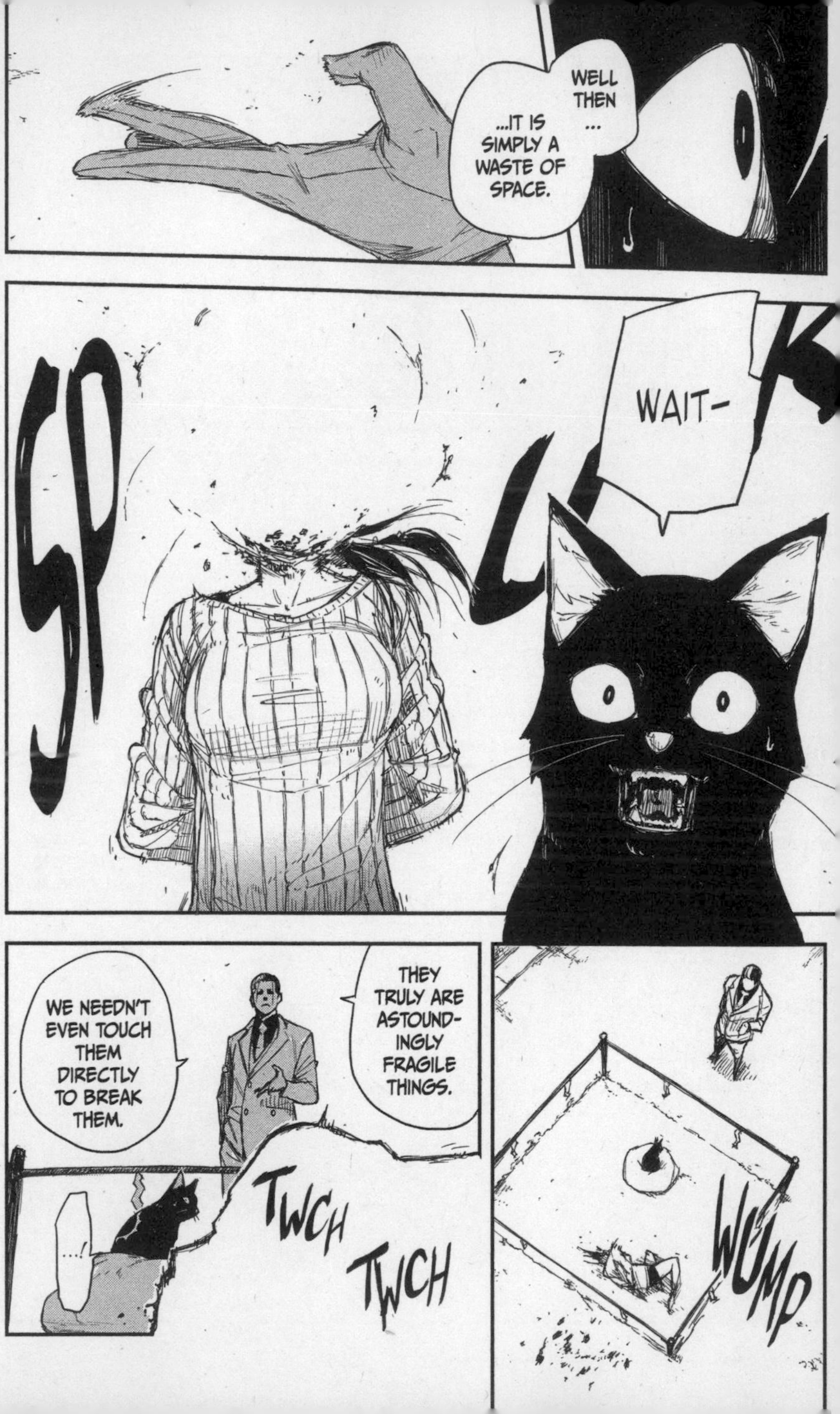
WELL THEN ...
...IT IS SIMPLY A WASTE OF SPACE.
WAIT-
SP
K
WUMP
THEY TRULY ARE ASTOUND-INGLY FRAGILE THINGS.
WE NEEDN'T EVEN TOUCH THEM DIRECTLY TO BREAK THEM.
...!
TWCH
TWCH

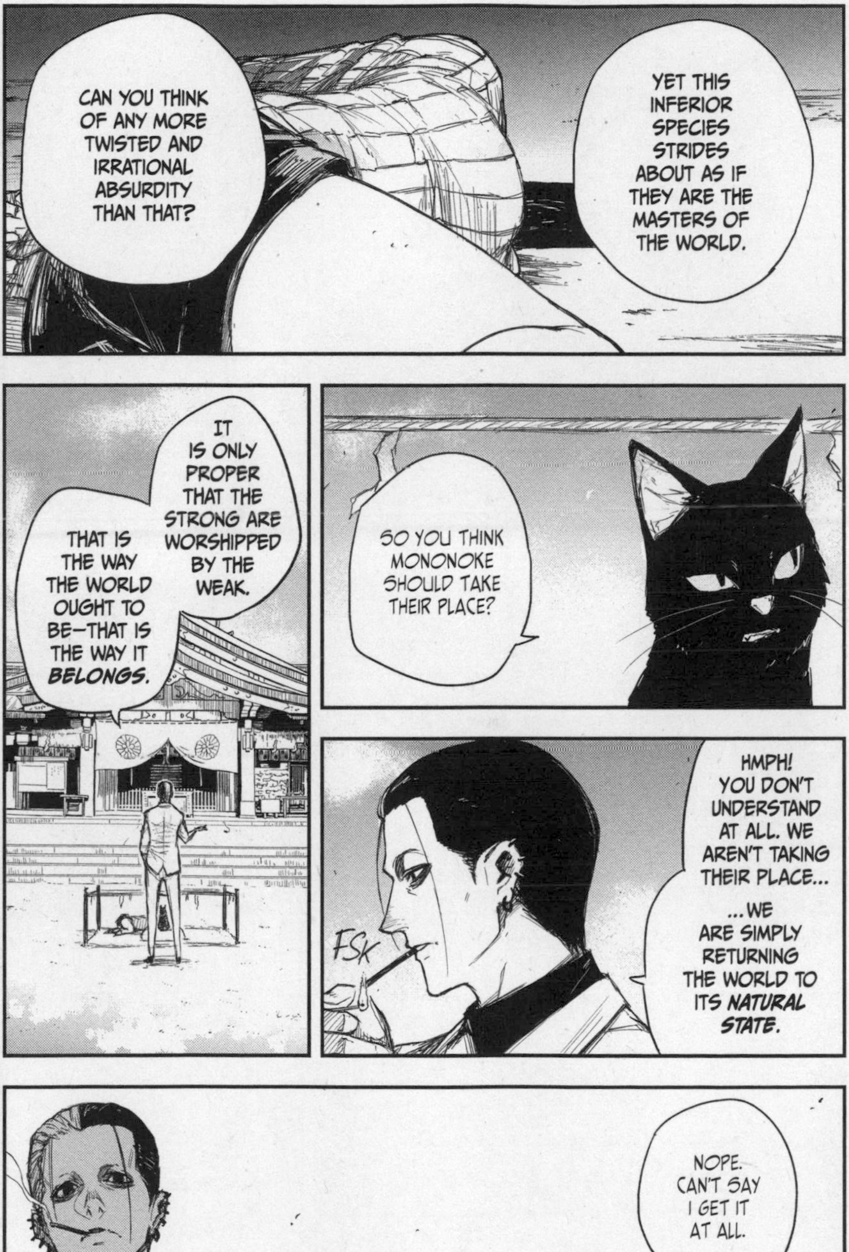
YET THIS INFERIOR SPECIES STRIDES ABOUT AS IF THEY ARE THE MASTERS OF THE WORLD.
CAN YOU THINK OF ANY MORE TWISTED AND IRRATIONAL ABSURDITY THAN THAT?
SO YOU THINK MONONOKE SHOULD TAKE THEIR PLACE?
HMPH! YOU DON'T UNDERSTAND AT ALL. WE AREN'T TAKING THEIR PLACE...
...WE ARE SIMPLY RETURNING THE WORLD TO ITS ***NATURAL STATE.***
FSK
IT IS ONLY PROPER THAT THE STRONG ARE WORSHIPPED BY THE WEAK.
THAT IS THE WAY THE WORLD OUGHT TO BE—THAT IS THE WAY IT ***BELONGS.***
NOPE. CAN'T SAY I GET IT AT ALL.

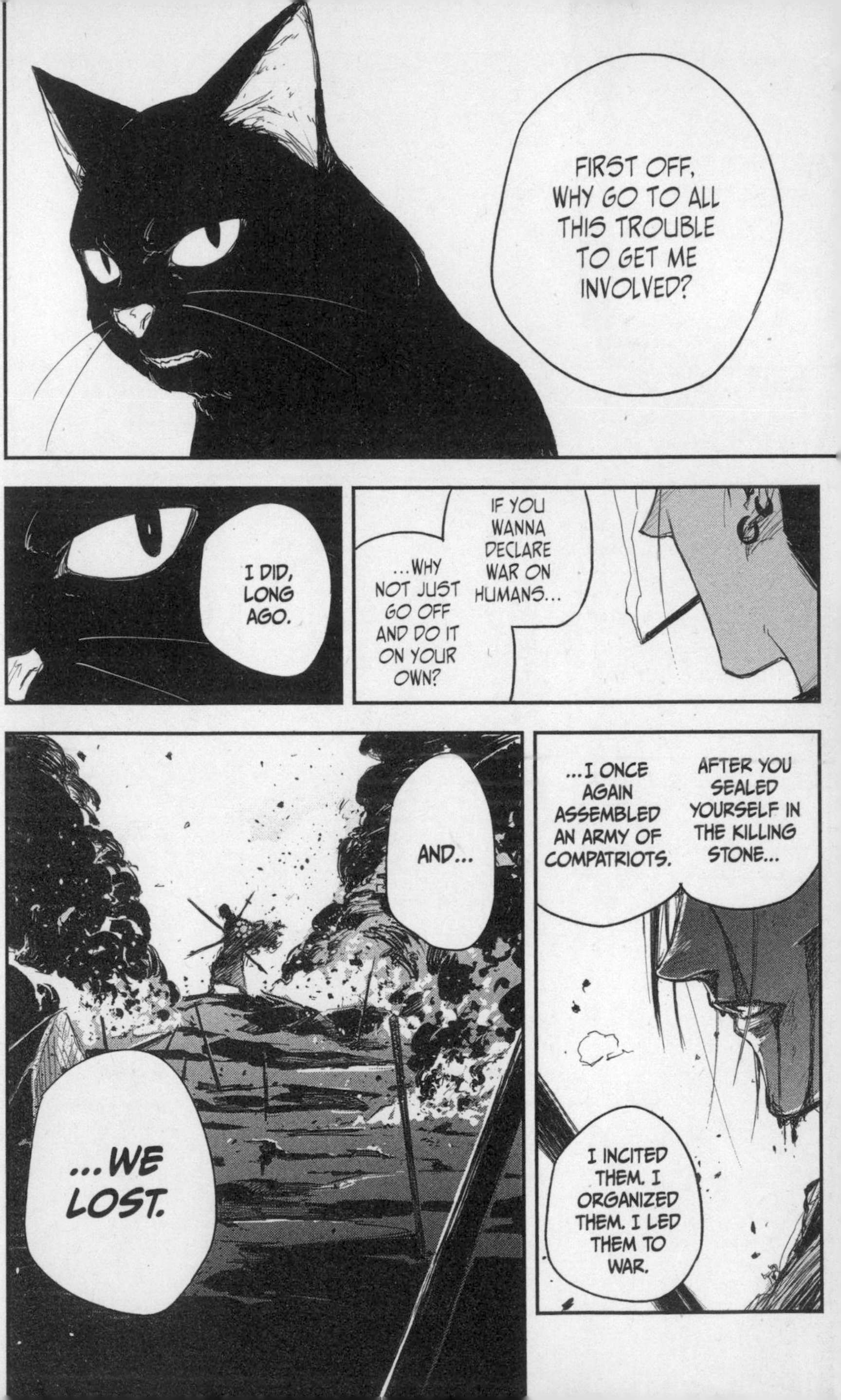
FIRST OFF, WHY GO TO ALL THIS TROUBLE TO GET ME INVOLVED?
IF YOU WANNA DECLARE WAR ON HUMANS...
...WHY NOT JUST GO OFF AND DO IT ON YOUR OWN?
I DID, LONG AGO.
AFTER YOU SEALED YOURSELF IN THE KILLING STONE...
...I ONCE AGAIN ASSEMBLED AN ARMY OF COMPATRIOTS.
I INCITED THEM. I ORGANIZED THEM. I LED THEM TO WAR.
AND...
...WE LOST.

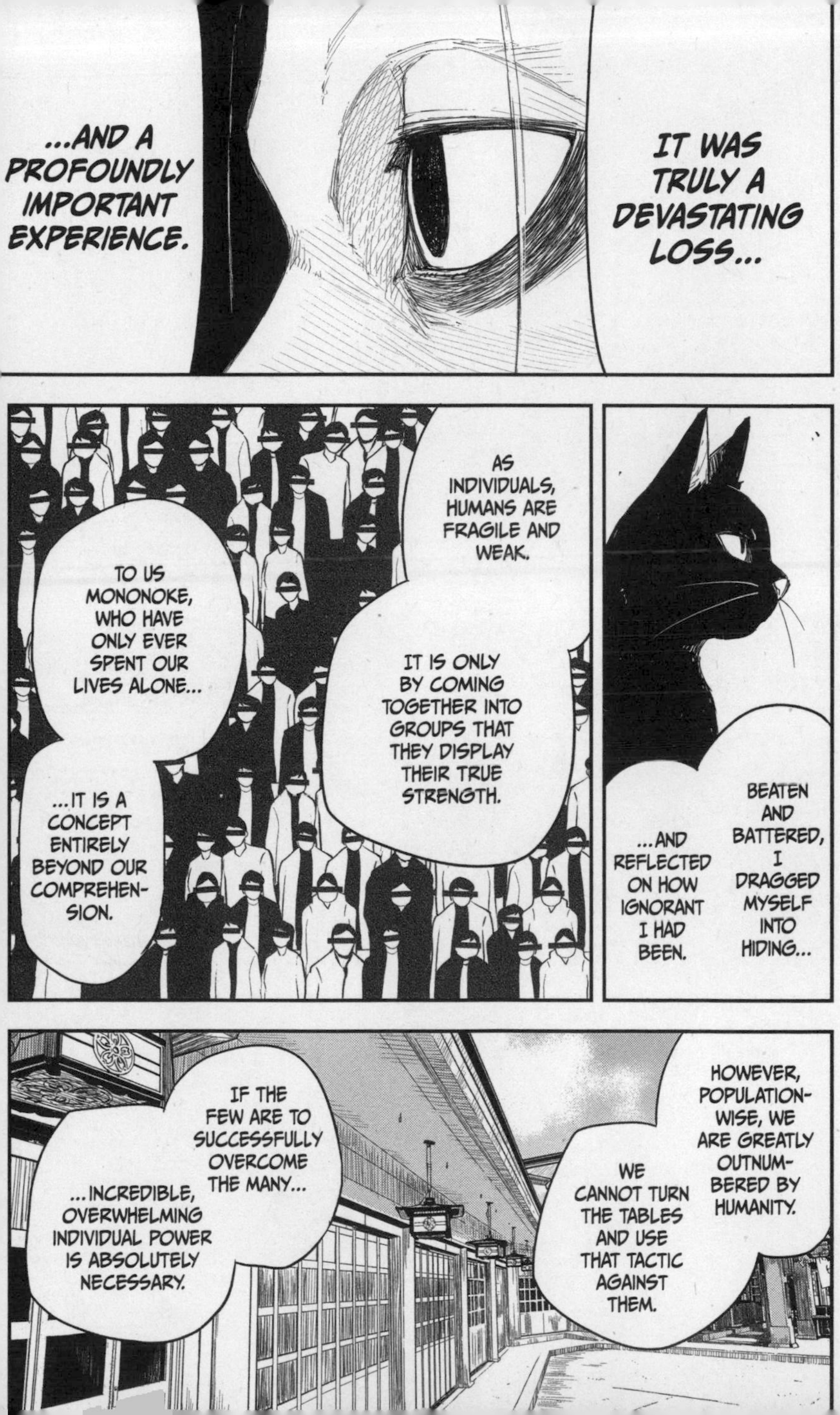
IT WAS TRULY A DEVASTATING LOSS...
...AND A PROFOUNDLY IMPORTANT EXPERIENCE.
BEATEN AND BATTERED, I DRAGGED MYSELF INTO HIDING...
...AND REFLECTED ON HOW IGNORANT I HAD BEEN.
AS INDIVIDUALS, HUMANS ARE FRAGILE AND WEAK.
IT IS ONLY BY COMING TOGETHER INTO GROUPS THAT THEY DISPLAY THEIR TRUE STRENGTH.
TO US MONONOKE, WHO HAVE ONLY EVER SPENT OUR LIVES ALONE...
...IT IS A CONCEPT ENTIRELY BEYOND OUR COMPREHENSION.
HOWEVER, POPULATION-WISE, WE ARE GREATLY OUTNUMBERED BY HUMANITY.
WE CANNOT TURN THE TABLES AND USE THAT TACTIC AGAINST THEM.
IF THE FEW ARE TO SUCCESSFULLY OVERCOME THE MANY...
...INCREDIBLE, OVERWHELMING INDIVIDUAL POWER IS ABSOLUTELY NECESSARY.

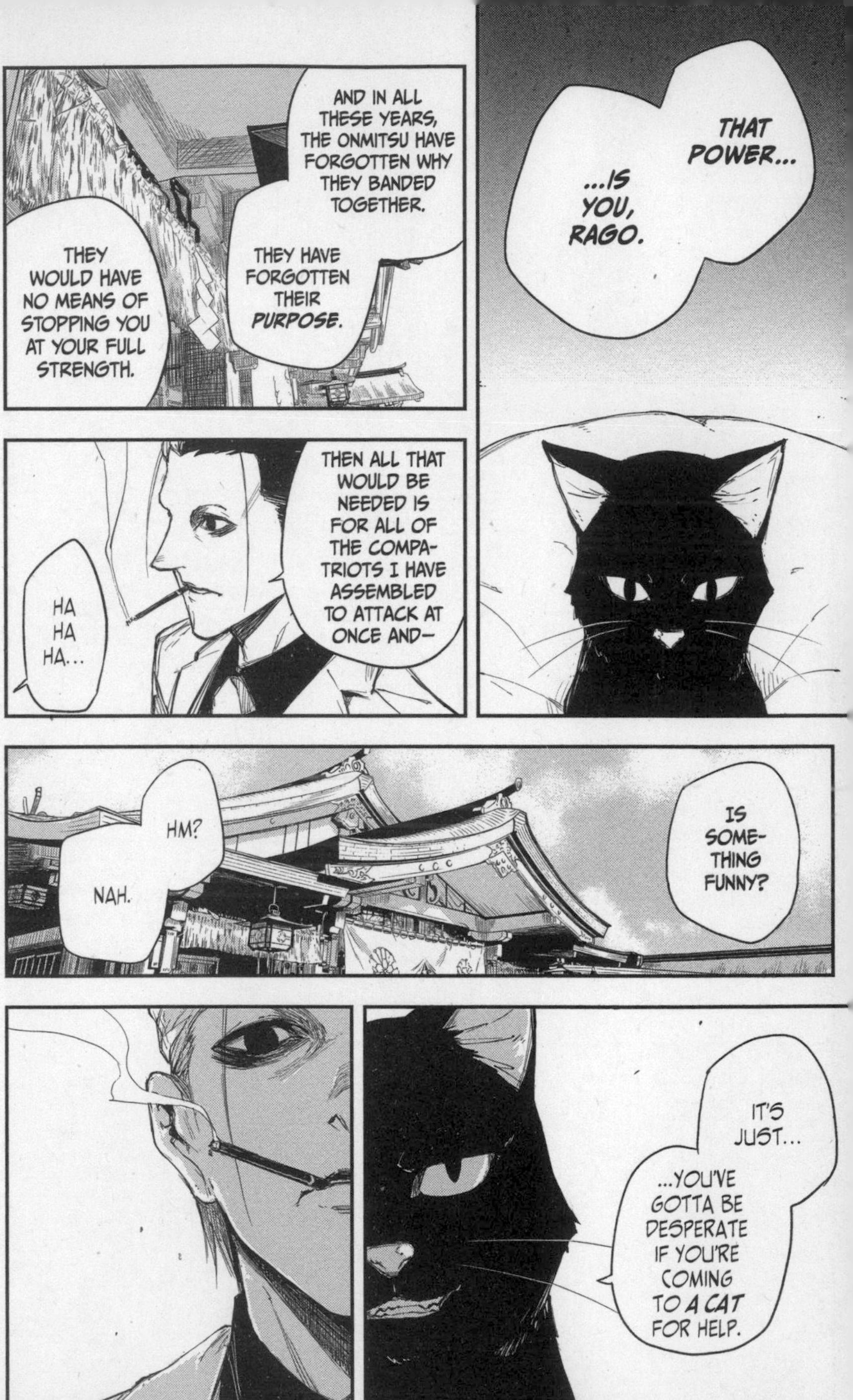
THAT POWER...
...IS YOU, RAGO.
AND IN ALL THESE YEARS, THE ONMITSU HAVE FORGOTTEN WHY THEY BANDED TOGETHER.
THEY HAVE FORGOTTEN THEIR *PURPOSE*.
THEY WOULD HAVE NO MEANS OF STOPPING YOU AT YOUR FULL STRENGTH.
THEN ALL THAT WOULD BE NEEDED IS FOR ALL OF THE COMPATRIOTS I HAVE ASSEMBLED TO ATTACK AT ONCE AND—
HA HA HA...
IS SOMETHING FUNNY?
HM?
NAH.
IT'S JUST...
...YOU'VE GOTTA BE DESPERATE IF YOU'RE COMING TO *A CAT* FOR HELP.

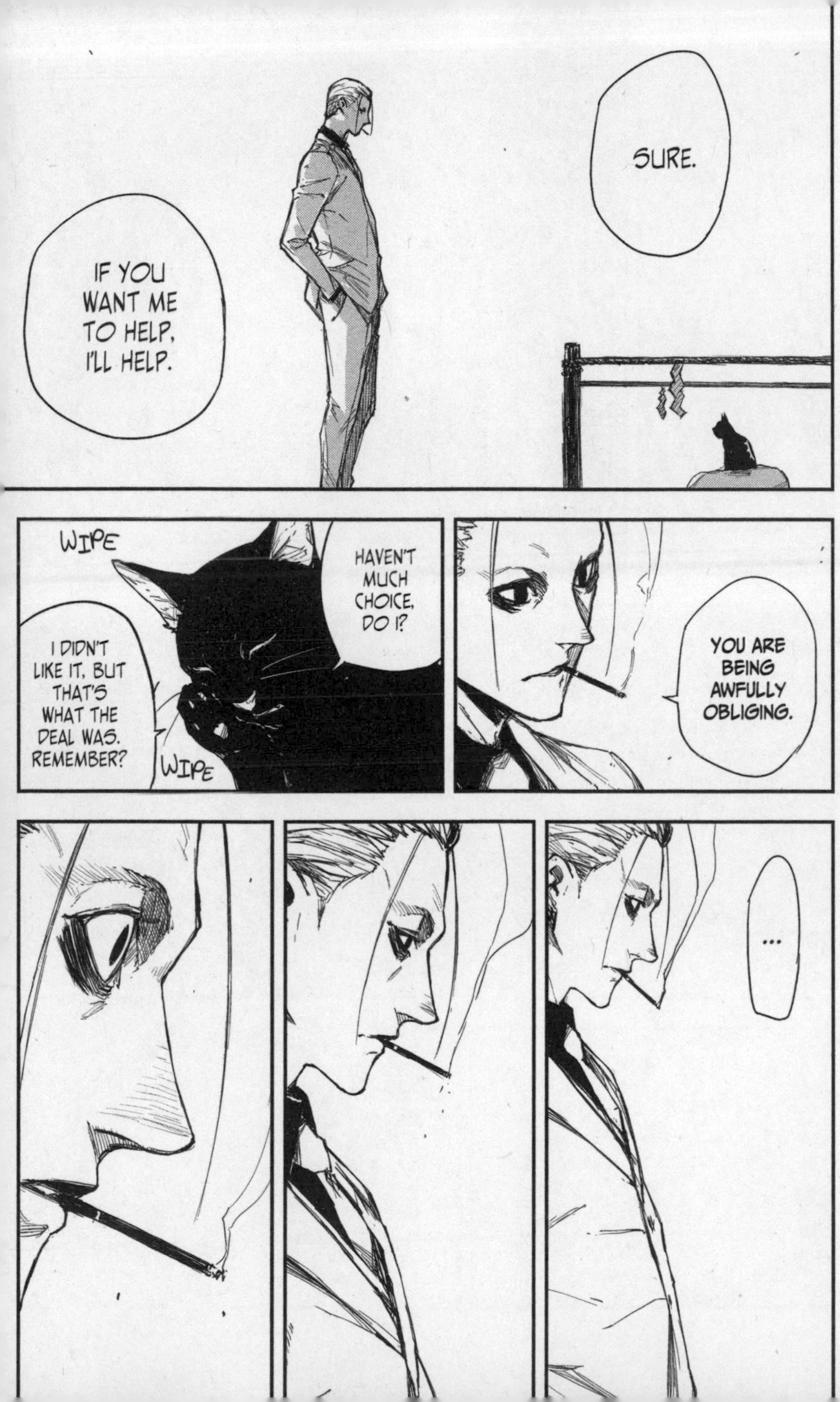
SURE.
IF YOU WANT ME TO HELP, I'LL HELP.
YOU ARE BEING AWFULLY OBLIGING.
HAVEN'T MUCH CHOICE, DO I?
WIPE
I DIDN'T LIKE IT, BUT THAT'S WHAT THE DEAL WAS. REMEMBER?
WIPE
...

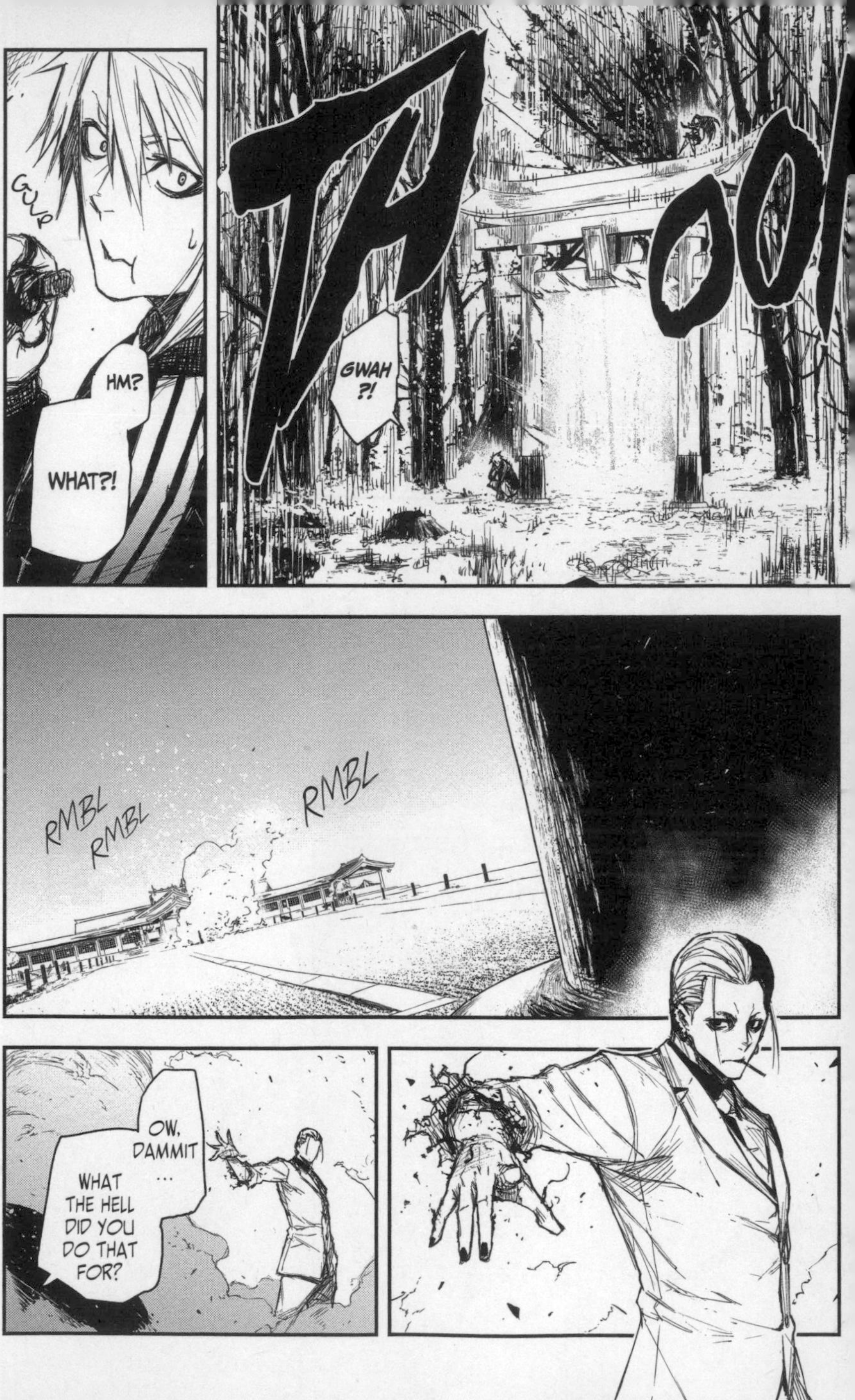

TAOO
GWAH ?!
GULP
HM?
WHAT?!
RMBL
RMBL
RMBL
OW, DAMMIT …
WHAT THE HELL DID YOU DO THAT FOR?

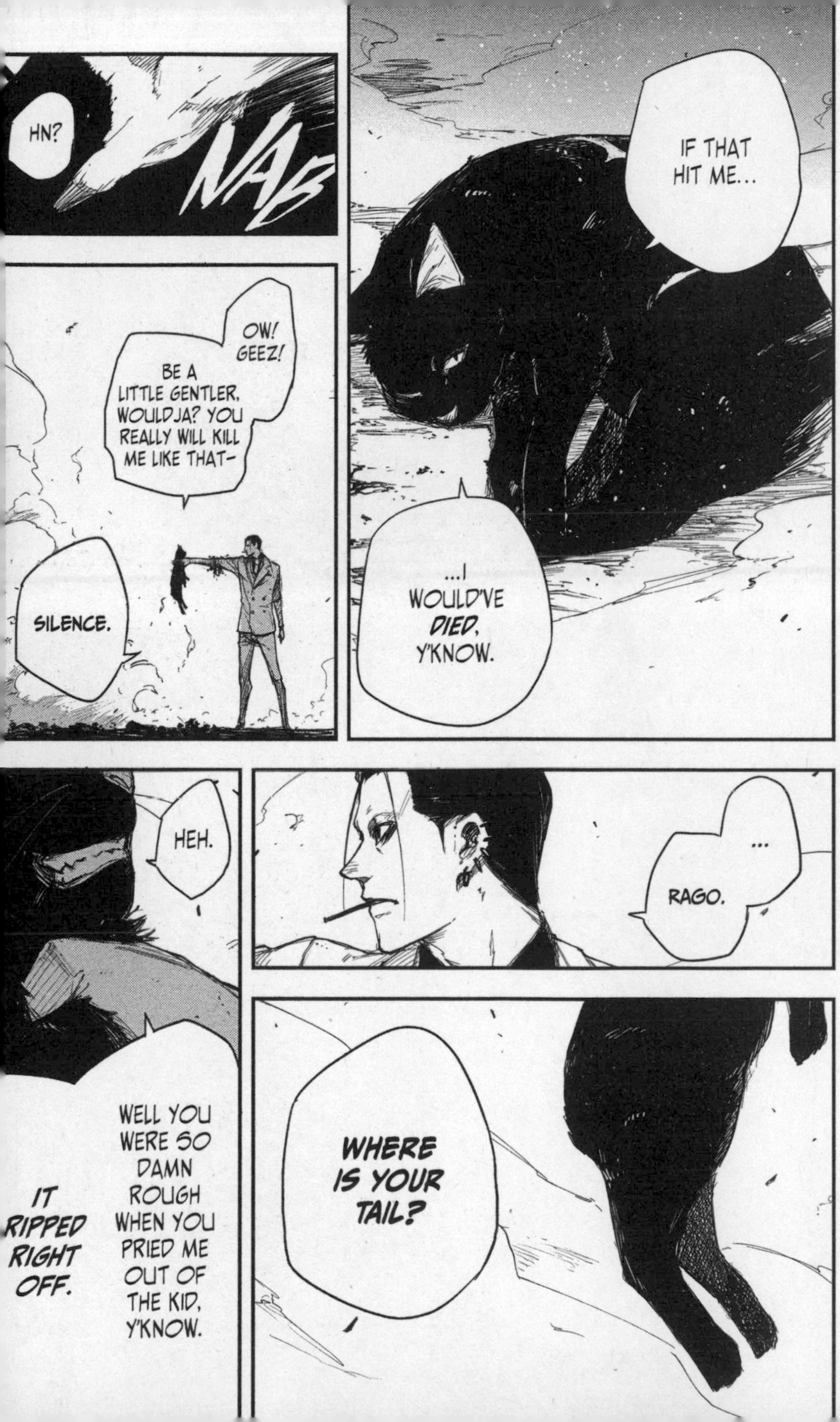
IF THAT HIT ME...
...I WOULD'VE *DIED*, Y'KNOW.
NAB
HN?
OW! GEEZ!
BE A LITTLE GENTLER, WOULDJA? YOU REALLY WILL KILL ME LIKE THAT-
SILENCE.
... RAGO.
WHERE IS YOUR TAIL?
HEH.
WELL YOU WERE SO DAMN ROUGH WHEN YOU PRIED ME OUT OF THE KID, Y'KNOW.
IT RIPPED RIGHT OFF.

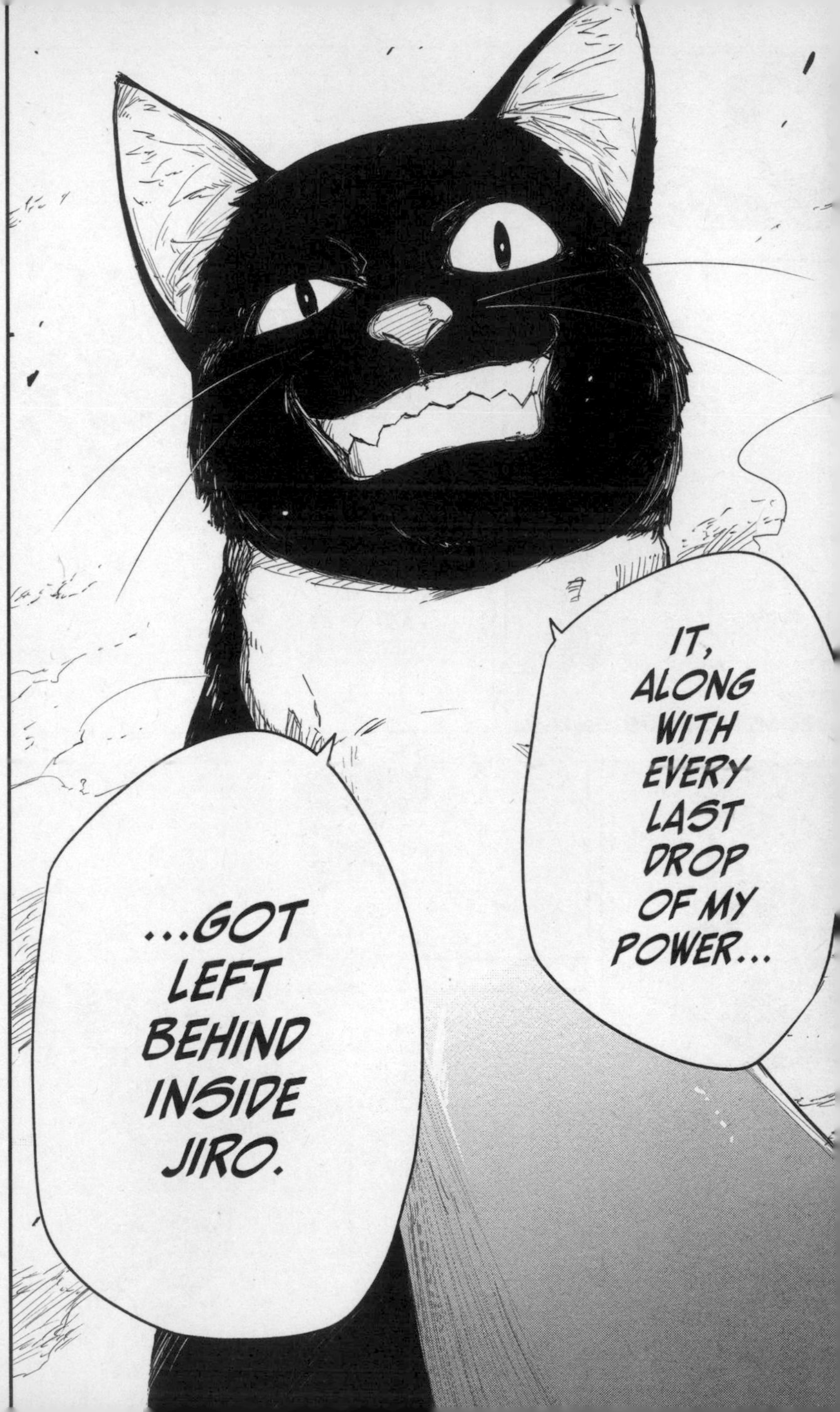
IT, ALONG WITH EVERY LAST DROP OF MY POWER...
...GOT LEFT BEHIND INSIDE JIRO.

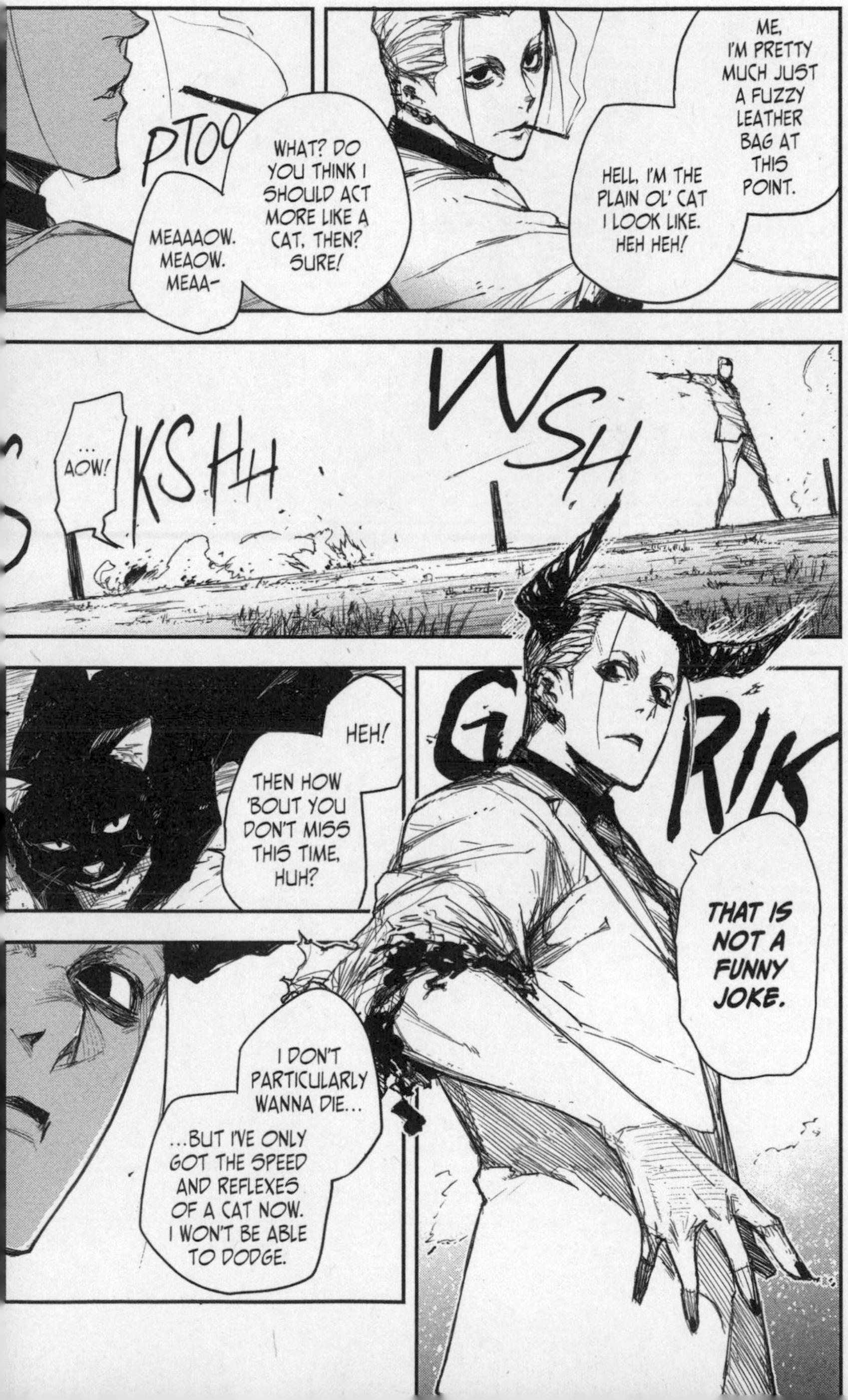
ME, I'M PRETTY MUCH JUST A FUZZY LEATHER BAG AT THIS POINT.
HELL, I'M THE PLAIN OL' CAT I LOOK LIKE. HEH HEH!
WHAT? DO YOU THINK I SHOULD ACT MORE LIKE A CAT, THEN? SURE!
PTOO
MEAAAOW. MEAOW. MEAA-
WSH
KSHH
... AOW!
GRIK
THAT IS NOT A FUNNY JOKE.
HEH!
THEN HOW 'BOUT YOU DON'T MISS THIS TIME, HUH?
I DON'T PARTICULARLY WANNA DIE...
...BUT I'VE ONLY GOT THE SPEED AND REFLEXES OF A CAT NOW. I WON'T BE ABLE TO DODGE.

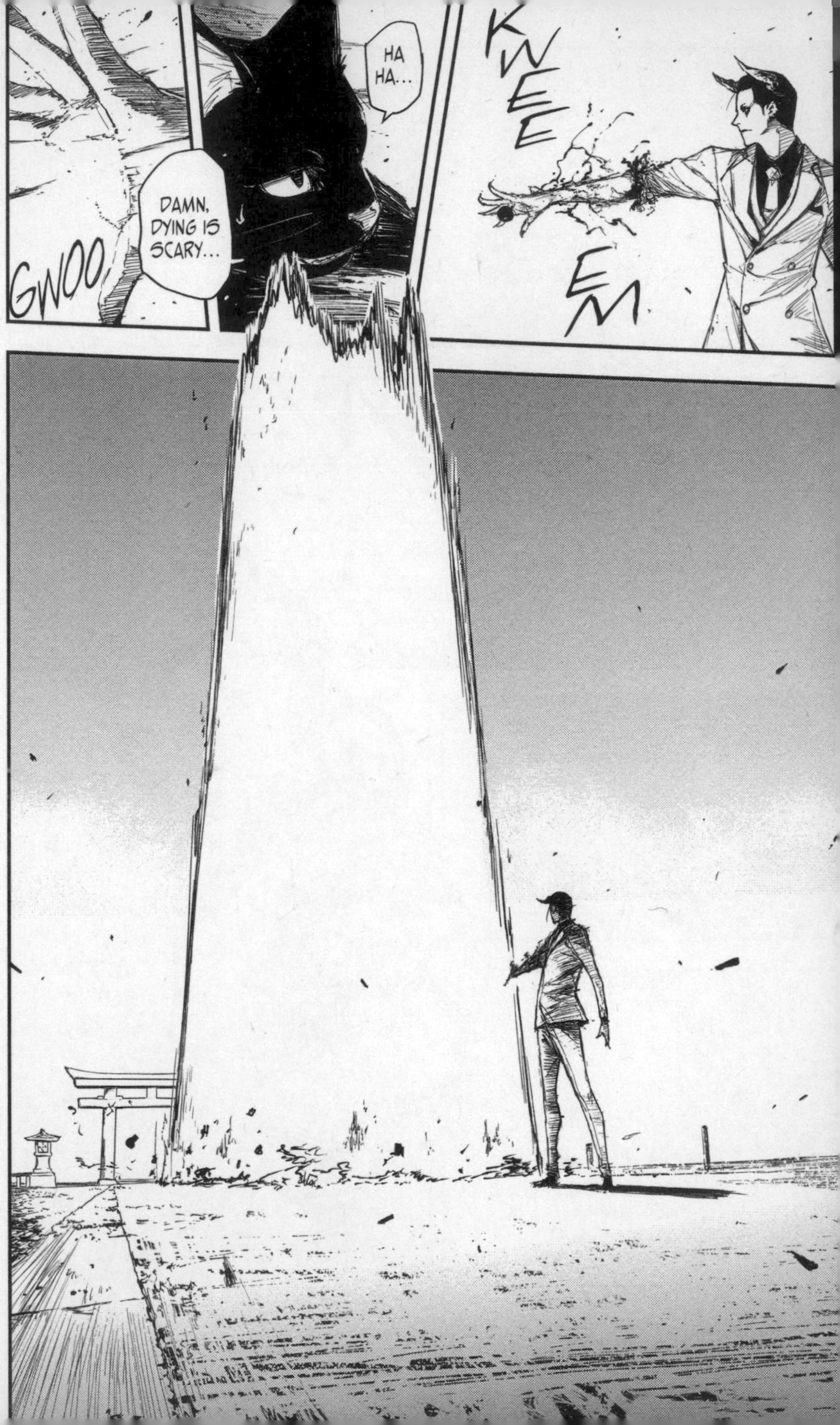
KWEE
EM
HA HA...
DAMN, DYING IS SCARY...
GWOO

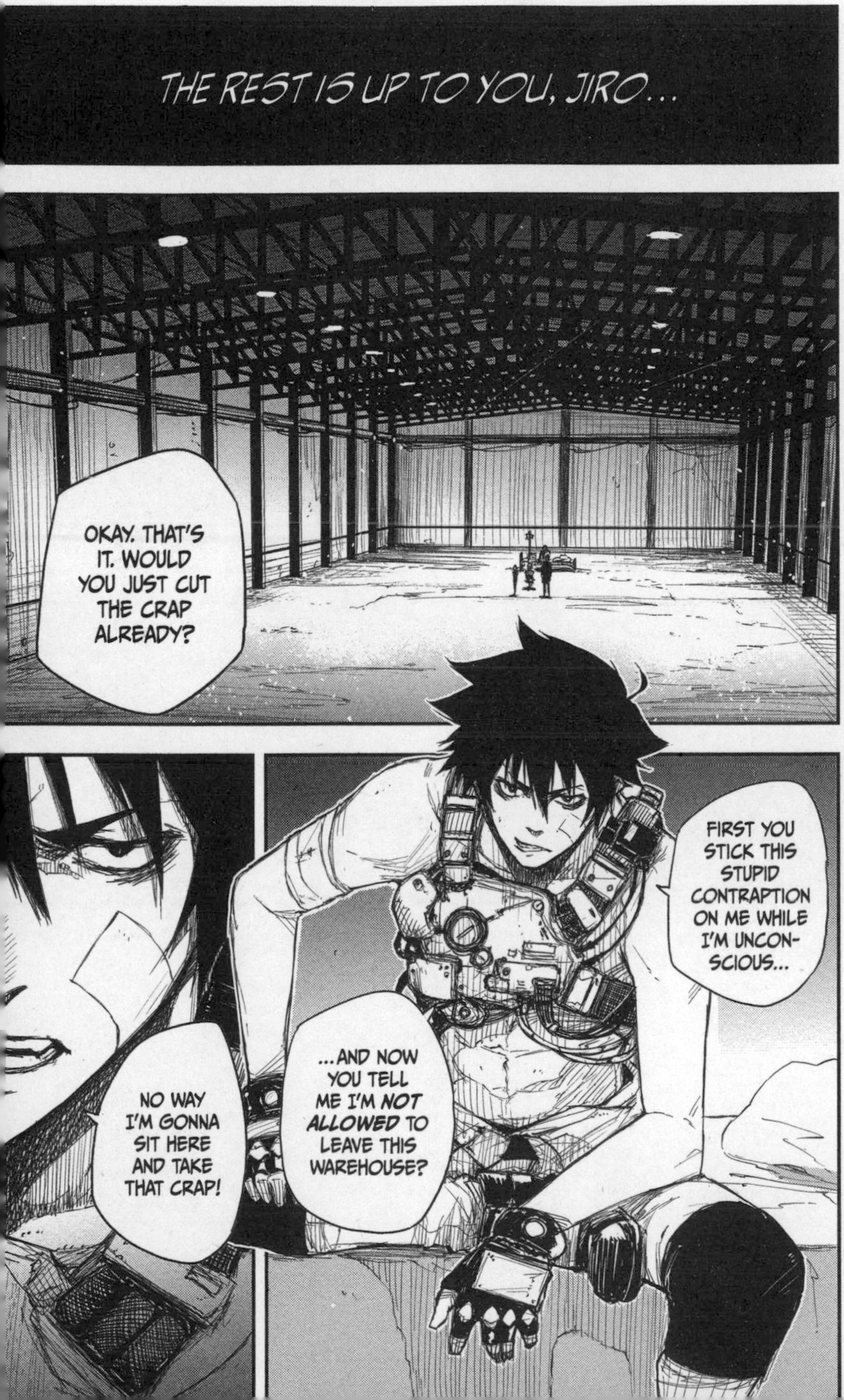
THE REST IS UP TO YOU, JIRO...
OKAY. THAT'S IT. WOULD YOU JUST CUT THE CRAP ALREADY?
FIRST YOU STICK THIS STUPID CONTRAPTION ON ME WHILE I'M UNCON-SCIOUS...
...AND NOW YOU TELL ME I'M *NOT ALLOWED* TO LEAVE THIS WAREHOUSE?
NO WAY I'M GONNA SIT HERE AND TAKE THAT CRAP!

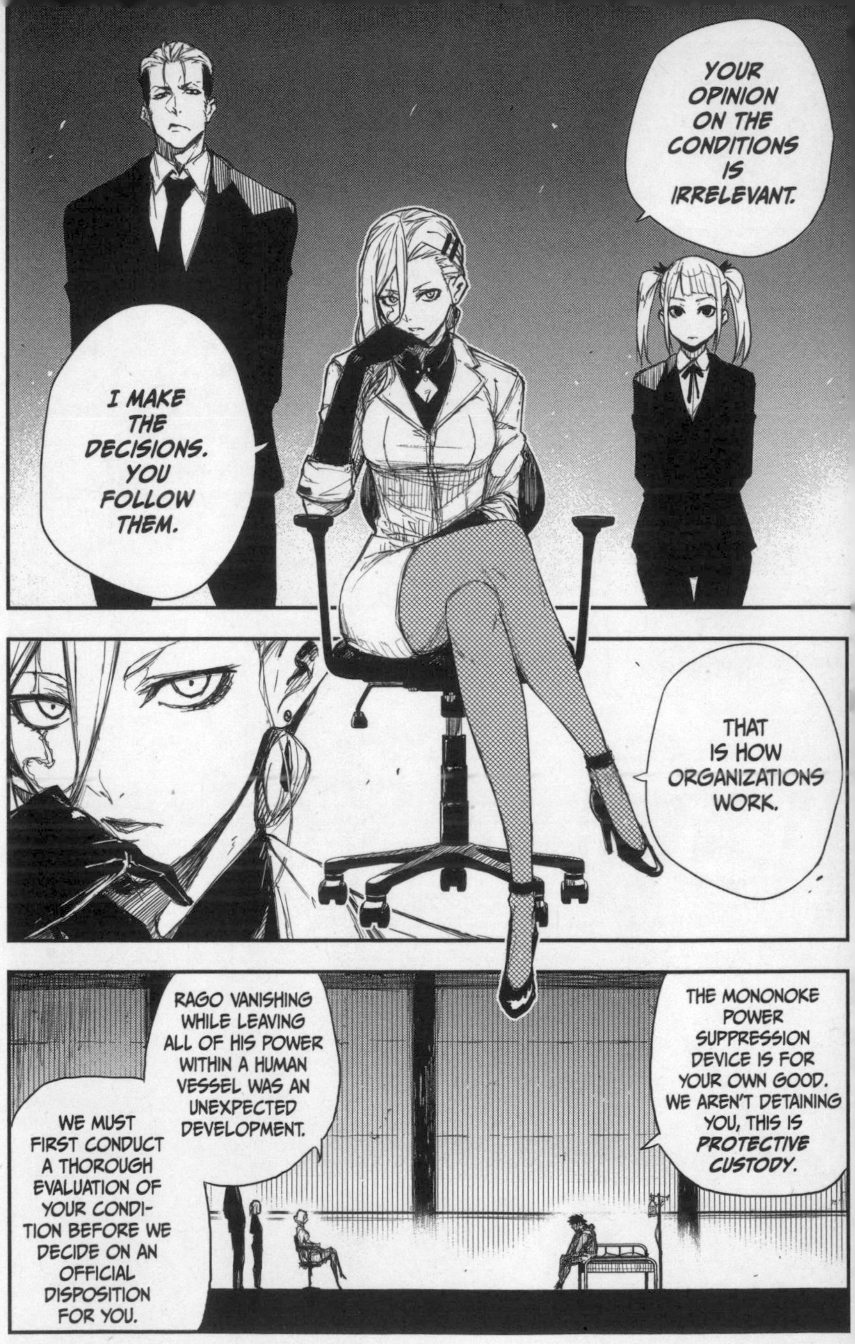
YOUR OPINION ON THE CONDITIONS IS IRRELEVANT.
I MAKE THE DECISIONS. YOU FOLLOW THEM.
THAT IS HOW ORGANIZATIONS WORK.
THE MONONOKE POWER SUPPRESSION DEVICE IS FOR YOUR OWN GOOD. WE AREN'T DETAINING YOU, THIS IS *PROTECTIVE CUSTODY.*
RAGO VANISHING WHILE LEAVING ALL OF HIS POWER WITHIN A HUMAN VESSEL WAS AN UNEXPECTED DEVELOPMENT.
WE MUST FIRST CONDUCT A THOROUGH EVALUATION OF YOUR CONDITION BEFORE WE DECIDE ON AN OFFICIAL DISPOSITION FOR YOU.

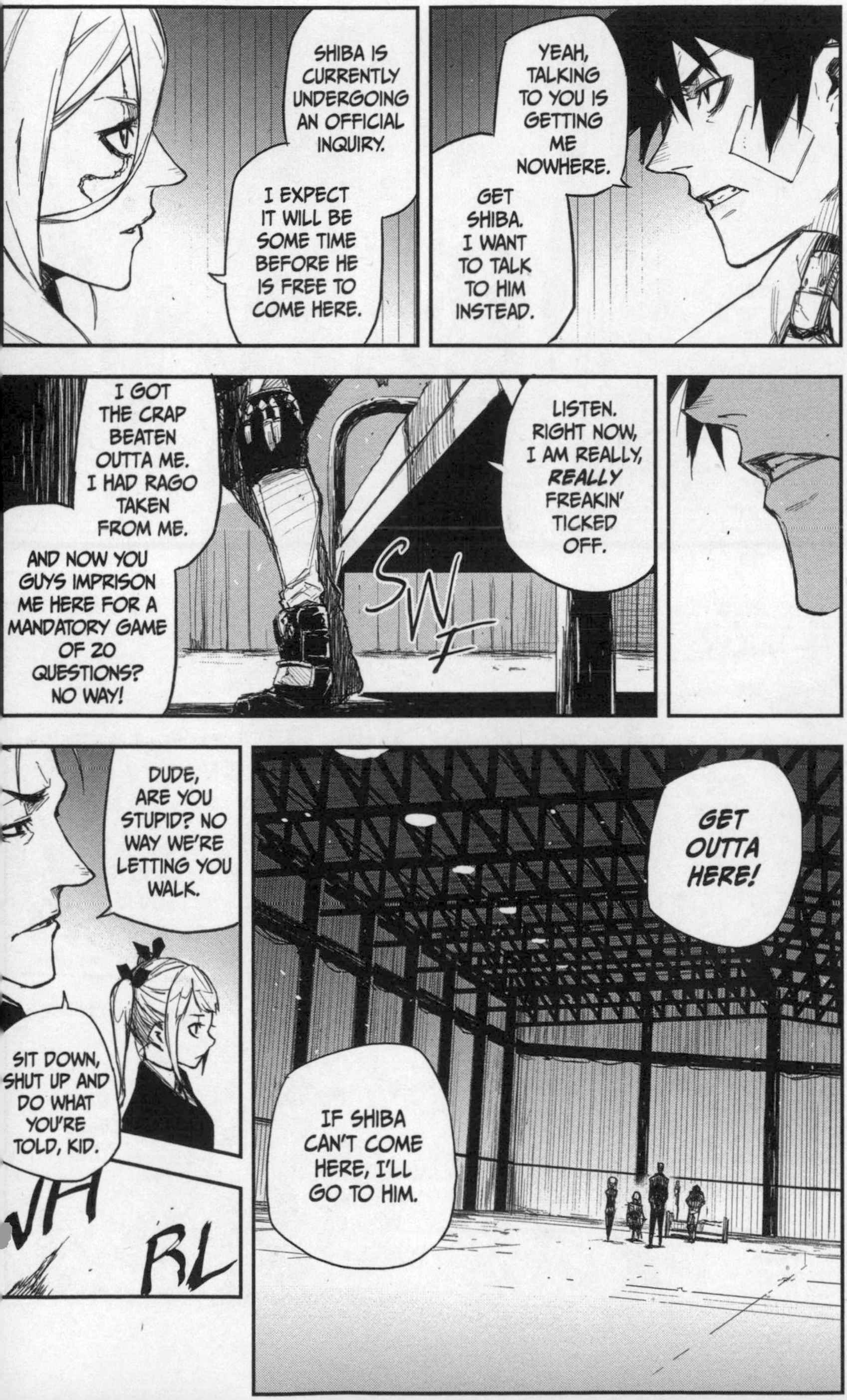
YEAH, TALKING TO YOU IS GETTING ME NOWHERE.
GET SHIBA. I WANT TO TALK TO HIM INSTEAD.
SHIBA IS CURRENTLY UNDERGOING AN OFFICIAL INQUIRY.
I EXPECT IT WILL BE SOME TIME BEFORE HE IS FREE TO COME HERE.
LISTEN. RIGHT NOW, I AM REALLY, *REALLY* FREAKIN' TICKED OFF.
SWF
I GOT THE CRAP BEATEN OUTTA ME. I HAD RAGO TAKEN FROM ME.
AND NOW YOU GUYS IMPRISON ME HERE FOR A MANDATORY GAME OF 20 QUESTIONS? NO WAY!
GET OUTTA HERE!
IF SHIBA CAN'T COME HERE, I'LL GO TO HIM.
DUDE, ARE YOU STUPID? NO WAY WE'RE LETTING YOU WALK.
SIT DOWN, SHUT UP AND DO WHAT YOU'RE TOLD, KID.
WHRL

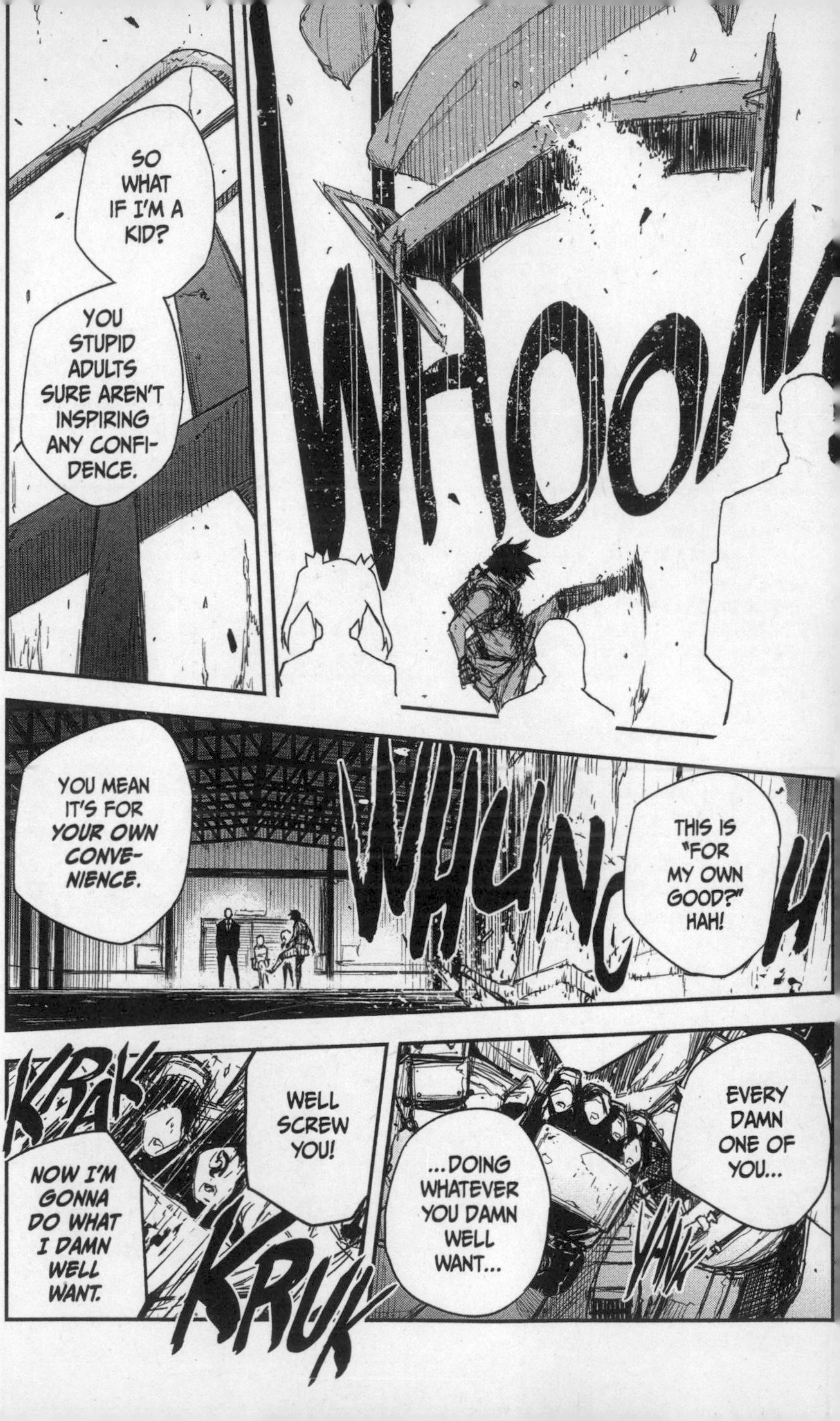
WHOOM
SO WHAT IF I'M A KID?
YOU STUPID ADULTS SURE AREN'T INSPIRING ANY CONFI-DENCE.
THIS IS "FOR MY OWN GOOD?" HAH!
WHUNCH
YOU MEAN IT'S FOR YOUR OWN CONVE-NIENCE.
EVERY DAMN ONE OF YOU...
...DOING WHATEVER YOU DAMN WELL WANT...
YANK
WELL SCREW YOU!
KRAK
NOW I'M GONNA DO WHAT I DAMN WELL WANT.
KRUK

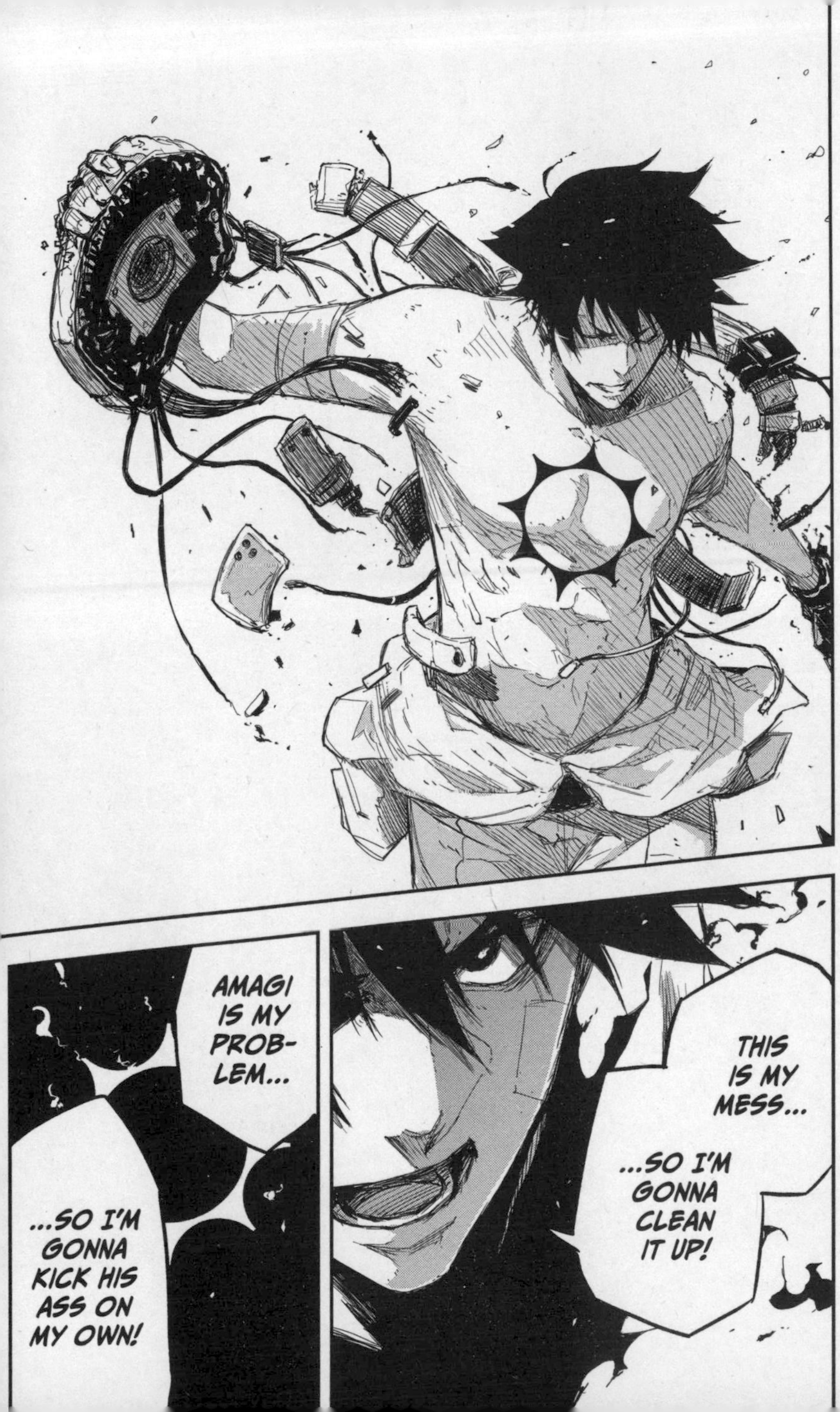
THIS IS MY MESS...
...SO I'M GONNA CLEAN IT UP!
AMAGI IS MY PROB-LEM...
...SO I'M GONNA KICK HIS ASS ON MY OWN!

BLACK TORCH

#13 One

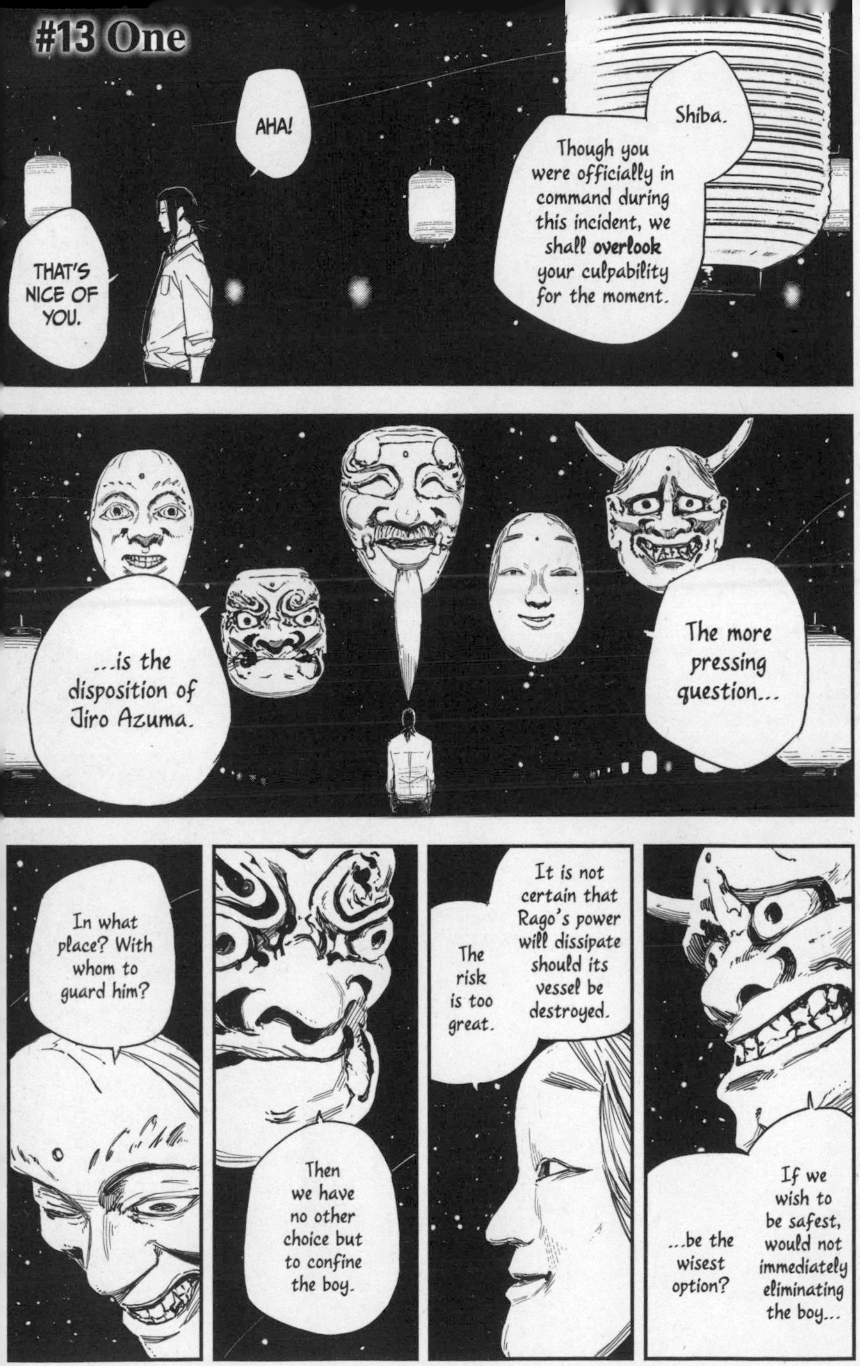

Shiba.
Though you were officially in command during this incident, we shall **overlook** your culpability for the moment.
AHA!
THAT'S NICE OF YOU.
The more pressing question...
...is the disposition of Jiro Azuma.
If we wish to be safest, would not immediately eliminating the boy...
...be the wisest option?
It is not certain that Rago's power will dissipate should its vessel be destroyed.
The risk is too great.
Then we have no other choice but to confine the boy.
In what place? With whom to guard him?

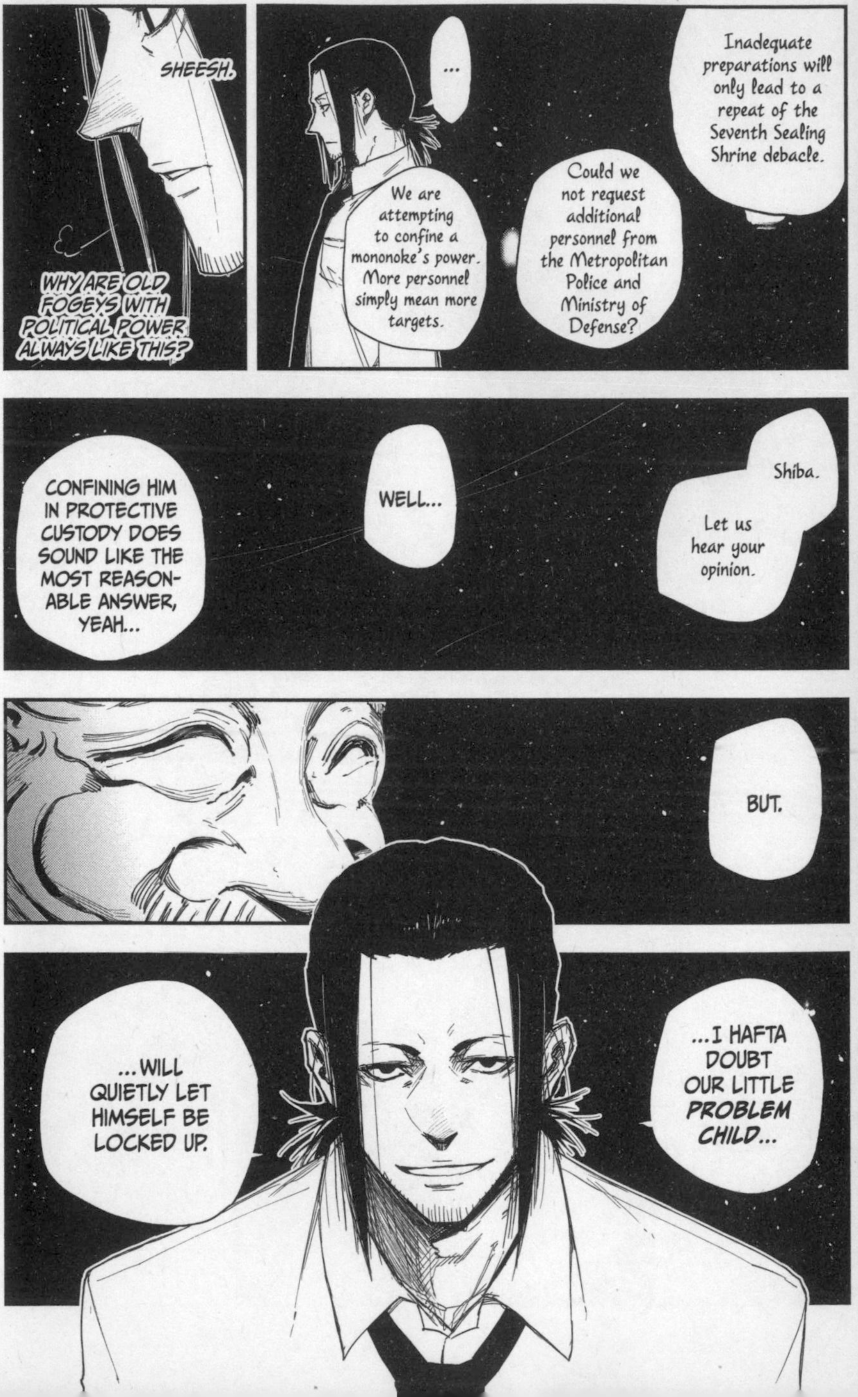
Inadequate preparations will only lead to a repeat of the Seventh Sealing Shrine debacle.
Could we not request additional personnel from the Metropolitan Police and Ministry of Defense?
We are attempting to confine a mononoke's power. More personnel simply mean more targets.
...
SHEESH.
WHY ARE OLD FOGEYS WITH POLITICAL POWER ALWAYS LIKE THIS?
Shiba.
Let us hear your opinion.
WELL...
CONFINING HIM IN PROTECTIVE CUSTODY DOES SOUND LIKE THE MOST REASON-ABLE ANSWER, YEAH...
BUT.
...I HAFTA DOUBT OUR LITTLE PROBLEM CHILD...
...WILL QUIETLY LET HIMSELF BE LOCKED UP.

#13 One

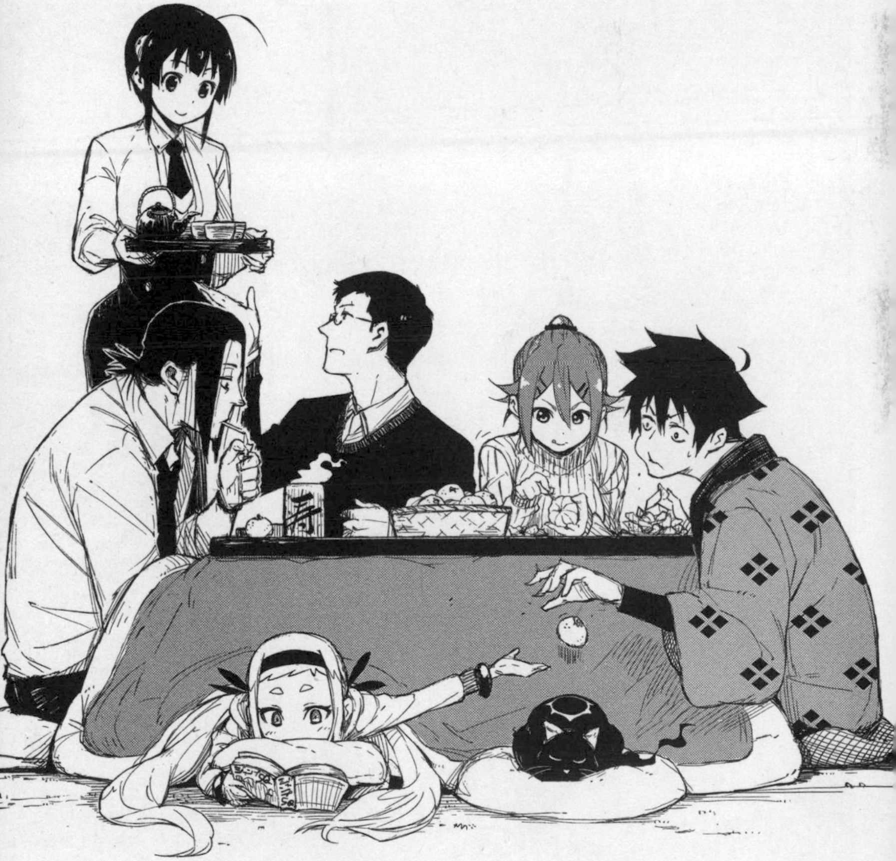

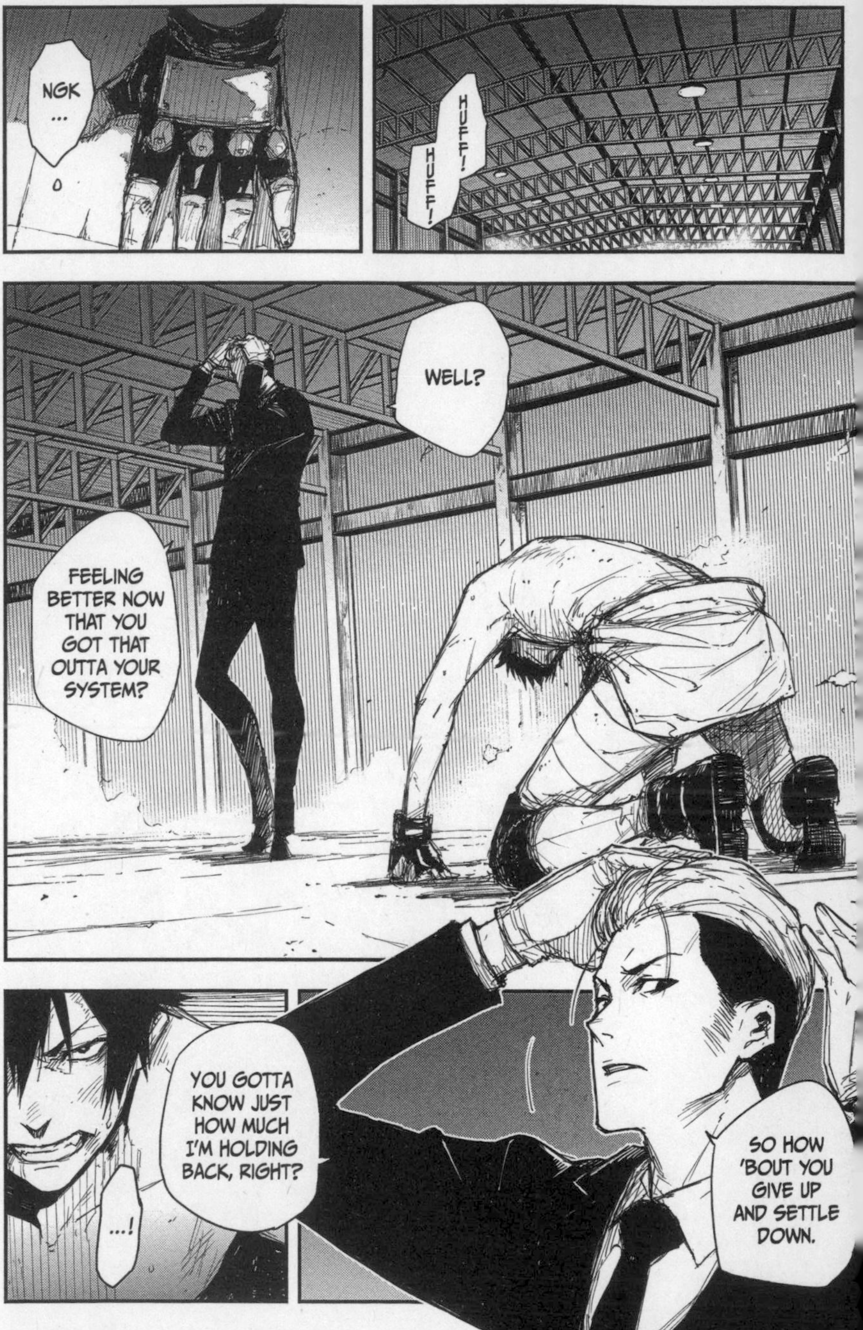
HUFF! HUFF!
NGK ...
WELL?
FEELING BETTER NOW THAT YOU GOT THAT OUTTA YOUR SYSTEM?
YOU GOTTA KNOW JUST HOW MUCH I'M HOLDING BACK, RIGHT?
SO HOW 'BOUT YOU GIVE UP AND SETTLE DOWN.
...!

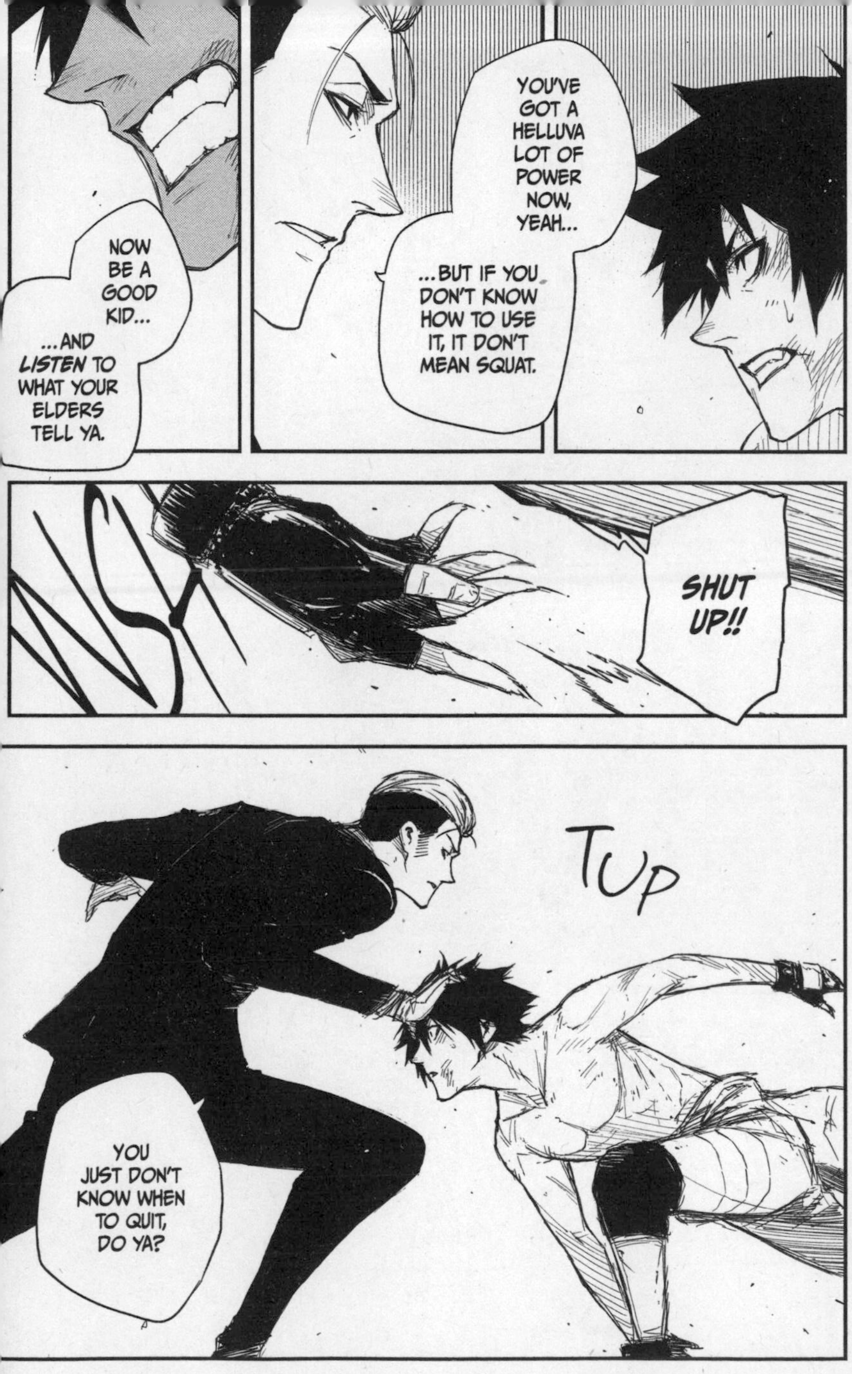
YOU'VE GOT A HELLUVA LOT OF POWER NOW, YEAH...
...BUT IF YOU DON'T KNOW HOW TO USE IT, IT DON'T MEAN SQUAT.
NOW BE A GOOD KID...
...AND *LISTEN* TO WHAT YOUR ELDERS TELL YA.
SHUT UP!!
TUP
YOU JUST DON'T KNOW WHEN TO QUIT, DO YA?

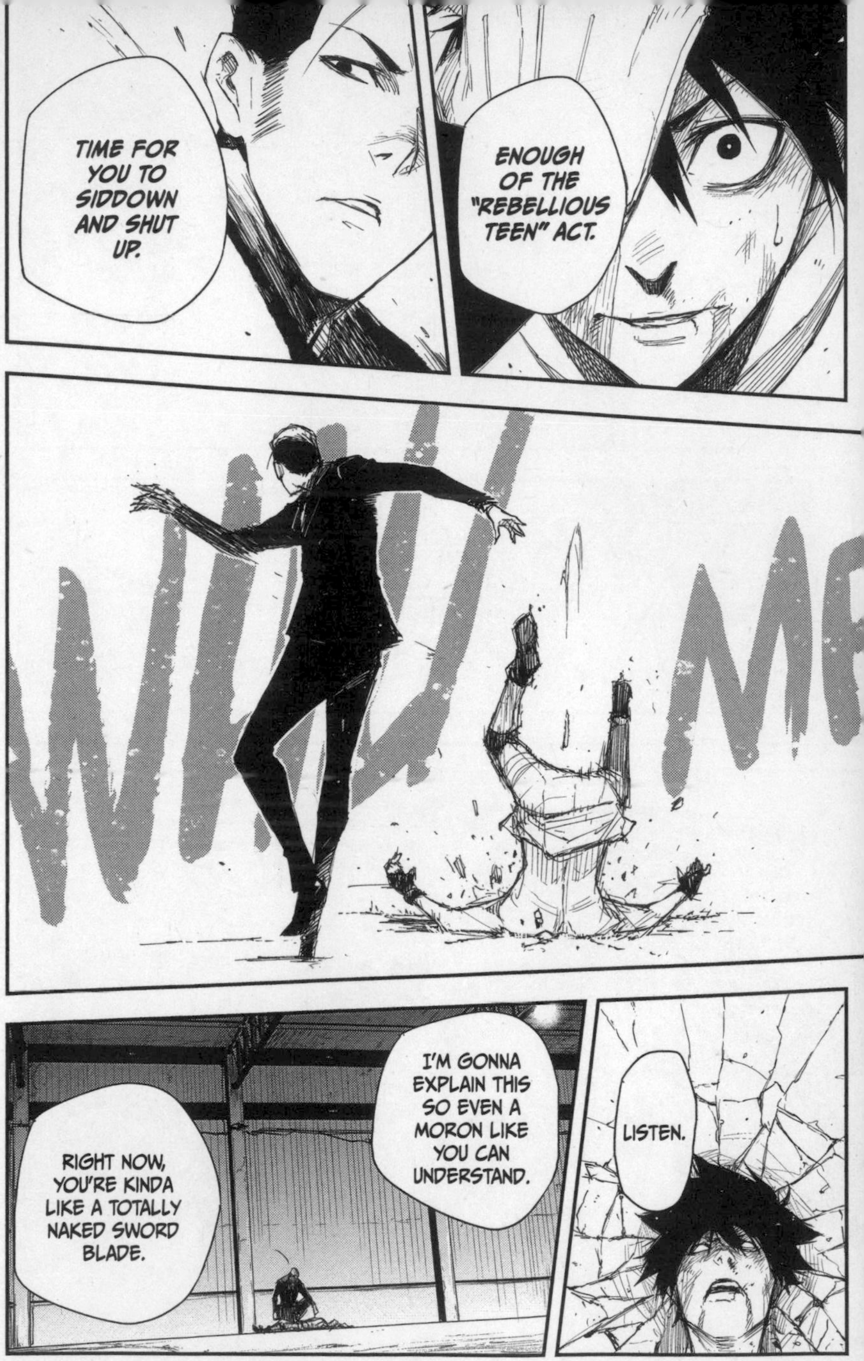
ENOUGH OF THE "REBELLIOUS TEEN" ACT.
TIME FOR YOU TO SIDDOWN AND SHUT UP.
LISTEN.
I'M GONNA EXPLAIN THIS SO EVEN A MORON LIKE YOU CAN UNDERSTAND.
RIGHT NOW, YOU'RE KINDA LIKE A TOTALLY NAKED SWORD BLADE.

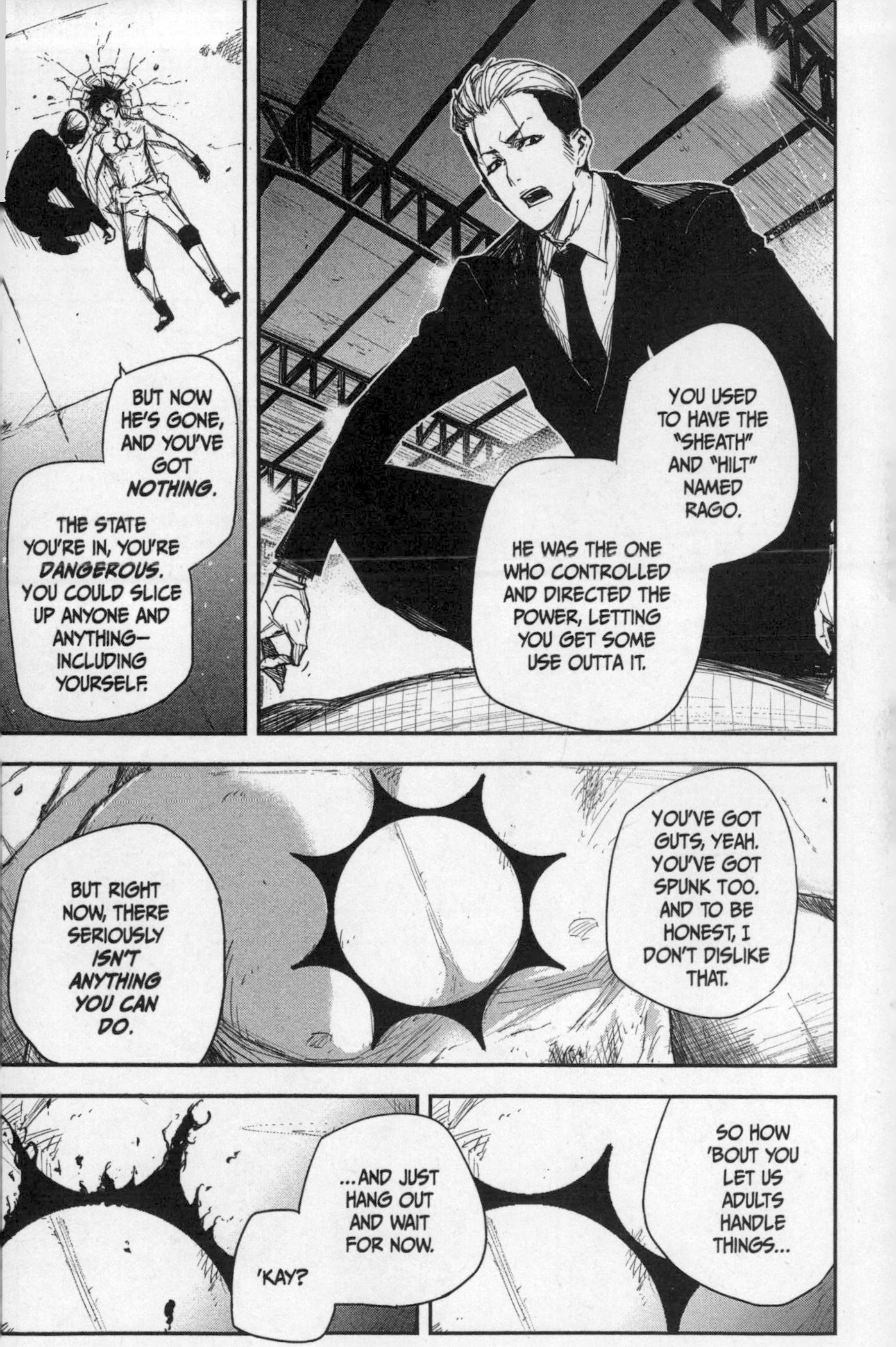
YOU USED TO HAVE THE "SHEATH" AND "HILT" NAMED RAGO.
HE WAS THE ONE WHO CONTROLLED AND DIRECTED THE POWER, LETTING YOU GET SOME USE OUTTA IT.
BUT NOW HE'S GONE, AND YOU'VE GOT *NOTHING*.
THE STATE YOU'RE IN, YOU'RE *DANGEROUS*. YOU COULD SLICE UP ANYONE AND ANYTHING—INCLUDING YOURSELF.
YOU'VE GOT GUTS, YEAH. YOU'VE GOT SPUNK TOO. AND TO BE HONEST, I DON'T DISLIKE THAT.
BUT RIGHT NOW, THERE SERIOUSLY *ISN'T ANYTHING YOU CAN DO*.
SO HOW 'BOUT YOU LET US ADULTS HANDLE THINGS...
...AND JUST HANG OUT AND WAIT FOR NOW.
'KAY?

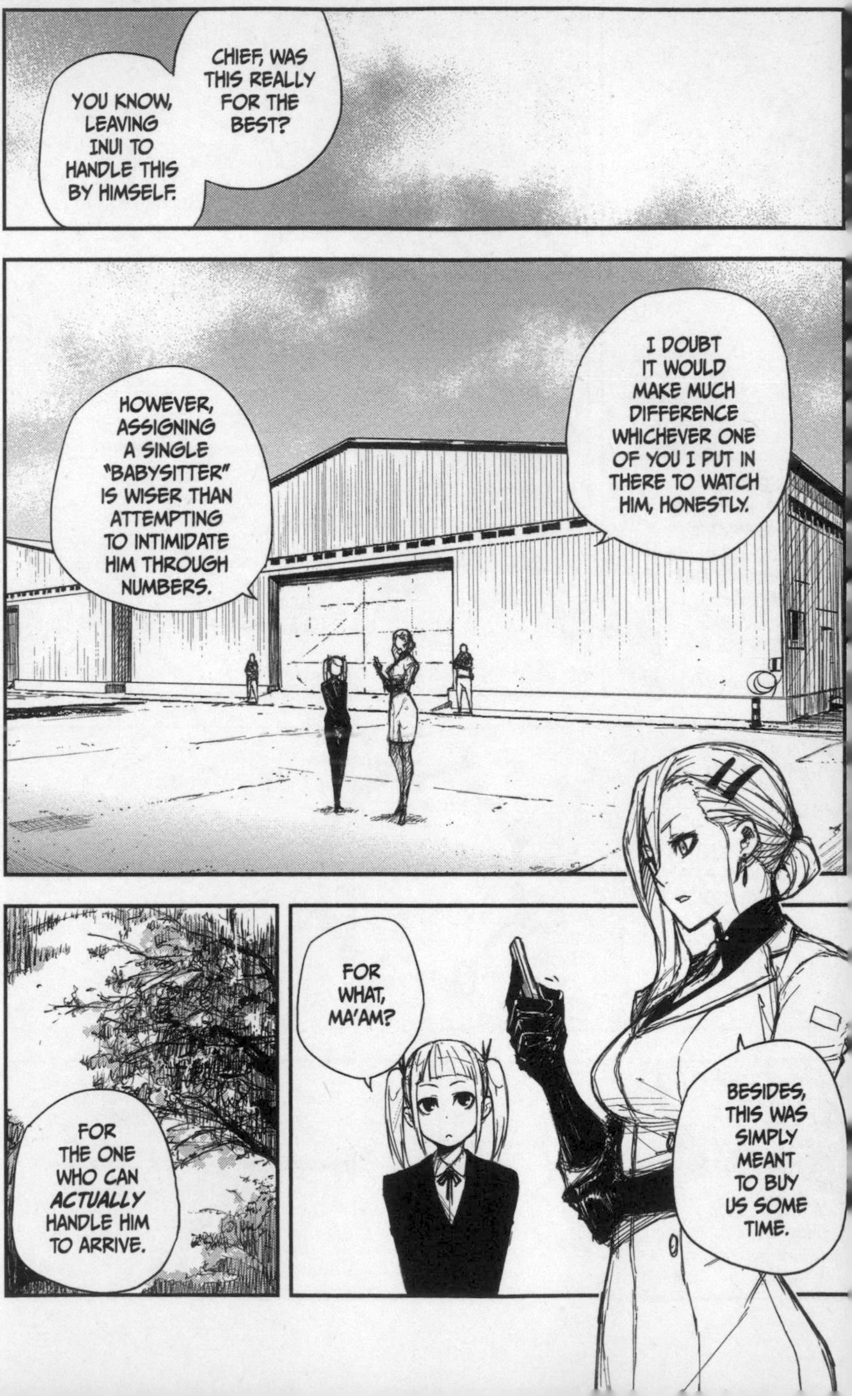

CHIEF, WAS THIS REALLY FOR THE BEST?
YOU KNOW, LEAVING INUI TO HANDLE THIS BY HIMSELF.
I DOUBT IT WOULD MAKE MUCH DIFFERENCE WHICHEVER ONE OF YOU I PUT IN THERE TO WATCH HIM, HONESTLY.
HOWEVER, ASSIGNING A SINGLE "BABYSITTER" IS WISER THAN ATTEMPTING TO INTIMIDATE HIM THROUGH NUMBERS.
BESIDES, THIS WAS SIMPLY MEANT TO BUY US SOME TIME.
FOR WHAT, MA'AM?
FOR THE ONE WHO CAN *ACTUALLY* HANDLE HIM TO ARRIVE.

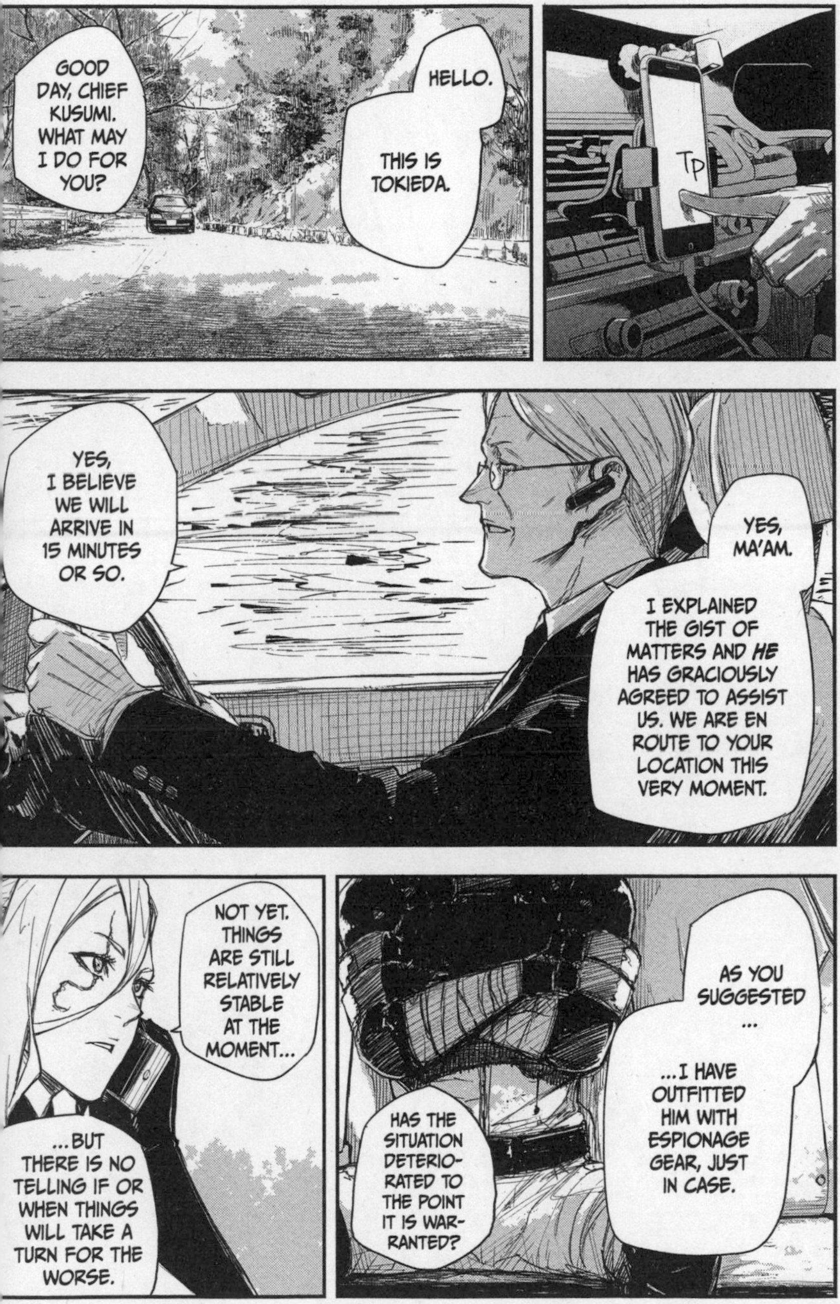
TP
HELLO.
THIS IS TOKIEDA.
GOOD DAY, CHIEF KUSUMI. WHAT MAY I DO FOR YOU?
YES, MA'AM.
I EXPLAINED THE GIST OF MATTERS AND *HE* HAS GRACIOUSLY AGREED TO ASSIST US. WE ARE EN ROUTE TO YOUR LOCATION THIS VERY MOMENT.
YES, I BELIEVE WE WILL ARRIVE IN 15 MINUTES OR SO.
AS YOU SUGGESTED ...
...I HAVE OUTFITTED HIM WITH ESPIONAGE GEAR, JUST IN CASE.
HAS THE SITUATION DETERIO-RATED TO THE POINT IT IS WAR-RANTED?
NOT YET. THINGS ARE STILL RELATIVELY STABLE AT THE MOMENT...
...BUT THERE IS NO TELLING IF OR WHEN THINGS WILL TAKE A TURN FOR THE WORSE.

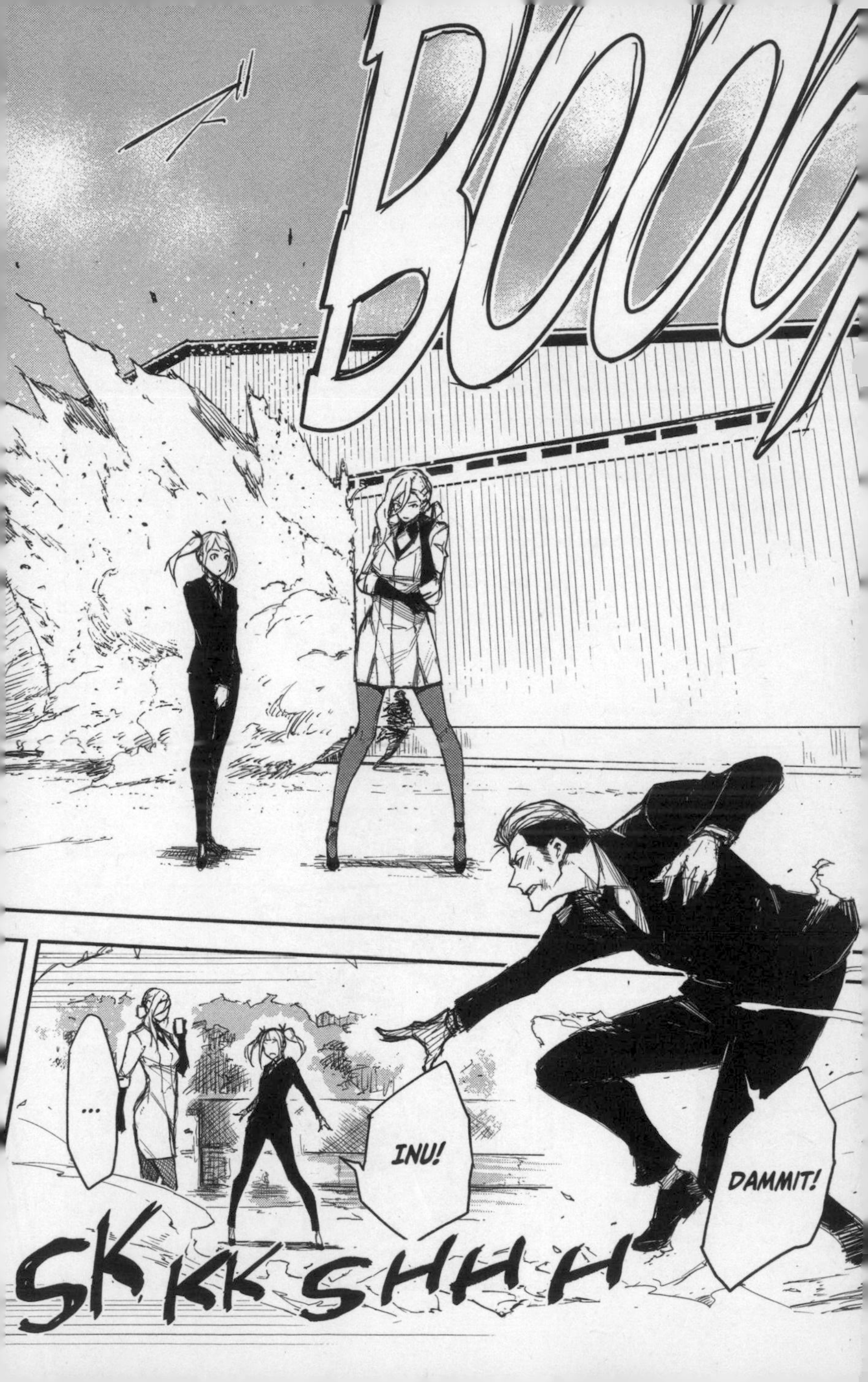
DAMMIT!
INU!
...
SKKSHHH

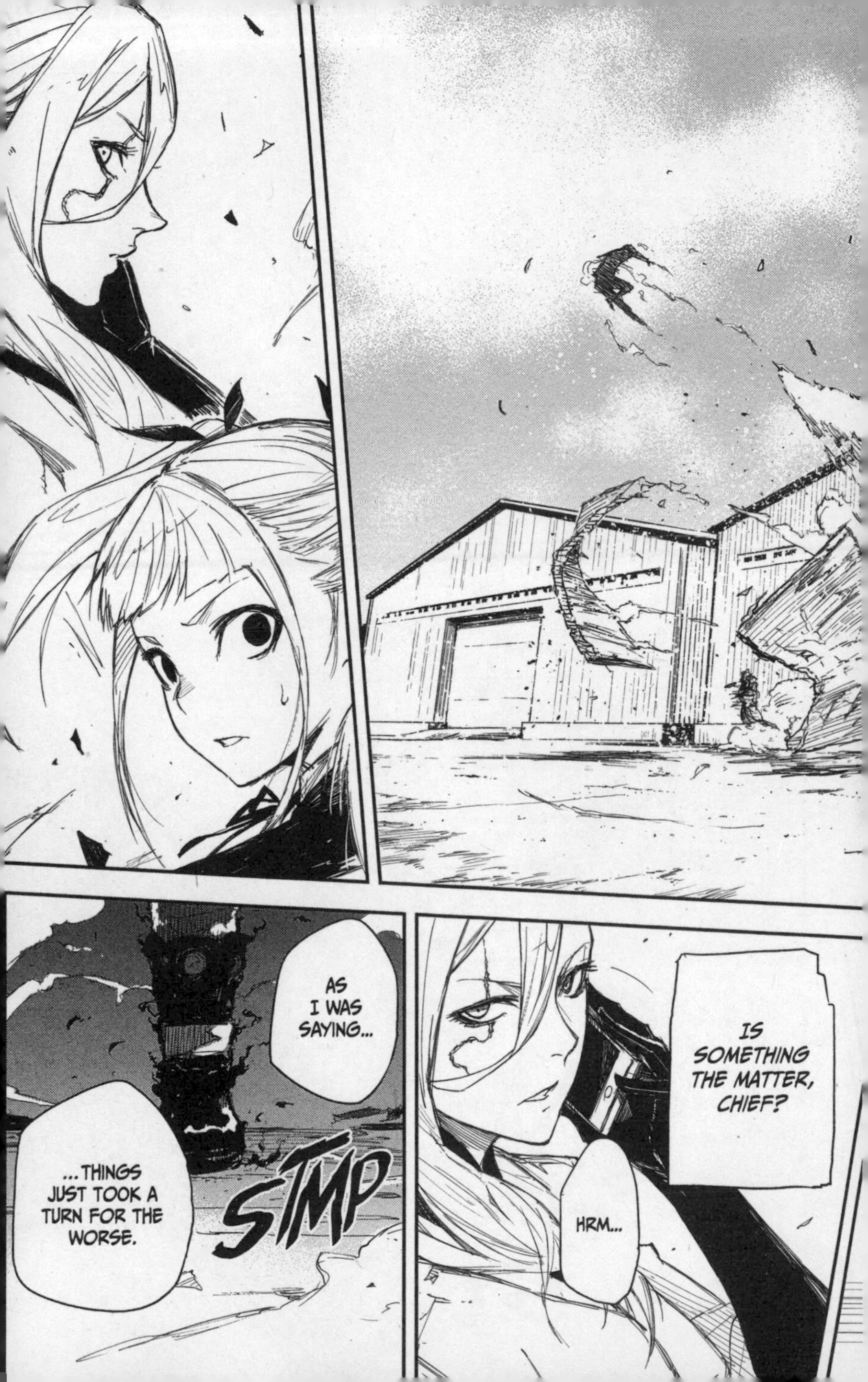
IS SOMETHING THE MATTER, CHIEF?
HRM...
AS I WAS SAYING...
...THINGS JUST TOOK A TURN FOR THE WORSE.
STMP

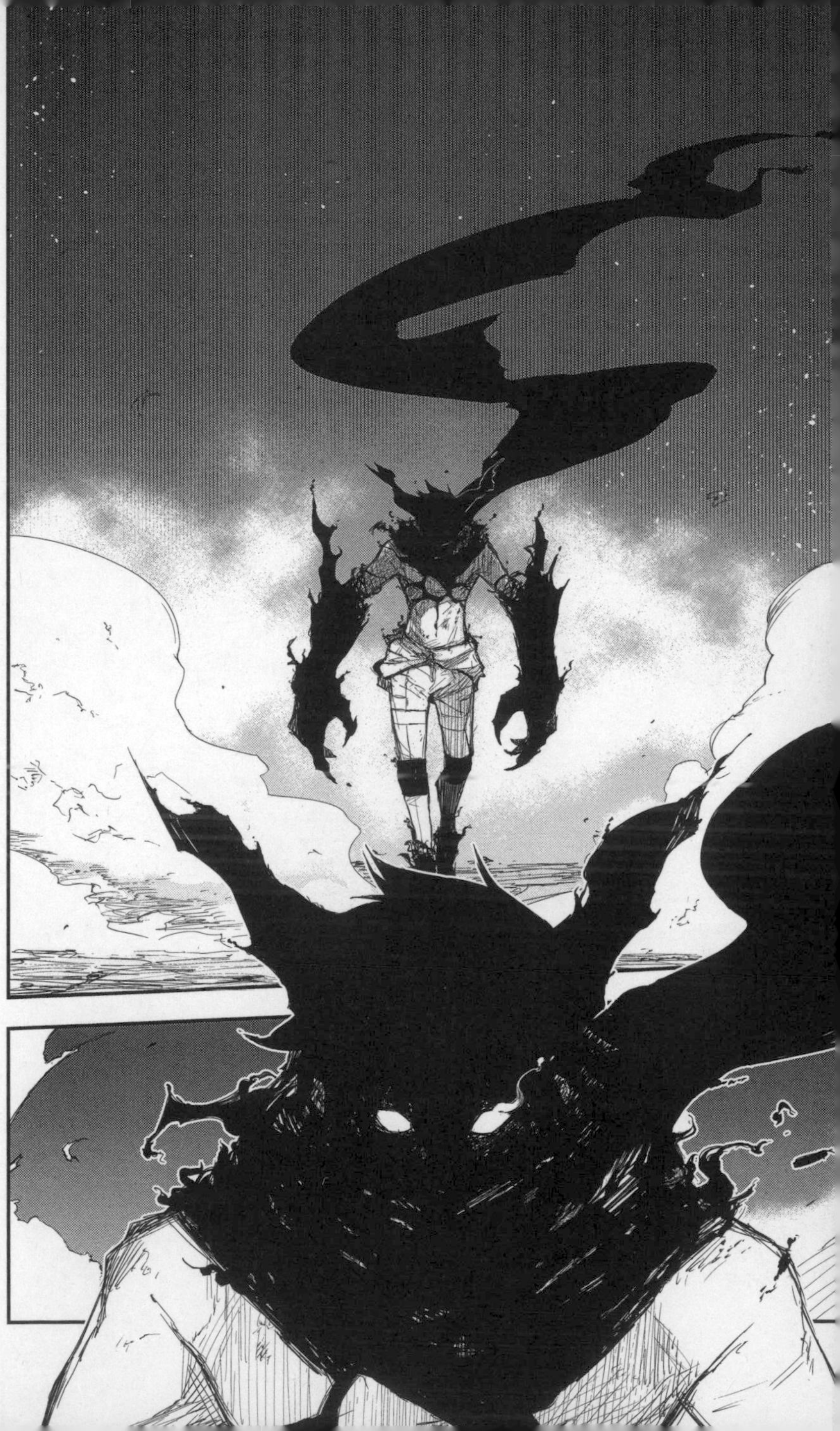

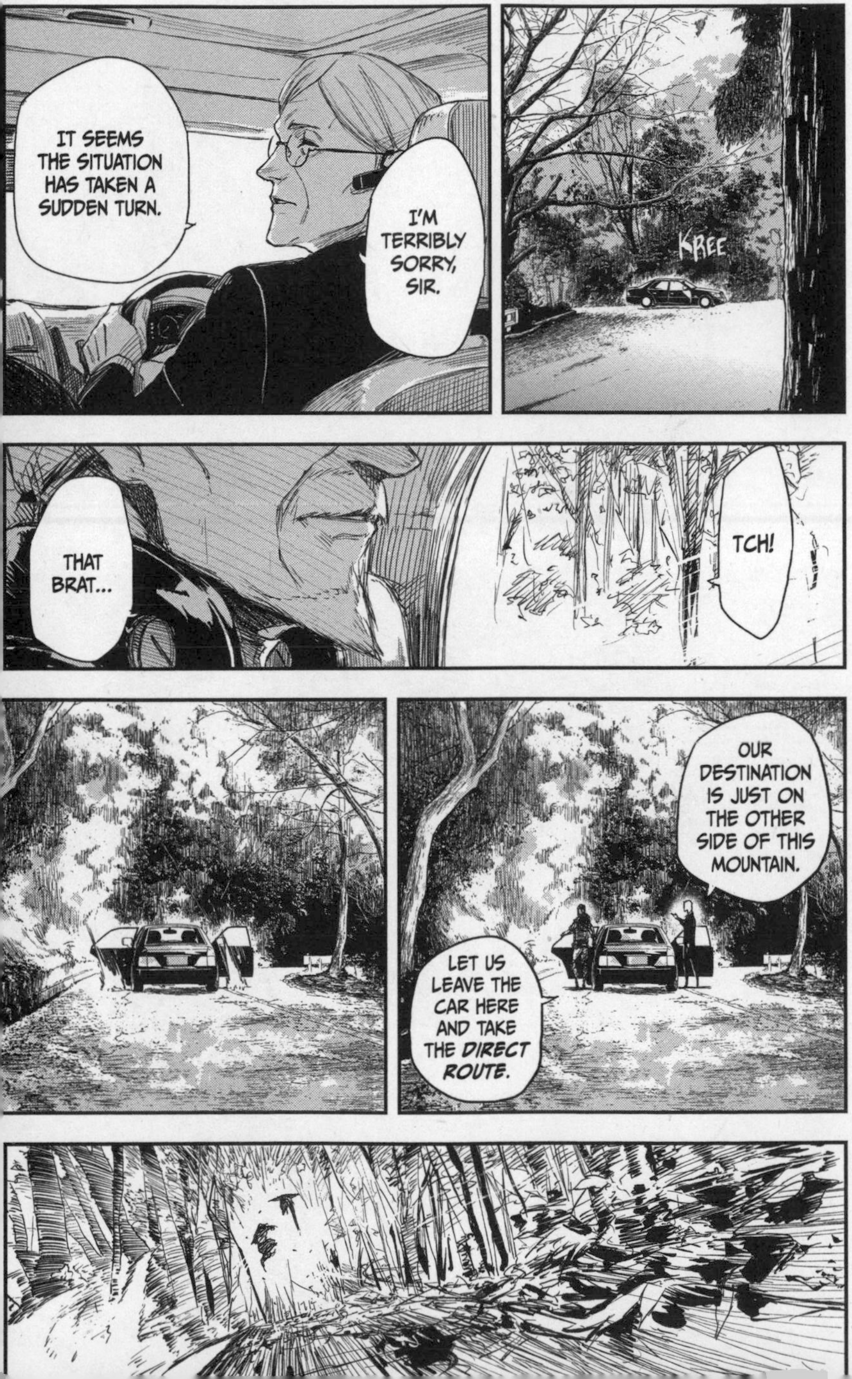
KREE
IT SEEMS THE SITUATION HAS TAKEN A SUDDEN TURN.
I'M TERRIBLY SORRY, SIR.
TCH!
THAT BRAT...
OUR DESTINATION IS JUST ON THE OTHER SIDE OF THIS MOUNTAIN.
LET US LEAVE THE CAR HERE AND TAKE THE *DIRECT ROUTE*.

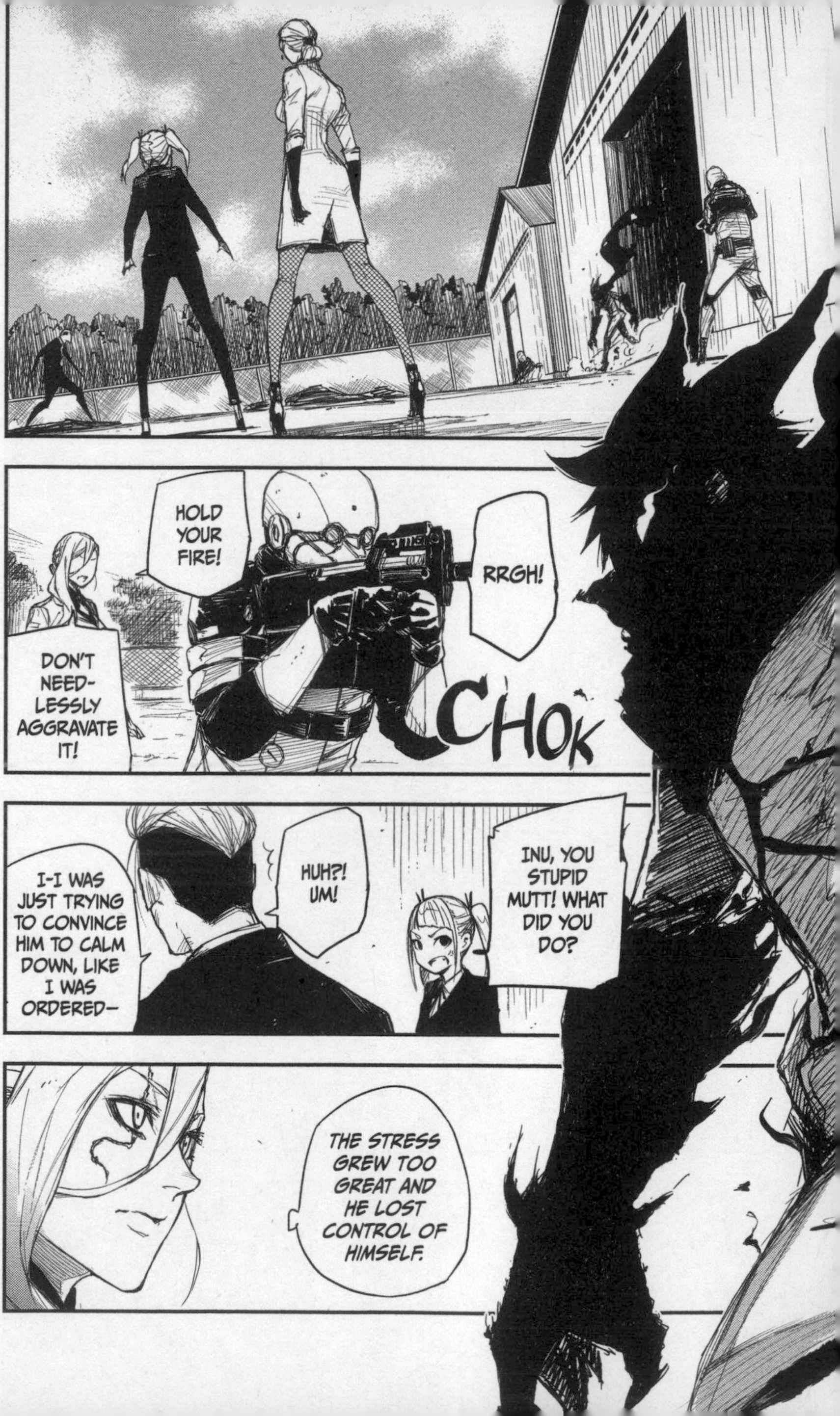
RRGH!
HOLD YOUR FIRE!
CHOK
DON'T NEED-LESSLY AGGRAVATE IT!
INU, YOU STUPID MUTT! WHAT DID YOU DO?
HUH?! UM!
I-I WAS JUST TRYING TO CONVINCE HIM TO CALM DOWN, LIKE I WAS ORDERED—
THE STRESS GREW TOO GREAT AND HE LOST CONTROL OF HIMSELF.

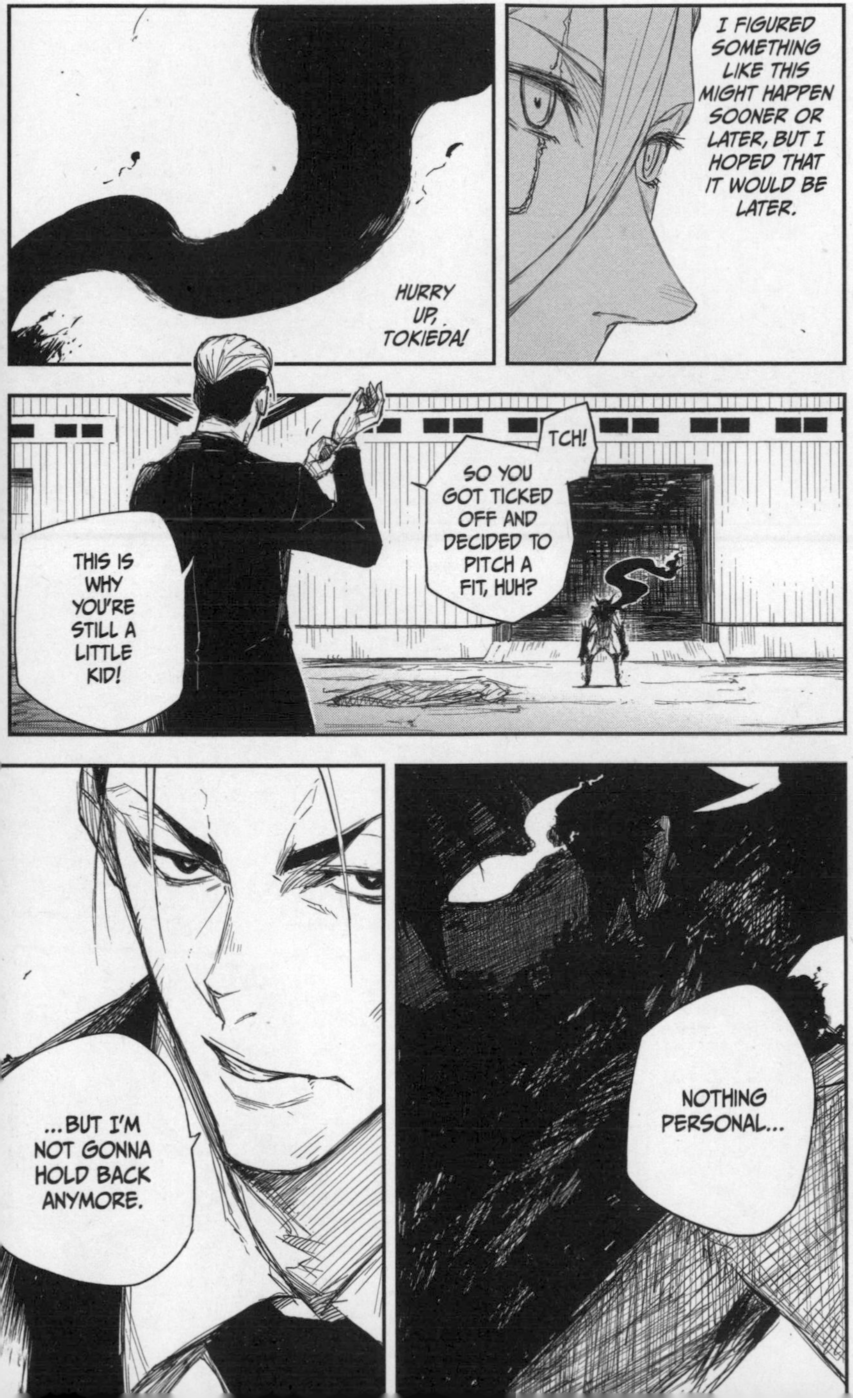
I FIGURED SOMETHING LIKE THIS MIGHT HAPPEN SOONER OR LATER, BUT I HOPED THAT IT WOULD BE LATER.
HURRY UP, TOKIEDA!
TCH!
SO YOU GOT TICKED OFF AND DECIDED TO PITCH A FIT, HUH?
THIS IS WHY YOU'RE STILL A LITTLE KID!
NOTHING PERSONAL...
...BUT I'M NOT GONNA HOLD BACK ANYMORE.

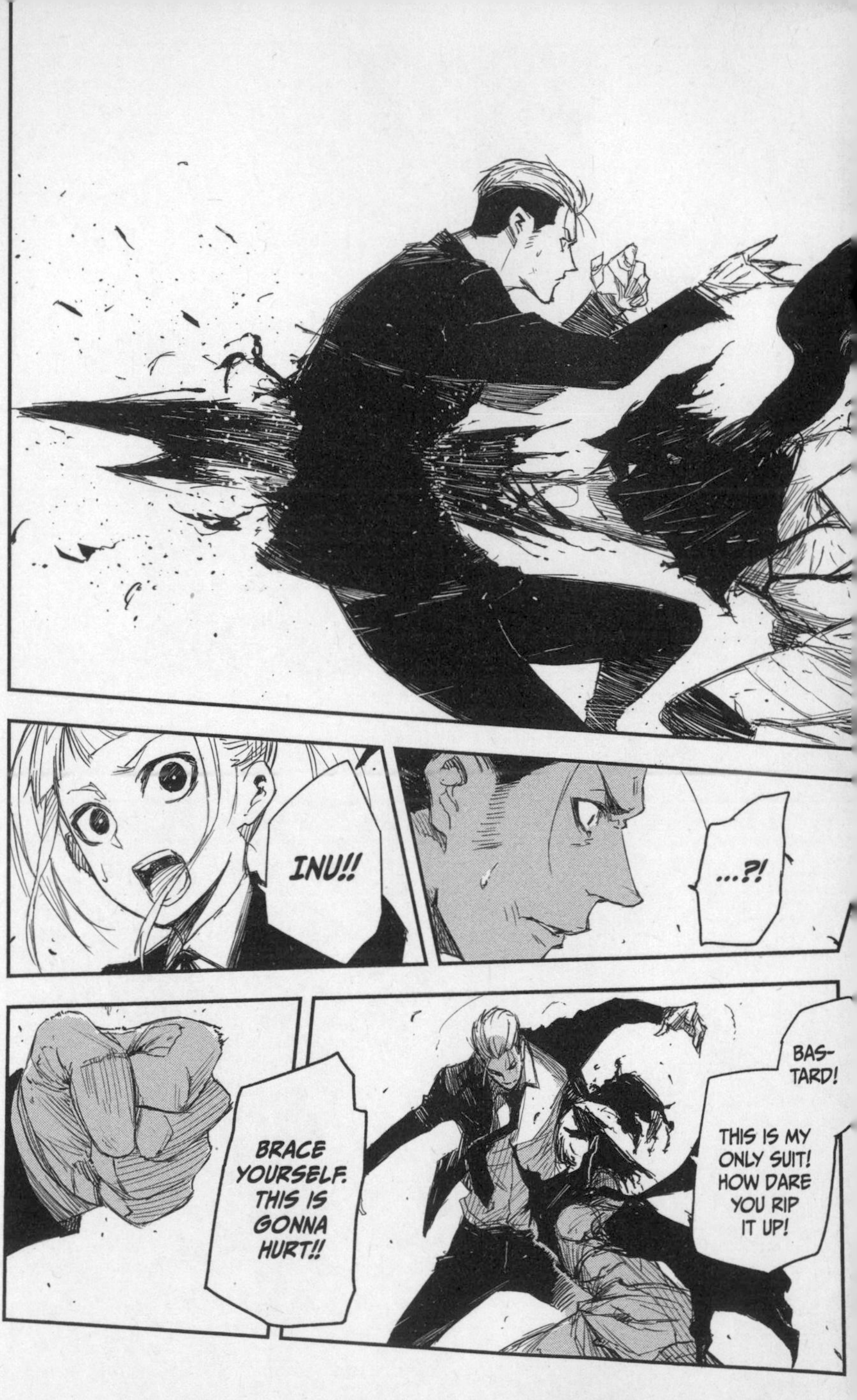
...?!
INU!!
BASTARD!
THIS IS MY ONLY SUIT! HOW DARE YOU RIP IT UP!
BRACE YOURSELF. THIS IS GONNA HURT!!

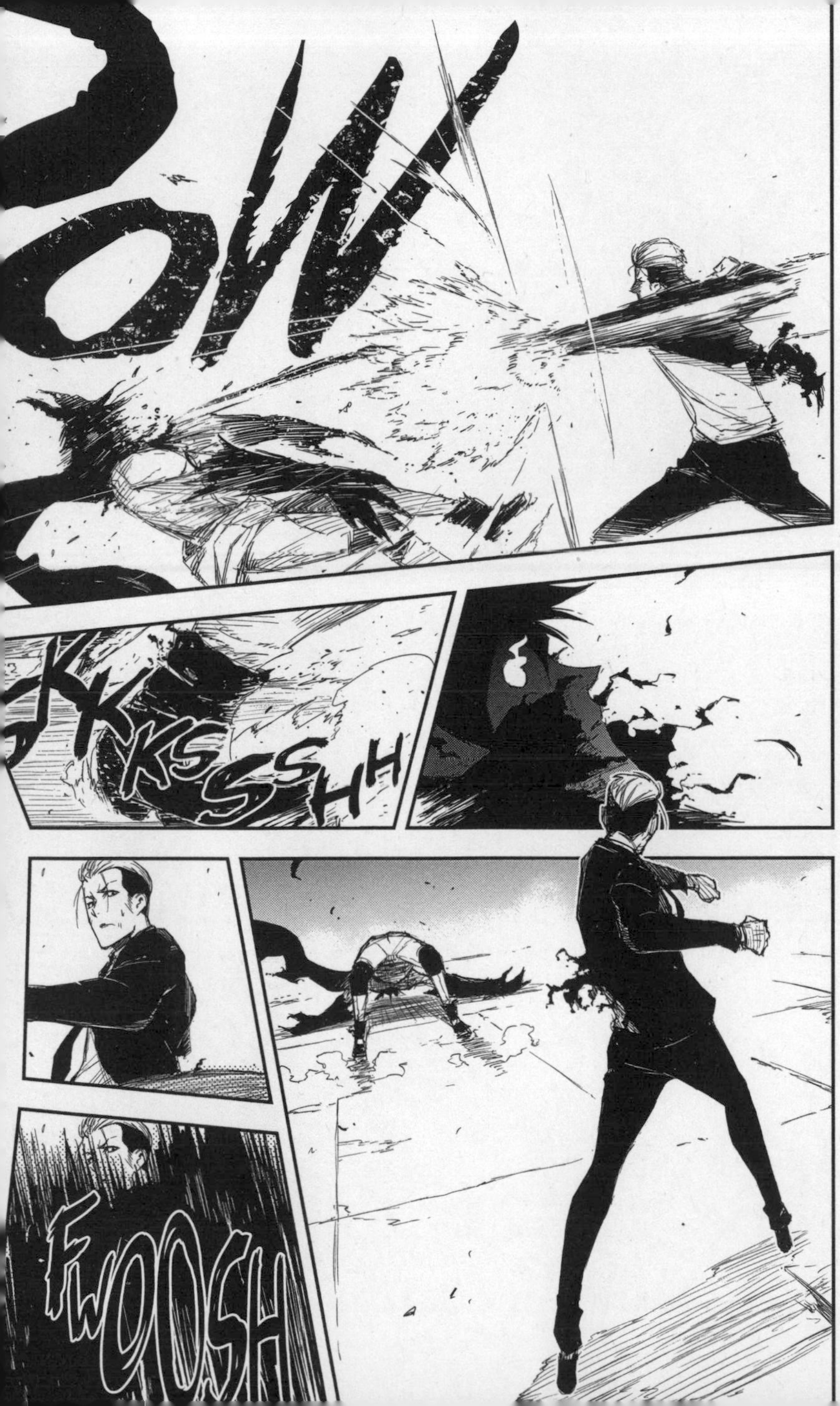
OW
KKKSSSHH
FWOOSH

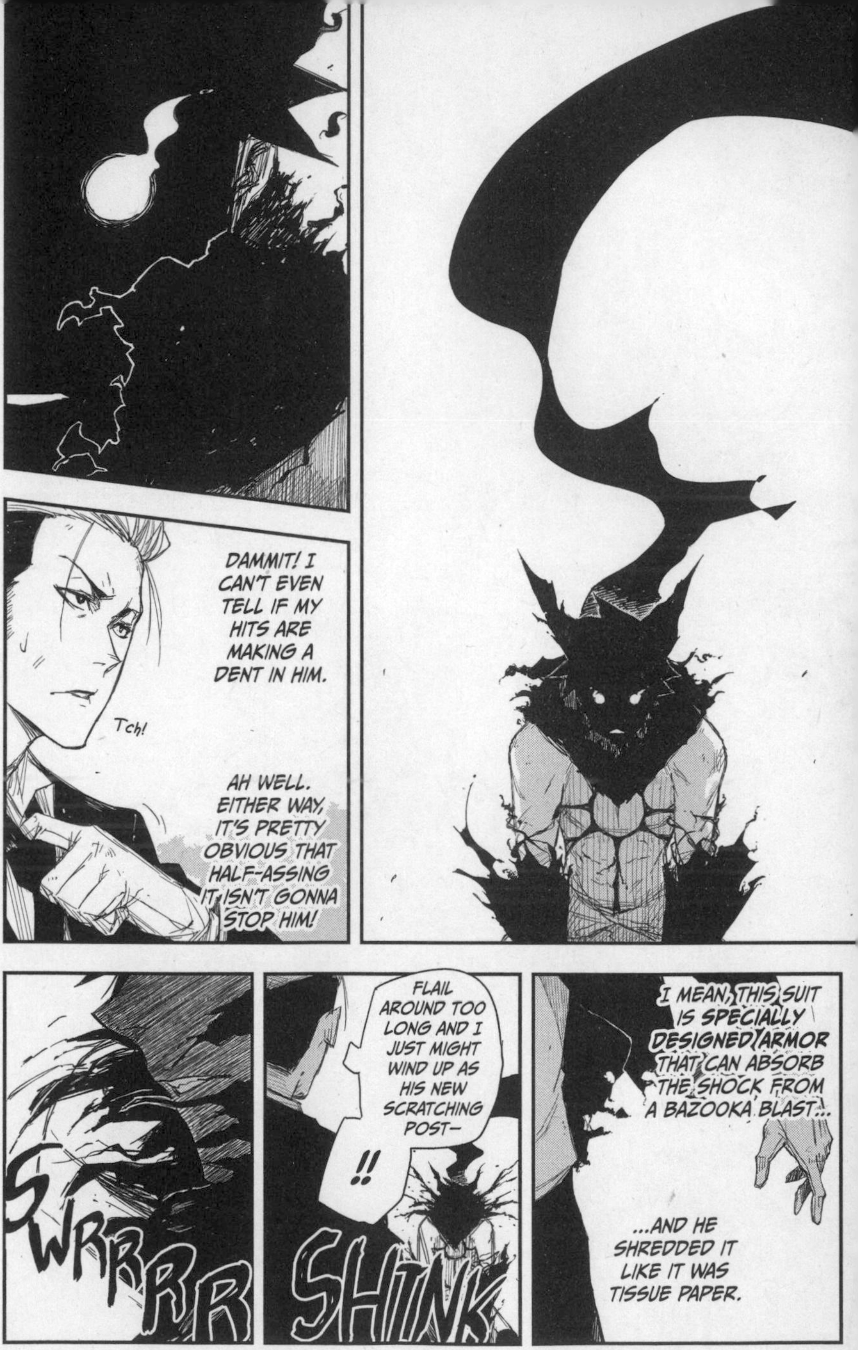
DAMMIT! I CAN'T EVEN TELL IF MY HITS ARE MAKING A DENT IN HIM.
Tch!
AH WELL. EITHER WAY, IT'S PRETTY OBVIOUS THAT HALF-ASSING IT ISN'T GONNA STOP HIM!
I MEAN, THIS SUIT IS SPECIALLY DESIGNED ARMOR THAT CAN ABSORB THE SHOCK FROM A BAZOOKA BLAST...
...AND HE SHREDDED IT LIKE IT WAS TISSUE PAPER.
FLAIL AROUND TOO LONG AND I JUST MIGHT WIND UP AS HIS NEW SCRATCHING POST–
!!
SHINK
SWRRRR

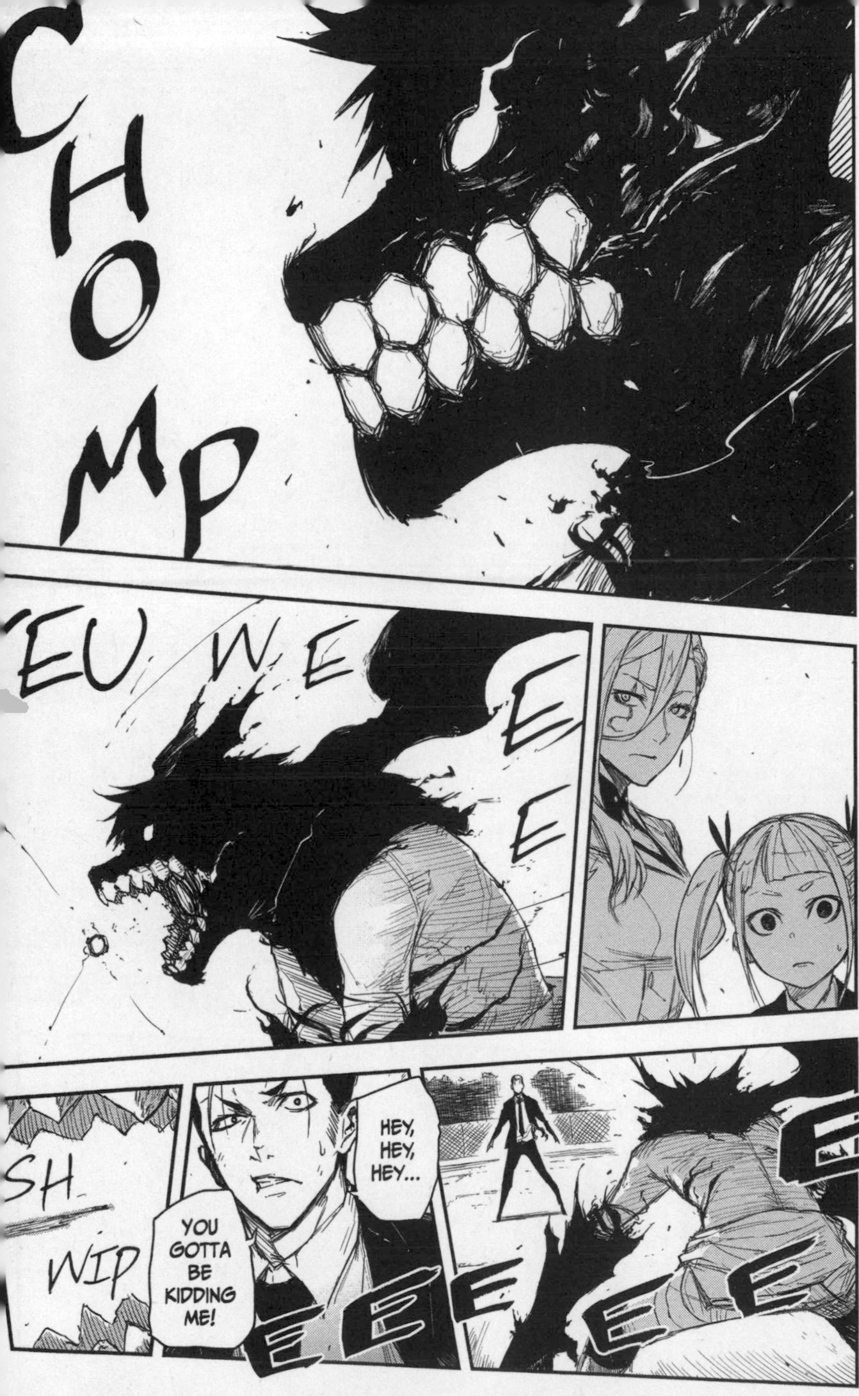
CHOMP
EU WEEEE
HEY, HEY, HEY...
YOU GOTTA BE KIDDING ME!
SHWIP

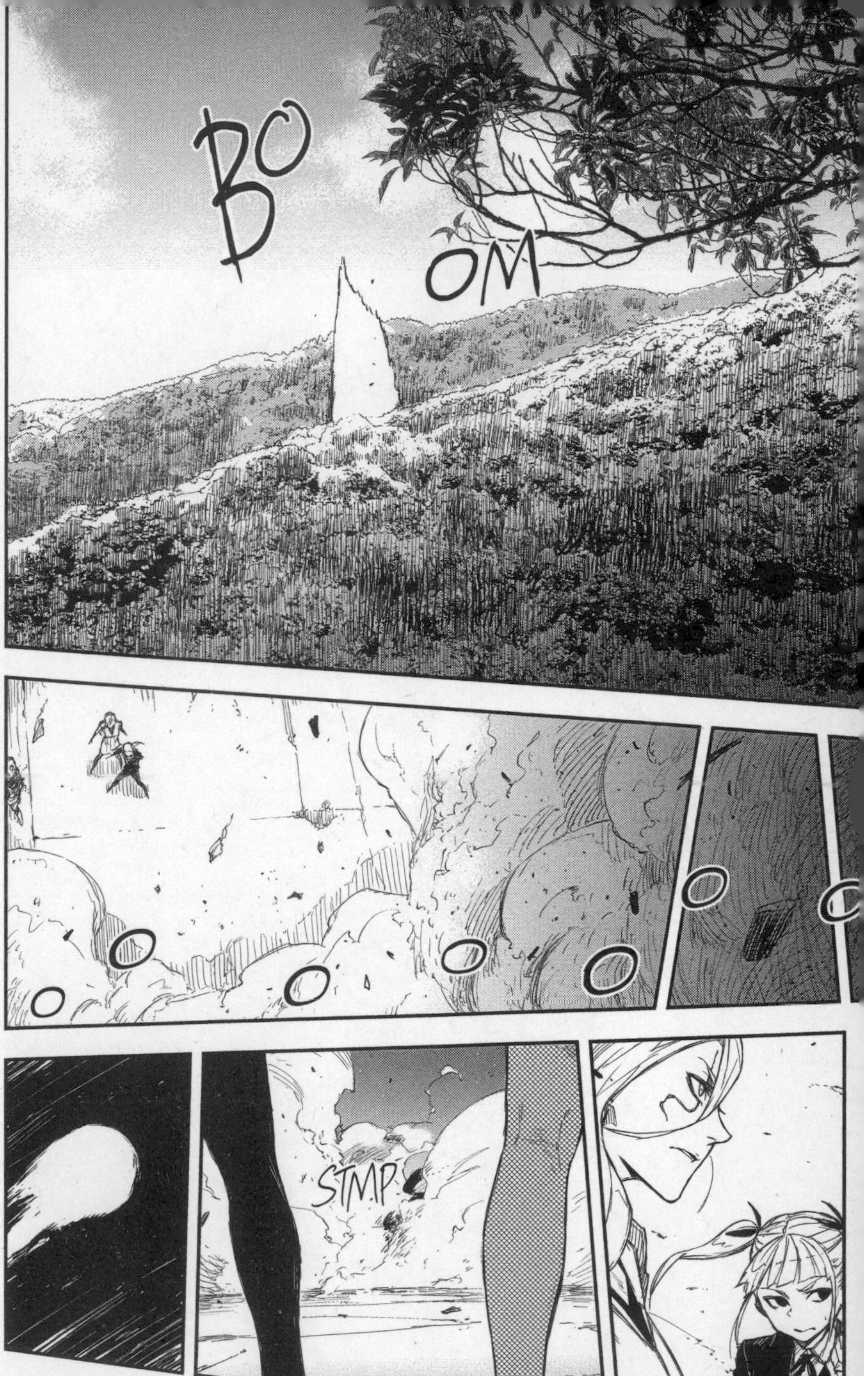
BOOM
STMP

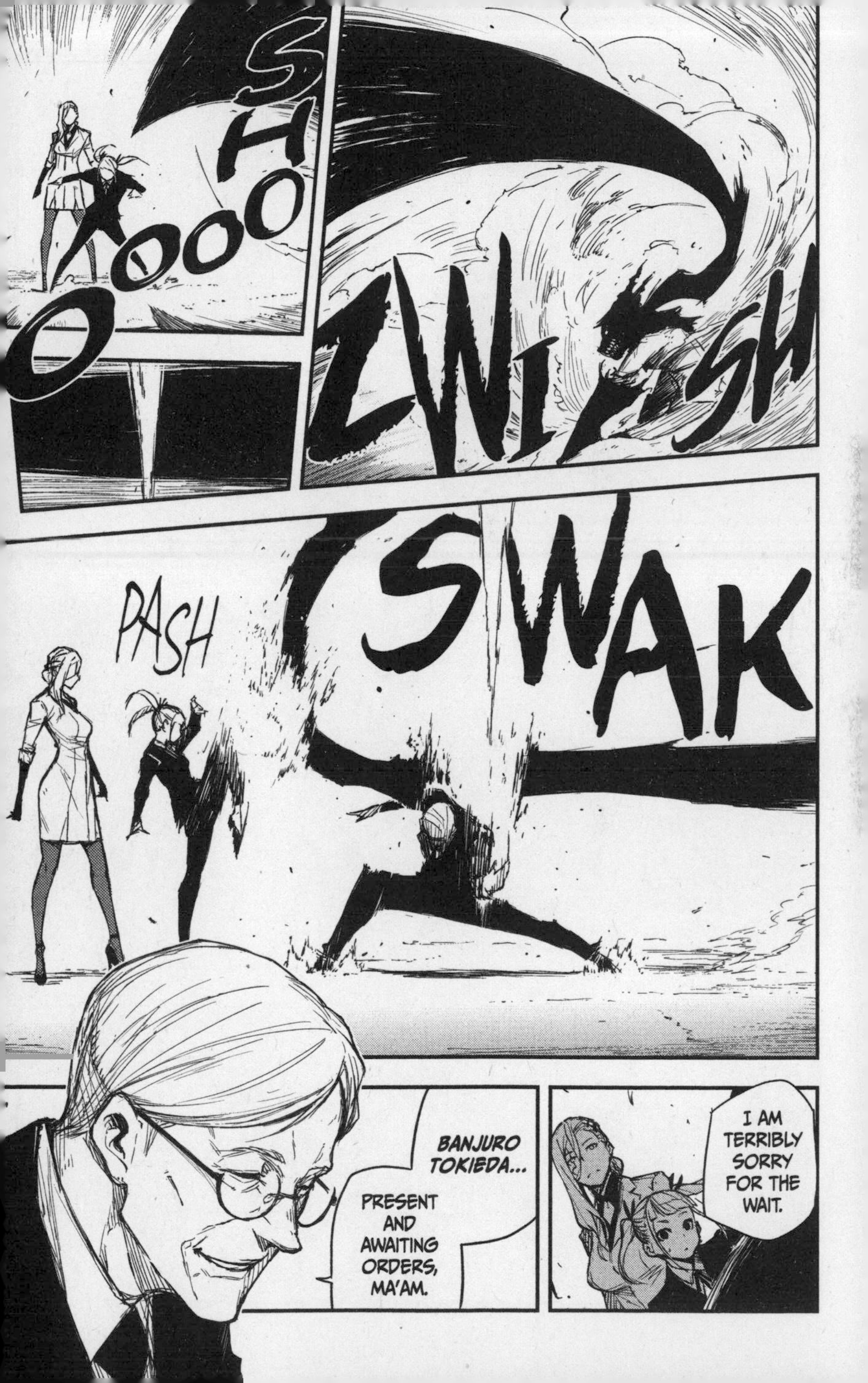
ZWASH
SHOOOOO
SWAK
PASH
I AM TERRIBLY SORRY FOR THE WAIT.
BANJURO TOKIEDA...
PRESENT AND AWAITING ORDERS, MA'AM.

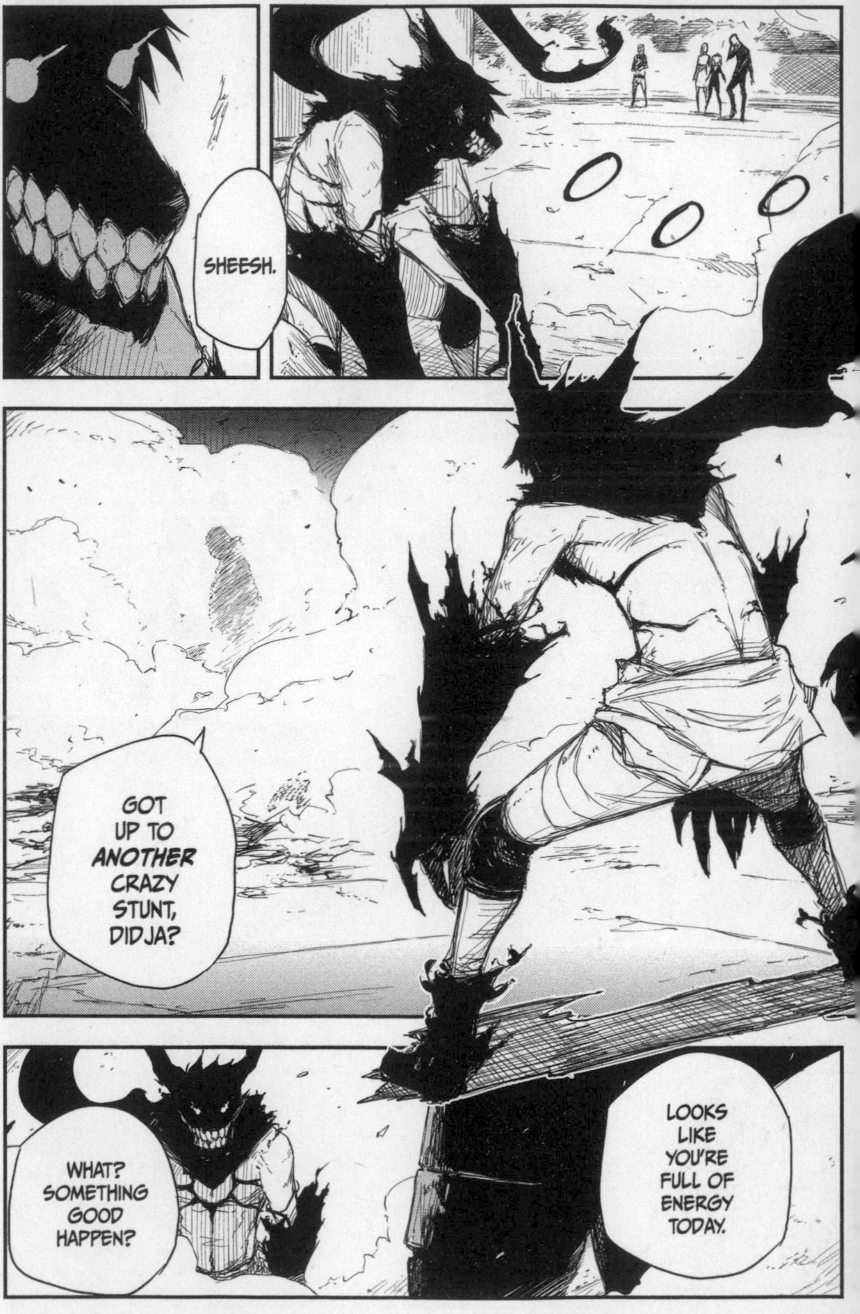
SHEESH.
GOT UP TO ANOTHER CRAZY STUNT, DIDJA?
LOOKS LIKE YOU'RE FULL OF ENERGY TODAY.
WHAT? SOMETHING GOOD HAPPEN?

JIRO.

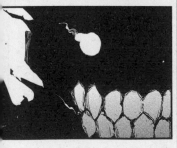

WELL?

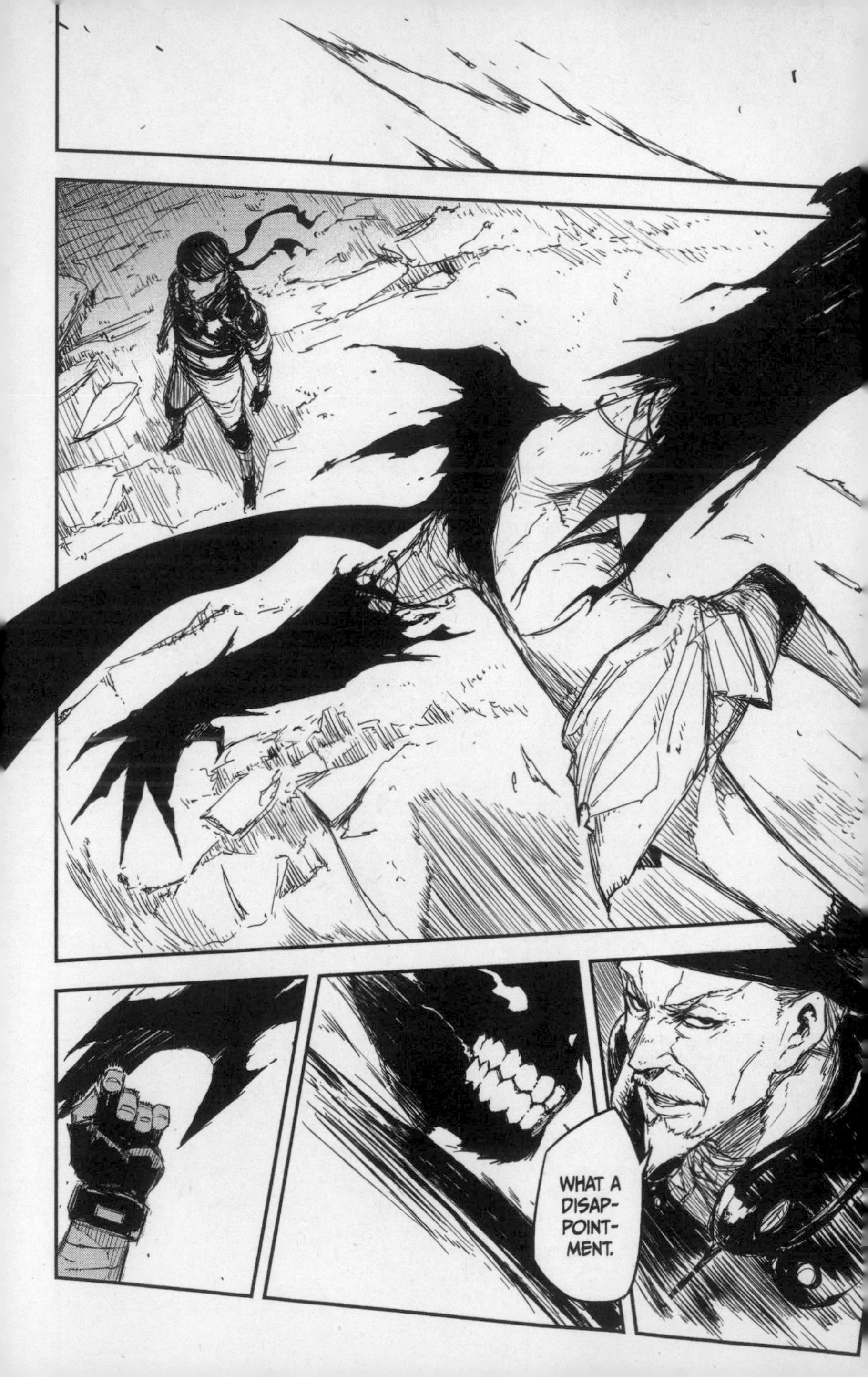
WHAT A DISAP- POINT- MENT.

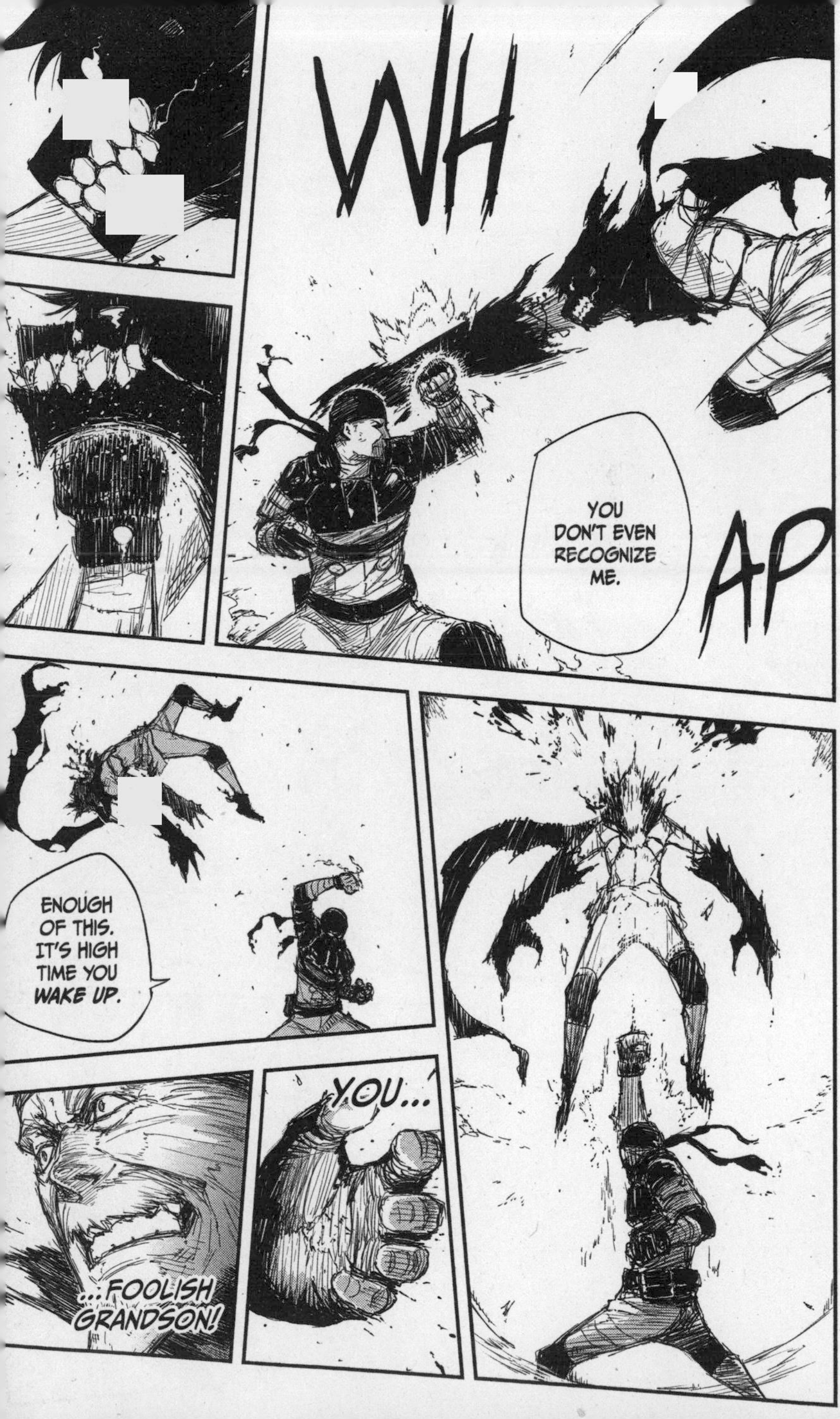
WHAP
YOU DON'T EVEN RECOGNIZE ME.
ENOUGH OF THIS. IT'S HIGH TIME YOU WAKE UP.
YOU...
...FOOLISH GRANDSON!

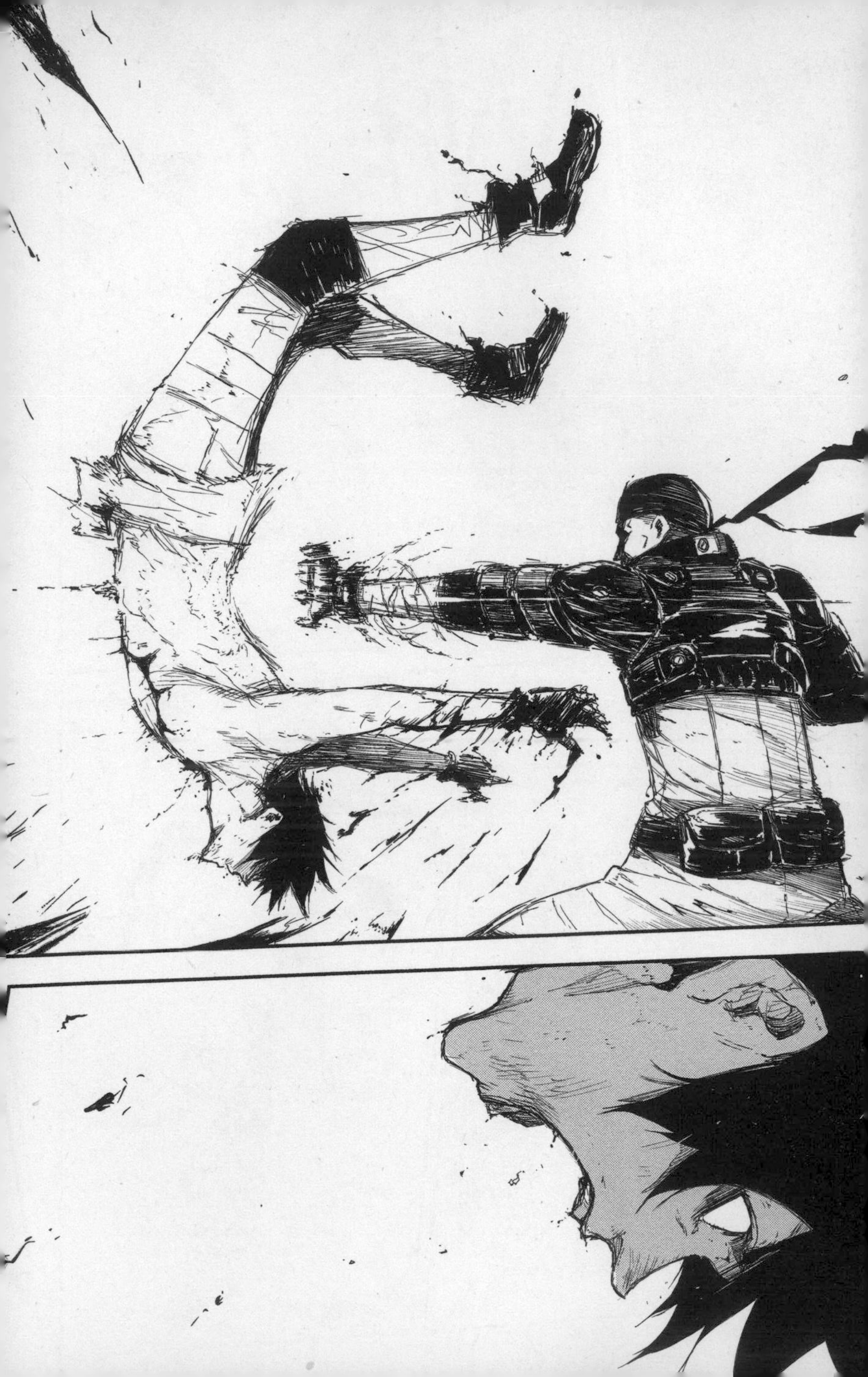

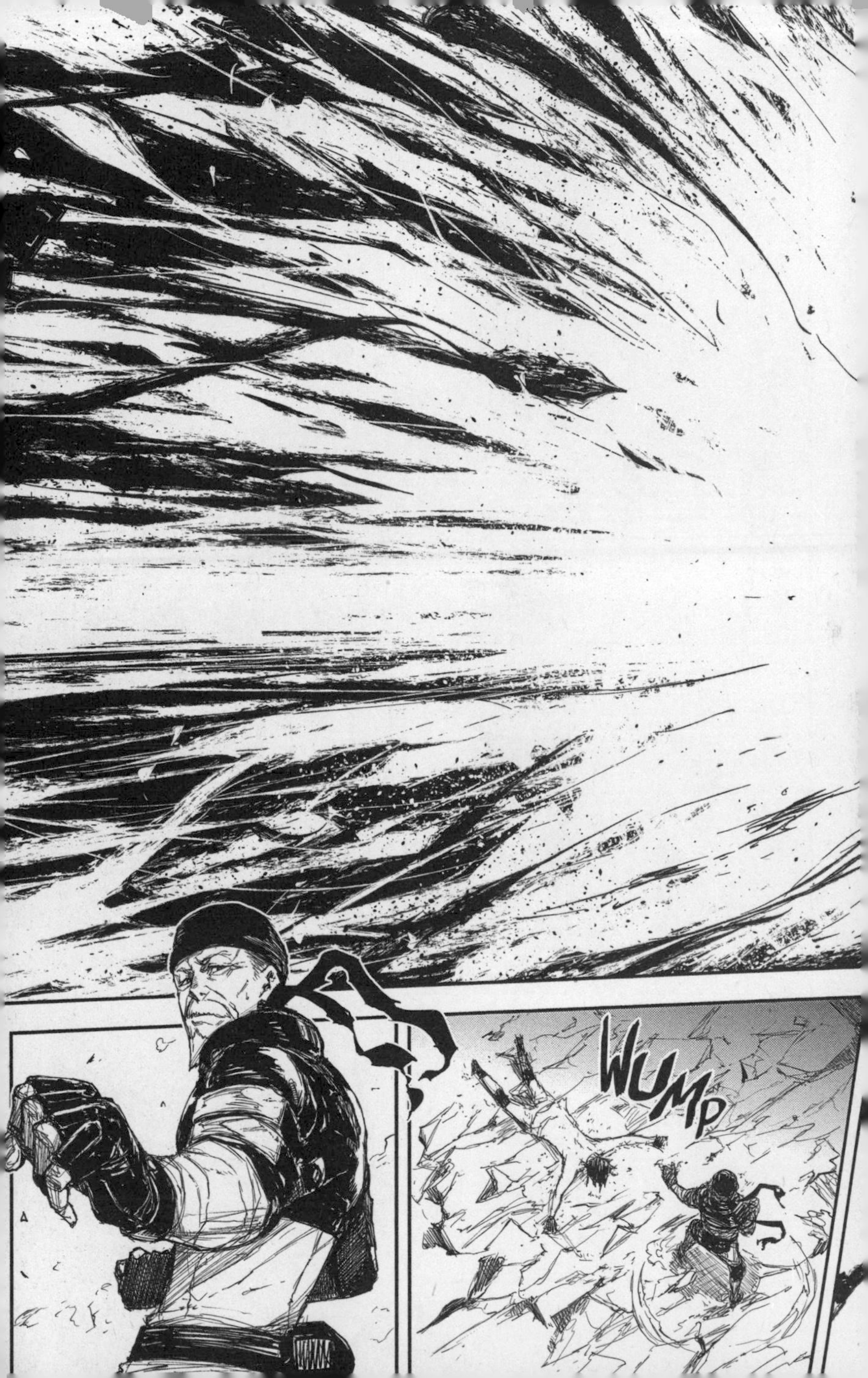
WUMP

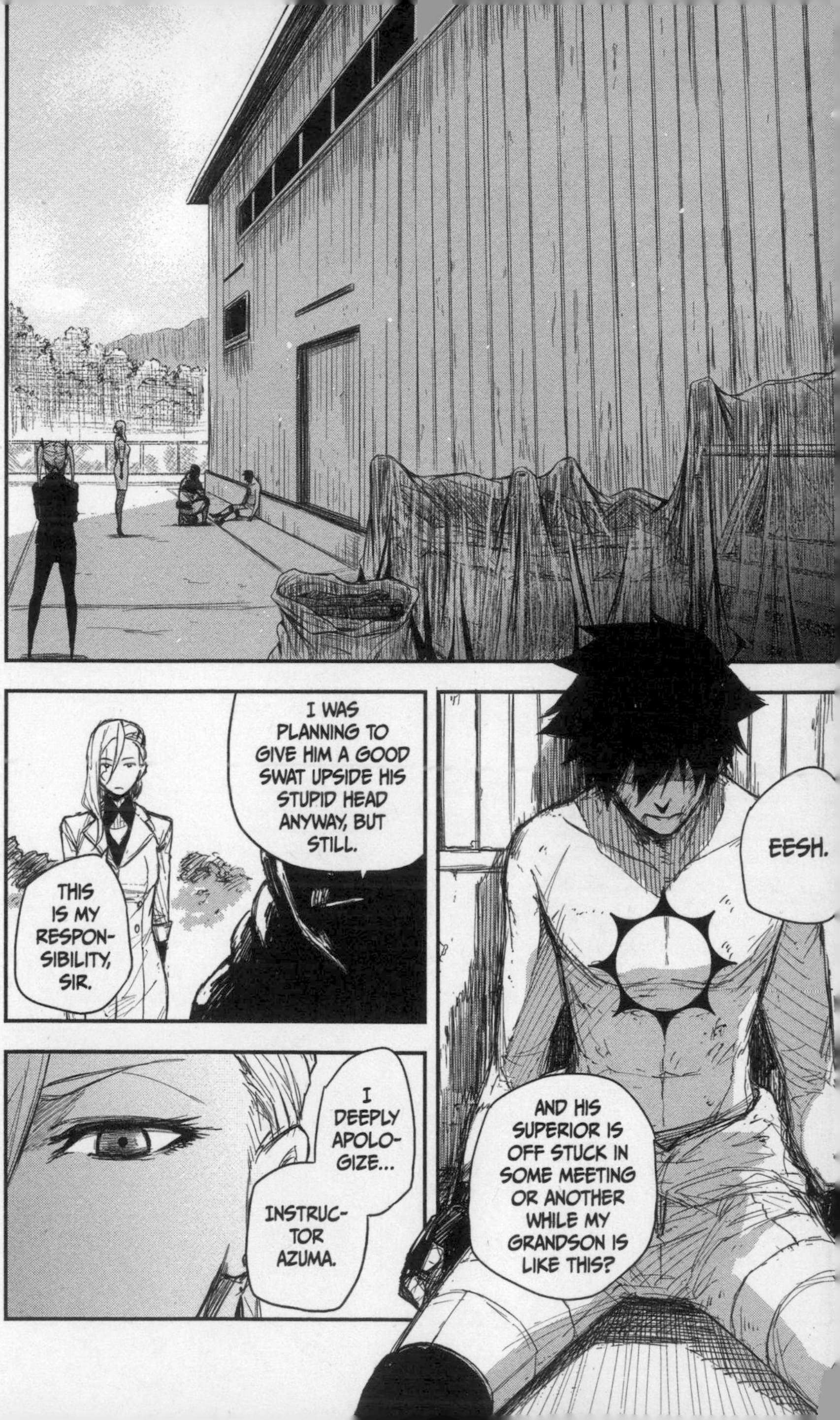
EESH.
AND HIS SUPERIOR IS OFF STUCK IN SOME MEETING OR ANOTHER WHILE MY GRANDSON IS LIKE THIS?
I WAS PLANNING TO GIVE HIM A GOOD SWAT UPSIDE HIS STUPID HEAD ANYWAY, BUT STILL.
THIS IS MY RESPONSIBILITY, SIR.
I DEEPLY APOLOGIZE...
INSTRUCTOR AZUMA.

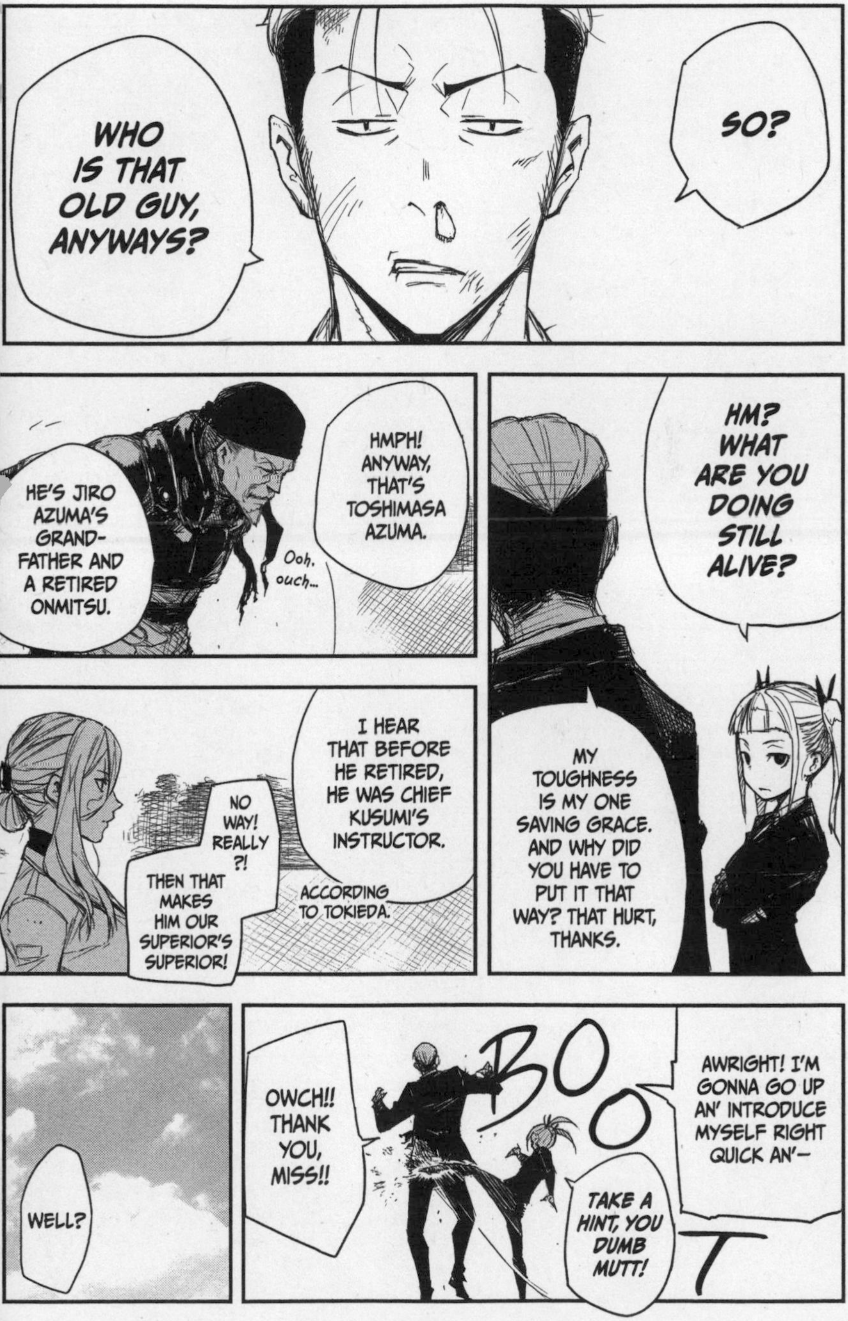
SO?
WHO IS THAT OLD GUY, ANYWAYS?
HM? WHAT ARE YOU DOING STILL ALIVE?
MY TOUGHNESS IS MY ONE SAVING GRACE. AND WHY DID YOU HAVE TO PUT IT THAT WAY? THAT HURT, THANKS.
HMPH! ANYWAY, THAT'S TOSHIMASA AZUMA.
Ooh. ouch...
HE'S JIRO AZUMA'S GRAND-FATHER AND A RETIRED ONMITSU.
I HEAR THAT BEFORE HE RETIRED, HE WAS CHIEF KUSUMI'S INSTRUCTOR.
ACCORDING TO TOKIEDA.
NO WAY! REALLY?!
THEN THAT MAKES HIM OUR SUPERIOR'S SUPERIOR!
AWRIGHT! I'M GONNA GO UP AN' INTRODUCE MYSELF RIGHT QUICK AN'—
TAKE A HINT, YOU DUMB MUTT!
BOOT
OWCH!! THANK YOU, MISS!!
WELL?

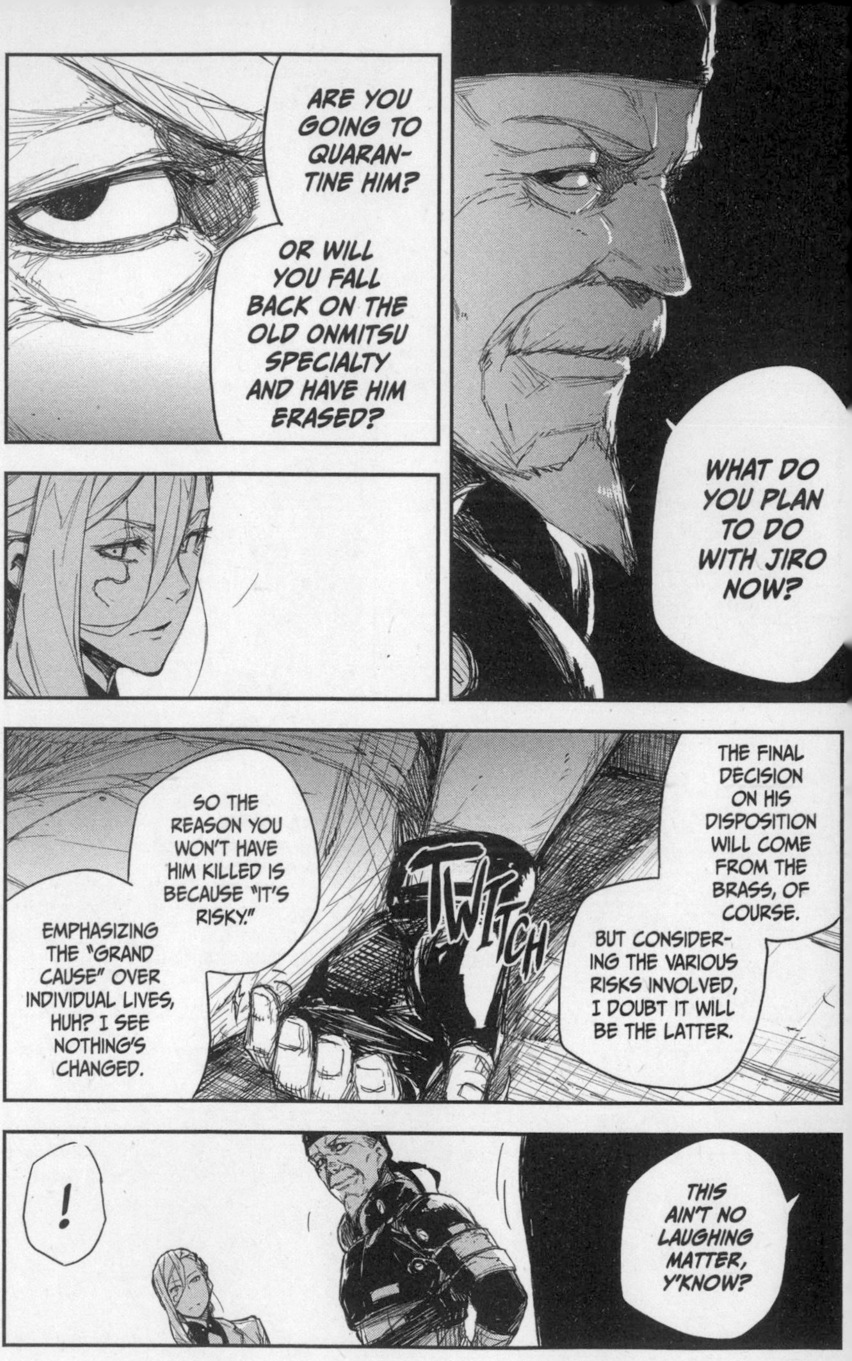
WHAT DO YOU PLAN TO DO WITH JIRO NOW?
ARE YOU GOING TO QUARAN-TINE HIM?
OR WILL YOU FALL BACK ON THE OLD ONMITSU SPECIALTY AND HAVE HIM ERASED?
THE FINAL DECISION ON HIS DISPOSITION WILL COME FROM THE BRASS, OF COURSE.
BUT CONSIDER-ING THE VARIOUS RISKS INVOLVED, I DOUBT IT WILL BE THE LATTER.
TWITCH
SO THE REASON YOU WON'T HAVE HIM KILLED IS BECAUSE "IT'S RISKY."
EMPHASIZING THE "GRAND CAUSE" OVER INDIVIDUAL LIVES, HUH? I SEE NOTHING'S CHANGED.
THIS AIN'T NO LAUGHING MATTER, Y'KNOW?
!

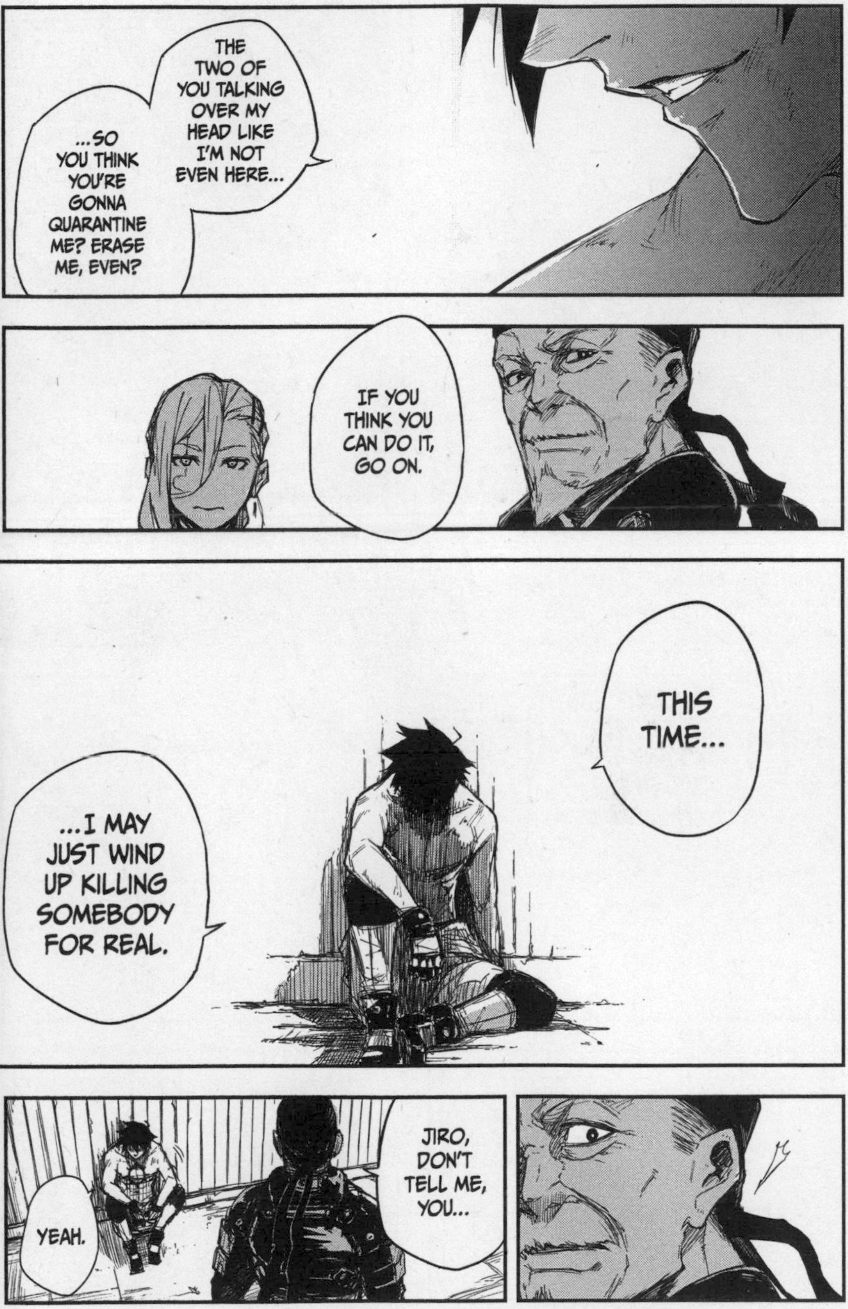
THE TWO OF YOU TALKING OVER MY HEAD LIKE I'M NOT EVEN HERE...
...SO YOU THINK YOU'RE GONNA QUARANTINE ME? ERASE ME, EVEN?
IF YOU THINK YOU CAN DO IT, GO ON.
THIS TIME...
...I MAY JUST WIND UP KILLING SOMEBODY FOR REAL.
JIRO, DON'T TELL ME, YOU...
YEAH.

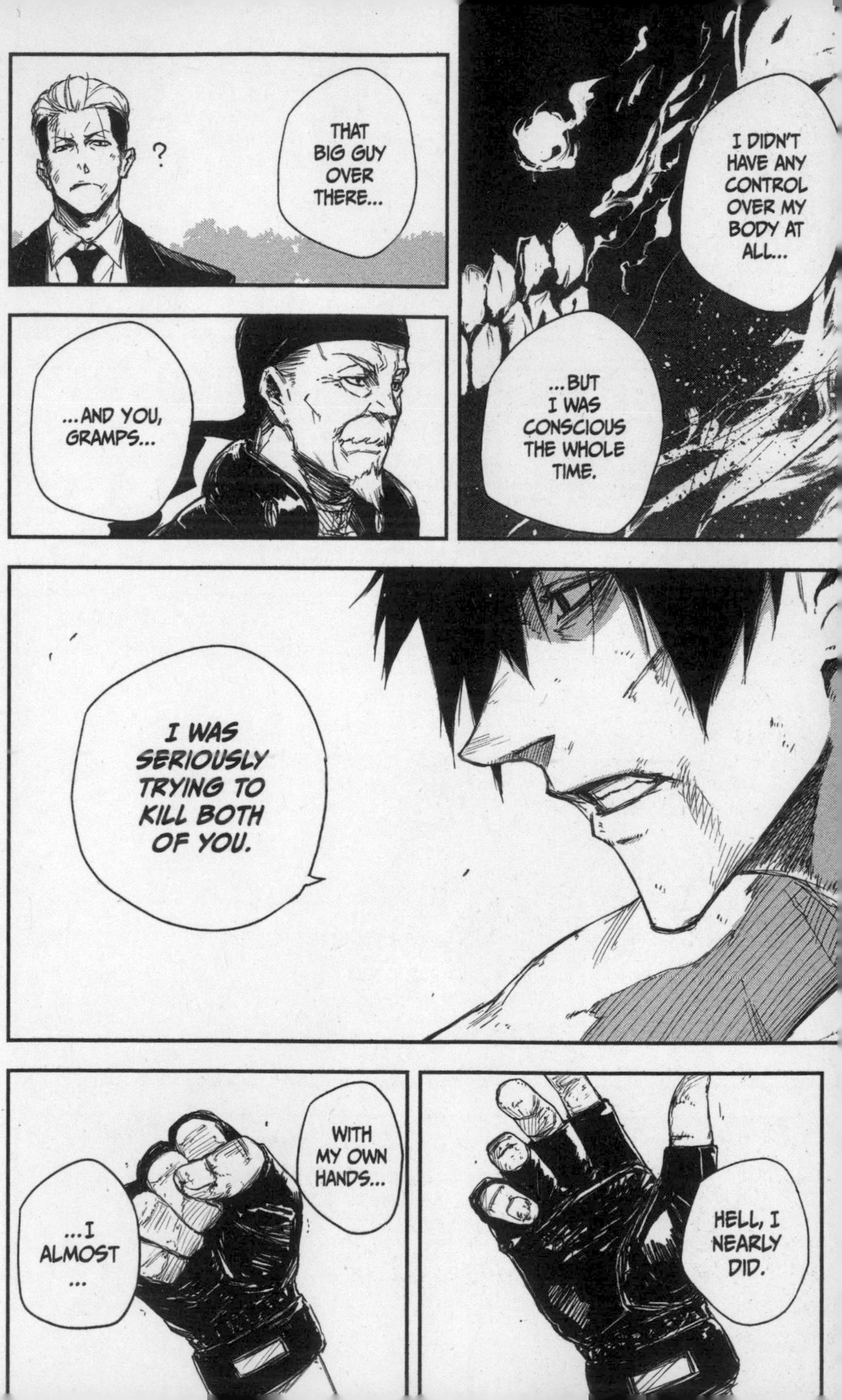
I DIDN'T HAVE ANY CONTROL OVER MY BODY AT ALL...
...BUT I WAS CONSCIOUS THE WHOLE TIME.
THAT BIG GUY OVER THERE...
?
...AND YOU, GRAMPS...
I WAS SERIOUSLY TRYING TO KILL BOTH OF YOU.
HELL, I NEARLY DID.
WITH MY OWN HANDS...
...I ALMOST ...

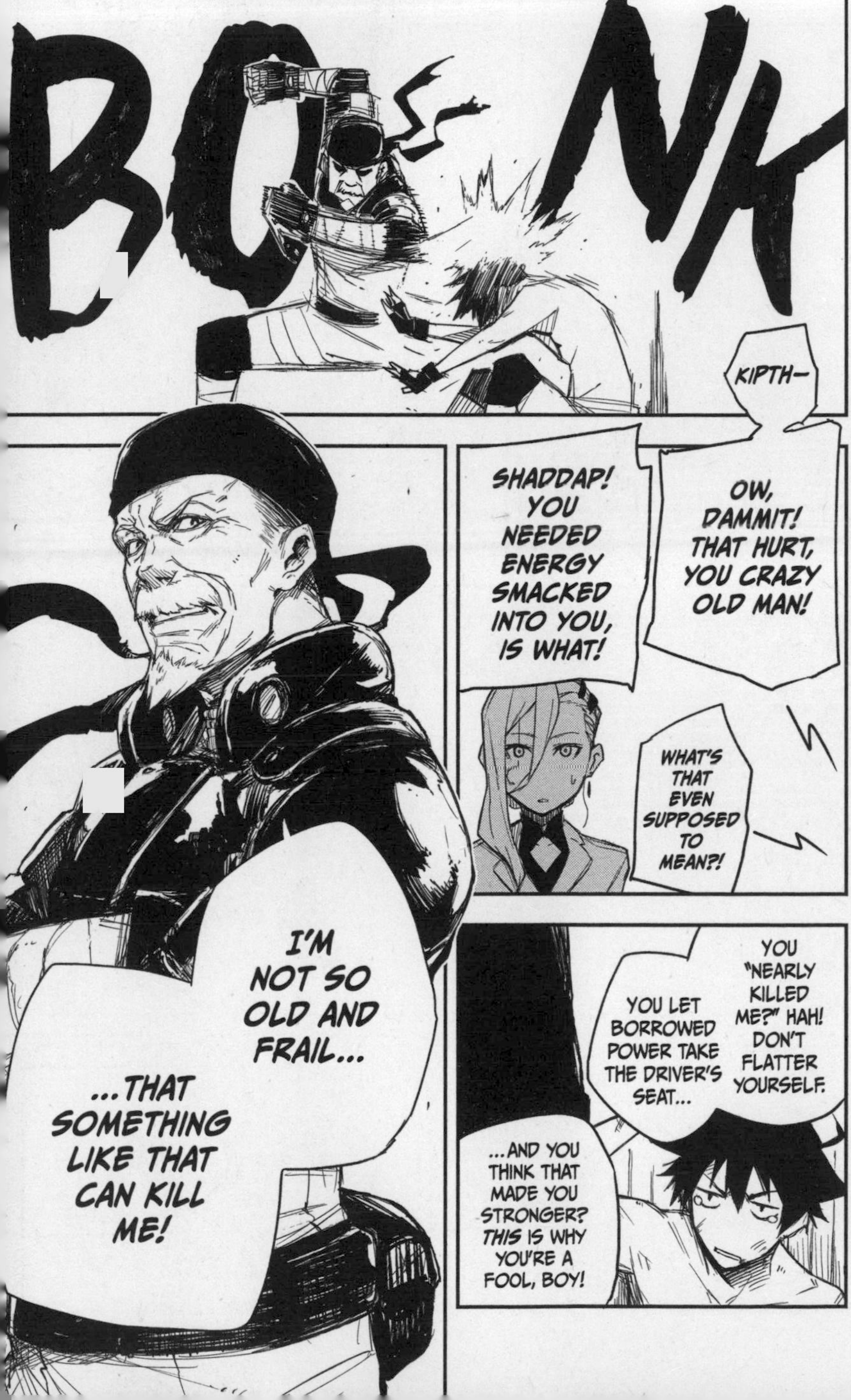
BONK
KIPTH—
OW, DAMMIT! THAT HURT, YOU CRAZY OLD MAN!
SHADDAP! YOU NEEDED ENERGY SMACKED INTO YOU, IS WHAT!
WHAT'S THAT EVEN SUPPOSED TO MEAN?!
YOU "NEARLY KILLED ME?" HAH! DON'T FLATTER YOURSELF.
YOU LET BORROWED POWER TAKE THE DRIVER'S SEAT...
...AND YOU THINK THAT MADE YOU STRONGER? THIS IS WHY YOU'RE A FOOL, BOY!
I'M NOT SO OLD AND FRAIL...
...THAT SOMETHING LIKE THAT CAN KILL ME!

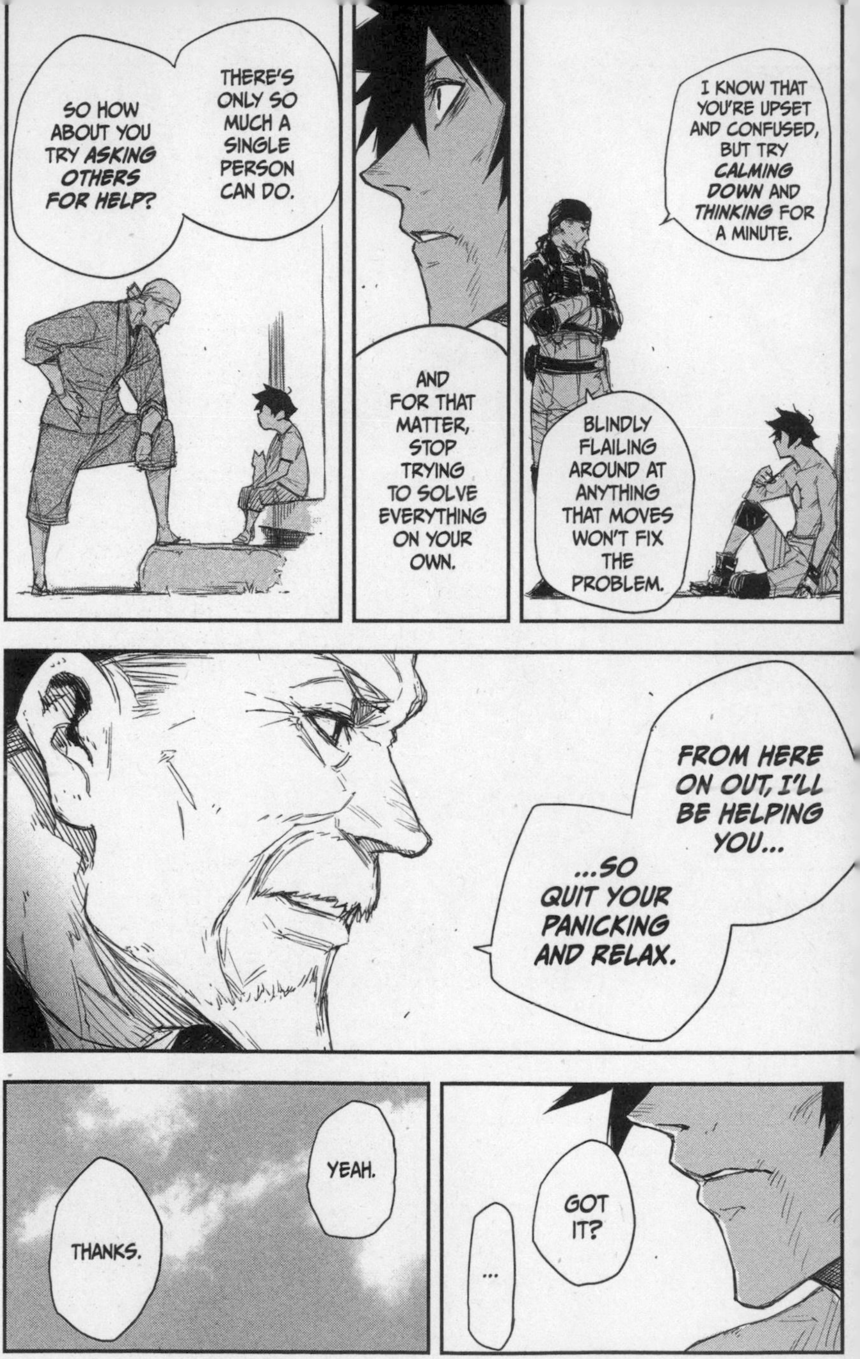
I KNOW THAT YOU'RE UPSET AND CONFUSED, BUT TRY *CALMING DOWN* AND *THINKING* FOR A MINUTE.
BLINDLY FLAILING AROUND AT ANYTHING THAT MOVES WON'T FIX THE PROBLEM.
AND FOR THAT MATTER, STOP TRYING TO SOLVE EVERYTHING ON YOUR OWN.
THERE'S ONLY SO MUCH A SINGLE PERSON CAN DO.
SO HOW ABOUT YOU TRY *ASKING OTHERS FOR HELP?*
FROM HERE ON OUT, I'LL BE HELPING YOU...
...SO QUIT YOUR PANICKING AND RELAX.
GOT IT?
...
YEAH.
THANKS.

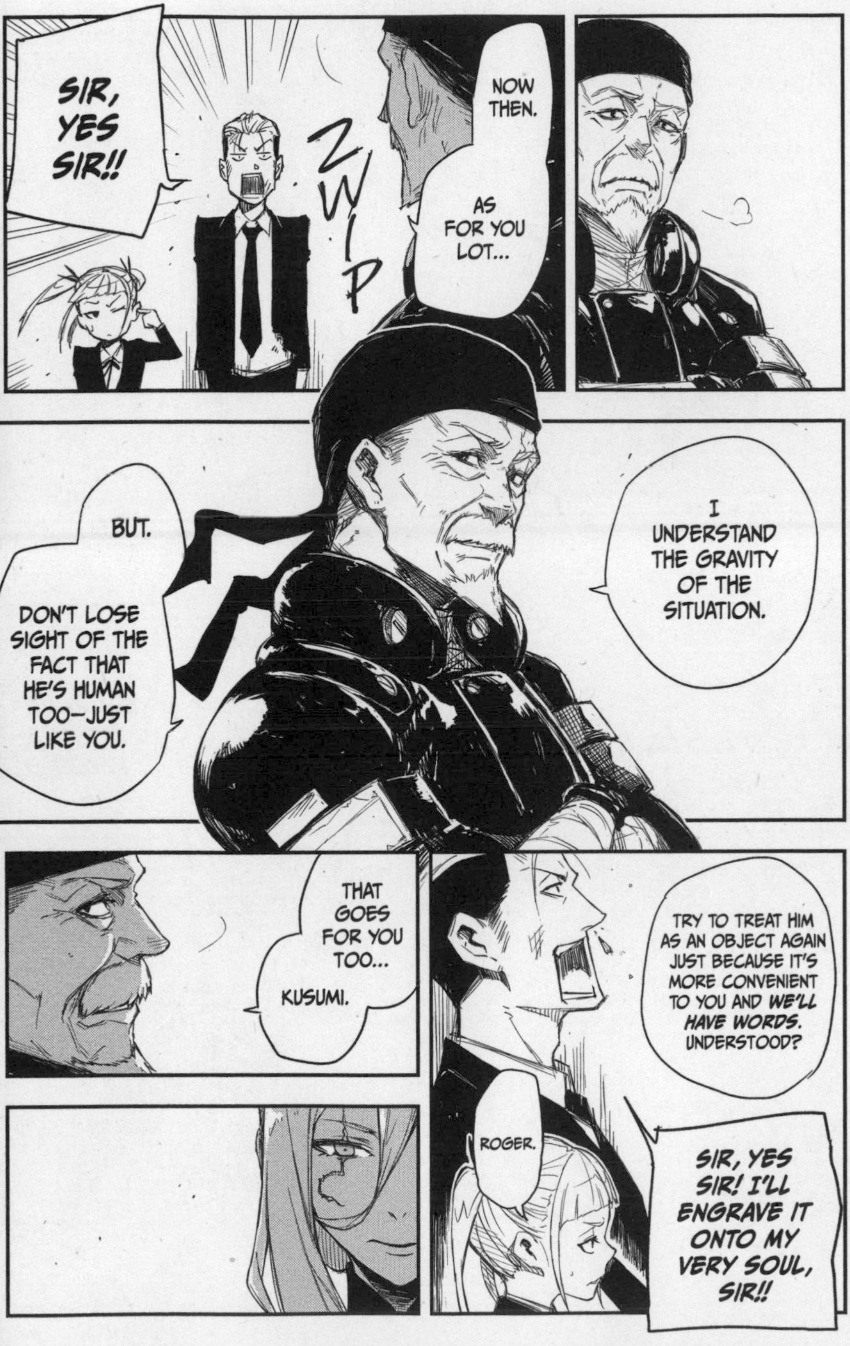
NOW THEN.
AS FOR YOU LOT...
ZWIP
SIR, YES SIR!!
I UNDERSTAND THE GRAVITY OF THE SITUATION.
BUT.
DON'T LOSE SIGHT OF THE FACT THAT HE'S HUMAN TOO—JUST LIKE YOU.
TRY TO TREAT HIM AS AN OBJECT AGAIN JUST BECAUSE IT'S MORE CONVENIENT TO YOU AND *WE'LL HAVE WORDS.* UNDERSTOOD?
SIR, YES SIR! I'LL ENGRAVE IT ONTO MY VERY SOUL, SIR!!
ROGER.
THAT GOES FOR YOU TOO...
KUSUMI.

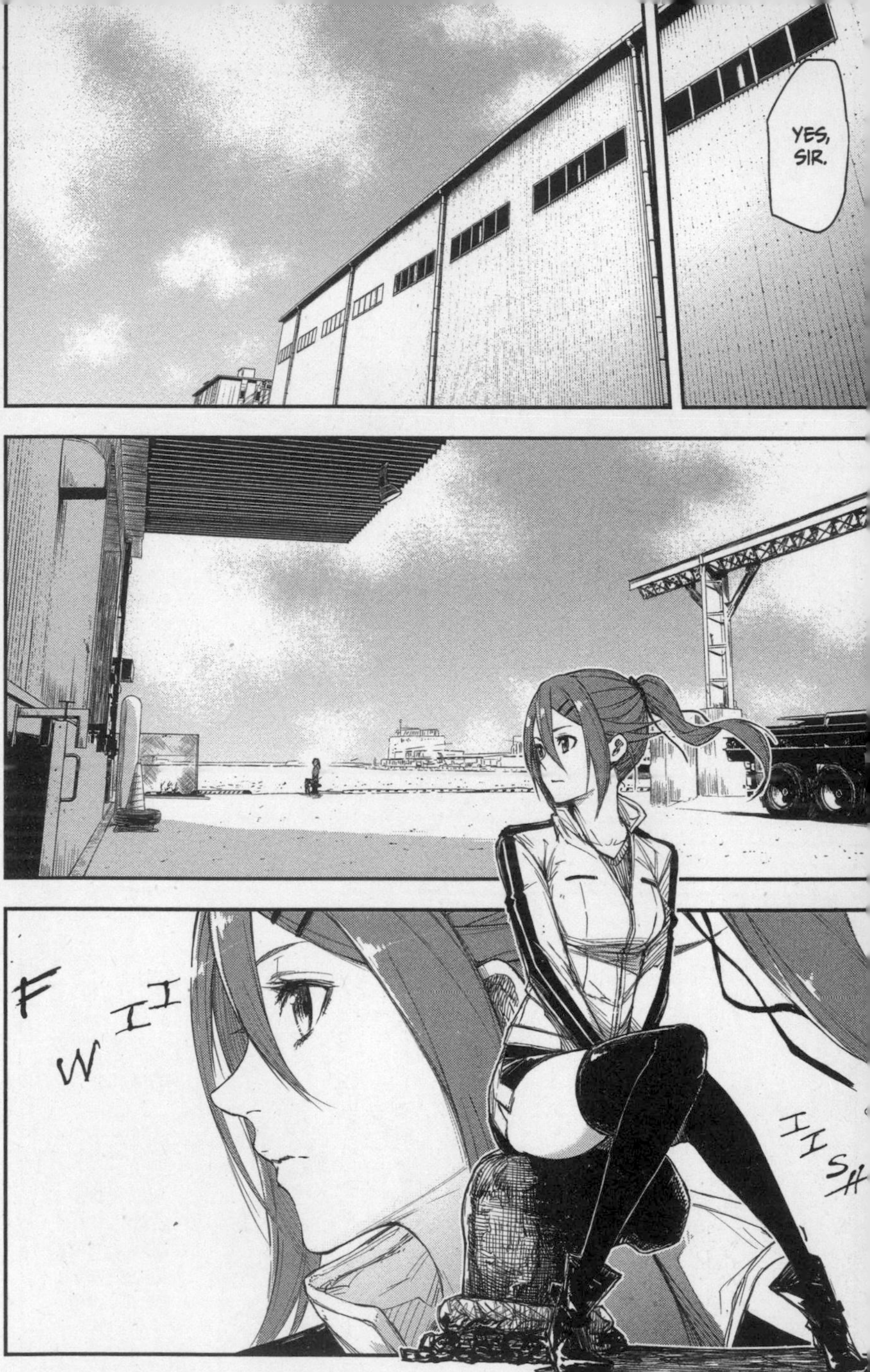
YES, SIR.
FWIISH

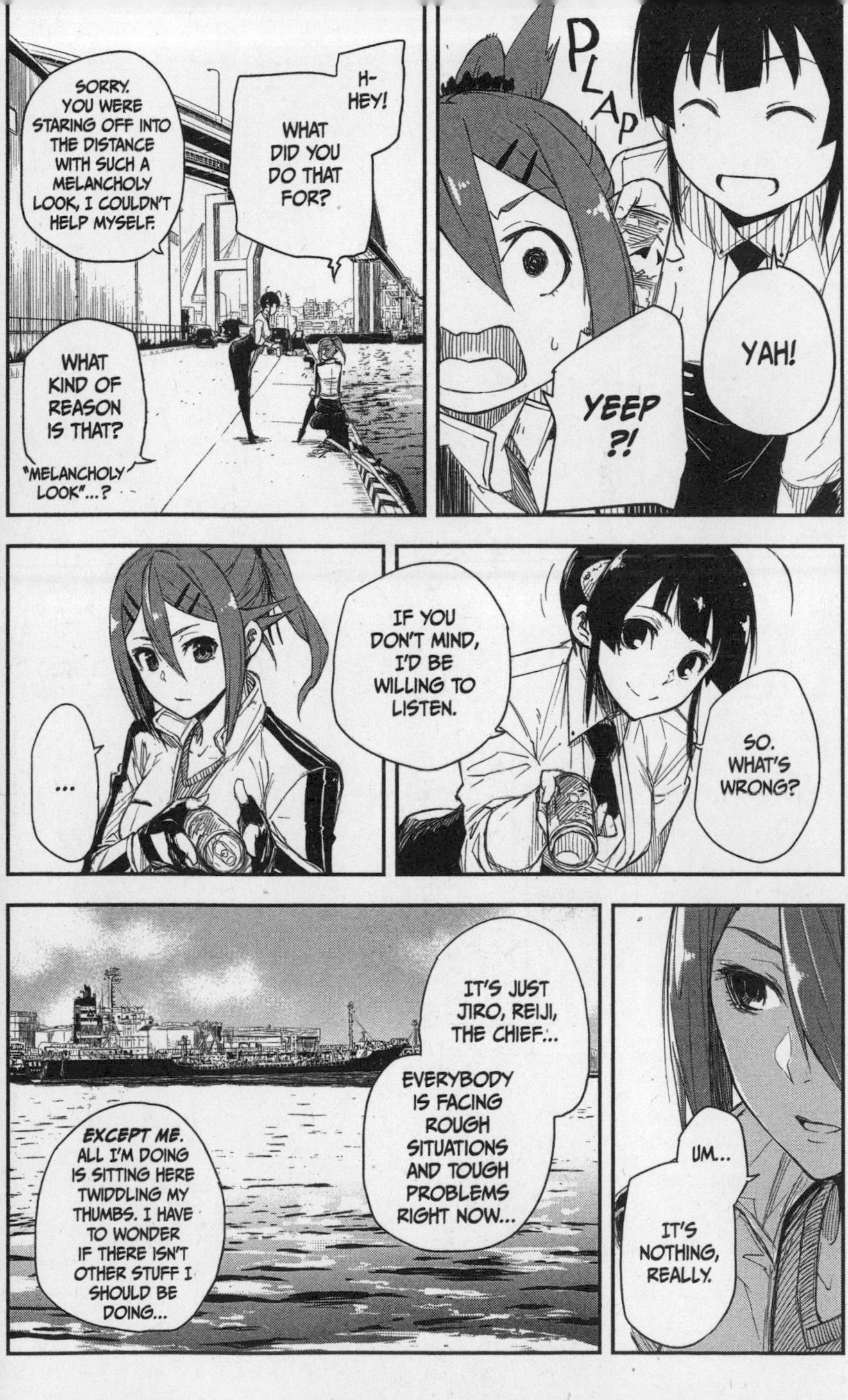
PLAP
YAH!
YEEP ?!
H- HEY!
WHAT DID YOU DO THAT FOR?
SORRY. YOU WERE STARING OFF INTO THE DISTANCE WITH SUCH A MELANCHOLY LOOK, I COULDN'T HELP MYSELF.
WHAT KIND OF REASON IS THAT?
"MELANCHOLY LOOK"...?
SO. WHAT'S WRONG?
IF YOU DON'T MIND, I'D BE WILLING TO LISTEN.
...
UM...
IT'S NOTHING, REALLY.
IT'S JUST JIRO, REIJI, THE CHIEF...
EVERYBODY IS FACING ROUGH SITUATIONS AND TOUGH PROBLEMS RIGHT NOW...
EXCEPT ME. ALL I'M DOING IS SITTING HERE TWIDDLING MY THUMBS. I HAVE TO WONDER IF THERE ISN'T OTHER STUFF I SHOULD BE DOING...

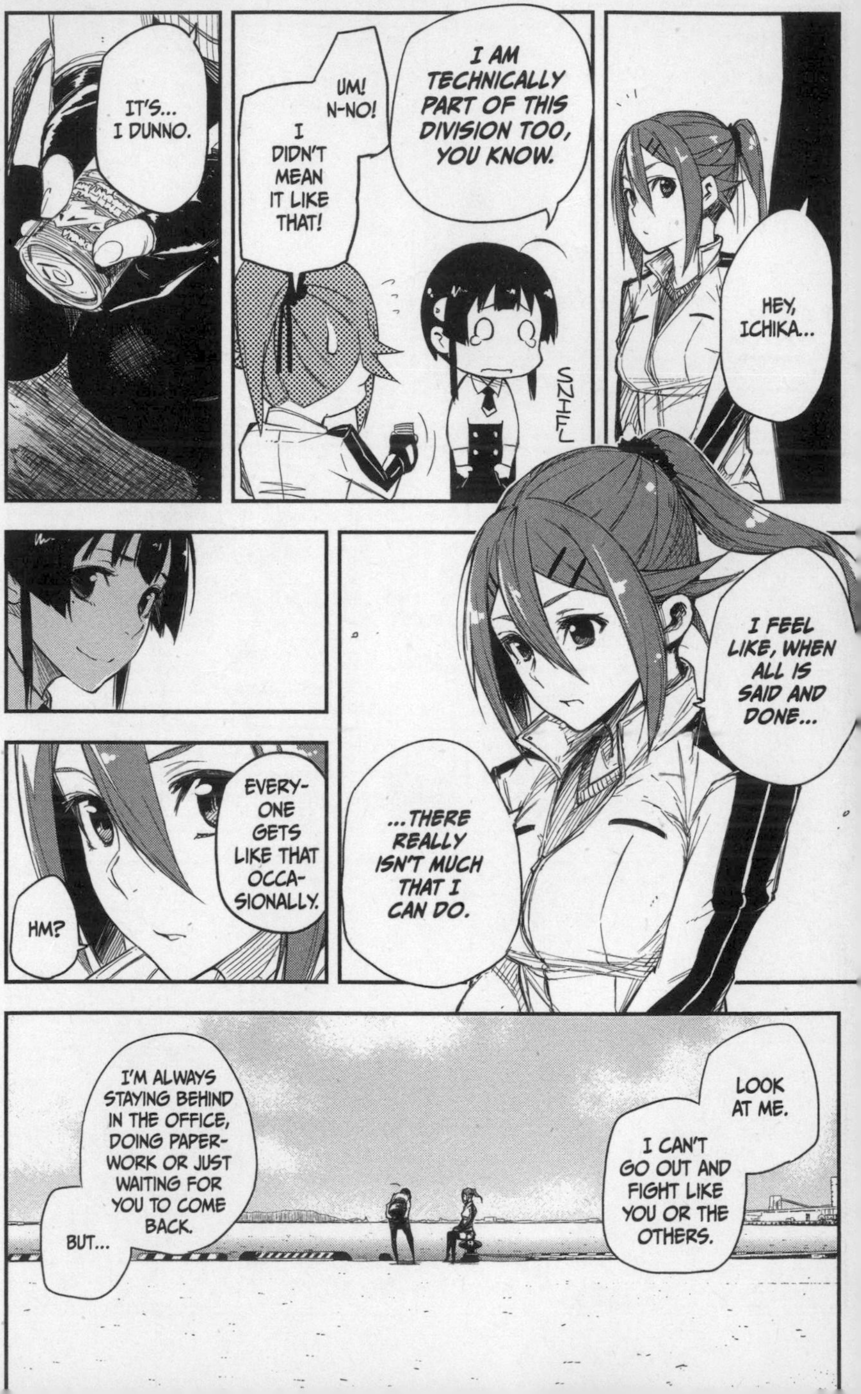
HEY, ICHIKA...
I AM TECHNICALLY PART OF THIS DIVISION TOO, YOU KNOW.
UM! N-NO! I DIDN'T MEAN IT LIKE THAT!
SNIFF
IT'S... I DUNNO.
I FEEL LIKE, WHEN ALL IS SAID AND DONE...
...THERE REALLY ISN'T MUCH THAT I CAN DO.
EVERY-ONE GETS LIKE THAT OCCA-SIONALLY.
HM?
LOOK AT ME.
I CAN'T GO OUT AND FIGHT LIKE YOU OR THE OTHERS.
I'M ALWAYS STAYING BEHIND IN THE OFFICE, DOING PAPER-WORK OR JUST WAITING FOR YOU TO COME BACK.
BUT...

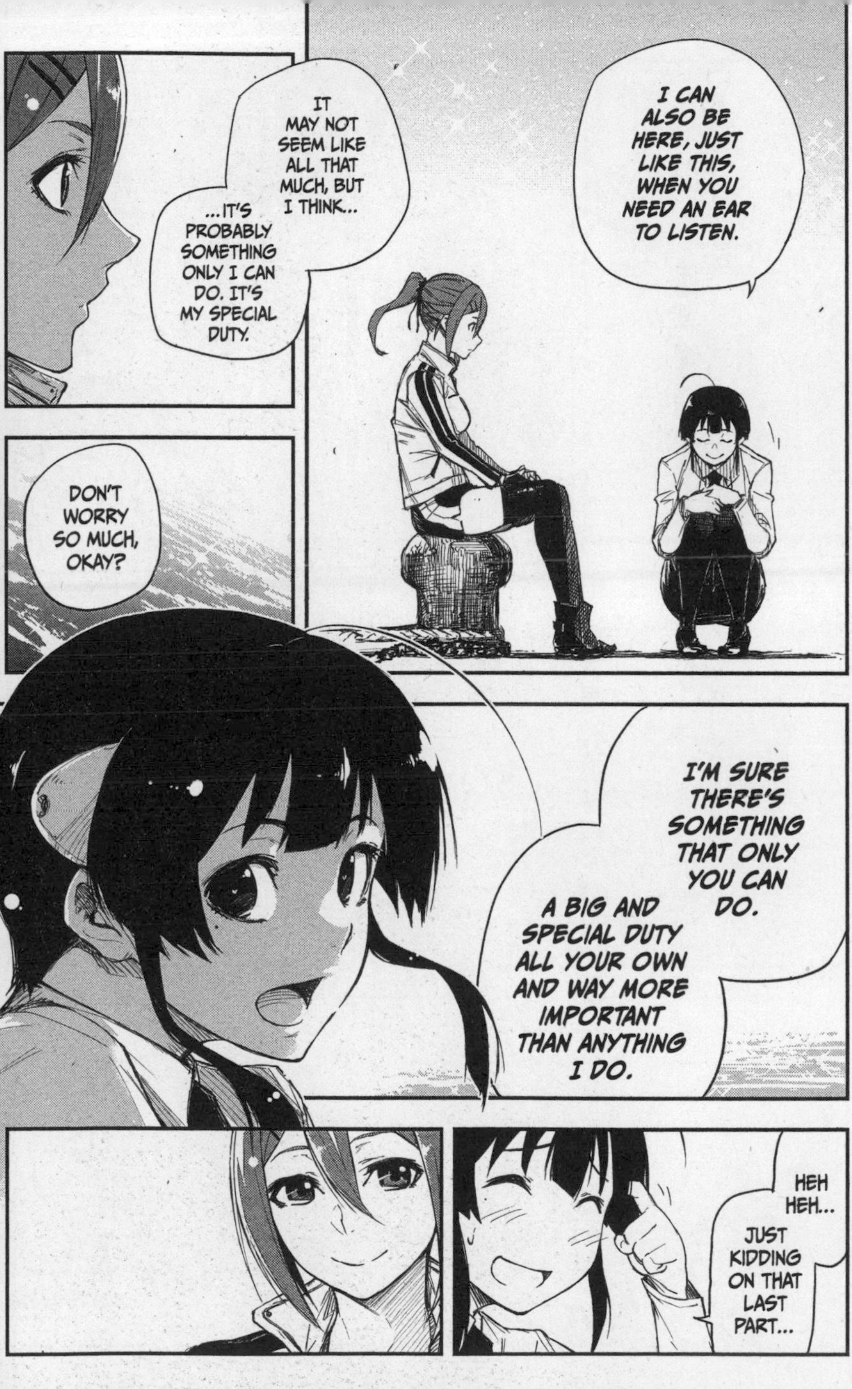
I CAN ALSO BE HERE, JUST LIKE THIS, WHEN YOU NEED AN EAR TO LISTEN.
IT MAY NOT SEEM LIKE ALL THAT MUCH, BUT I THINK...
...IT'S PROBABLY SOMETHING ONLY I CAN DO. IT'S MY SPECIAL DUTY.
DON'T WORRY SO MUCH, OKAY?
I'M SURE THERE'S SOMETHING THAT ONLY YOU CAN DO.
A BIG AND SPECIAL DUTY ALL YOUR OWN AND WAY MORE IMPORTANT THAN ANYTHING I DO.
HEH HEH...
JUST KIDDING ON THAT LAST PART...

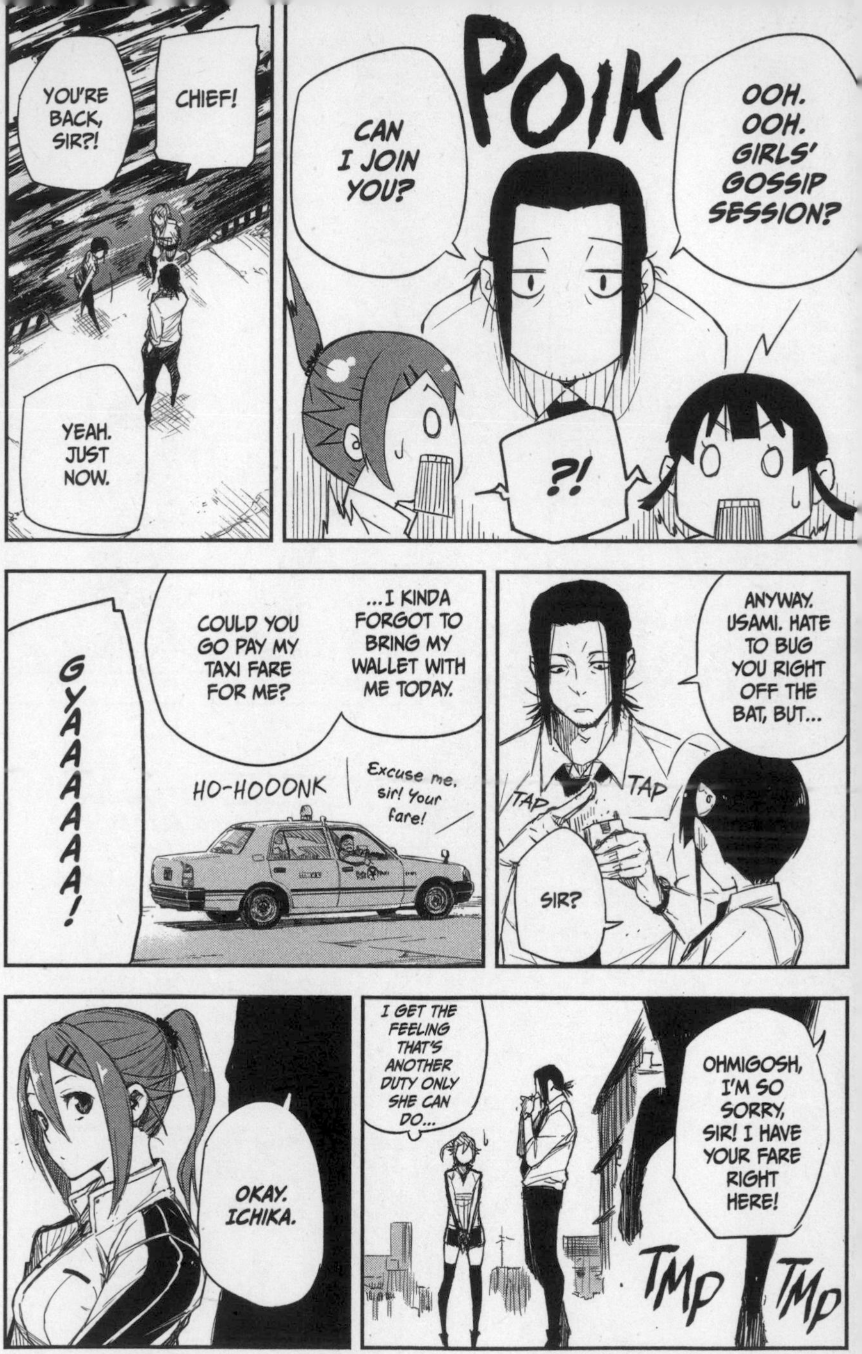

OOH. OOH. GIRLS' GOSSIP SESSION?
POIK
CAN I JOIN YOU?
?!
CHIEF!
YOU'RE BACK, SIR?!
YEAH. JUST NOW.
ANYWAY. USAMI. HATE TO BUG YOU RIGHT OFF THE BAT, BUT...
TAP
TAP
SIR?
...I KINDA FORGOT TO BRING MY WALLET WITH ME TODAY.
COULD YOU GO PAY MY TAXI FARE FOR ME?
Excuse me, sir! Your fare!
HO-HOOONK
GYAAAAAAA!
OHMIGOSH, I'M SO SORRY, SIR! I HAVE YOUR FARE RIGHT HERE!
I GET THE FEELING THAT'S ANOTHER DUTY ONLY SHE CAN DO...
TMP
TMP
OKAY. ICHIKA.

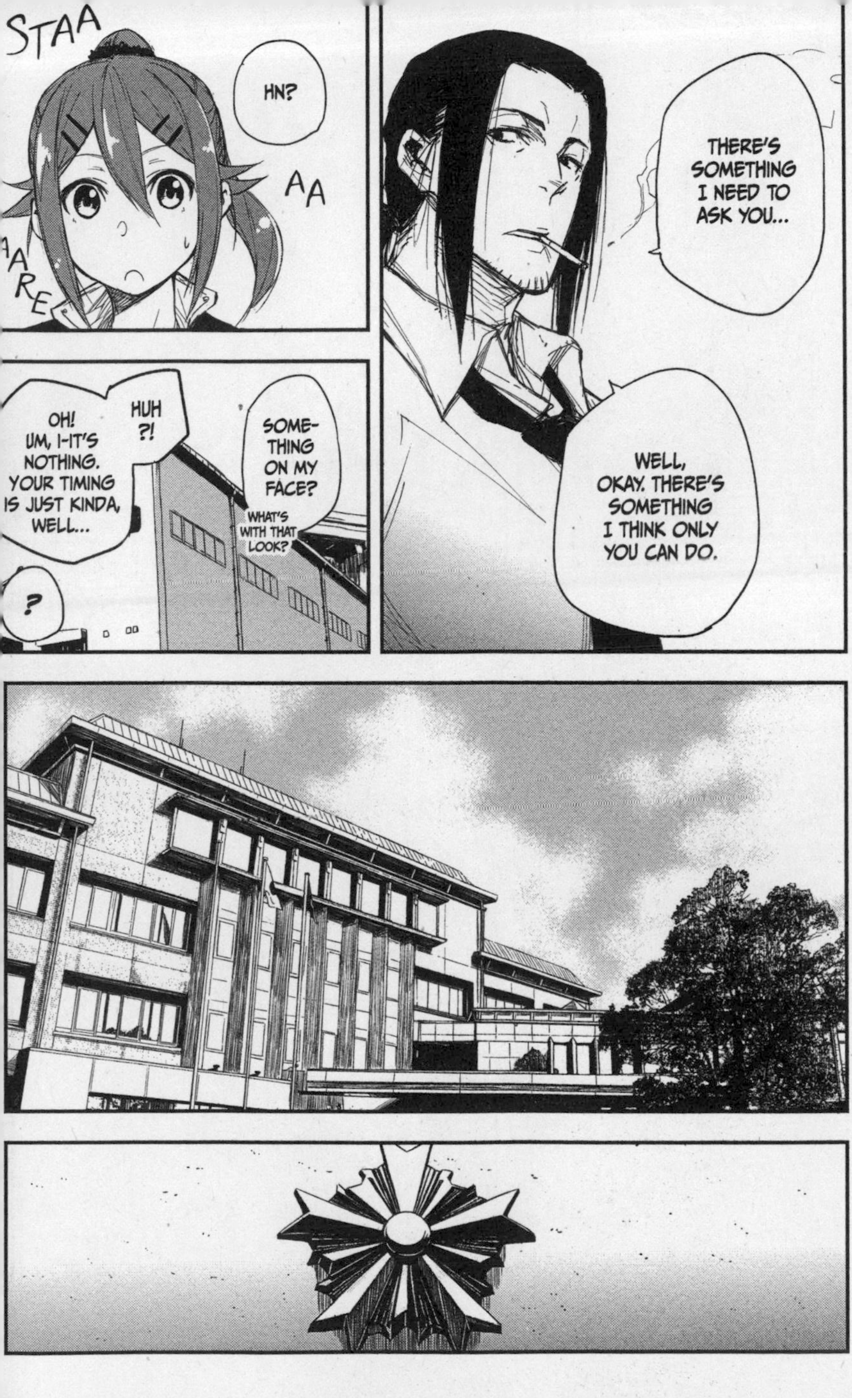
THERE'S SOMETHING I NEED TO ASK YOU...
WELL, OKAY. THERE'S SOMETHING I THINK ONLY YOU CAN DO.
HN?
STAA AA AARE
SOME-THING ON MY FACE?
WHAT'S WITH THAT LOOK?
HUH ?!
OH! UM, I-IT'S NOTHING. YOUR TIMING IS JUST KINDA, WELL...
?

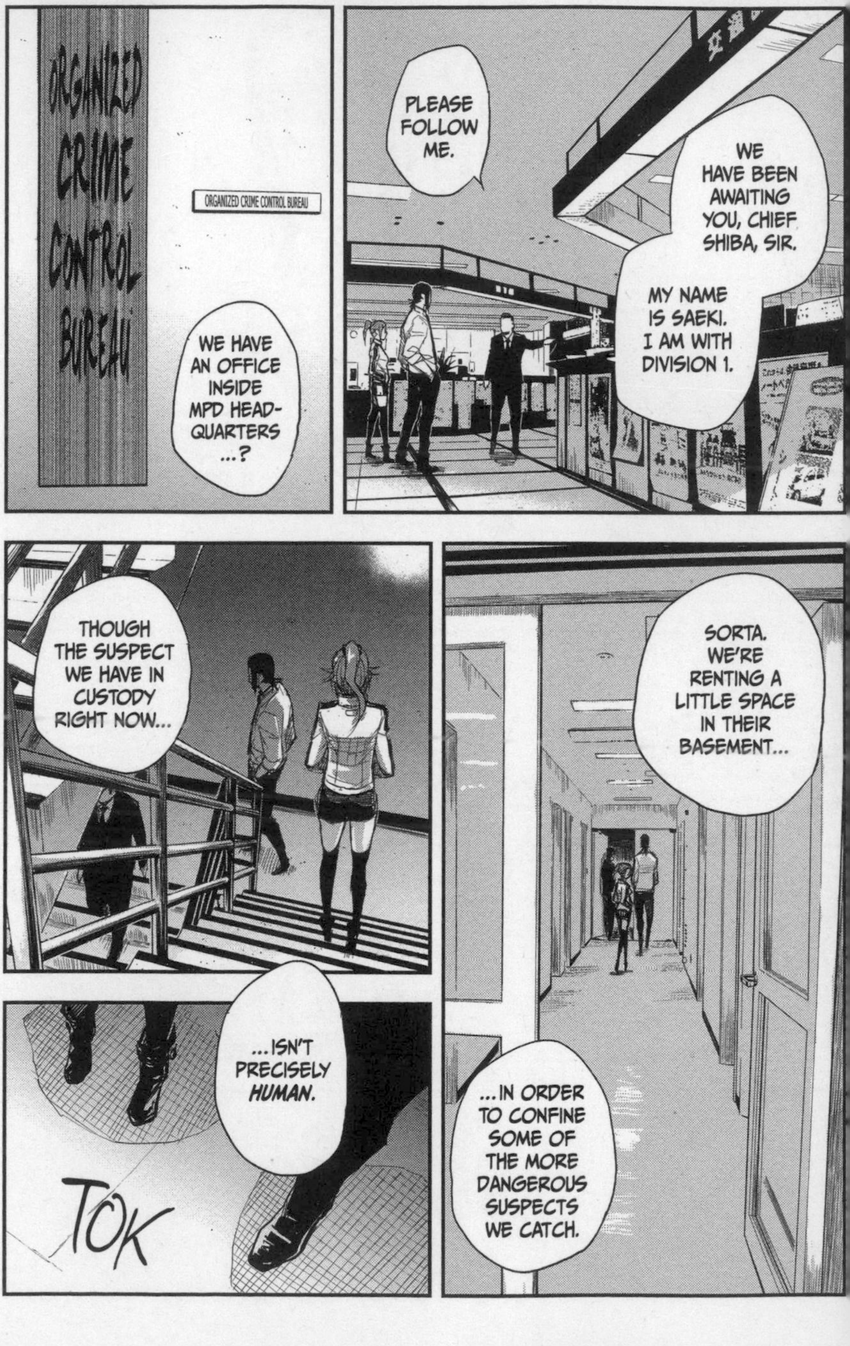
WE HAVE BEEN AWAITING YOU, CHIEF SHIBA, SIR.
MY NAME IS SAEKI. I AM WITH DIVISION 1.
PLEASE FOLLOW ME.
ORGANIZED CRIME CONTROL BUREAU
ORGANIZED CRIME CONTROL BUREAU
WE HAVE AN OFFICE INSIDE MPD HEAD-QUARTERS ...?
SORTA. WE'RE RENTING A LITTLE SPACE IN THEIR BASEMENT...
...IN ORDER TO CONFINE SOME OF THE MORE DANGEROUS SUSPECTS WE CATCH.
THOUGH THE SUSPECT WE HAVE IN CUSTODY RIGHT NOW...
...ISN'T PRECISELY *HUMAN.*
TOK

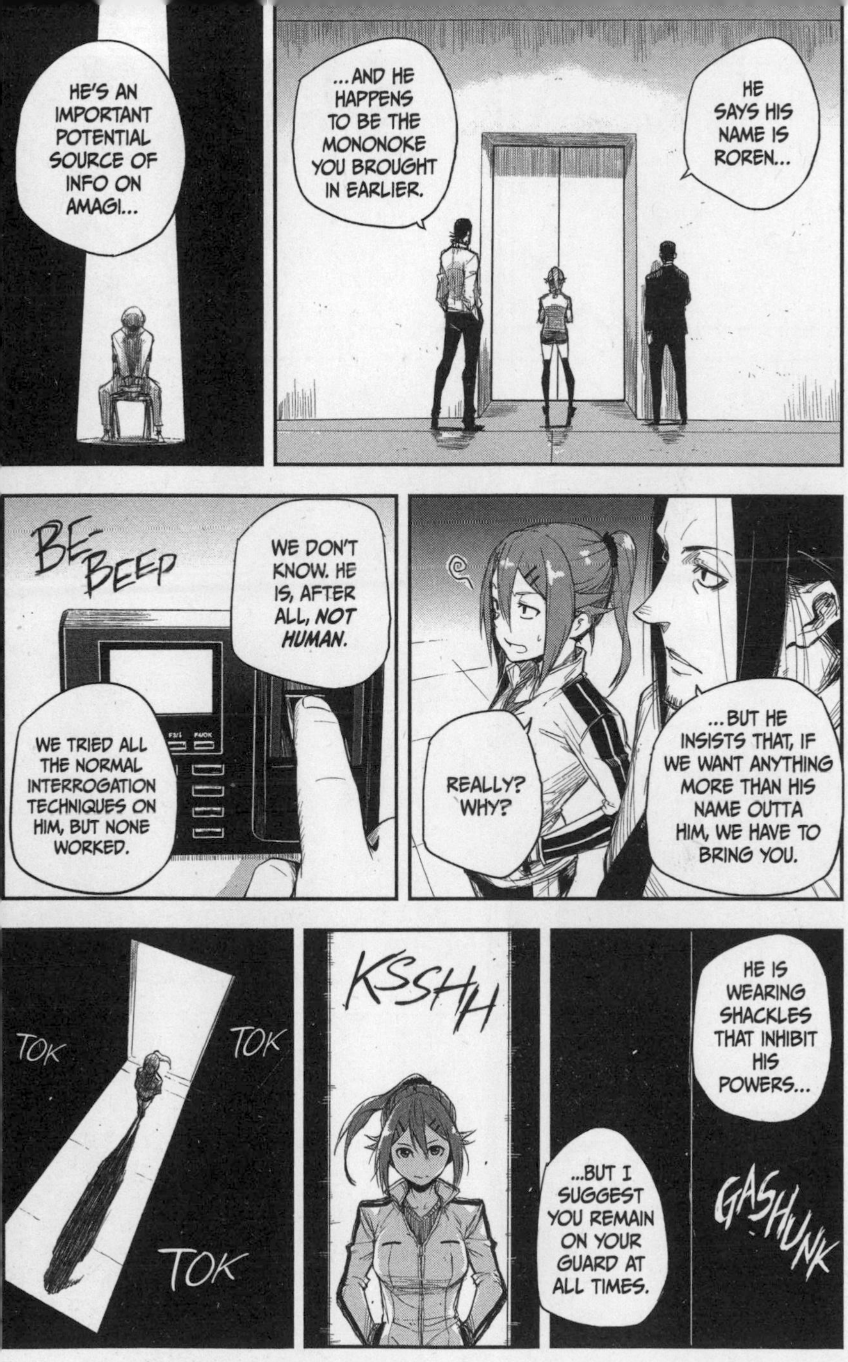
HE SAYS HIS NAME IS ROREN...
...AND HE HAPPENS TO BE THE MONONOKE YOU BROUGHT IN EARLIER.
HE'S AN IMPORTANT POTENTIAL SOURCE OF INFO ON AMAGI...
...BUT HE INSISTS THAT, IF WE WANT ANYTHING MORE THAN HIS NAME OUTTA HIM, WE HAVE TO BRING YOU.
REALLY? WHY?
BE-BEEP
WE DON'T KNOW. HE IS, AFTER ALL, *NOT HUMAN*.
WE TRIED ALL THE NORMAL INTERROGATION TECHNIQUES ON HIM, BUT NONE WORKED.
HE IS WEARING SHACKLES THAT INHIBIT HIS POWERS...
GASHUNK
...BUT I SUGGEST YOU REMAIN ON YOUR GUARD AT ALL TIMES.
KSSHH
TOK
TOK
TOK

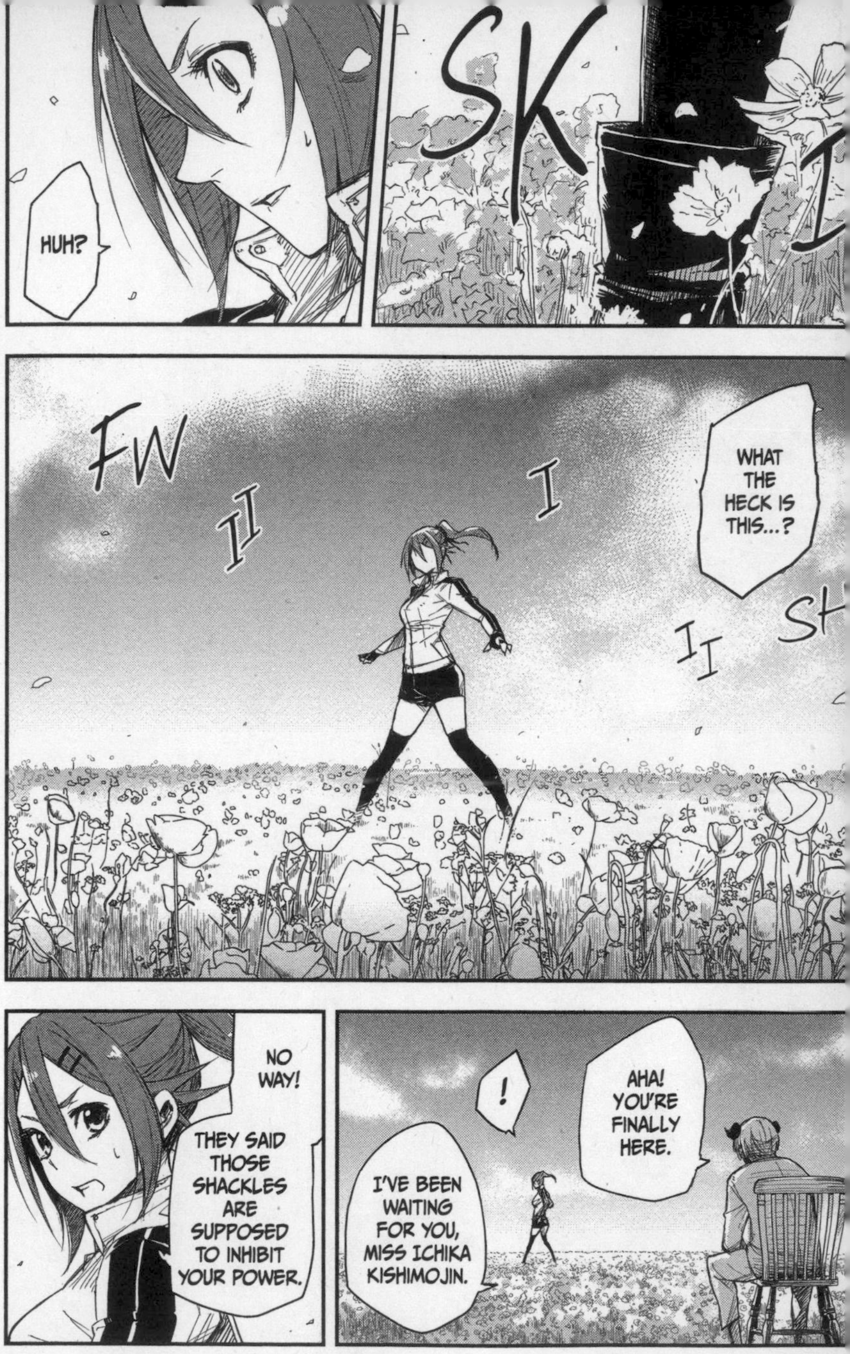
SKI
HUH?
WHAT THE HECK IS THIS...?
SH
II
FW
II
I
AHA! YOU'RE FINALLY HERE.
!
I'VE BEEN WAITING FOR YOU, MISS ICHIKA KISHIMOJIN.
NO WAY!
THEY SAID THOSE SHACKLES ARE SUPPOSED TO INHIBIT YOUR POWER.

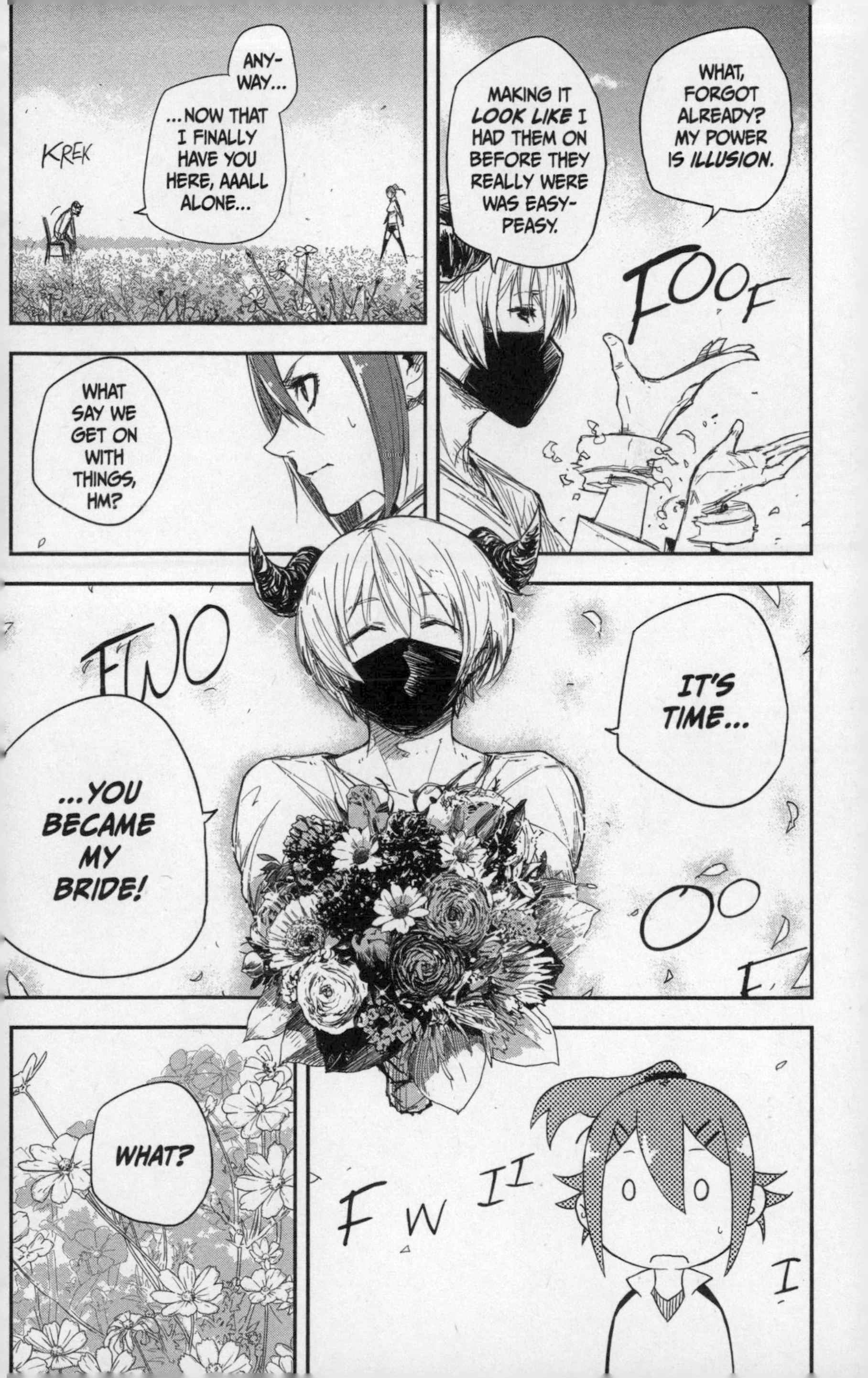
WHAT, FORGOT ALREADY? MY POWER IS *ILLUSION*.
MAKING IT *LOOK LIKE* I HAD THEM ON BEFORE THEY REALLY WERE WAS EASY-PEASY.
FOOF
ANY-WAY...
...NOW THAT I FINALLY HAVE YOU HERE, AAALL ALONE...
KREK
WHAT SAY WE GET ON WITH THINGS, HM?
IT'S TIME...
...YOU BECAME MY BRIDE!
OOF
FWO
FWII
I
WHAT?

BLACK TORCH

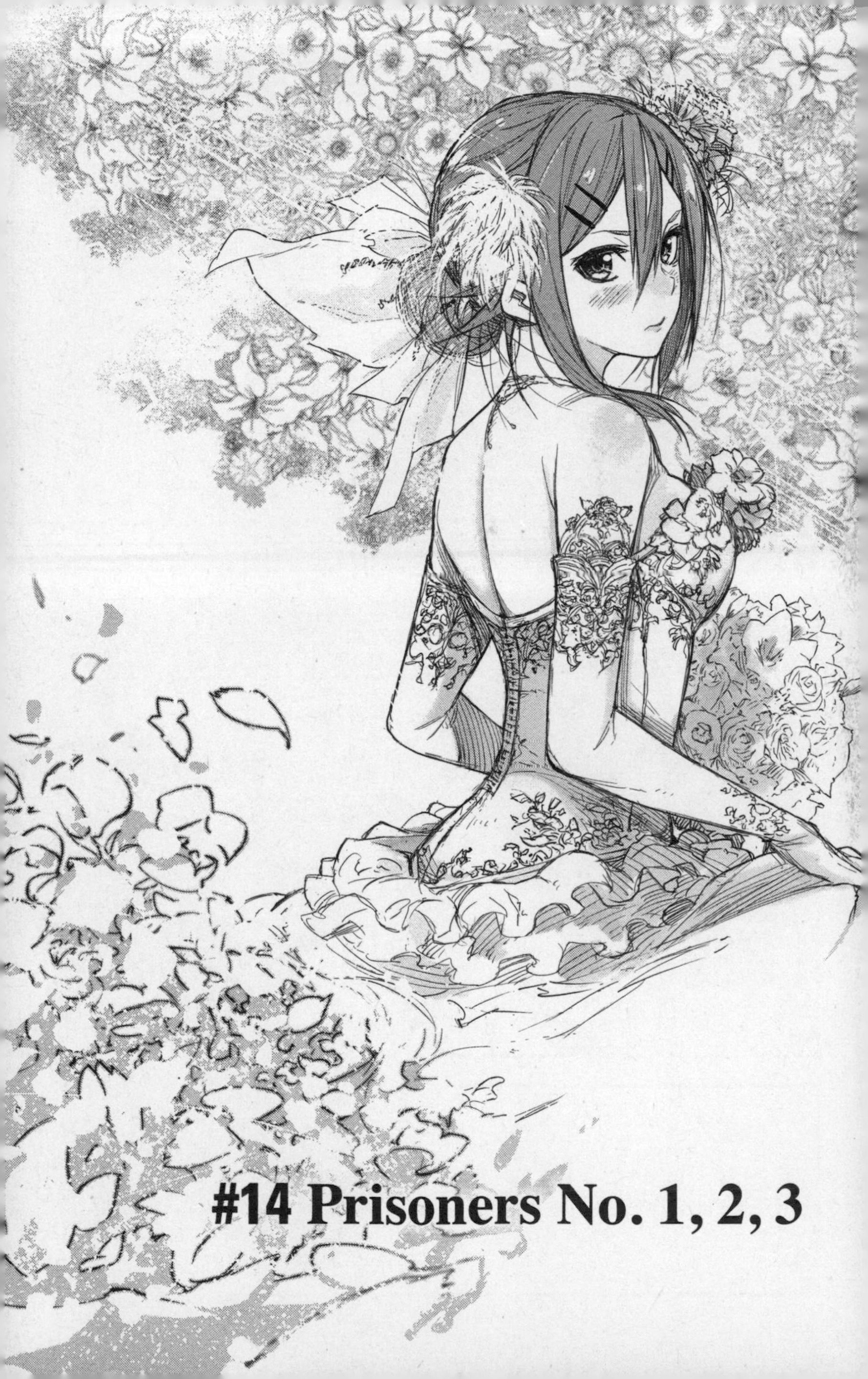

#14 Prisoners No. 1, 2, 3

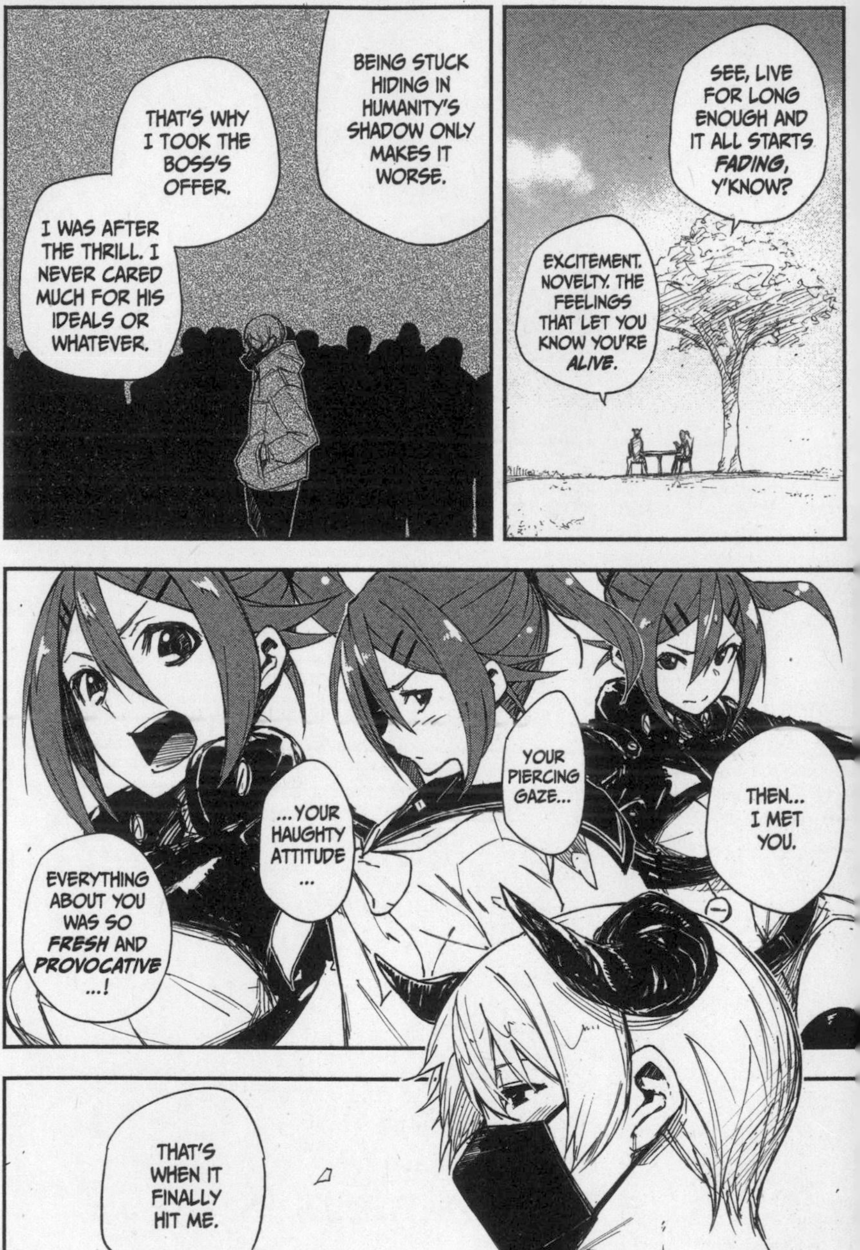
SEE, LIVE FOR LONG ENOUGH AND IT ALL STARTS *FADING*, Y'KNOW?
EXCITEMENT. NOVELTY. THE FEELINGS THAT LET YOU KNOW YOU'RE *ALIVE*.
BEING STUCK HIDING IN HUMANITY'S SHADOW ONLY MAKES IT WORSE.
THAT'S WHY I TOOK THE BOSS'S OFFER.
I WAS AFTER THE THRILL. I NEVER CARED MUCH FOR HIS IDEALS OR WHATEVER.
THEN... I MET YOU.
YOUR PIERCING GAZE...
...YOUR HAUGHTY ATTITUDE ...
EVERYTHING ABOUT YOU WAS SO *FRESH* AND *PROVOCATIVE* ...!
THAT'S WHEN IT FINALLY HIT ME.

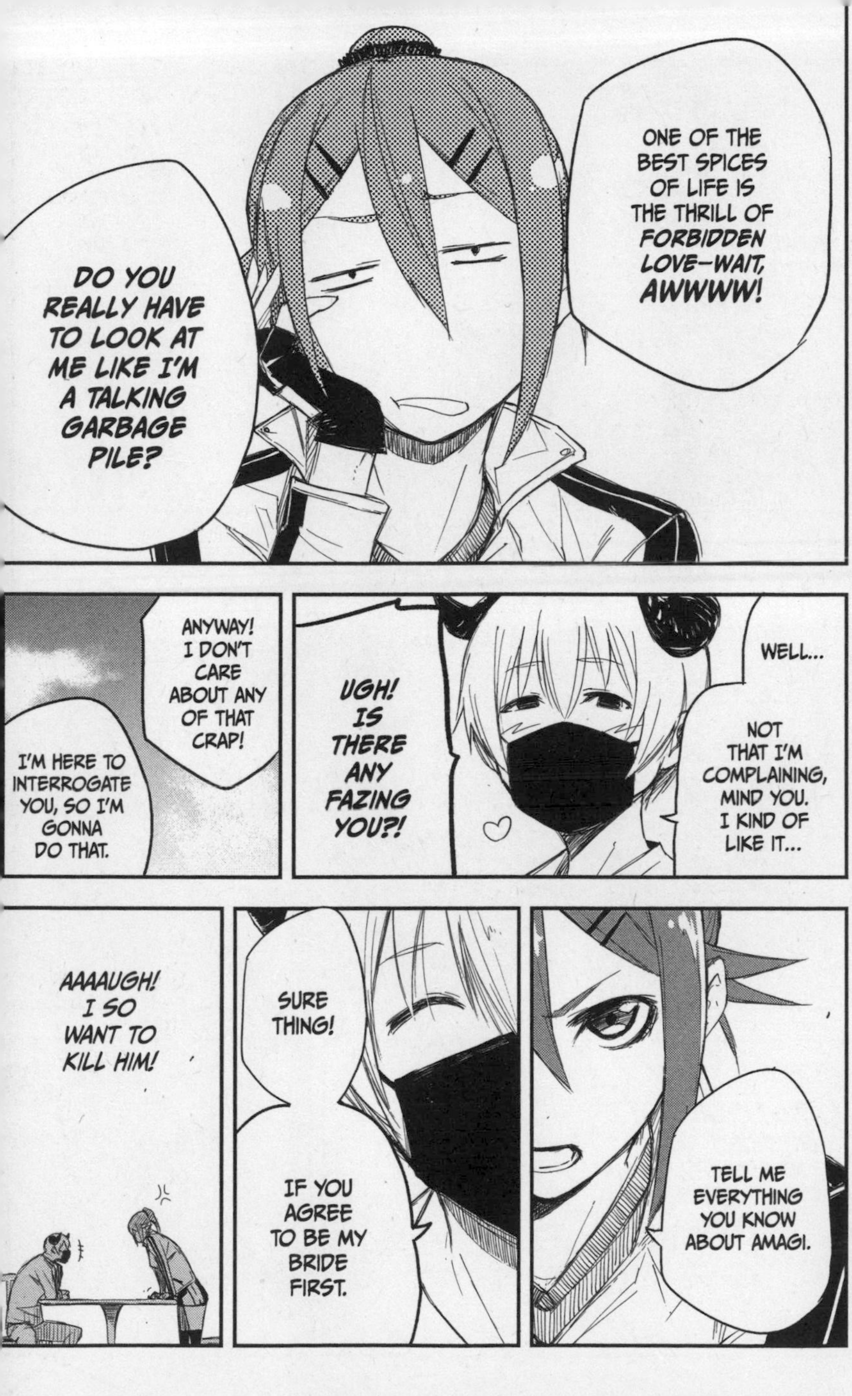
ONE OF THE BEST SPICES OF LIFE IS THE THRILL OF FORBIDDEN LOVE—WAIT, AWWWW!
DO YOU REALLY HAVE TO LOOK AT ME LIKE I'M A TALKING GARBAGE PILE?
WELL...
NOT THAT I'M COMPLAINING, MIND YOU. I KIND OF LIKE IT...
UGH! IS THERE ANY FAZING YOU?!
ANYWAY! I DON'T CARE ABOUT ANY OF THAT CRAP!
I'M HERE TO INTERROGATE YOU, SO I'M GONNA DO THAT.
TELL ME EVERYTHING YOU KNOW ABOUT AMAGI.
SURE THING!
IF YOU AGREE TO BE MY BRIDE FIRST.
AAAAUGH! I SO WANT TO KILL HIM!

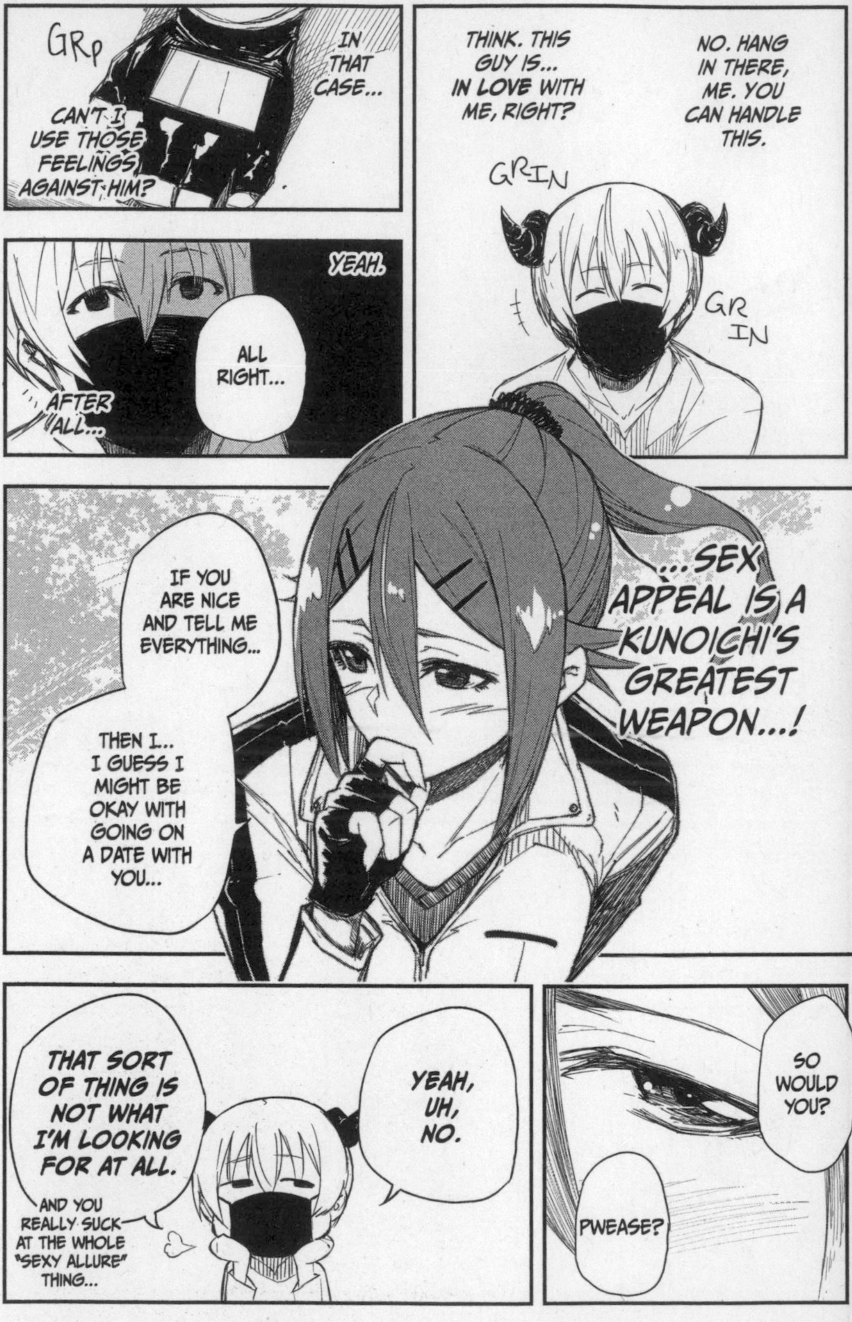
NO. HANG IN THERE, ME. YOU CAN HANDLE THIS.
THINK. THIS GUY IS... IN LOVE WITH ME, RIGHT?
GRIN
GRIN
IN THAT CASE...
GRp
CAN'T I USE THOSE FEELINGS AGAINST HIM?
YEAH.
ALL RIGHT...
AFTER ALL...
...SEX APPEAL IS A KUNOICHI'S GREATEST WEAPON...!
IF YOU ARE NICE AND TELL ME EVERYTHING...
THEN I... I GUESS I MIGHT BE OKAY WITH GOING ON A DATE WITH YOU...
SO WOULD YOU?
PWEASE?
YEAH, UH, NO.
THAT SORT OF THING IS NOT WHAT I'M LOOKING FOR AT ALL.
AND YOU REALLY SUCK AT THE WHOLE "SEXY ALLURE" THING...

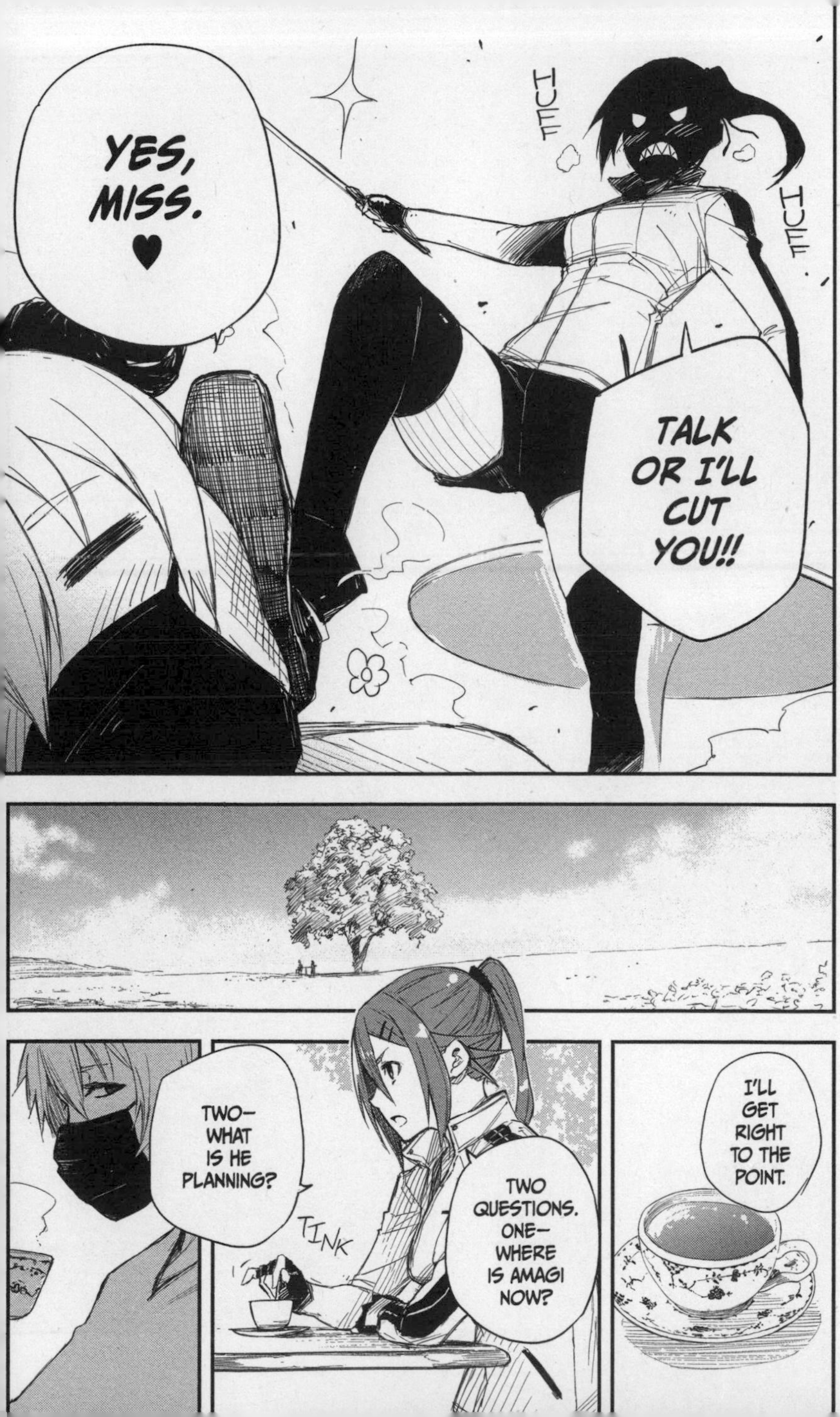
HUFF
HUFF
TALK OR I'LL CUT YOU!!
YES, MISS. ♥
I'LL GET RIGHT TO THE POINT.
TWO QUESTIONS. ONE— WHERE IS AMAGI NOW?
TINK
TWO— WHAT IS HE PLANNING?

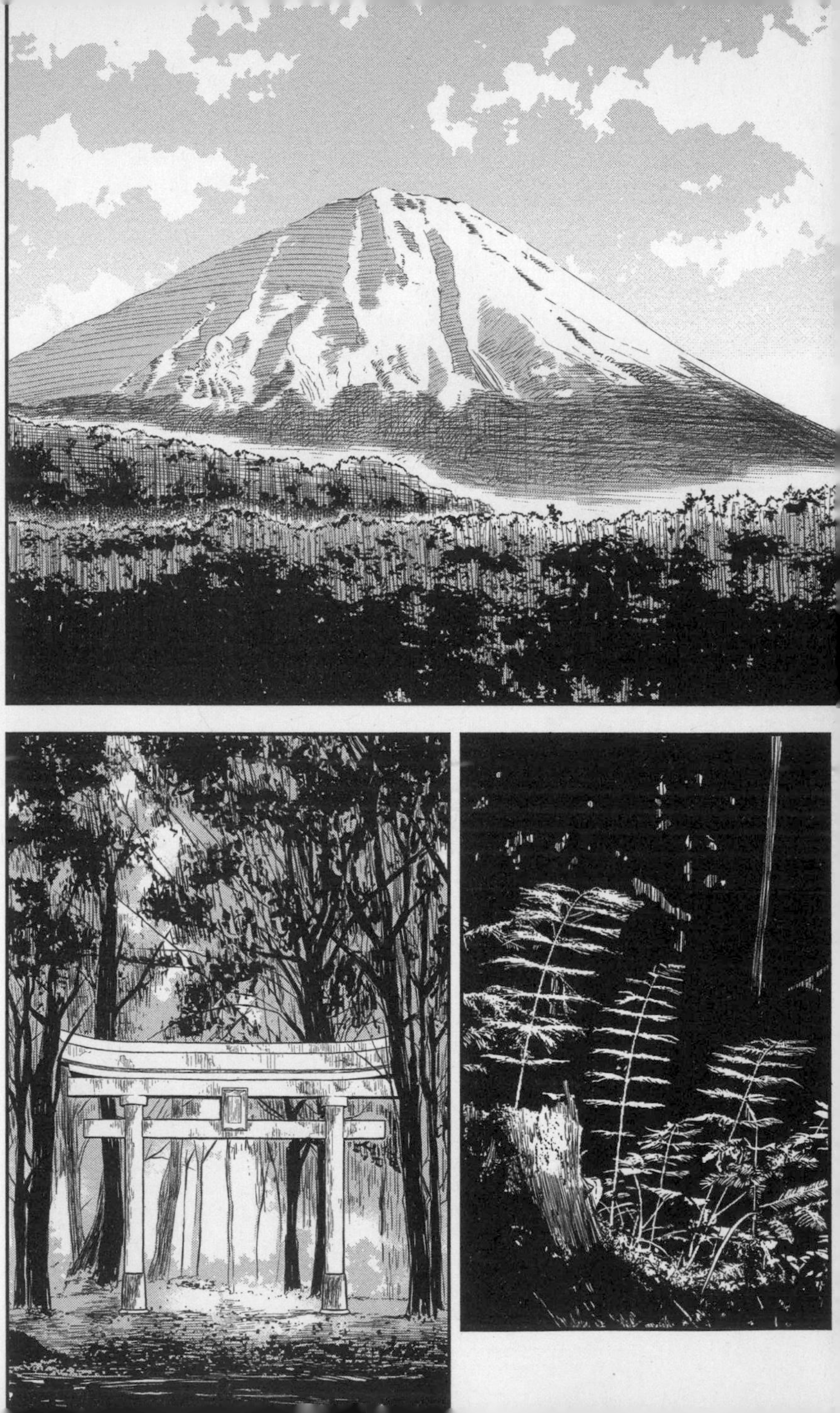

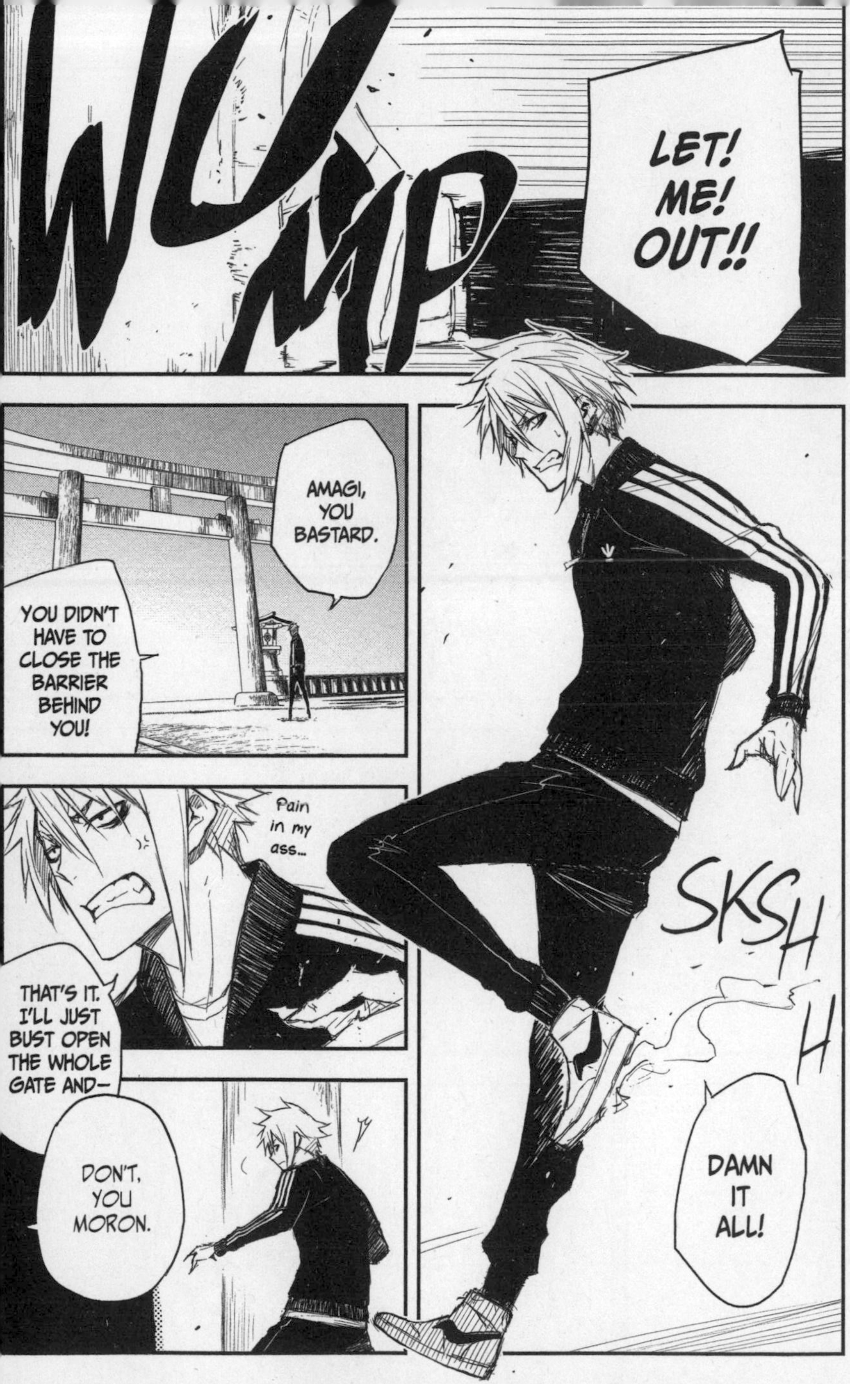

LET! ME! OUT!!
WUMP
SKSHH
DAMN IT ALL!
AMAGI, YOU BASTARD.
YOU DIDN'T HAVE TO CLOSE THE BARRIER BEHIND YOU!
Pain in my ass...
THAT'S IT. I'LL JUST BUST OPEN THE WHOLE GATE AND—
DON'T, YOU MORON.

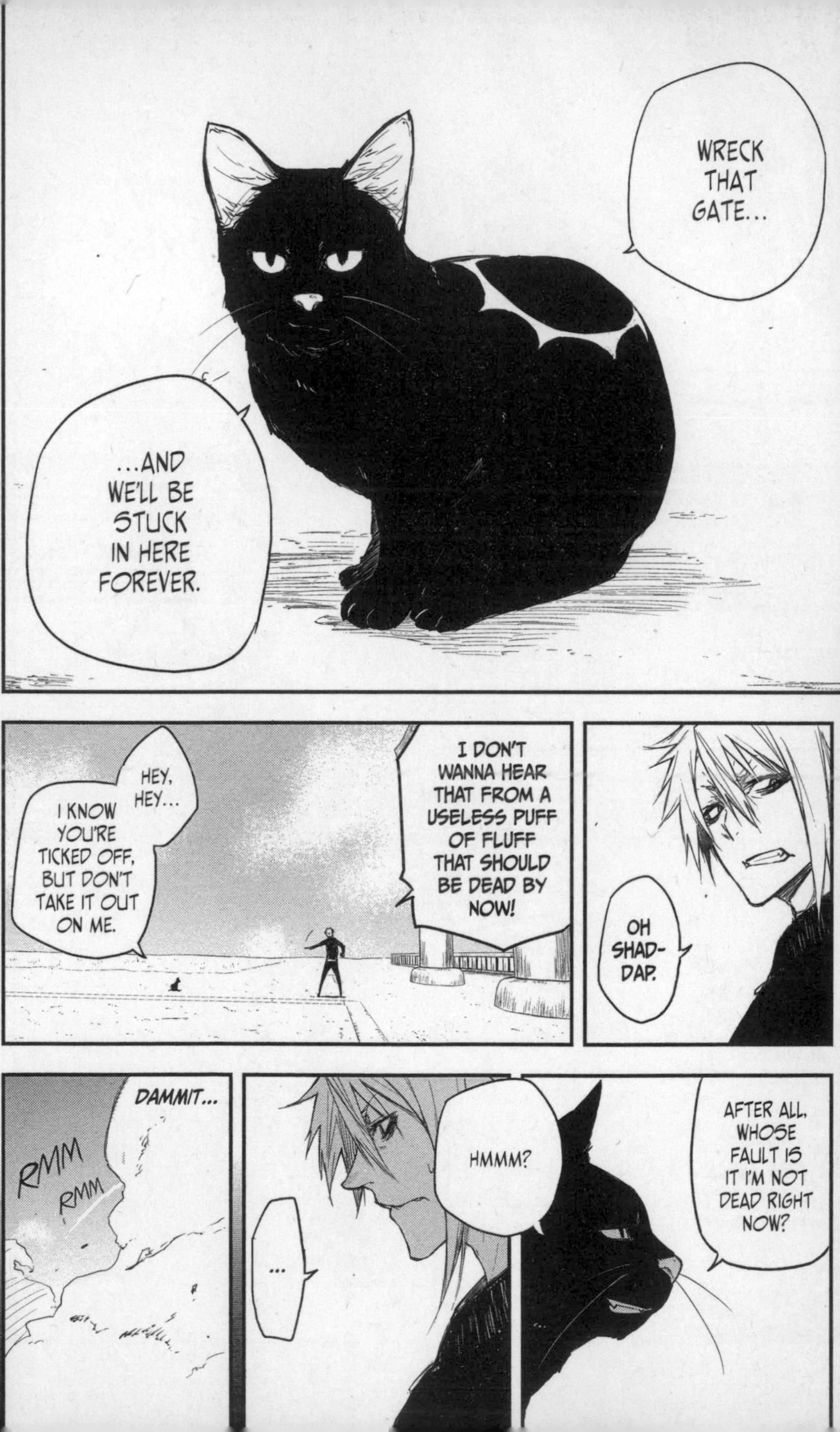
WRECK THAT GATE...
...AND WE'LL BE STUCK IN HERE FOREVER.
OH SHAD-DAP.
I DON'T WANNA HEAR THAT FROM A USELESS PUFF OF FLUFF THAT SHOULD BE DEAD BY NOW!
HEY, HEY...
I KNOW YOU'RE TICKED OFF, BUT DON'T TAKE IT OUT ON ME.
AFTER ALL, WHOSE FAULT IS IT I'M NOT DEAD RIGHT NOW?
HMMM?
...
DAMMIT...
RMM RMM

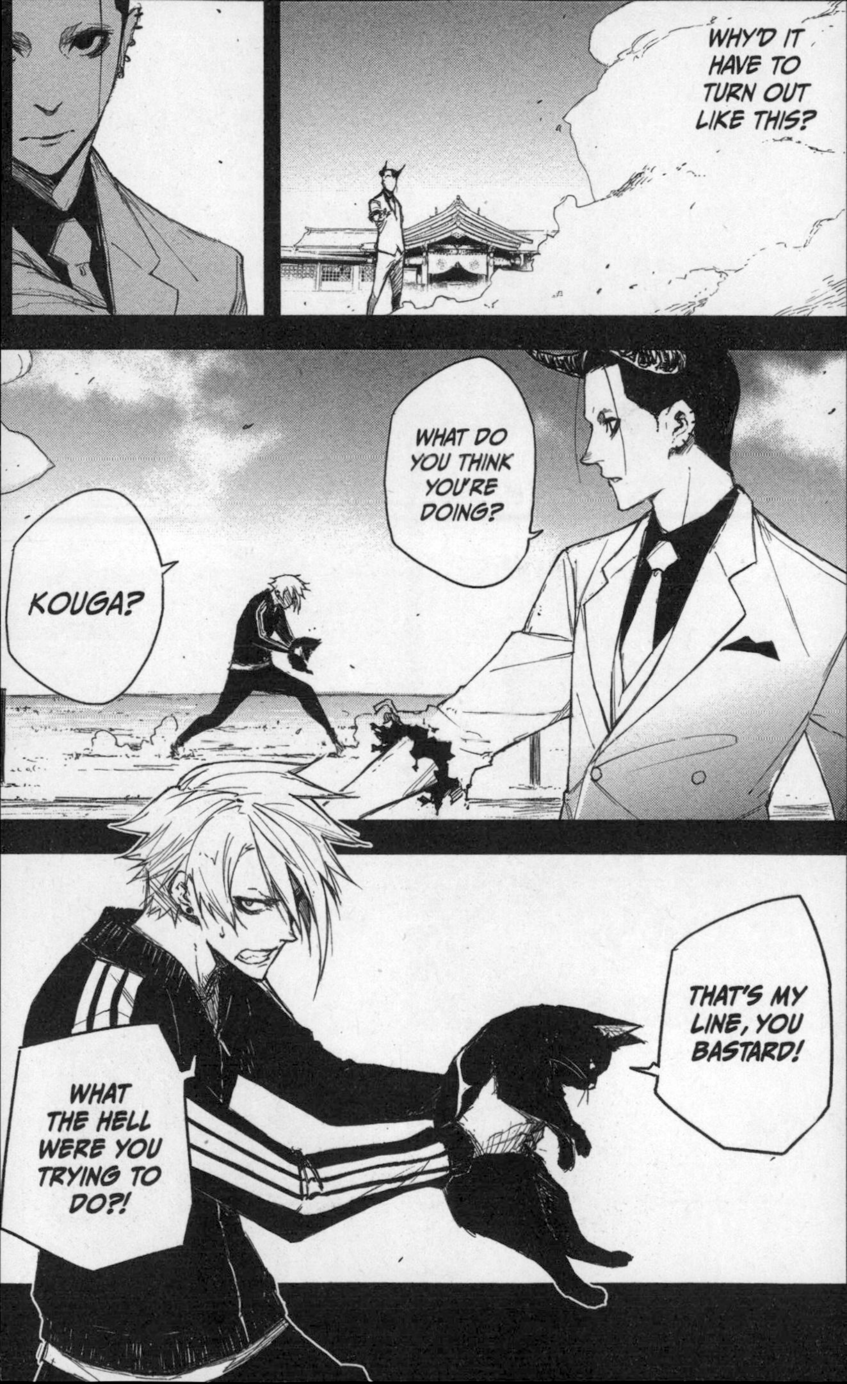
WHY'D IT HAVE TO TURN OUT LIKE THIS?
WHAT DO YOU THINK YOU'RE DOING?
KOUGA?
THAT'S MY LINE, YOU BASTARD!
WHAT THE HELL WERE YOU TRYING TO DO?!

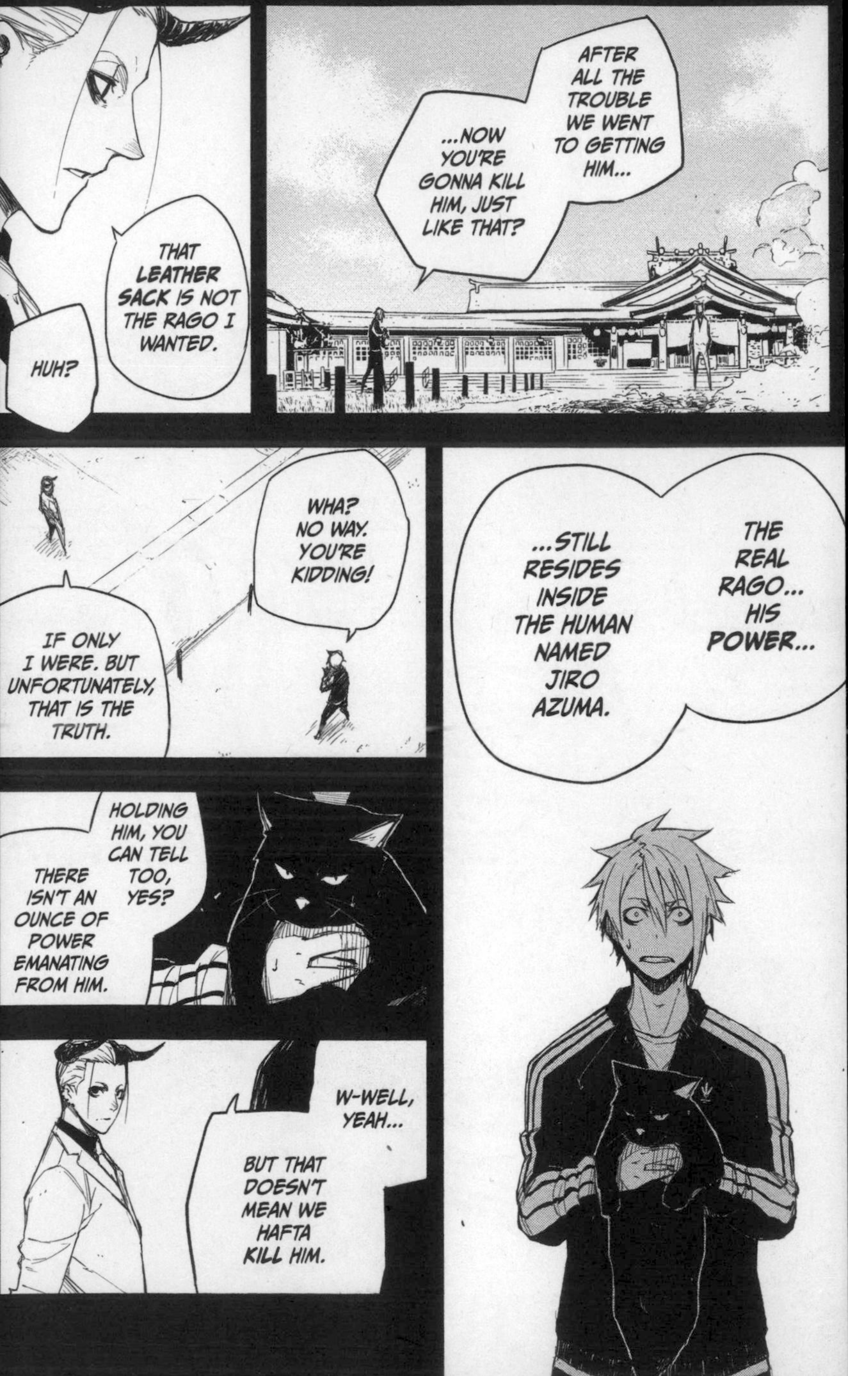
AFTER ALL THE TROUBLE WE WENT TO GETTING HIM...
...NOW YOU'RE GONNA KILL HIM, JUST LIKE THAT?
THAT LEATHER SACK IS NOT THE RAGO I WANTED.
HUH?
THE REAL RAGO... HIS POWER...
...STILL RESIDES INSIDE THE HUMAN NAMED JIRO AZUMA.
WHA? NO WAY. YOU'RE KIDDING!
IF ONLY I WERE. BUT UNFORTUNATELY, THAT IS THE TRUTH.
HOLDING HIM, YOU CAN TELL TOO, YES?
THERE ISN'T AN OUNCE OF POWER EMANATING FROM HIM.
W-WELL, YEAH...
BUT THAT DOESN'T MEAN WE HAFTA KILL HIM.

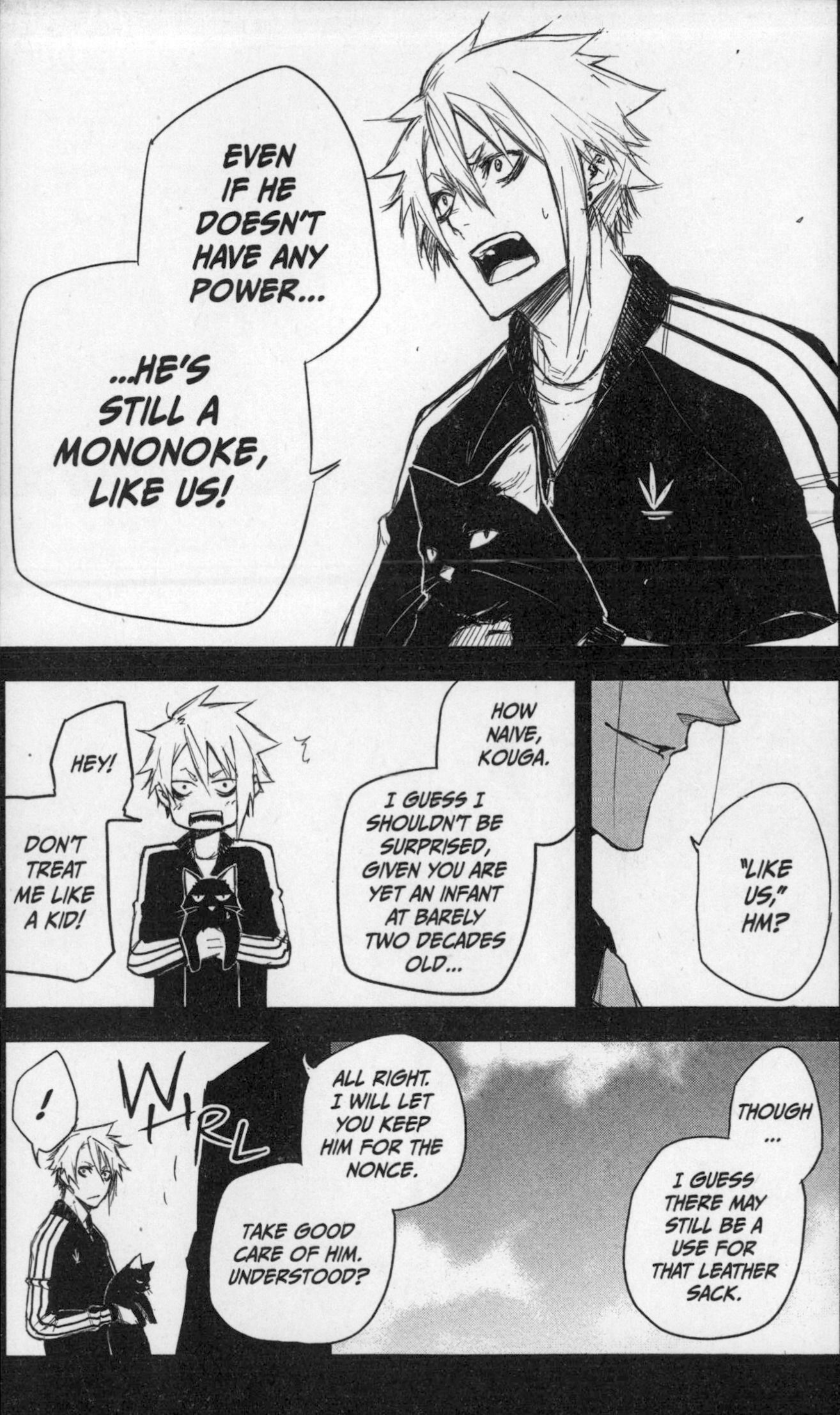
EVEN IF HE DOESN'T HAVE ANY POWER...
...HE'S STILL A MONONOKE, LIKE US!
"LIKE US," HM?
HOW NAIVE, KOUGA.
I GUESS I SHOULDN'T BE SURPRISED, GIVEN YOU ARE YET AN INFANT AT BARELY TWO DECADES OLD...
HEY!
DON'T TREAT ME LIKE A KID!
THOUGH...
I GUESS THERE MAY STILL BE A USE FOR THAT LEATHER SACK.
ALL RIGHT. I WILL LET YOU KEEP HIM FOR THE NONCE.
TAKE GOOD CARE OF HIM. UNDERSTOOD?
WHIRL
!

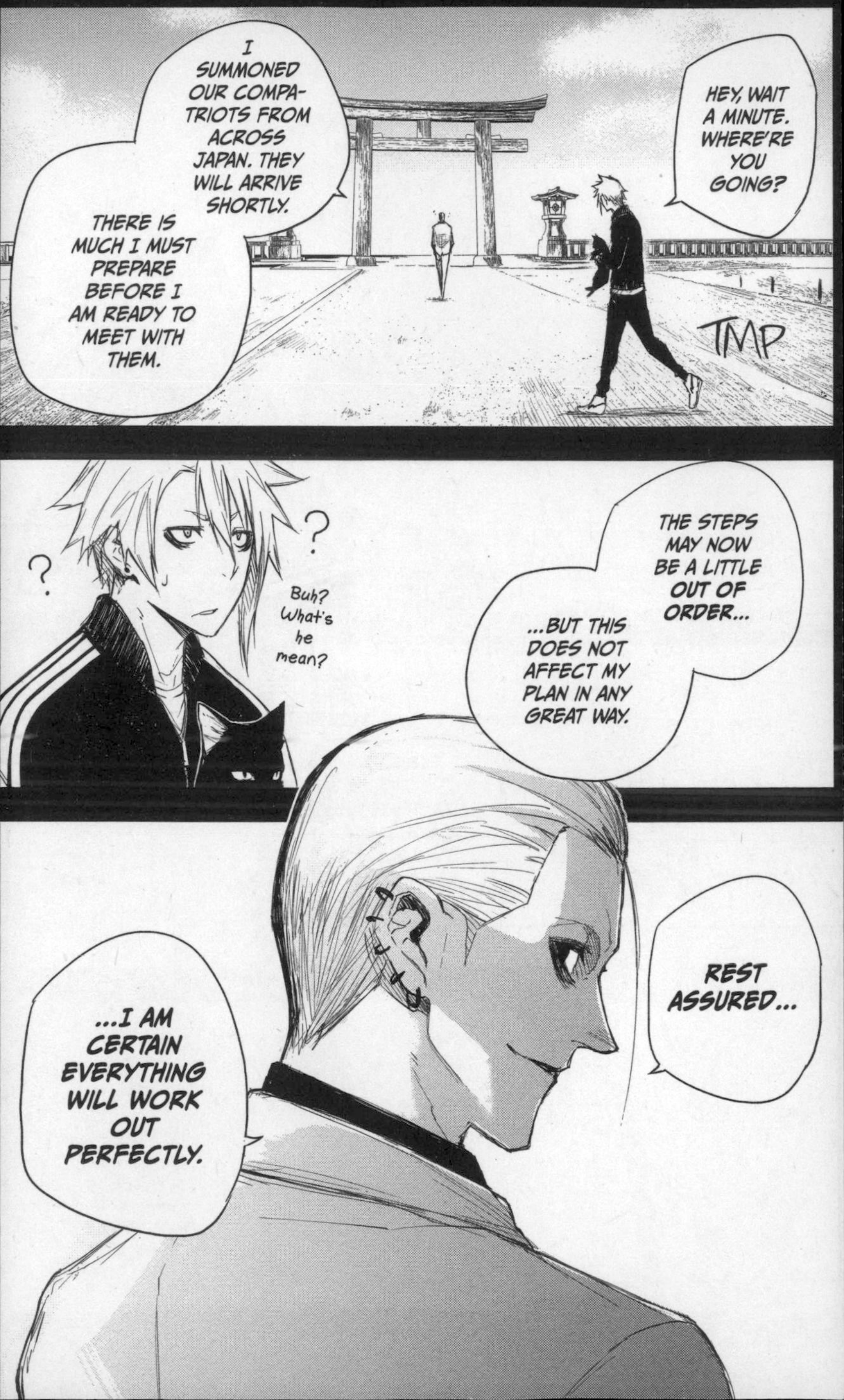
HEY, WAIT A MINUTE. WHERE'RE YOU GOING?
I SUMMONED OUR COMPA-TRIOTS FROM ACROSS JAPAN. THEY WILL ARRIVE SHORTLY.
TMP
THERE IS MUCH I MUST PREPARE BEFORE I AM READY TO MEET WITH THEM.
THE STEPS MAY NOW BE A LITTLE OUT OF ORDER...
...BUT THIS DOES NOT AFFECT MY PLAN IN ANY GREAT WAY.
?
Buh? What's he mean?
?
REST ASSURED...
...I AM CERTAIN EVERYTHING WILL WORK OUT PERFECTLY.

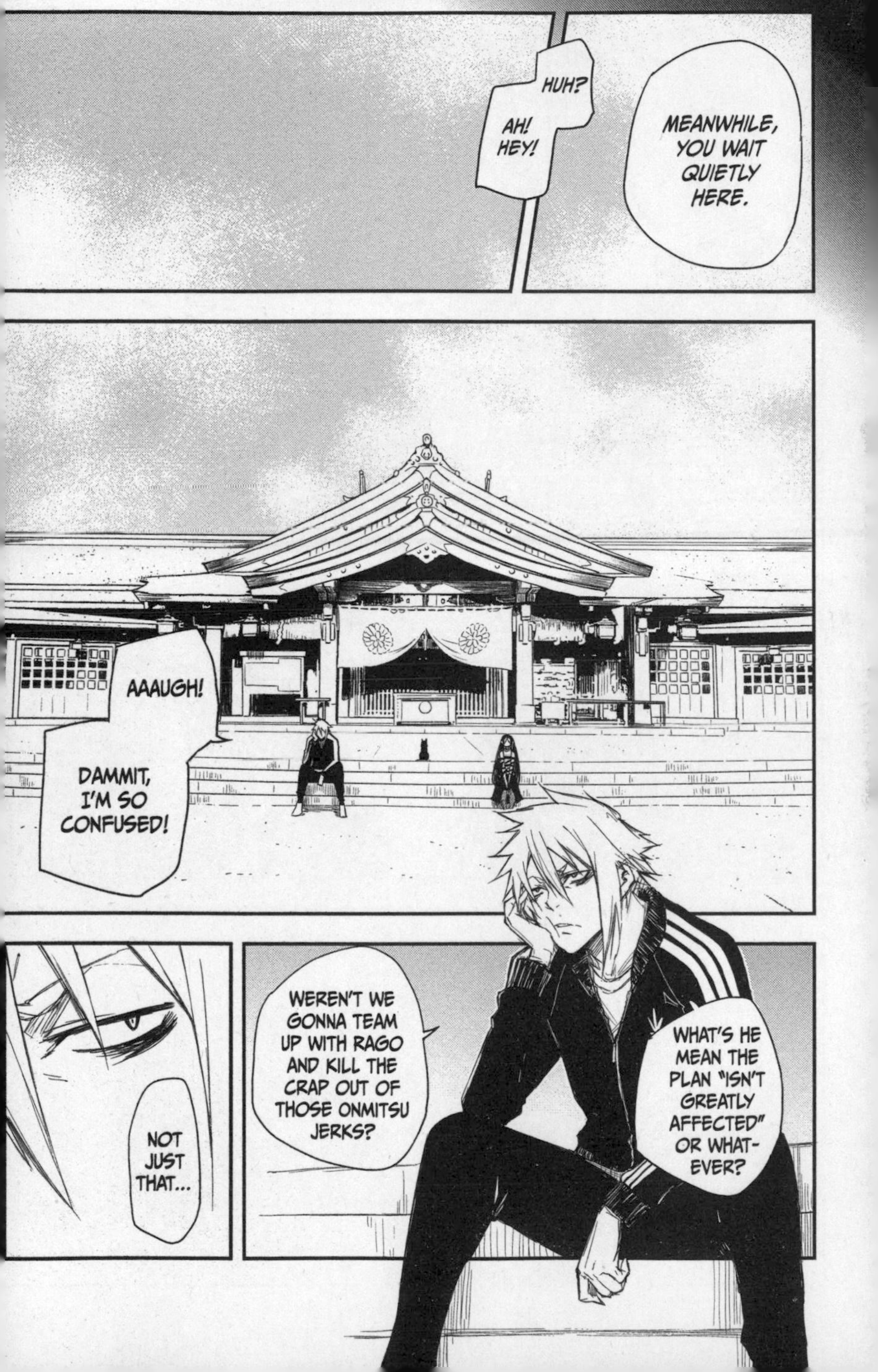

MEANWHILE, YOU WAIT QUIETLY HERE.
HUH?
AH! HEY!
AAAUGH!
DAMMIT, I'M SO CONFUSED!
WHAT'S HE MEAN THE PLAN "ISN'T GREATLY AFFECTED" OR WHAT-EVER?
WEREN'T WE GONNA TEAM UP WITH RAGO AND KILL THE CRAP OUT OF THOSE ONMITSU JERKS?
NOT JUST THAT...

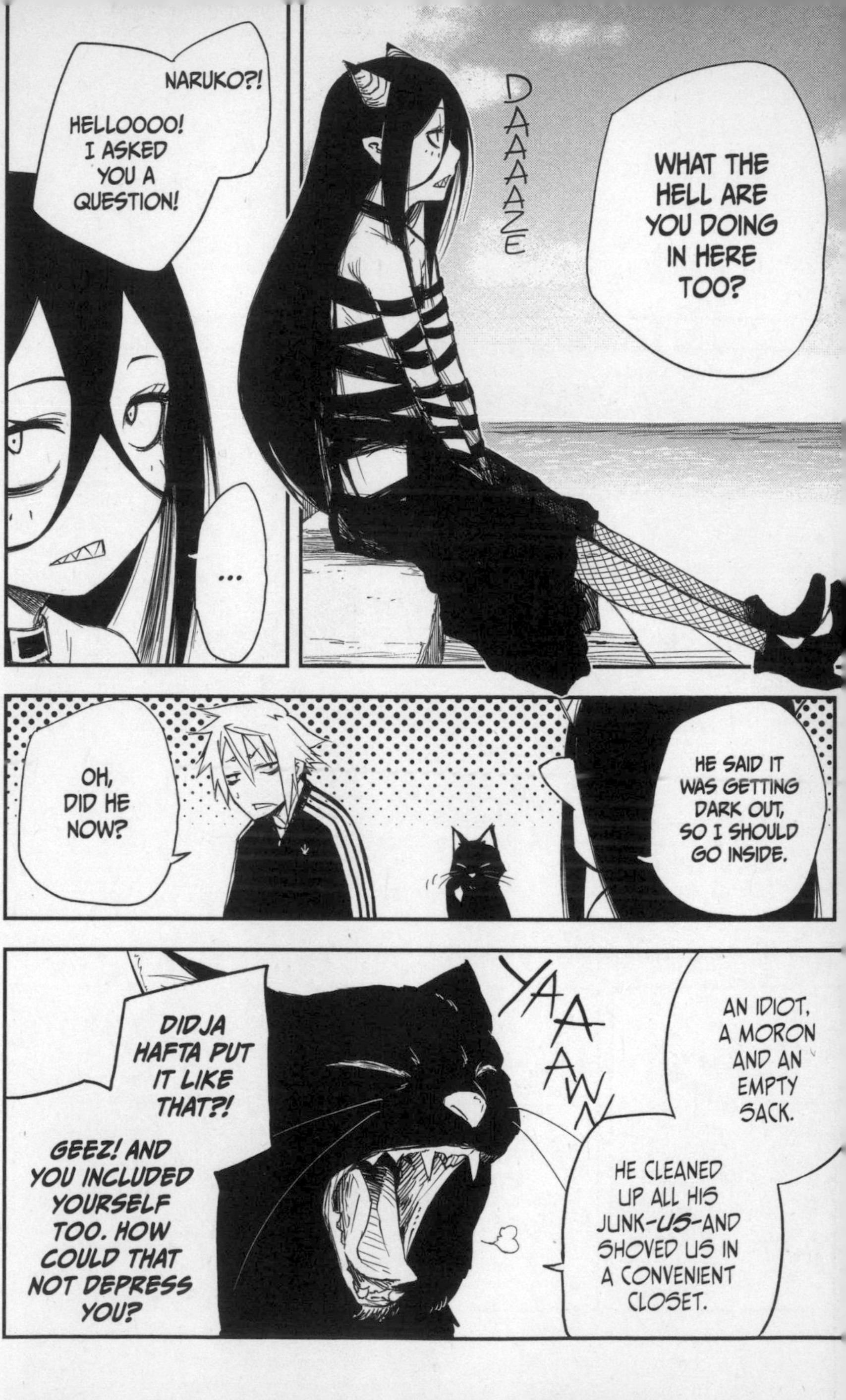
WHAT THE HELL ARE YOU DOING IN HERE TOO?
DAAAAZE
NARUKO?!
HELLOOOO! I ASKED YOU A QUESTION!
...
HE SAID IT WAS GETTING DARK OUT, SO I SHOULD GO INSIDE.
OH, DID HE NOW?
AN IDIOT, A MORON AND AN EMPTY SACK.
HE CLEANED UP ALL HIS JUNK-US-AND SHOVED US IN A CONVENIENT CLOSET.
YAAAWN
DIDJA HAFTA PUT IT LIKE THAT?!
GEEZ! AND YOU INCLUDED YOURSELF TOO. HOW COULD THAT NOT DEPRESS YOU?

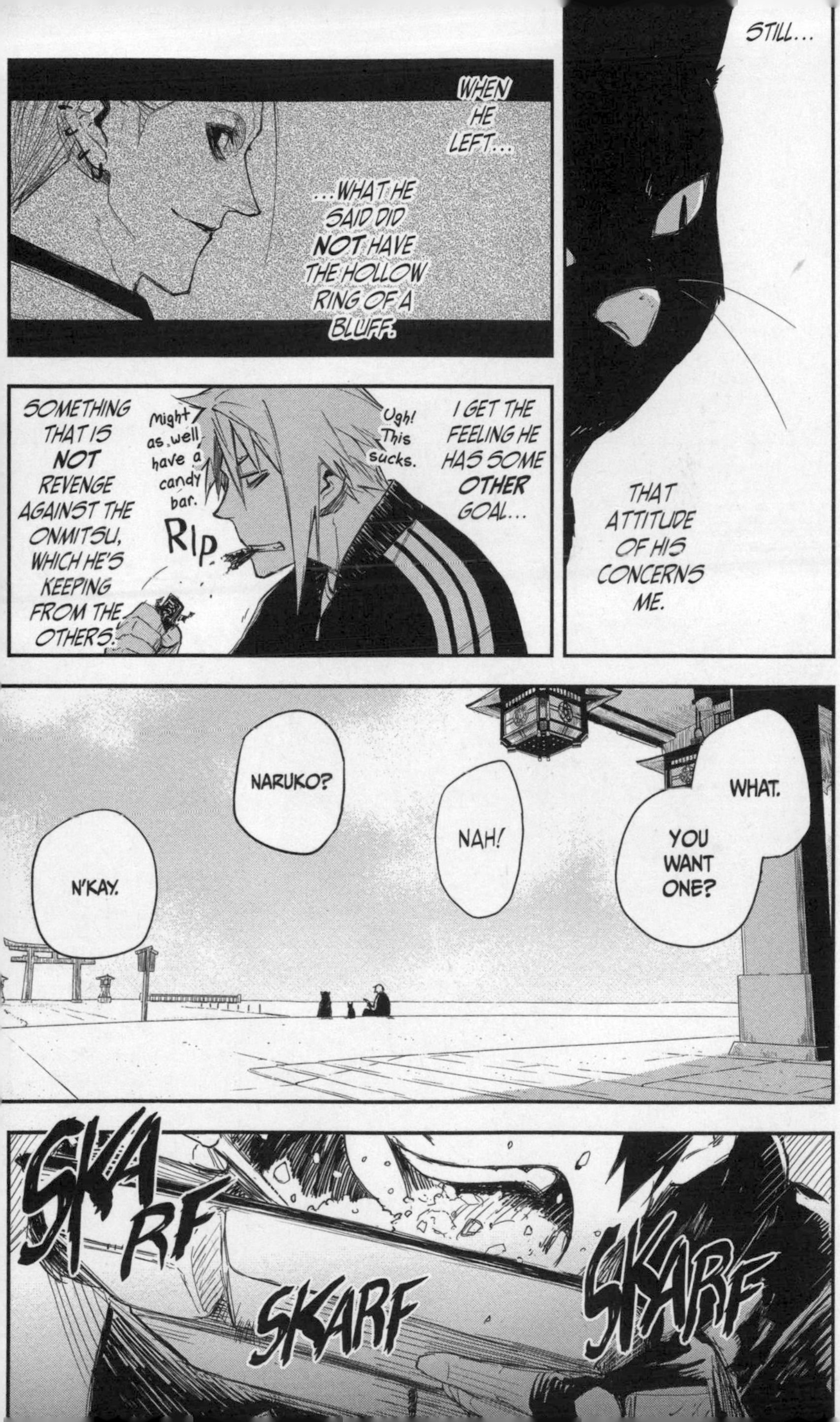
STILL…
THAT ATTITUDE OF HIS CONCERNS ME.
WHEN HE LEFT…
…WHAT HE SAID DID NOT HAVE THE HOLLOW RING OF A BLUFF.
I GET THE FEELING HE HAS SOME OTHER GOAL…
Ugh! This sucks.
Might as well have a candy bar.
RIP
SOMETHING THAT IS NOT REVENGE AGAINST THE ONMITSU, WHICH HE'S KEEPING FROM THE OTHERS.
WHAT.
YOU WANT ONE?
NAH!
NARUKO?
N'KAY.
SKARF
SKARF
SKARF

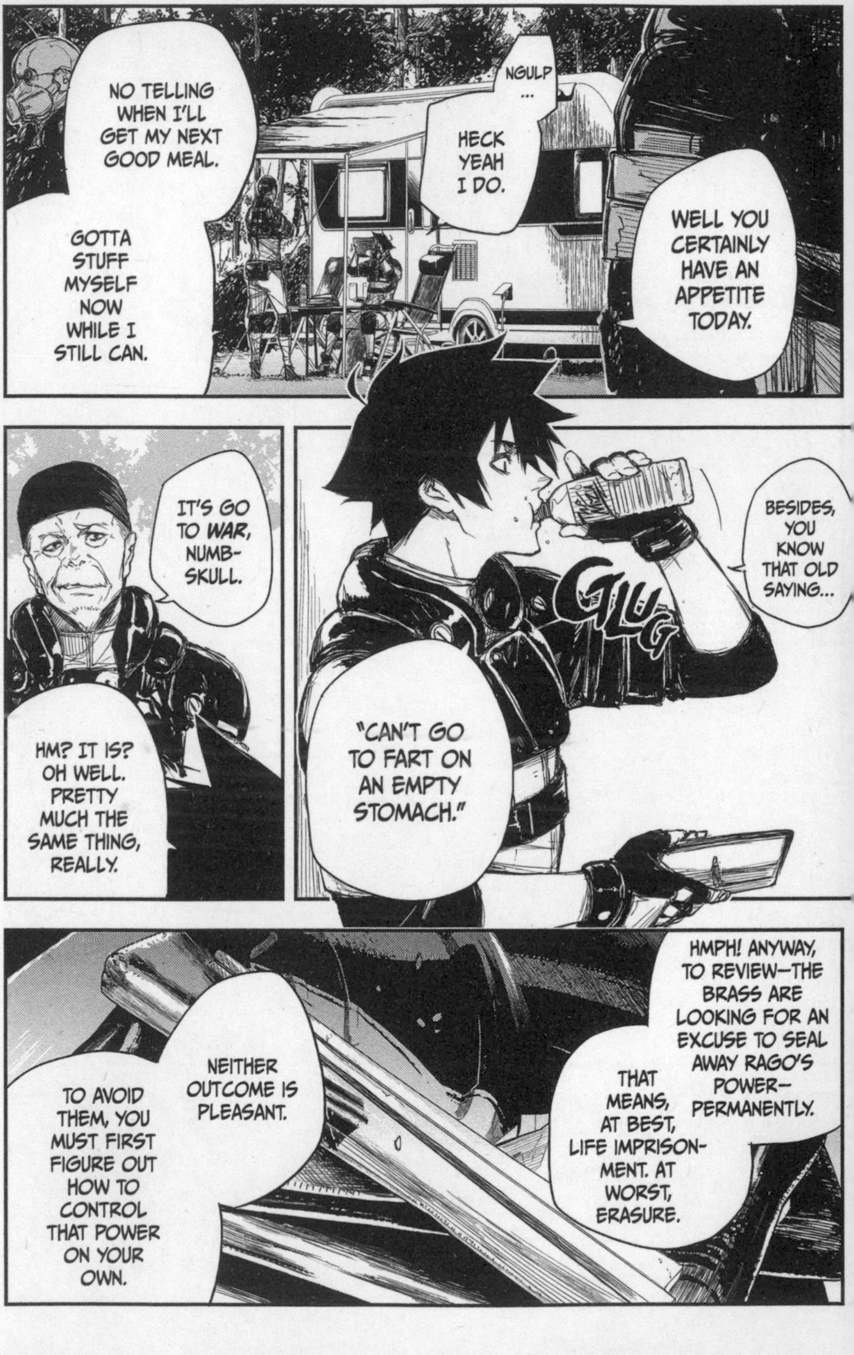
WELL YOU CERTAINLY HAVE AN APPETITE TODAY.
NGULP ...
HECK YEAH I DO.
NO TELLING WHEN I'LL GET MY NEXT GOOD MEAL.
GOTTA STUFF MYSELF NOW WHILE I STILL CAN.
BESIDES, YOU KNOW THAT OLD SAYING...
GLUG
"CAN'T GO TO FART ON AN EMPTY STOMACH."
IT'S GO TO *WAR*, NUMB-SKULL.
HM? IT IS? OH WELL. PRETTY MUCH THE SAME THING, REALLY.
HMPH! ANYWAY, TO REVIEW—THE BRASS ARE LOOKING FOR AN EXCUSE TO SEAL AWAY RAGO'S POWER—PERMANENTLY.
THAT MEANS, AT BEST, LIFE IMPRISON-MENT. AT WORST, ERASURE.
NEITHER OUTCOME IS PLEASANT.
TO AVOID THEM, YOU MUST FIRST FIGURE OUT HOW TO CONTROL THAT POWER ON YOUR OWN.

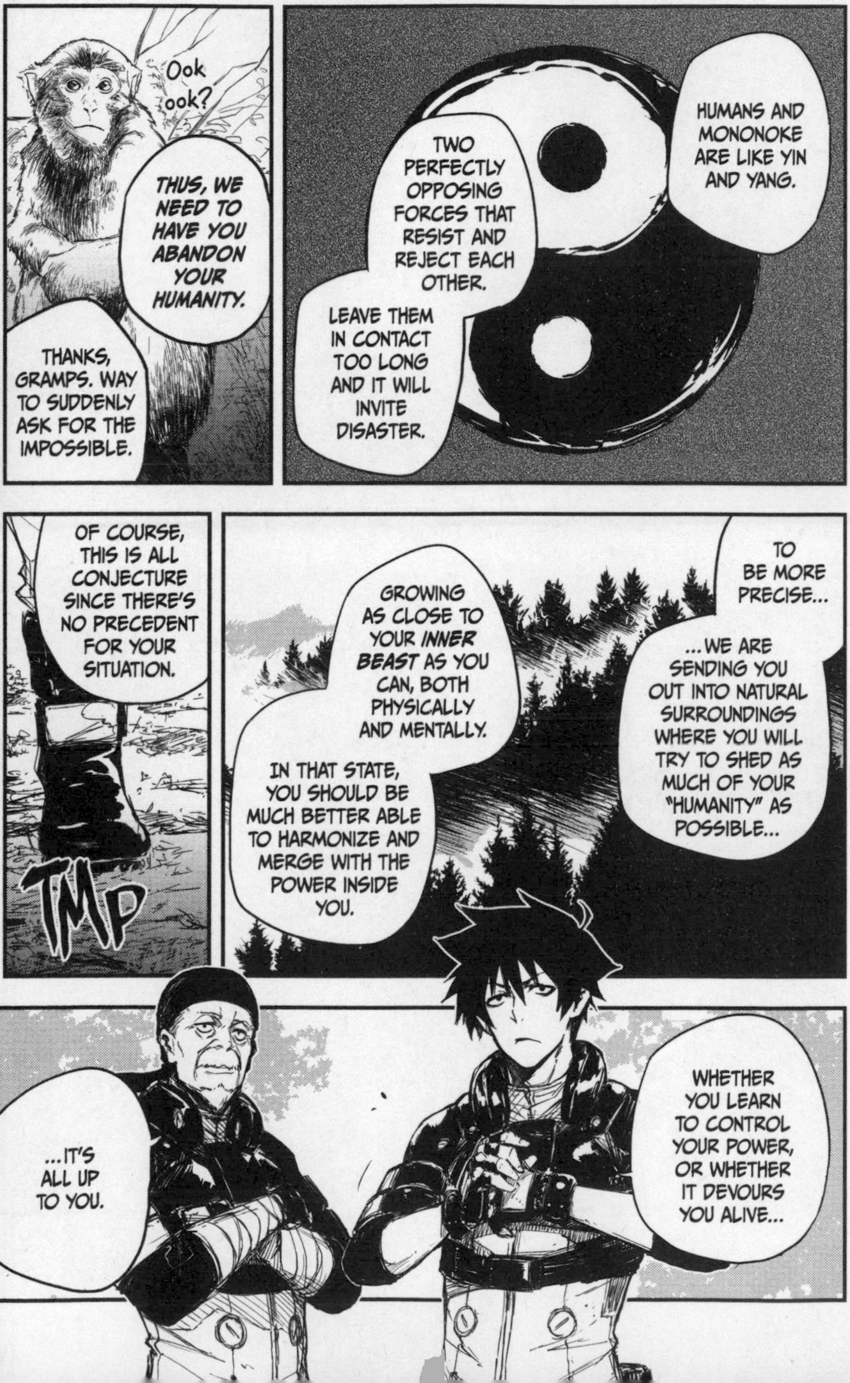
HUMANS AND MONONOKE ARE LIKE YIN AND YANG.
TWO PERFECTLY OPPOSING FORCES THAT RESIST AND REJECT EACH OTHER.
LEAVE THEM IN CONTACT TOO LONG AND IT WILL INVITE DISASTER.
THUS, WE NEED TO HAVE YOU ABANDON YOUR HUMANITY.
Ook ook?
THANKS, GRAMPS. WAY TO SUDDENLY ASK FOR THE IMPOSSIBLE.
TO BE MORE PRECISE...
...WE ARE SENDING YOU OUT INTO NATURAL SURROUNDINGS WHERE YOU WILL TRY TO SHED AS MUCH OF YOUR "HUMANITY" AS POSSIBLE...
GROWING AS CLOSE TO YOUR INNER BEAST AS YOU CAN, BOTH PHYSICALLY AND MENTALLY.
IN THAT STATE, YOU SHOULD BE MUCH BETTER ABLE TO HARMONIZE AND MERGE WITH THE POWER INSIDE YOU.
OF COURSE, THIS IS ALL CONJECTURE SINCE THERE'S NO PRECEDENT FOR YOUR SITUATION.
TMP
WHETHER YOU LEARN TO CONTROL YOUR POWER, OR WHETHER IT DEVOURS YOU ALIVE...
...IT'S ALL UP TO YOU.

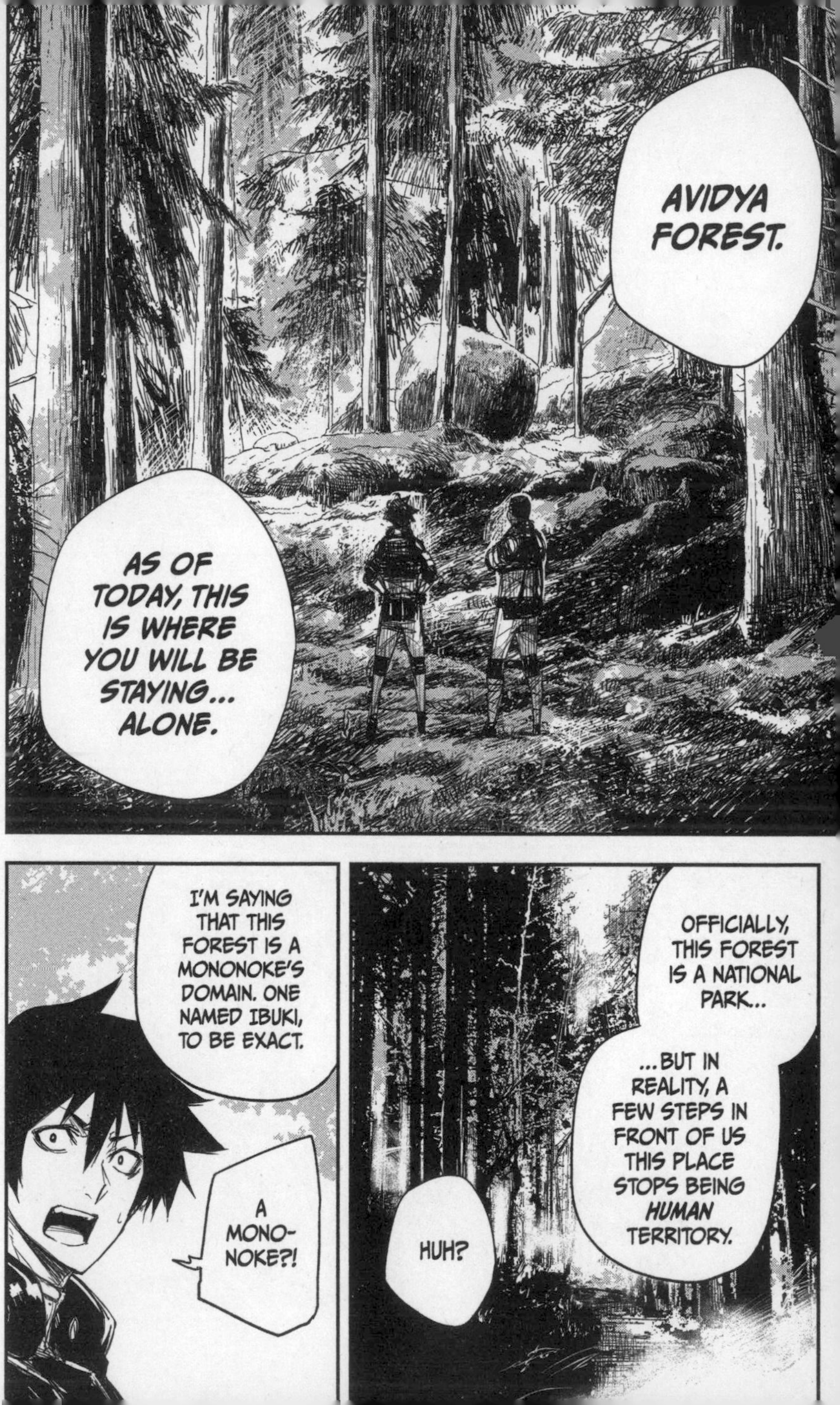
AVIDYA FOREST.
AS OF TODAY, THIS IS WHERE YOU WILL BE STAYING... ALONE.
OFFICIALLY, THIS FOREST IS A NATIONAL PARK...
...BUT IN REALITY, A FEW STEPS IN FRONT OF US THIS PLACE STOPS BEING *HUMAN* TERRITORY.
HUH?
I'M SAYING THAT THIS FOREST IS A MONONOKE'S DOMAIN. ONE NAMED IBUKI, TO BE EXACT.
A MONO-NOKE?!

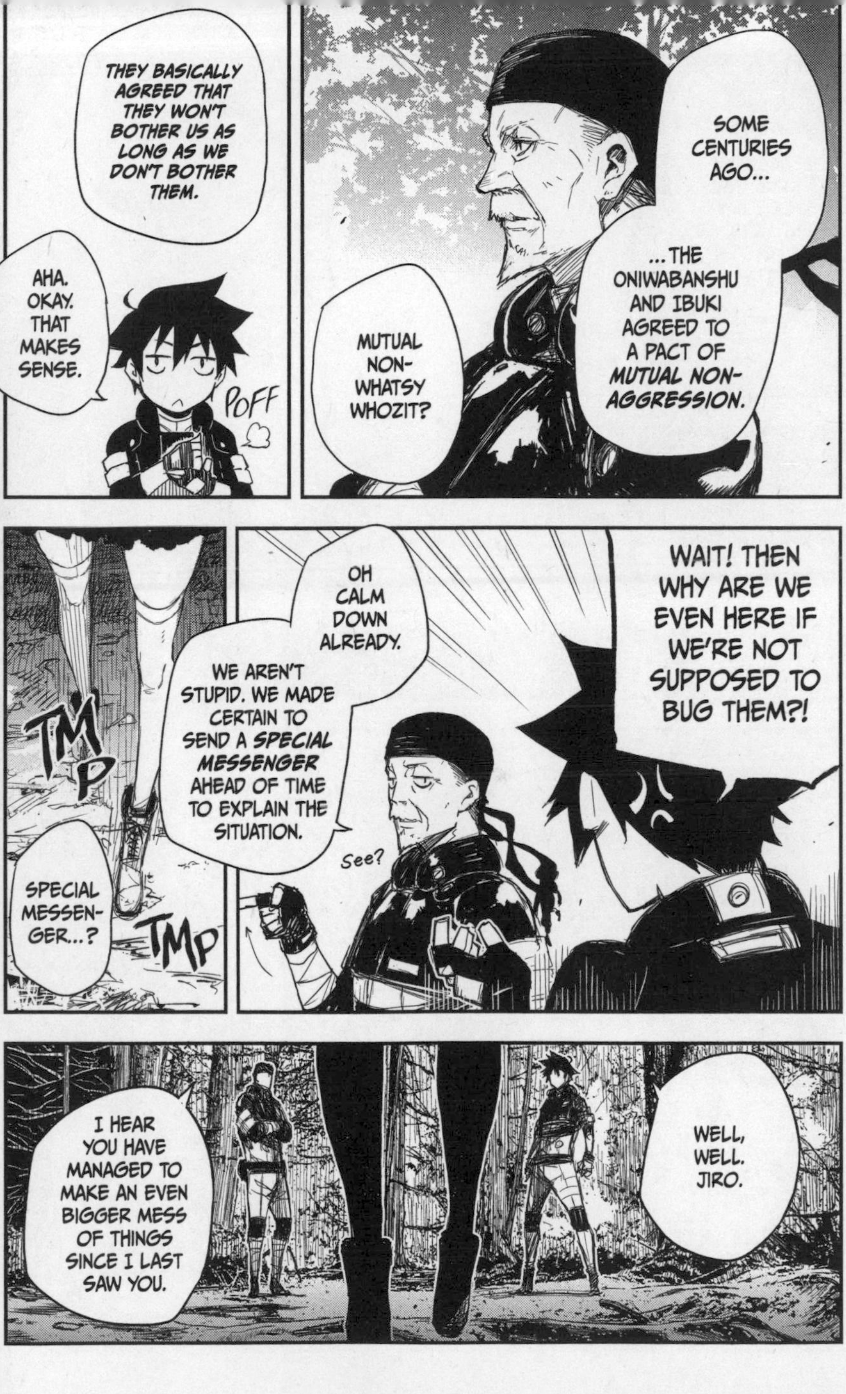
SOME CENTURIES AGO...
...THE ONIWABANSHU AND IBUKI AGREED TO A PACT OF MUTUAL NON-AGGRESSION.
MUTUAL NON-WHATSY WHOZIT?
THEY BASICALLY AGREED THAT THEY WON'T BOTHER US AS LONG AS WE DON'T BOTHER THEM.
AHA. OKAY. THAT MAKES SENSE.
POFF
WAIT! THEN WHY ARE WE EVEN HERE IF WE'RE NOT SUPPOSED TO BUG THEM?!
OH CALM DOWN ALREADY.
WE AREN'T STUPID. WE MADE CERTAIN TO SEND A SPECIAL MESSENGER AHEAD OF TIME TO EXPLAIN THE SITUATION.
See?
TMP
SPECIAL MESSENGER...?
TMP
WELL, WELL. JIRO.
I HEAR YOU HAVE MANAGED TO MAKE AN EVEN BIGGER MESS OF THINGS SINCE I LAST SAW YOU.

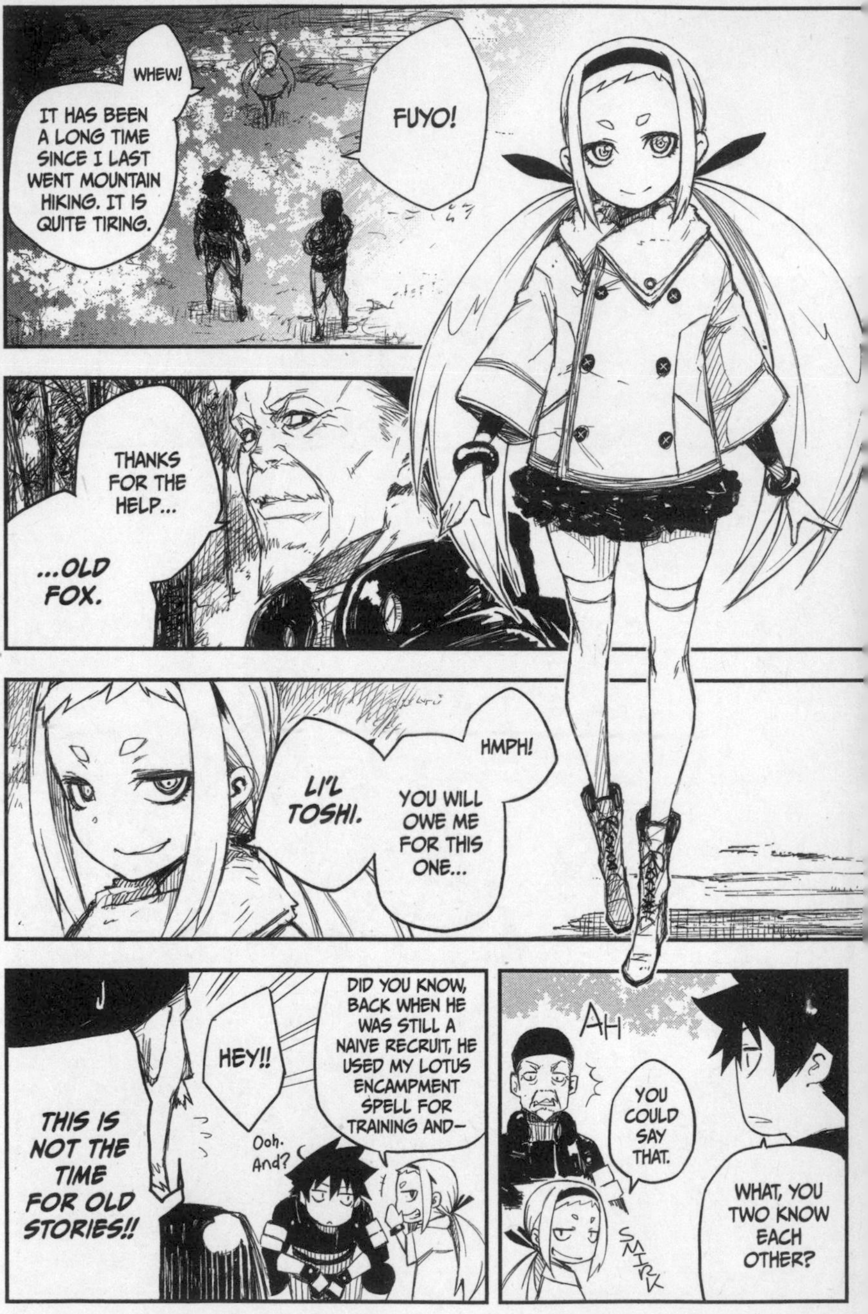
FUYO!
WHEW!
IT HAS BEEN A LONG TIME SINCE I LAST WENT MOUNTAIN HIKING. IT IS QUITE TIRING.
THANKS FOR THE HELP...
...OLD FOX.
HMPH!
YOU WILL OWE ME FOR THIS ONE...
LI'L TOSHI.
AH
WHAT, YOU TWO KNOW EACH OTHER?
YOU COULD SAY THAT.
SMIRK
DID YOU KNOW, BACK WHEN HE WAS STILL A NAIVE RECRUIT, HE USED MY LOTUS ENCAMPMENT SPELL FOR TRAINING AND—
Ooh. And?
HEY!!
THIS IS NOT THE TIME FOR OLD STORIES!!

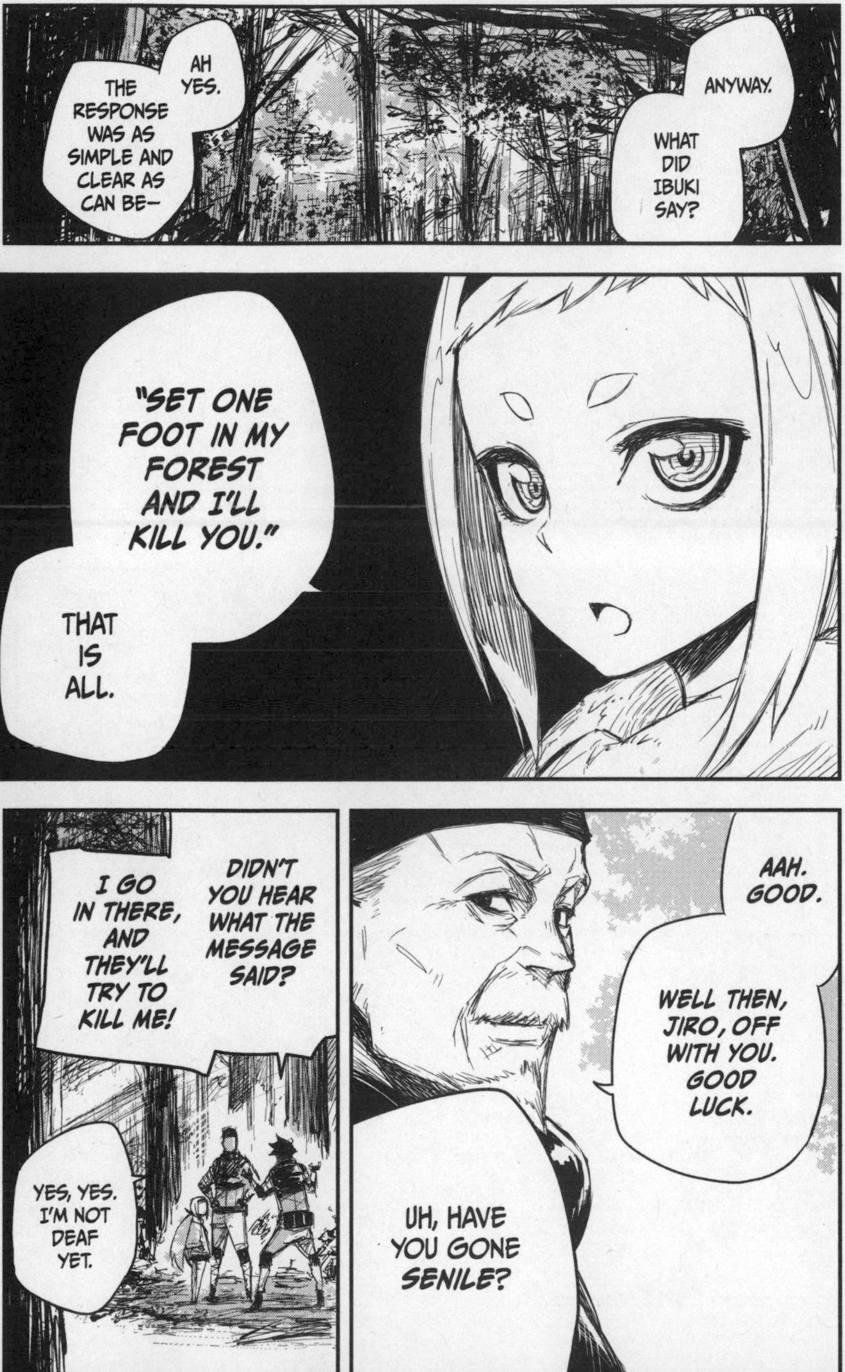
ANYWAY.
WHAT DID IBUKI SAY?
AH YES.
THE RESPONSE WAS AS SIMPLE AND CLEAR AS CAN BE—
"SET ONE FOOT IN MY FOREST AND I'LL KILL YOU."
THAT IS ALL.
AAH. GOOD.
WELL THEN, JIRO, OFF WITH YOU. GOOD LUCK.
UH, HAVE YOU GONE SENILE?
DIDN'T YOU HEAR WHAT THE MESSAGE SAID?
I GO IN THERE, AND THEY'LL TRY TO KILL ME!
YES, YES. I'M NOT DEAF YET.

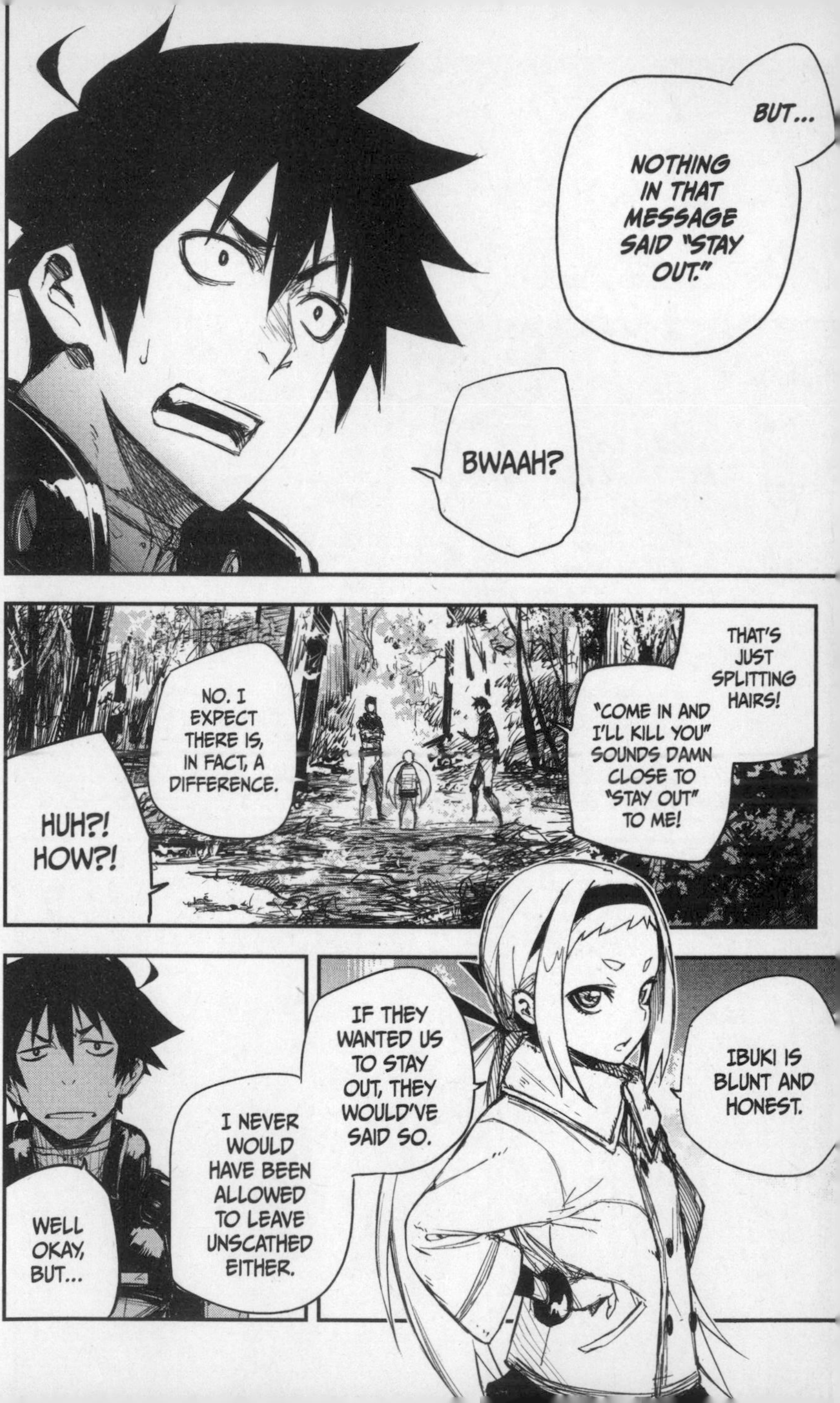
BUT...
NOTHING IN THAT MESSAGE SAID "STAY OUT."
BWAAH?
THAT'S JUST SPLITTING HAIRS!
"COME IN AND I'LL KILL YOU" SOUNDS DAMN CLOSE TO "STAY OUT" TO ME!
NO. I EXPECT THERE IS, IN FACT, A DIFFERENCE.
HUH?! HOW?!
IBUKI IS BLUNT AND HONEST.
IF THEY WANTED US TO STAY OUT, THEY WOULD'VE SAID SO.
I NEVER WOULD HAVE BEEN ALLOWED TO LEAVE UNSCATHED EITHER.
WELL OKAY, BUT...

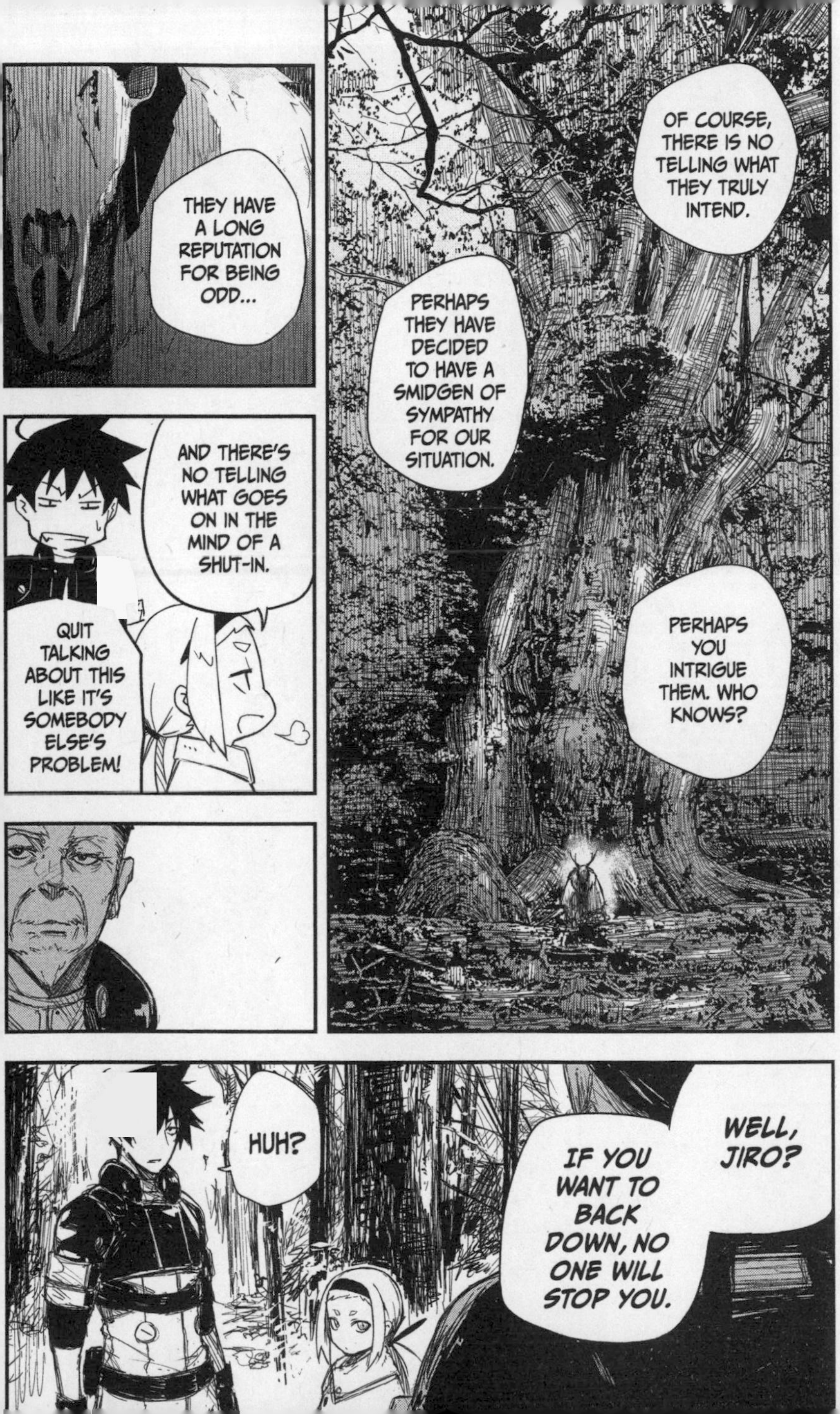
OF COURSE, THERE IS NO TELLING WHAT THEY TRULY INTEND.
PERHAPS THEY HAVE DECIDED TO HAVE A SMIDGEN OF SYMPATHY FOR OUR SITUATION.
PERHAPS YOU INTRIGUE THEM. WHO KNOWS?
THEY HAVE A LONG REPUTATION FOR BEING ODD...
AND THERE'S NO TELLING WHAT GOES ON IN THE MIND OF A SHUT-IN.
QUIT TALKING ABOUT THIS LIKE IT'S SOMEBODY ELSE'S PROBLEM!
WELL, JIRO?
IF YOU WANT TO BACK DOWN, NO ONE WILL STOP YOU.
HUH?

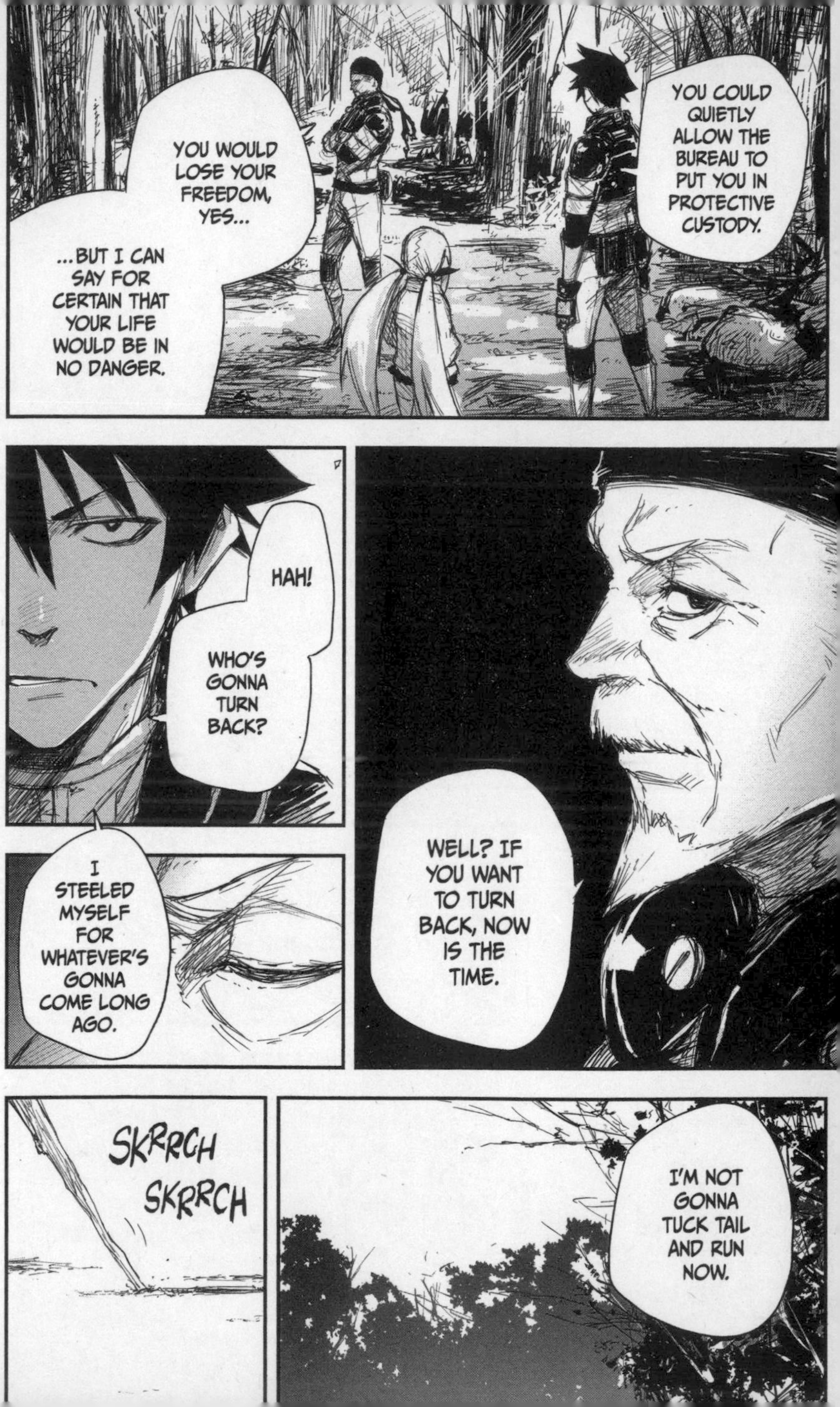
YOU COULD QUIETLY ALLOW THE BUREAU TO PUT YOU IN PROTECTIVE CUSTODY.
YOU WOULD LOSE YOUR FREEDOM, YES...
...BUT I CAN SAY FOR CERTAIN THAT YOUR LIFE WOULD BE IN NO DANGER.
WELL? IF YOU WANT TO TURN BACK, NOW IS THE TIME.
HAH!
WHO'S GONNA TURN BACK?
I STEELED MYSELF FOR WHATEVER'S GONNA COME LONG AGO.
I'M NOT GONNA TUCK TAIL AND RUN NOW.
SKRRCH
SKRRCH

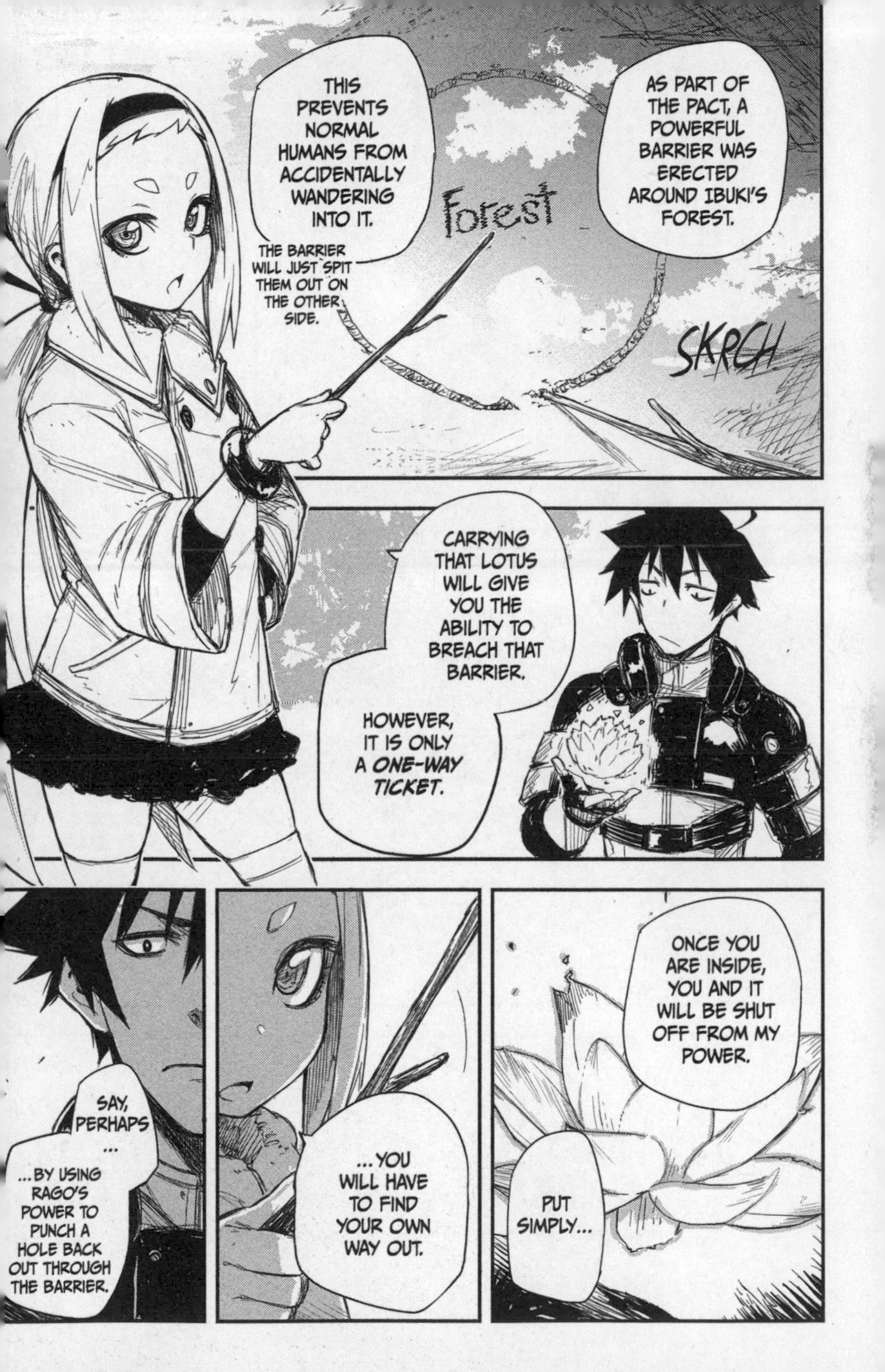
AS PART OF THE PACT, A POWERFUL BARRIER WAS ERECTED AROUND IBUKI'S FOREST.
Forest
SKRCH
THIS PREVENTS NORMAL HUMANS FROM ACCIDENTALLY WANDERING INTO IT.
THE BARRIER WILL JUST SPIT THEM OUT ON THE OTHER SIDE.
CARRYING THAT LOTUS WILL GIVE YOU THE ABILITY TO BREACH THAT BARRIER.
HOWEVER, IT IS ONLY A *ONE-WAY TICKET*.
ONCE YOU ARE INSIDE, YOU AND IT WILL BE SHUT OFF FROM MY POWER.
PUT SIMPLY...
...YOU WILL HAVE TO FIND YOUR OWN WAY OUT.
SAY, PERHAPS ...
...BY USING RAGO'S POWER TO PUNCH A HOLE BACK OUT THROUGH THE BARRIER.

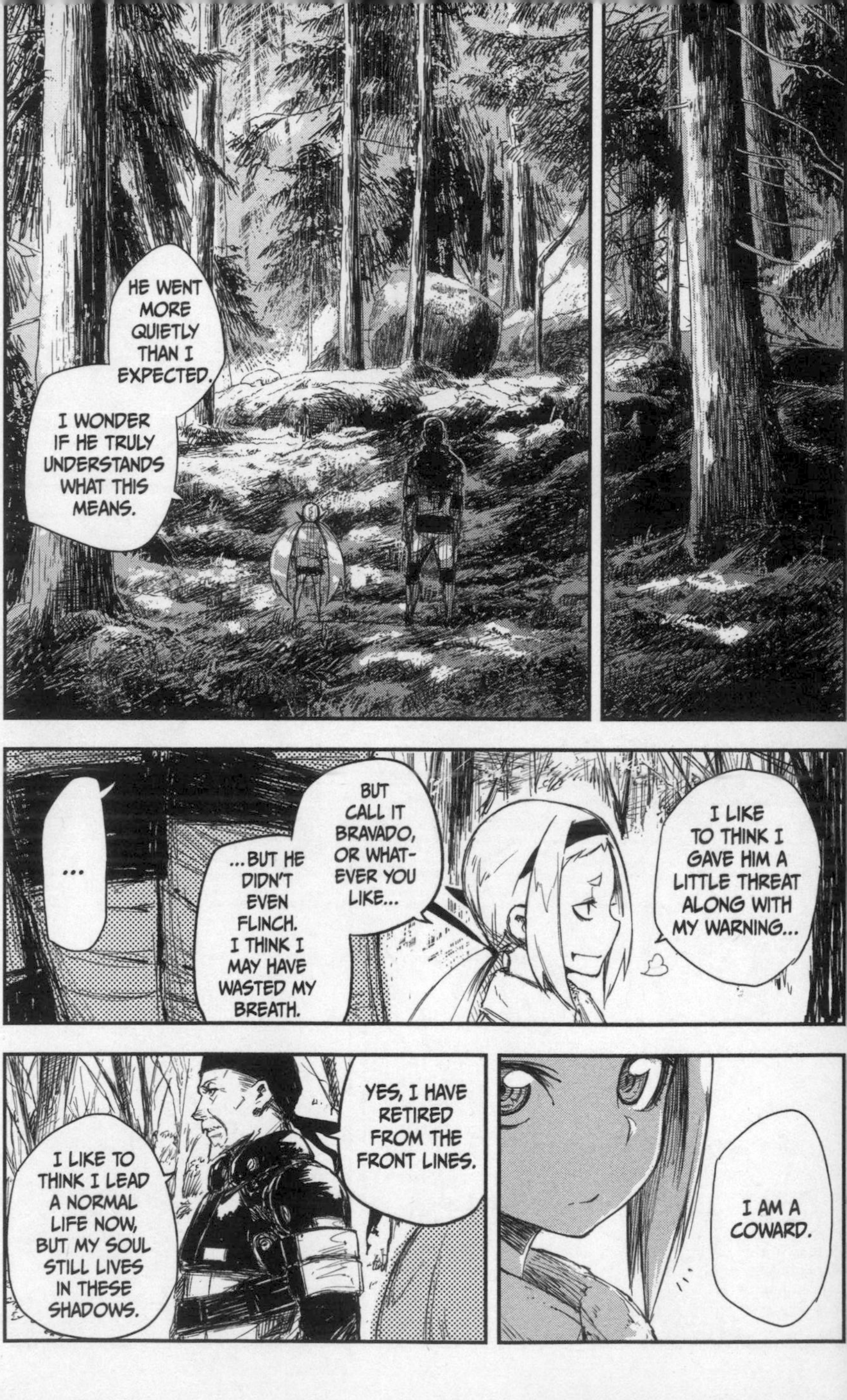
HE WENT MORE QUIETLY THAN I EXPECTED.
I WONDER IF HE TRULY UNDERSTANDS WHAT THIS MEANS.
I LIKE TO THINK I GAVE HIM A LITTLE THREAT ALONG WITH MY WARNING...
BUT CALL IT BRAVADO, OR WHAT-EVER YOU LIKE...
...BUT HE DIDN'T EVEN FLINCH. I THINK I MAY HAVE WASTED MY BREATH.
...
I AM A COWARD.
YES, I HAVE RETIRED FROM THE FRONT LINES.
I LIKE TO THINK I LEAD A NORMAL LIFE NOW, BUT MY SOUL STILL LIVES IN THESE SHADOWS.

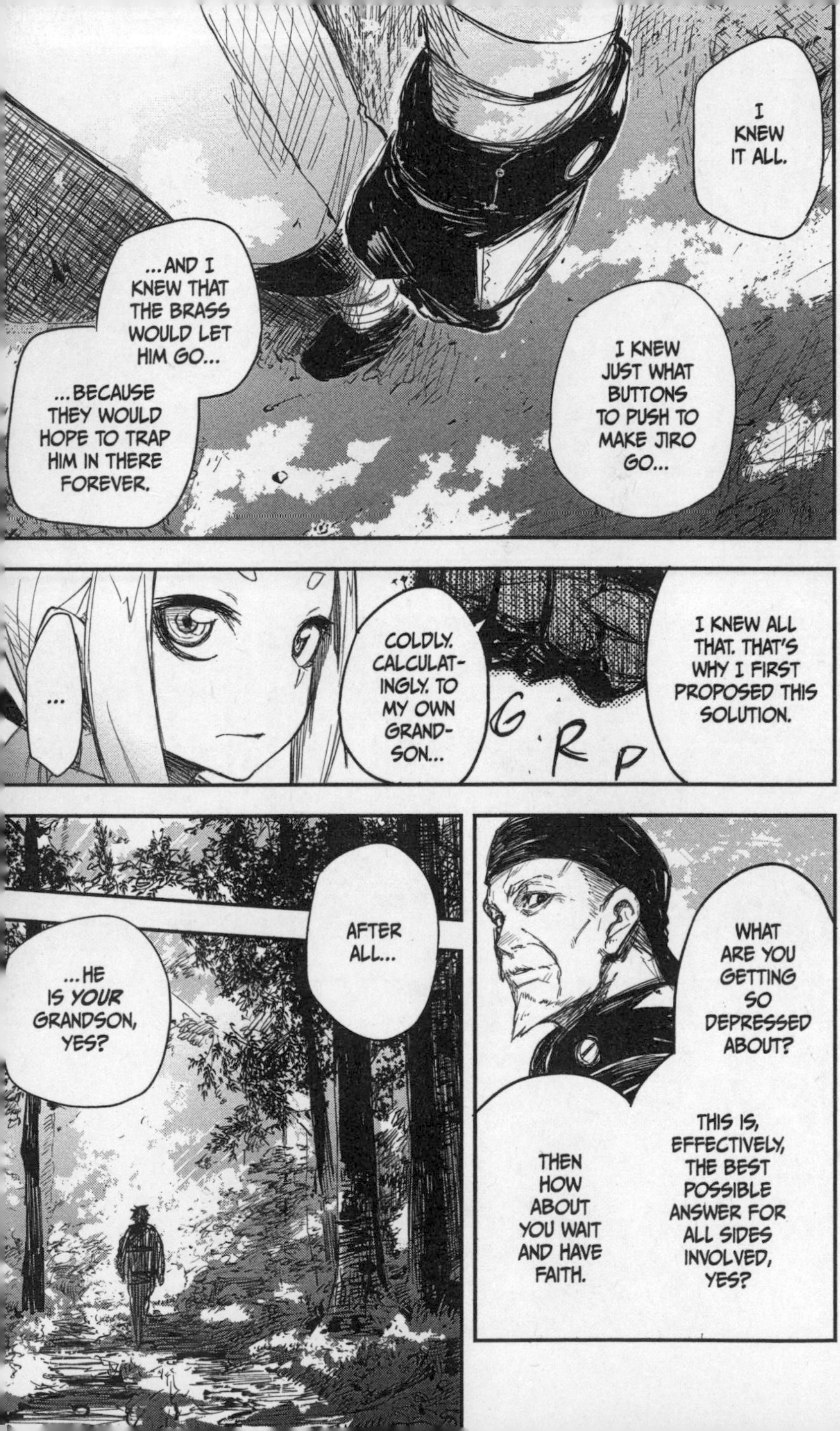
I KNEW IT ALL.
I KNEW JUST WHAT BUTTONS TO PUSH TO MAKE JIRO GO...
...AND I KNEW THAT THE BRASS WOULD LET HIM GO...
...BECAUSE THEY WOULD HOPE TO TRAP HIM IN THERE FOREVER.
I KNEW ALL THAT. THAT'S WHY I FIRST PROPOSED THIS SOLUTION.
GRP
COLDLY. CALCULAT-INGLY. TO MY OWN GRAND-SON...
...
WHAT ARE YOU GETTING SO DEPRESSED ABOUT?
THIS IS, EFFECTIVELY, THE BEST POSSIBLE ANSWER FOR ALL SIDES INVOLVED, YES?
THEN HOW ABOUT YOU WAIT AND HAVE FAITH.
AFTER ALL...
...HE IS *YOUR* GRANDSON, YES?

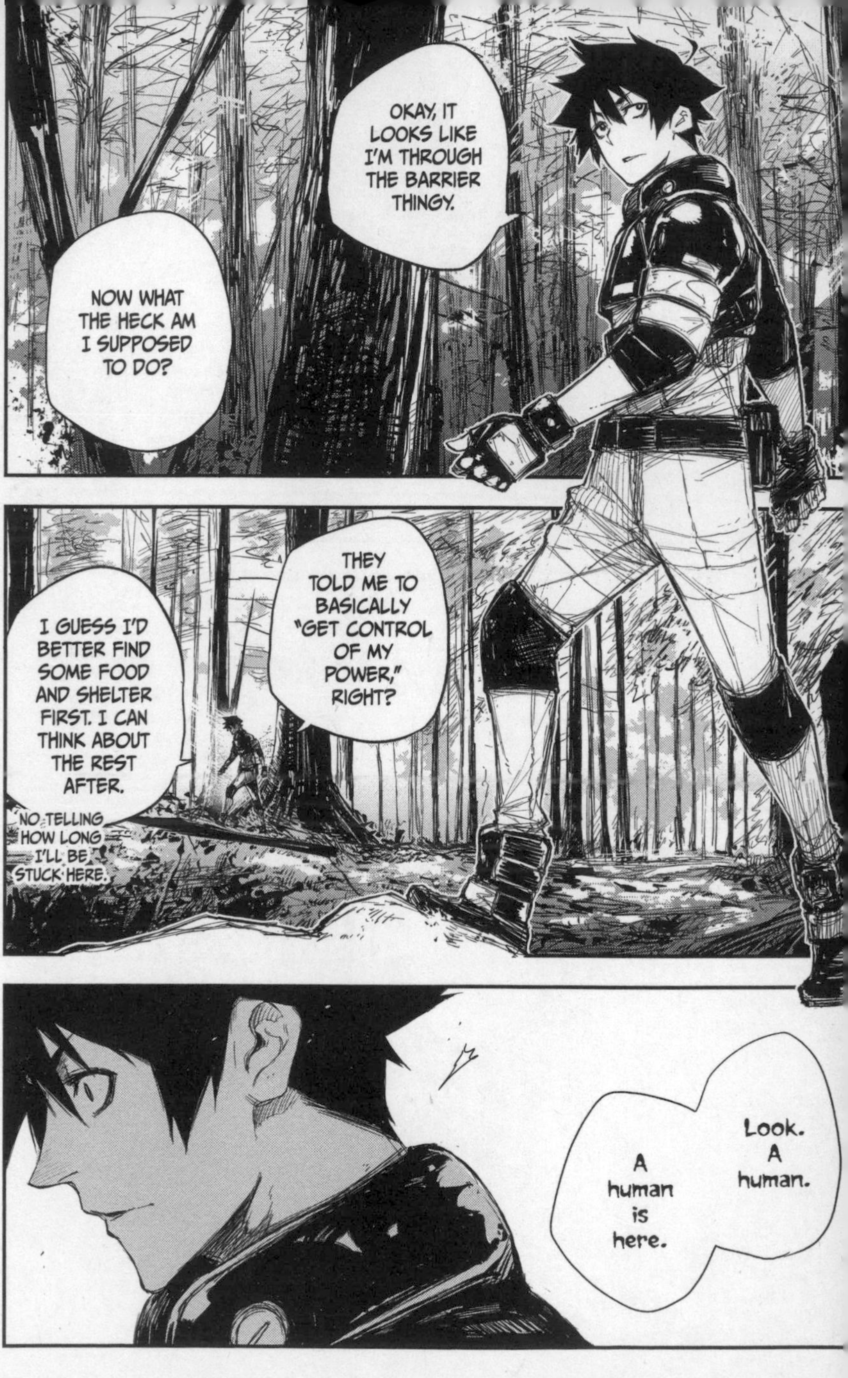
OKAY, IT LOOKS LIKE I'M THROUGH THE BARRIER THINGY.
NOW WHAT THE HECK AM I SUPPOSED TO DO?
THEY TOLD ME TO BASICALLY "GET CONTROL OF MY POWER," RIGHT?
I GUESS I'D BETTER FIND SOME FOOD AND SHELTER FIRST. I CAN THINK ABOUT THE REST AFTER.
NO TELLING HOW LONG I'LL BE STUCK HERE.
Look. A human.
A human is here.

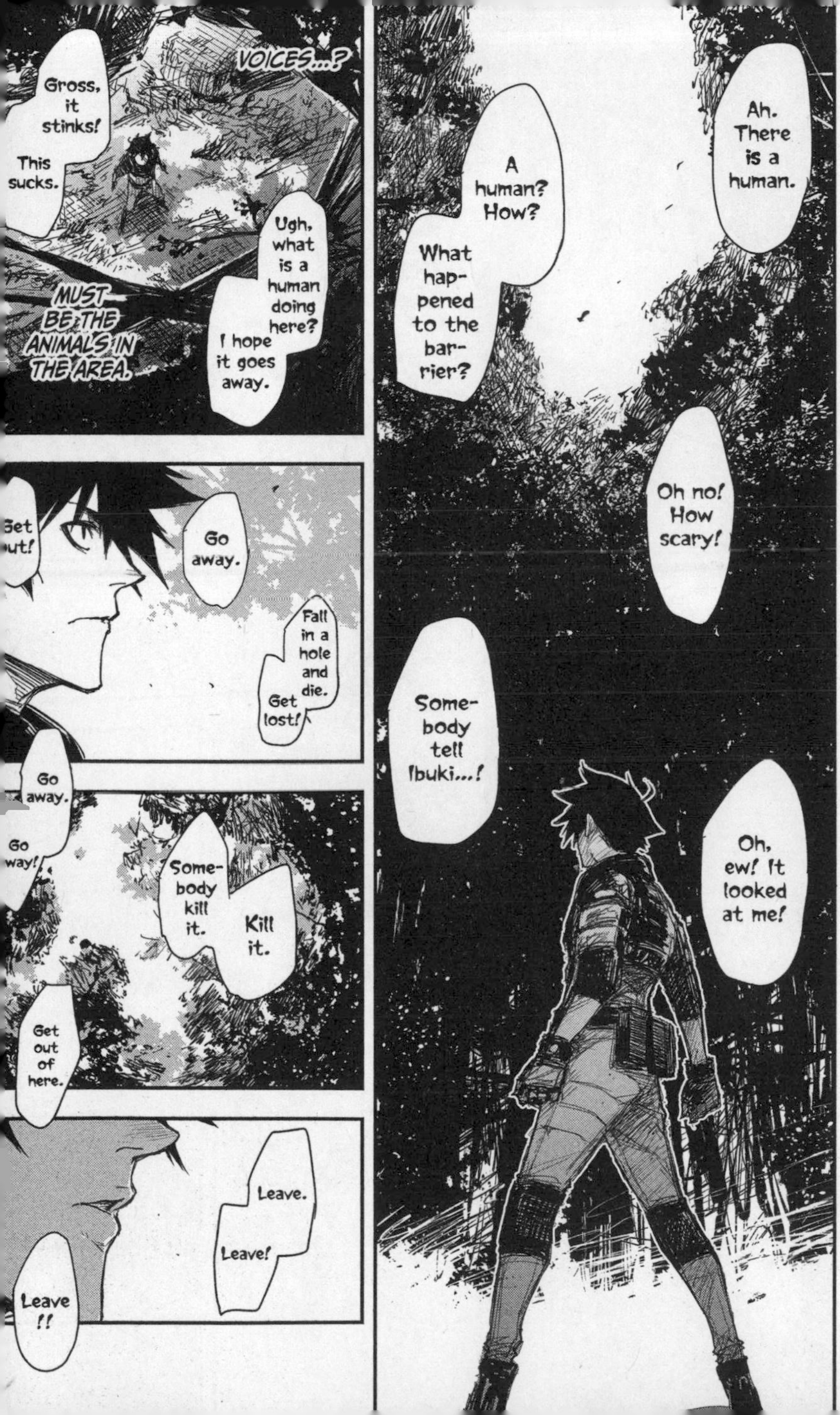

Ah. There is a human.
A human? How?
What happened to the barrier?
Oh no! How scary!
Somebody tell Ibuki...!
Oh, ew! It looked at me!
VOICES...?
Ugh, what is a human doing here?
I hope it goes away.
Gross, it stinks!
This sucks.
MUST BE THE ANIMALS IN THE AREA.
Go away.
Fall in a hole and die.
Get lost!
Get out!
Go away.
Somebody kill it.
Kill it.
Go away!
Get out of here.
Leave.
Leave!
Leave !!

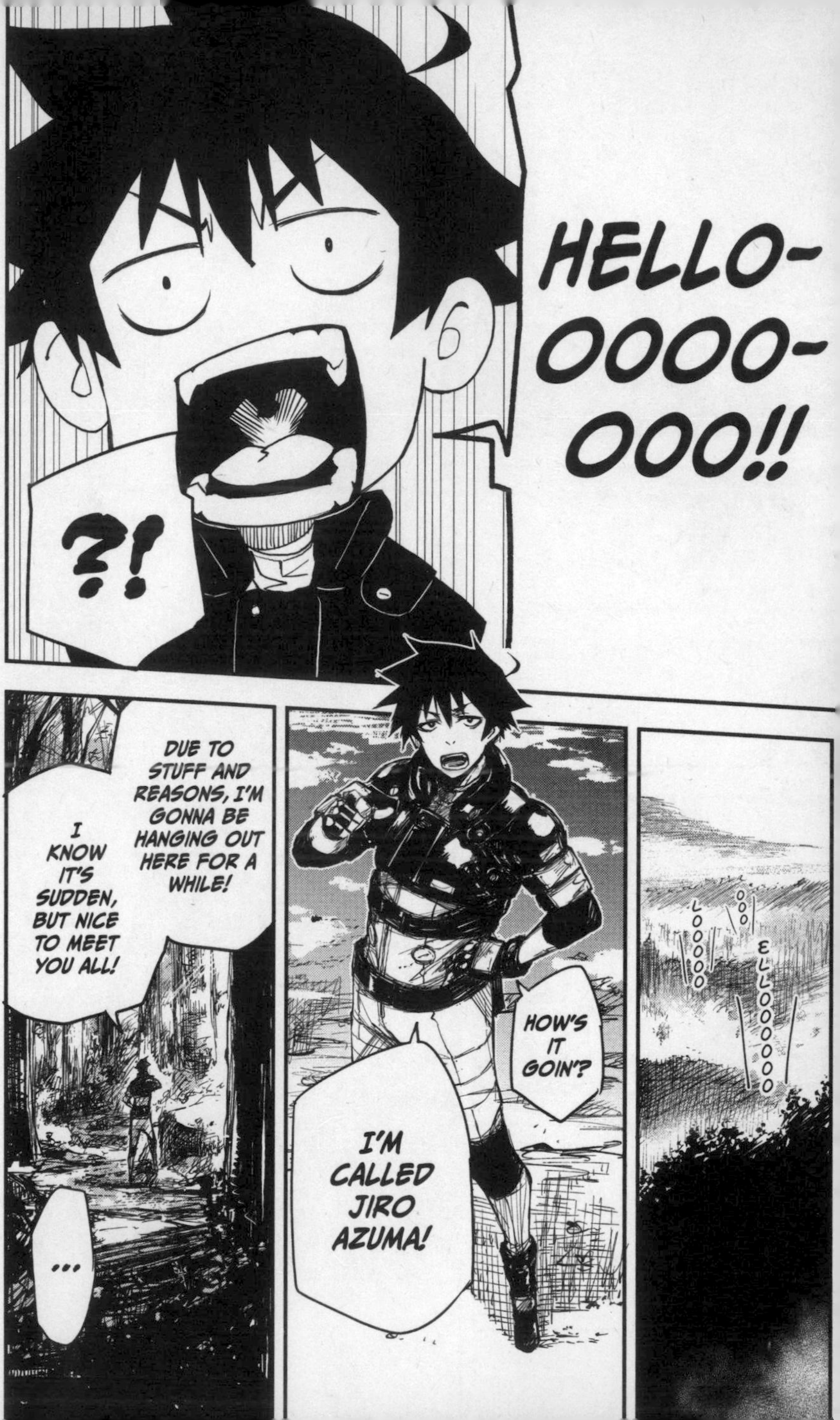
HELLO-OOOO-OOO!!
?!
ELLOOOOOOO
OOO
LOOOOO
HOW'S IT GOIN'?
I'M CALLED JIRO AZUMA!
DUE TO STUFF AND REASONS, I'M GONNA BE HANGING OUT HERE FOR A WHILE!
I KNOW IT'S SUDDEN, BUT NICE TO MEET YOU ALL!
...

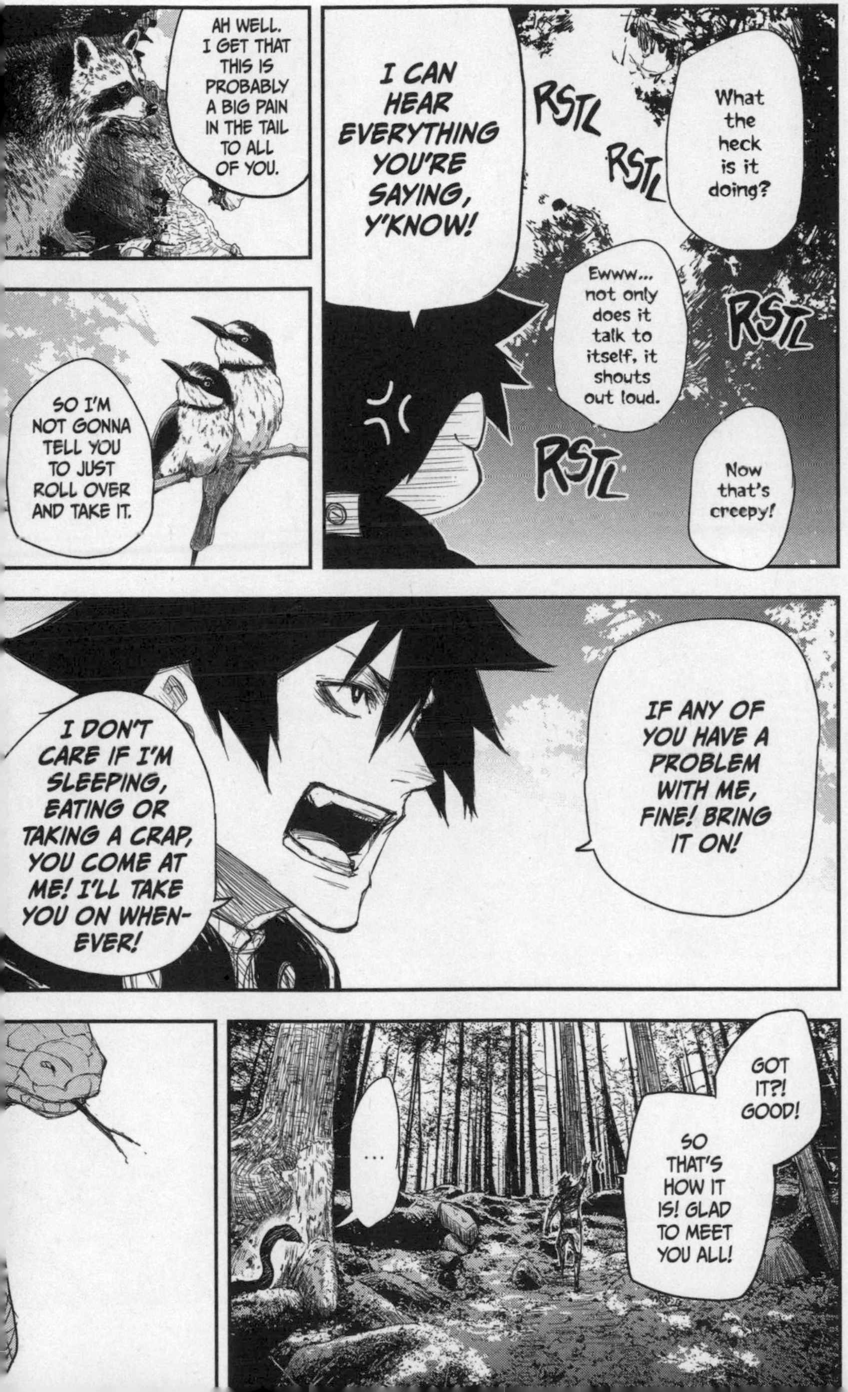
What the heck is it doing?
RSTL
RSTL
Ewww... not only does it talk to itself, it shouts out loud.
RSTL
RSTL
Now that's creepy!
I CAN HEAR EVERYTHING YOU'RE SAYING, Y'KNOW!
AH WELL. I GET THAT THIS IS PROBABLY A BIG PAIN IN THE TAIL TO ALL OF YOU.
SO I'M NOT GONNA TELL YOU TO JUST ROLL OVER AND TAKE IT.
IF ANY OF YOU HAVE A PROBLEM WITH ME, FINE! BRING IT ON!
I DON'T CARE IF I'M SLEEPING, EATING OR TAKING A CRAP, YOU COME AT ME! I'LL TAKE YOU ON WHEN-EVER!
GOT IT?! GOOD!
SO THAT'S HOW IT IS! GLAD TO MEET YOU ALL!
...

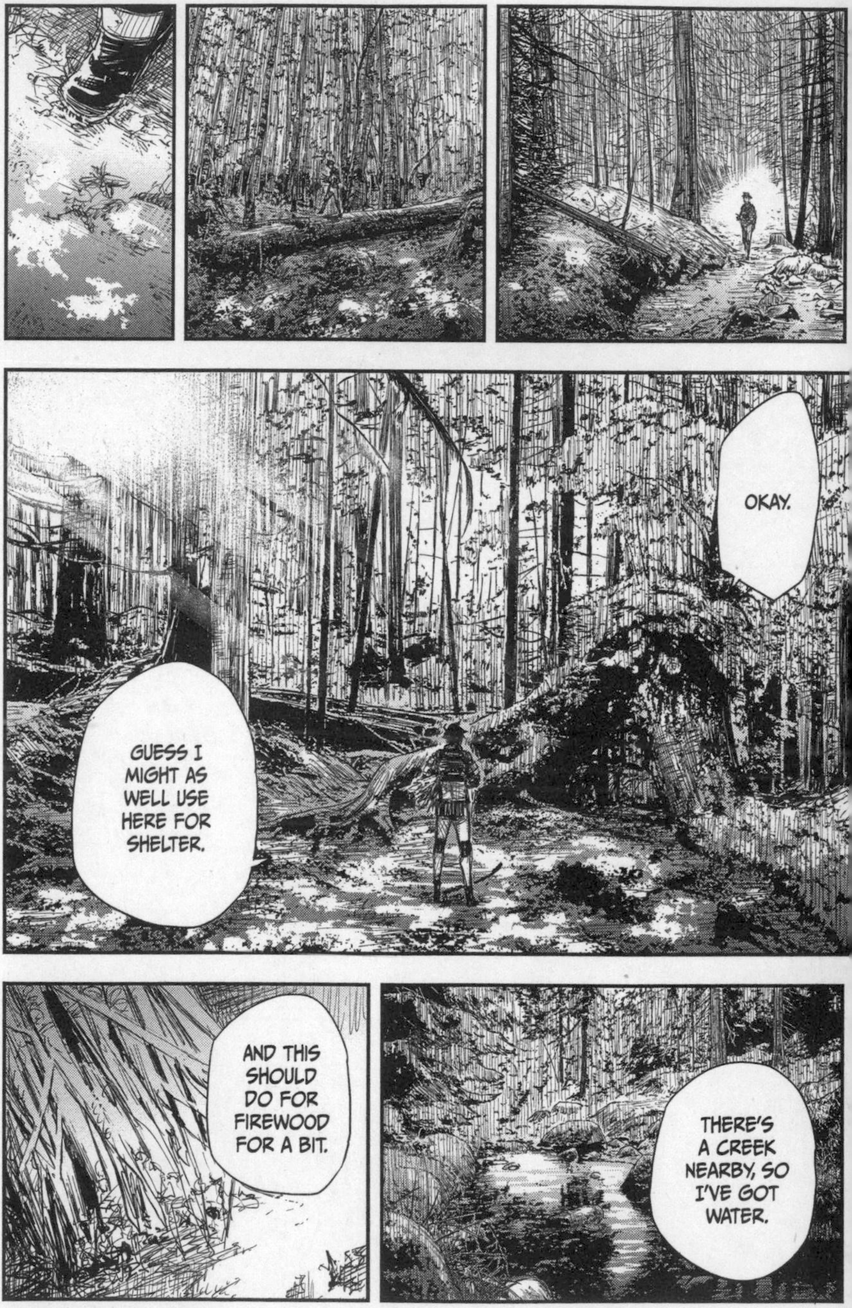
OKAY.
GUESS I MIGHT AS WELL USE HERE FOR SHELTER.
THERE'S A CREEK NEARBY, SO I'VE GOT WATER.
AND THIS SHOULD DO FOR FIREWOOD FOR A BIT.

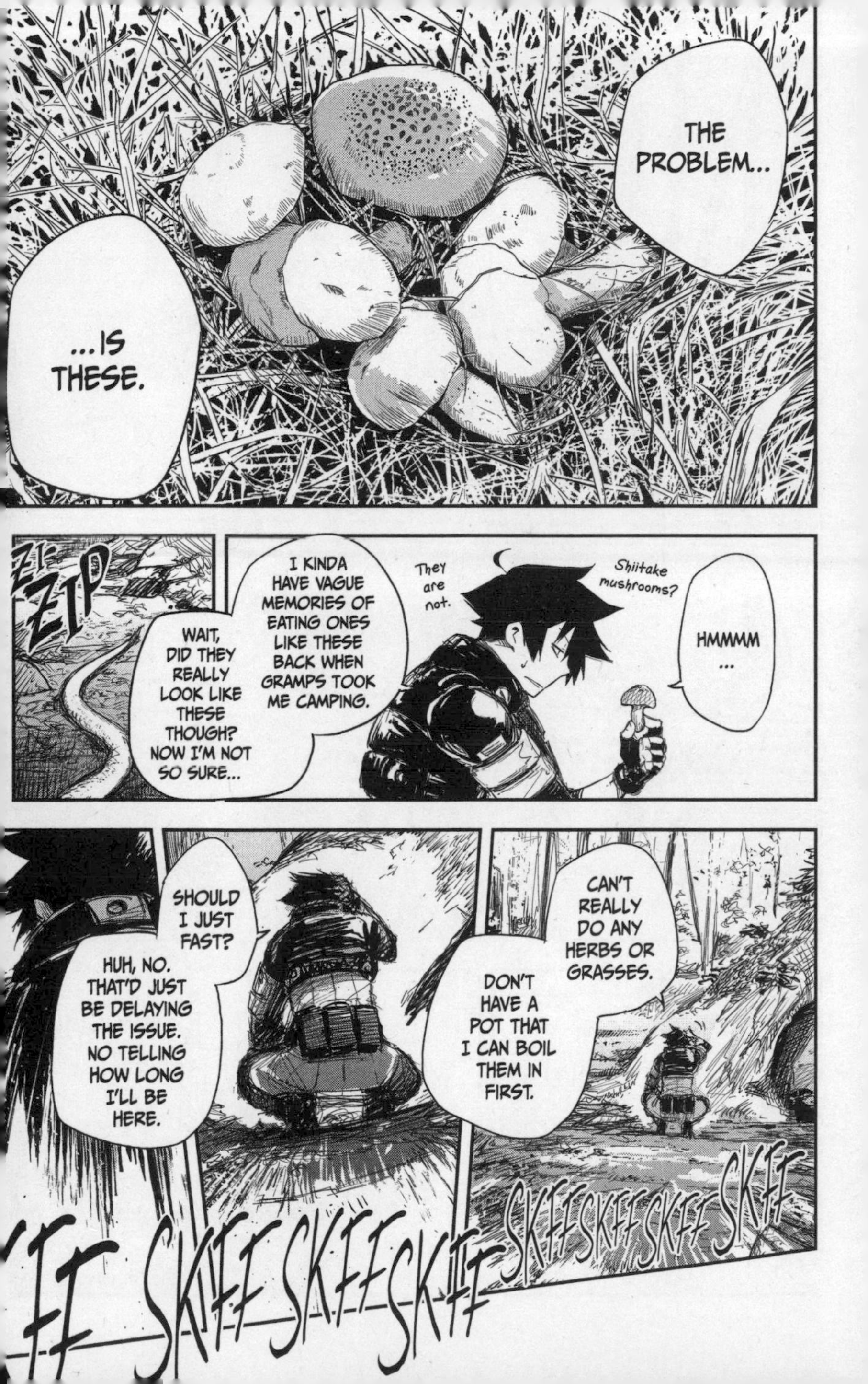
THE PROBLEM...
...IS THESE.
Shiitake mushrooms?
HMMMM ...
They are not.
I KINDA HAVE VAGUE MEMORIES OF EATING ONES LIKE THESE BACK WHEN GRAMPS TOOK ME CAMPING.
WAIT, DID THEY REALLY LOOK LIKE THESE THOUGH? NOW I'M NOT SO SURE...
ZI ZIP
CAN'T REALLY DO ANY HERBS OR GRASSES.
DON'T HAVE A POT THAT I CAN BOIL THEM IN FIRST.
SKFF SKFF SKFF SKFF
SHOULD I JUST FAST?
HUH, NO. THAT'D JUST BE DELAYING THE ISSUE. NO TELLING HOW LONG I'LL BE HERE.
SKFF SKFF SKFF FF

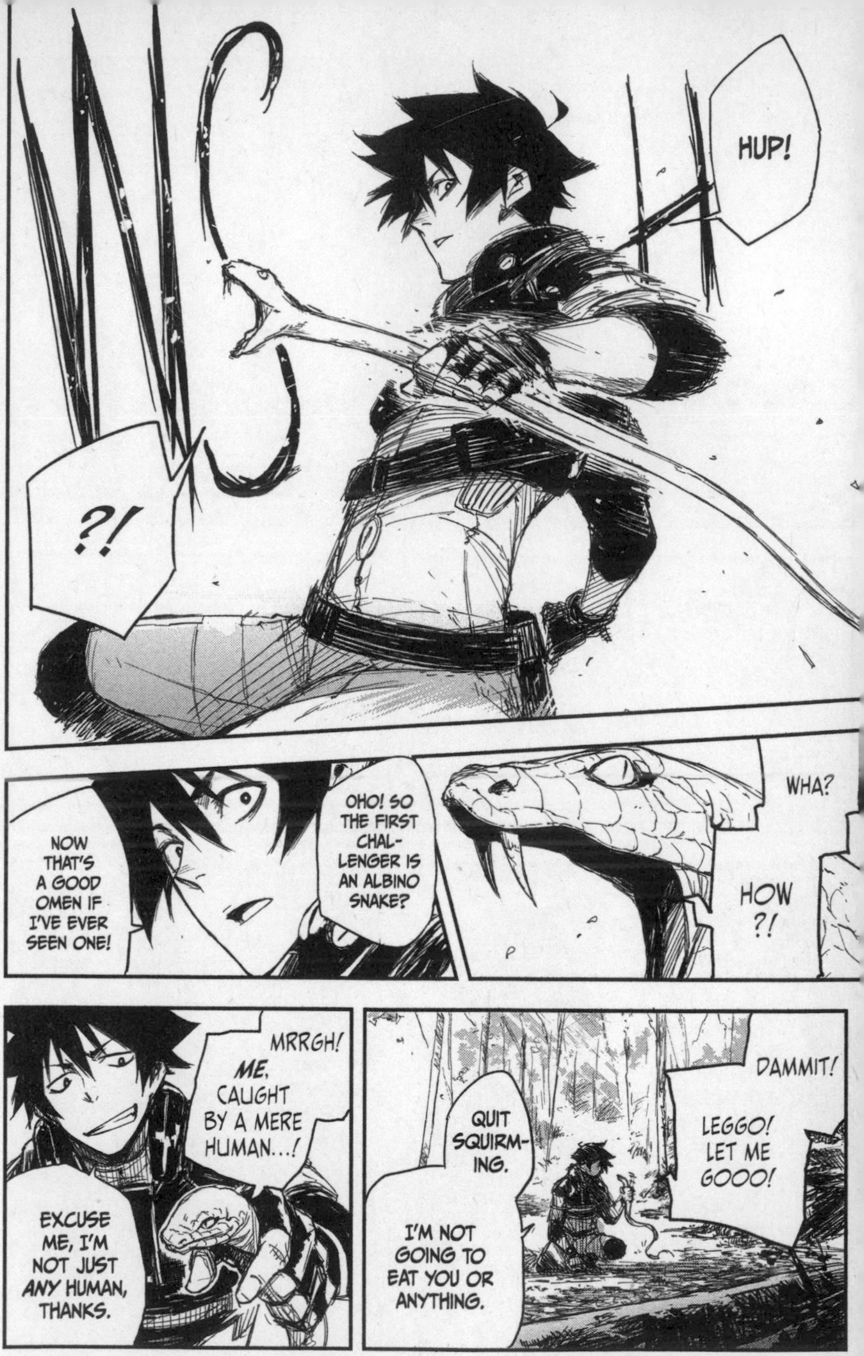

HUP!
?!
WHA?
HOW ?!
OHO! SO THE FIRST CHAL-LENGER IS AN ALBINO SNAKE?
NOW THAT'S A GOOD OMEN IF I'VE EVER SEEN ONE!
DAMMIT!
LEGGO! LET ME GOOO!
QUIT SQUIRM-ING.
I'M NOT GOING TO EAT YOU OR ANYTHING.
MRRGH!
ME, CAUGHT BY A MERE HUMAN...!
EXCUSE ME, I'M NOT JUST ANY HUMAN, THANKS.

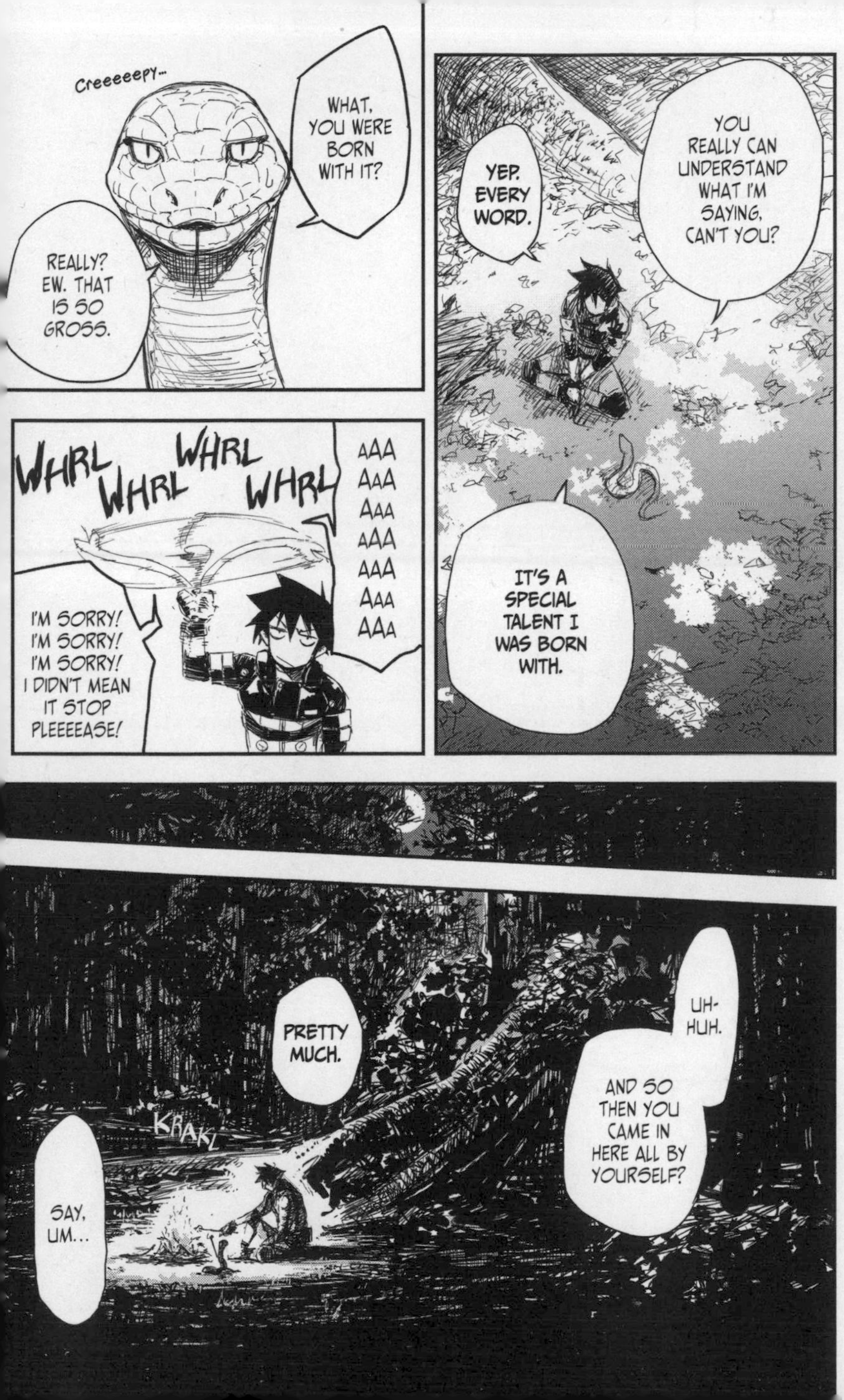
YOU REALLY CAN UNDERSTAND WHAT I'M SAYING, CAN'T YOU?
YEP. EVERY WORD.
IT'S A SPECIAL TALENT I WAS BORN WITH.
WHAT, YOU WERE BORN WITH IT?
Creeeeeepy...
REALLY? EW. THAT IS SO GROSS.
AAA AAA AAA AAA AAA AAA AAA
WHRL WHRL WHRL WHRL
I'M SORRY! I'M SORRY! I'M SORRY! I DIDN'T MEAN IT STOP PLEEEEASE!
UH-HUH.
AND SO THEN YOU CAME IN HERE ALL BY YOURSELF?
PRETTY MUCH.
KRAKL
SAY, UM...

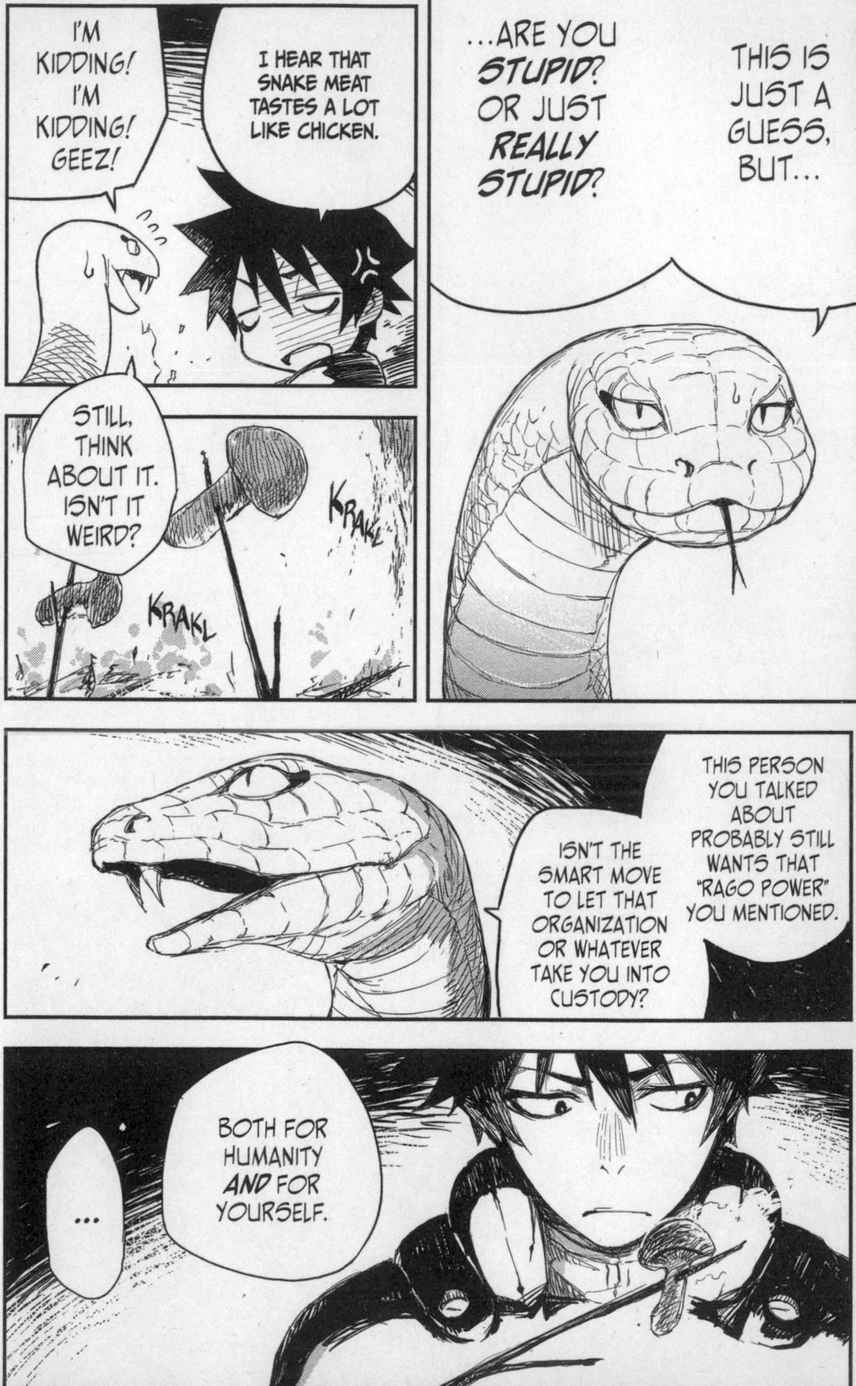
THIS IS JUST A GUESS, BUT...
...ARE YOU STUPID? OR JUST REALLY STUPID?
I HEAR THAT SNAKE MEAT TASTES A LOT LIKE CHICKEN.
I'M KIDDING! I'M KIDDING! GEEZ!
STILL, THINK ABOUT IT. ISN'T IT WEIRD?
KRAKL
KRAKL
THIS PERSON YOU TALKED ABOUT PROBABLY STILL WANTS THAT "RAGO POWER" YOU MENTIONED.
ISN'T THE SMART MOVE TO LET THAT ORGANIZATION OR WHATEVER TAKE YOU INTO CUSTODY?
BOTH FOR HUMANITY AND FOR YOURSELF.
...

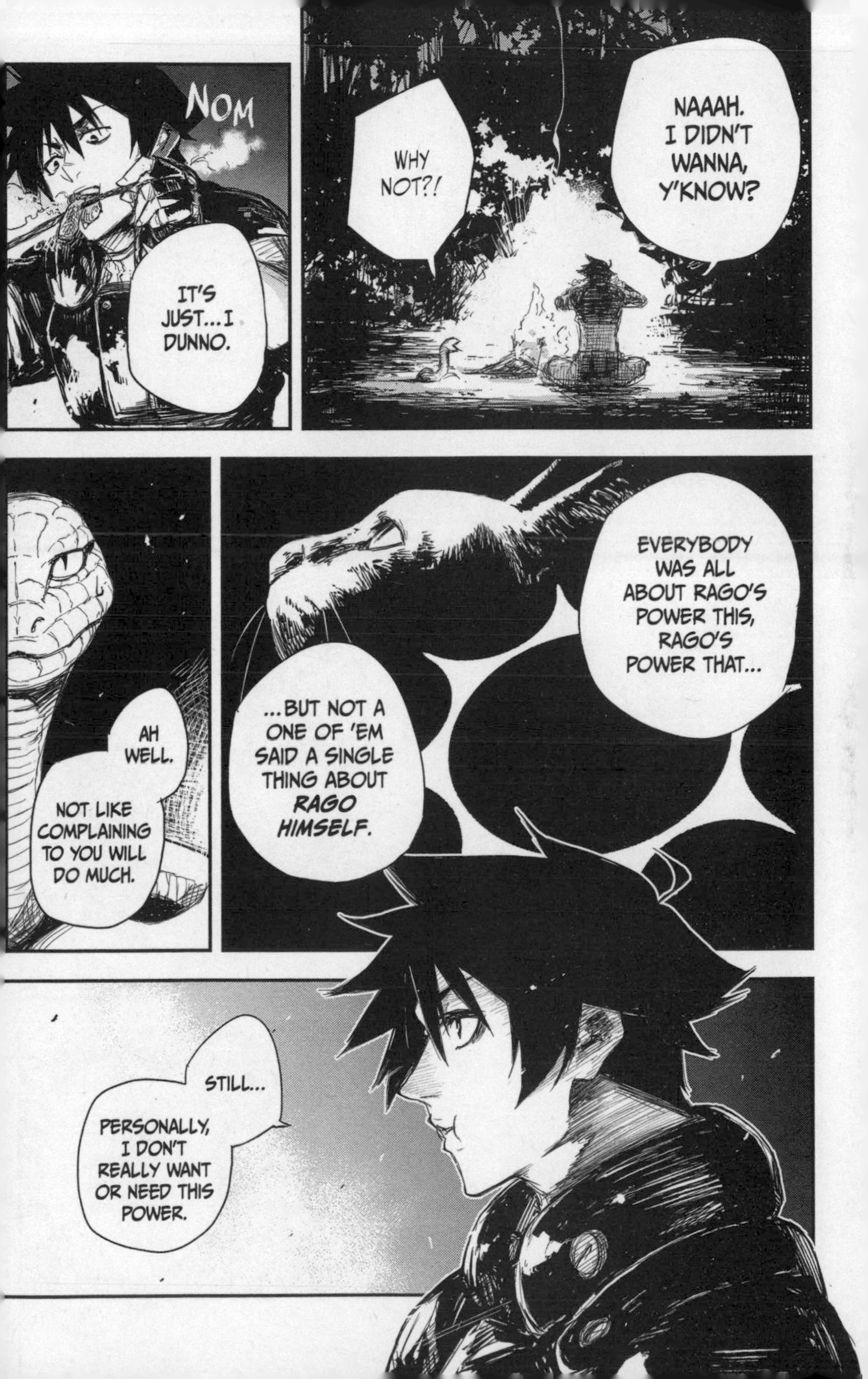
NAAAH. I DIDN'T WANNA, Y'KNOW?
WHY NOT?!
NOM
IT'S JUST...I DUNNO.
EVERYBODY WAS ALL ABOUT RAGO'S POWER THIS, RAGO'S POWER THAT...
...BUT NOT A ONE OF 'EM SAID A SINGLE THING ABOUT *RAGO HIMSELF*.
AH WELL.
NOT LIKE COMPLAINING TO YOU WILL DO MUCH.
STILL...
PERSONALLY, I DON'T REALLY WANT OR NEED THIS POWER.

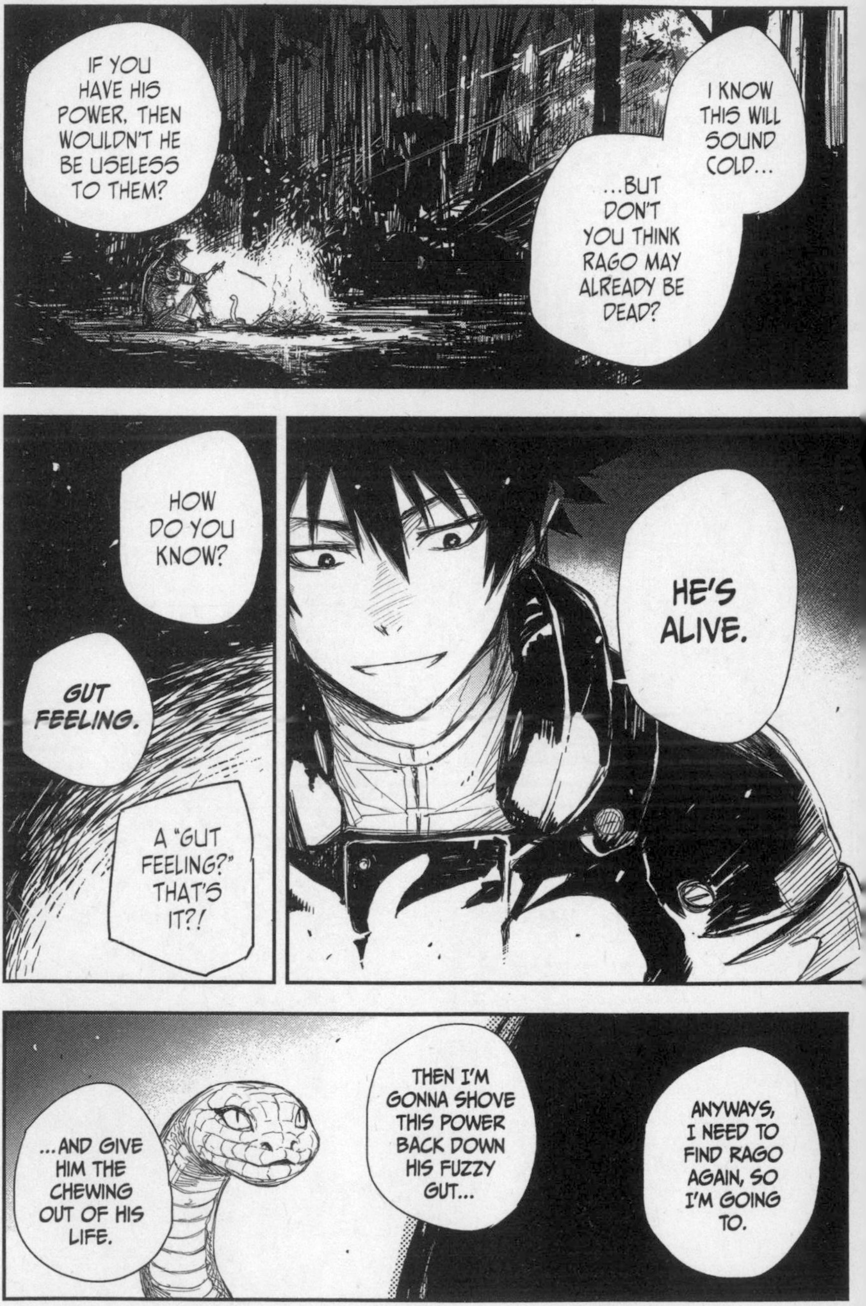
I KNOW THIS WILL SOUND COLD...
...BUT DON'T YOU THINK RAGO MAY ALREADY BE DEAD?
IF YOU HAVE HIS POWER, THEN WOULDN'T HE BE USELESS TO THEM?
HE'S ALIVE.
HOW DO YOU KNOW?
GUT FEELING.
A "GUT FEELING?" THAT'S IT?!
ANYWAYS, I NEED TO FIND RAGO AGAIN, SO I'M GOING TO.
THEN I'M GONNA SHOVE THIS POWER BACK DOWN HIS FUZZY GUT...
...AND GIVE HIM THE CHEWING OUT OF HIS LIFE.

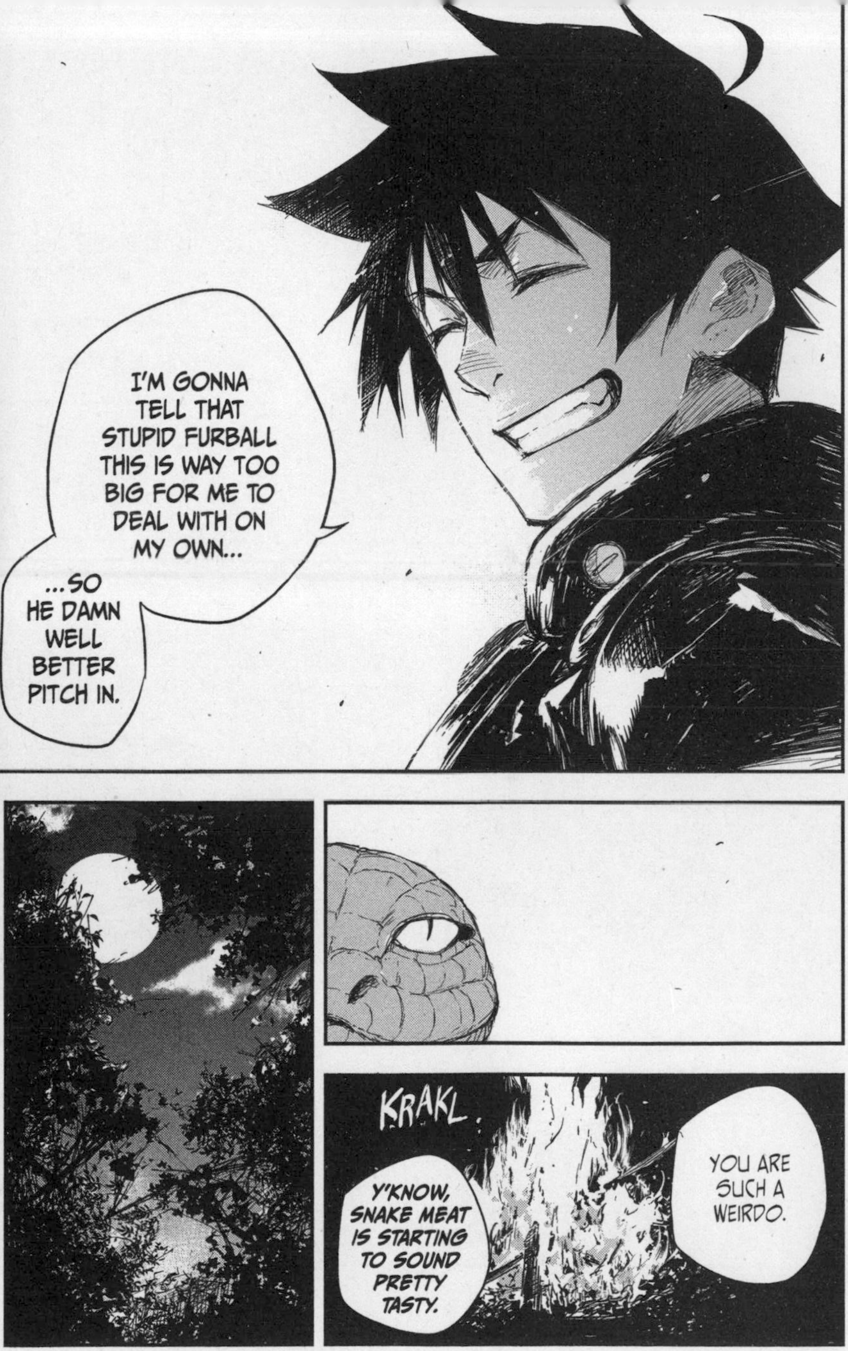
I'M GONNA TELL THAT STUPID FURBALL THIS IS WAY TOO BIG FOR ME TO DEAL WITH ON MY OWN...
...SO HE DAMN WELL BETTER PITCH IN.
KRAKL
YOU ARE SUCH A WEIRDO.
Y'KNOW, SNAKE MEAT IS STARTING TO SOUND PRETTY TASTY.

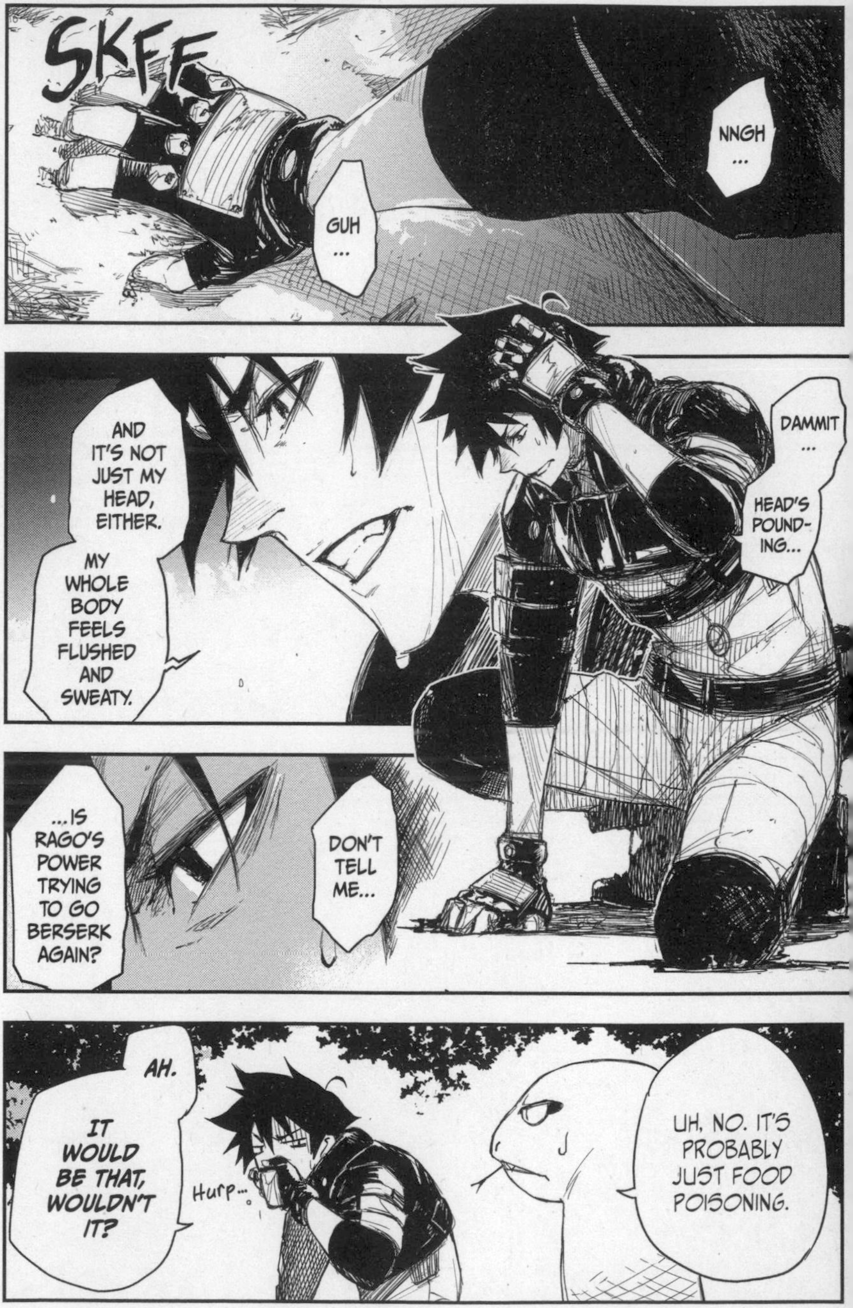
NNGH ...
GUH ...
SKFF
DAMMIT ...
HEAD'S POUNDING...
AND IT'S NOT JUST MY HEAD, EITHER.
MY WHOLE BODY FEELS FLUSHED AND SWEATY.
DON'T TELL ME...
...IS RAGO'S POWER TRYING TO GO BERSERK AGAIN?
UH, NO. IT'S PROBABLY JUST FOOD POISONING.
Hurp...
AH.
IT WOULD BE THAT, WOULDN'T IT?

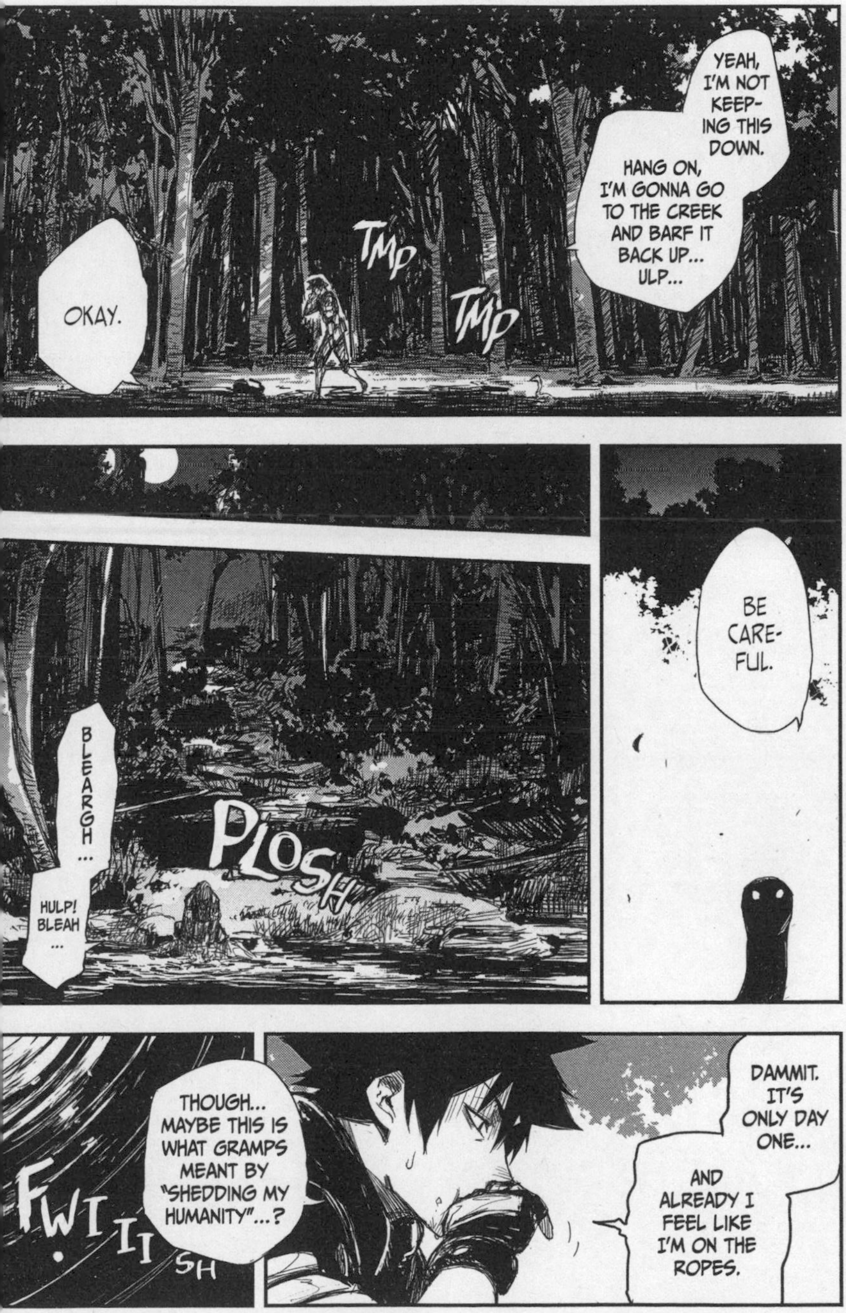
YEAH, I'M NOT KEEP-ING THIS DOWN.
HANG ON, I'M GONNA GO TO THE CREEK AND BARF IT BACK UP... ULP...
TMP
TMP
OKAY.
BE CARE-FUL.
PLOSH
BLEARGH...
HULP! BLEAH...
DAMMIT. IT'S ONLY DAY ONE...
AND ALREADY I FEEL LIKE I'M ON THE ROPES.
THOUGH... MAYBE THIS IS WHAT GRAMPS MEANT BY "SHEDDING MY HUMANITY"...?
FWIIISH

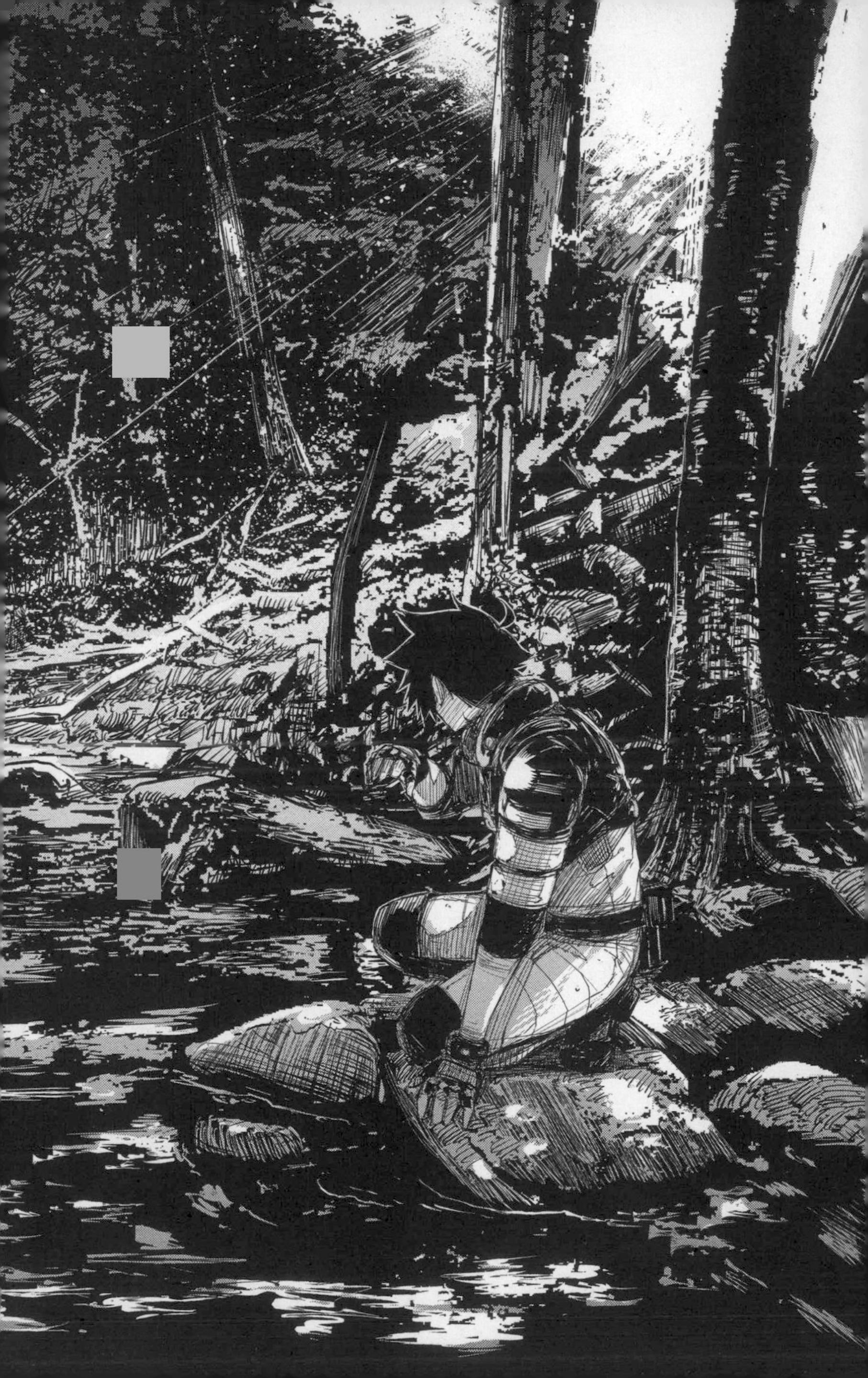

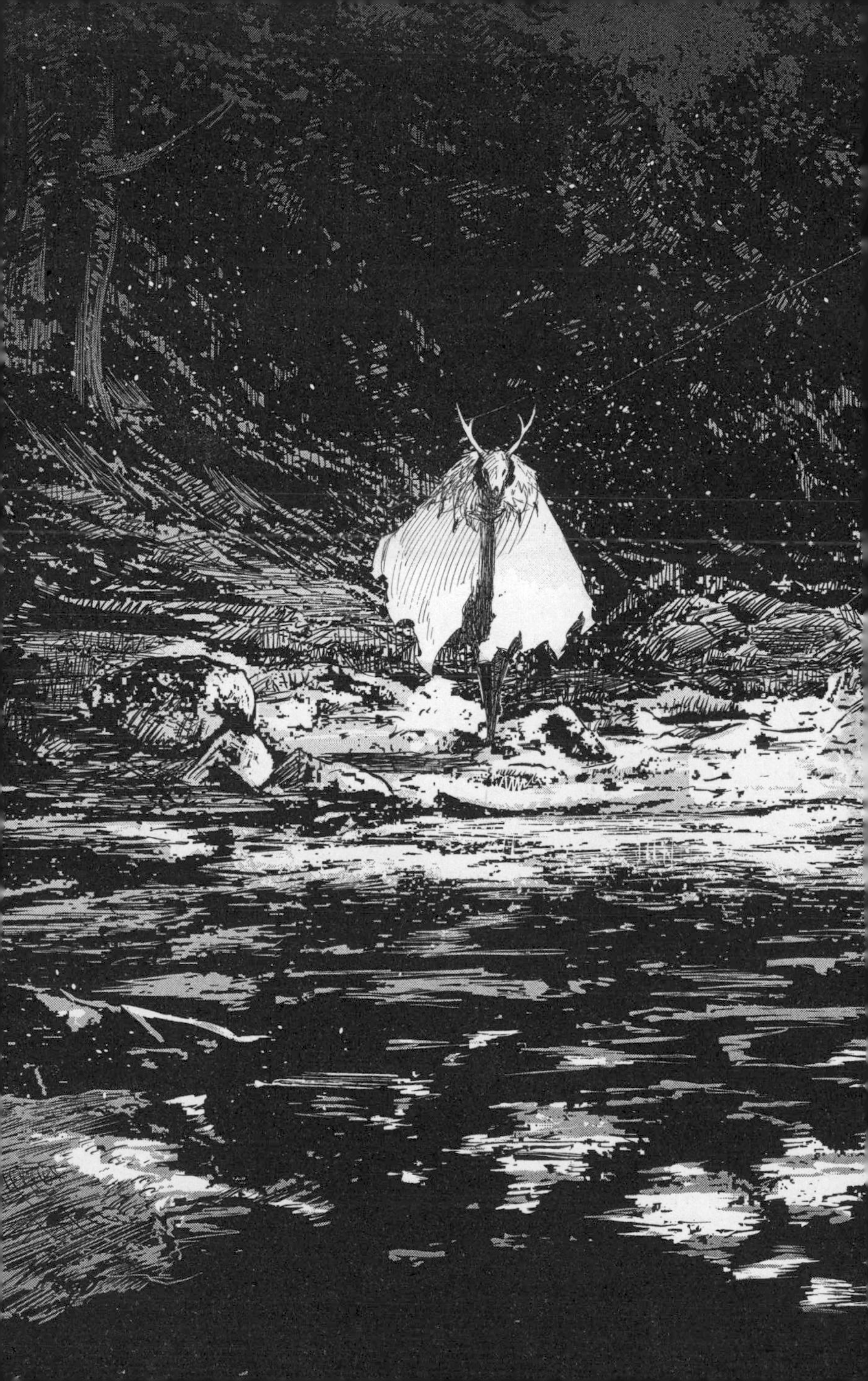

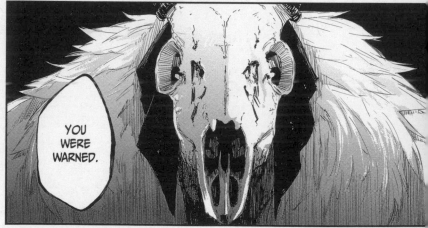

YOU WERE WARNED.

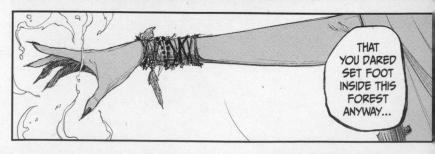

THAT YOU DARED SET FOOT INSIDE THIS FOREST ANYWAY...

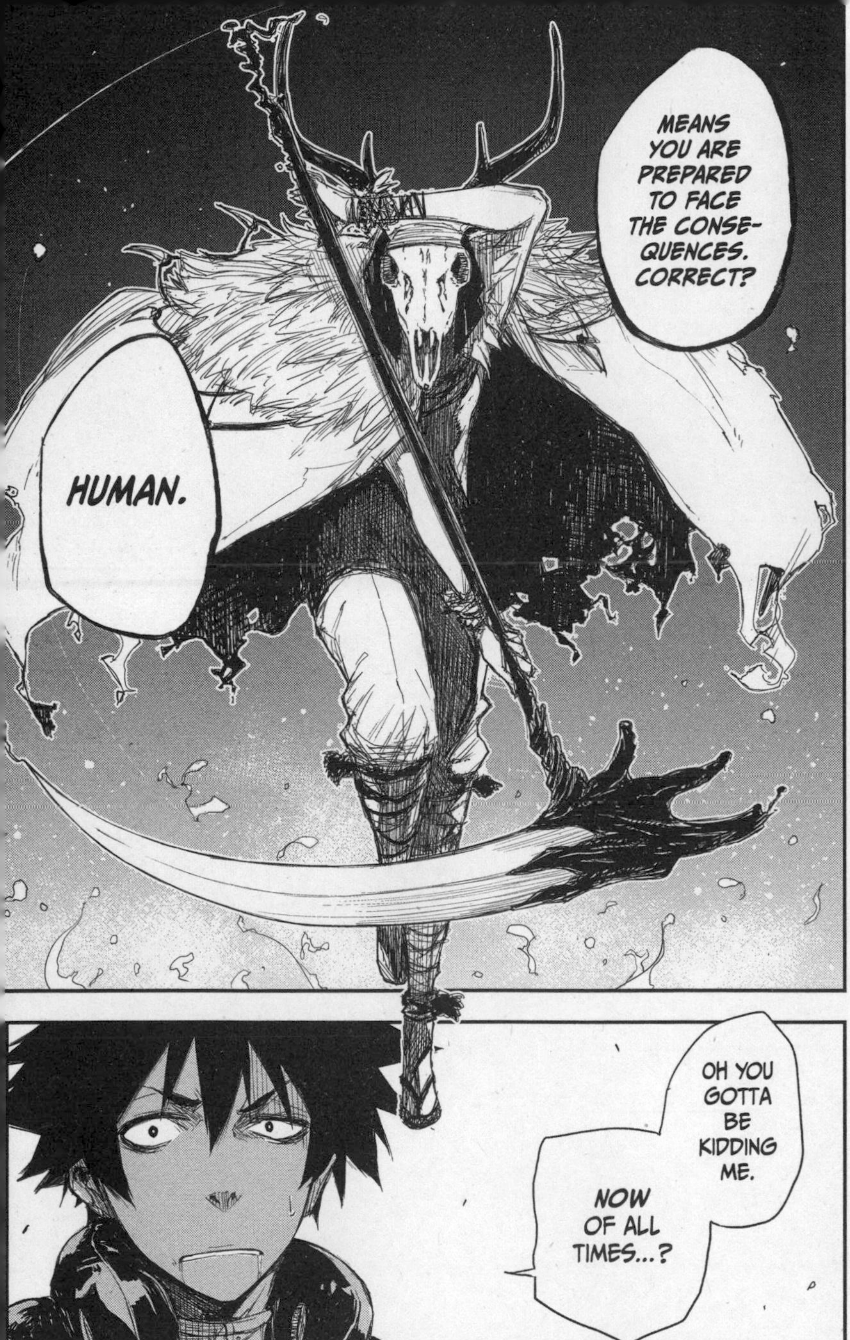
MEANS YOU ARE PREPARED TO FACE THE CONSE- QUENCES. CORRECT?
HUMAN.
OH YOU GOTTA BE KIDDING ME.
NOW OF ALL TIMES...?

BLACK TORCH

#15 Deadly Skillz

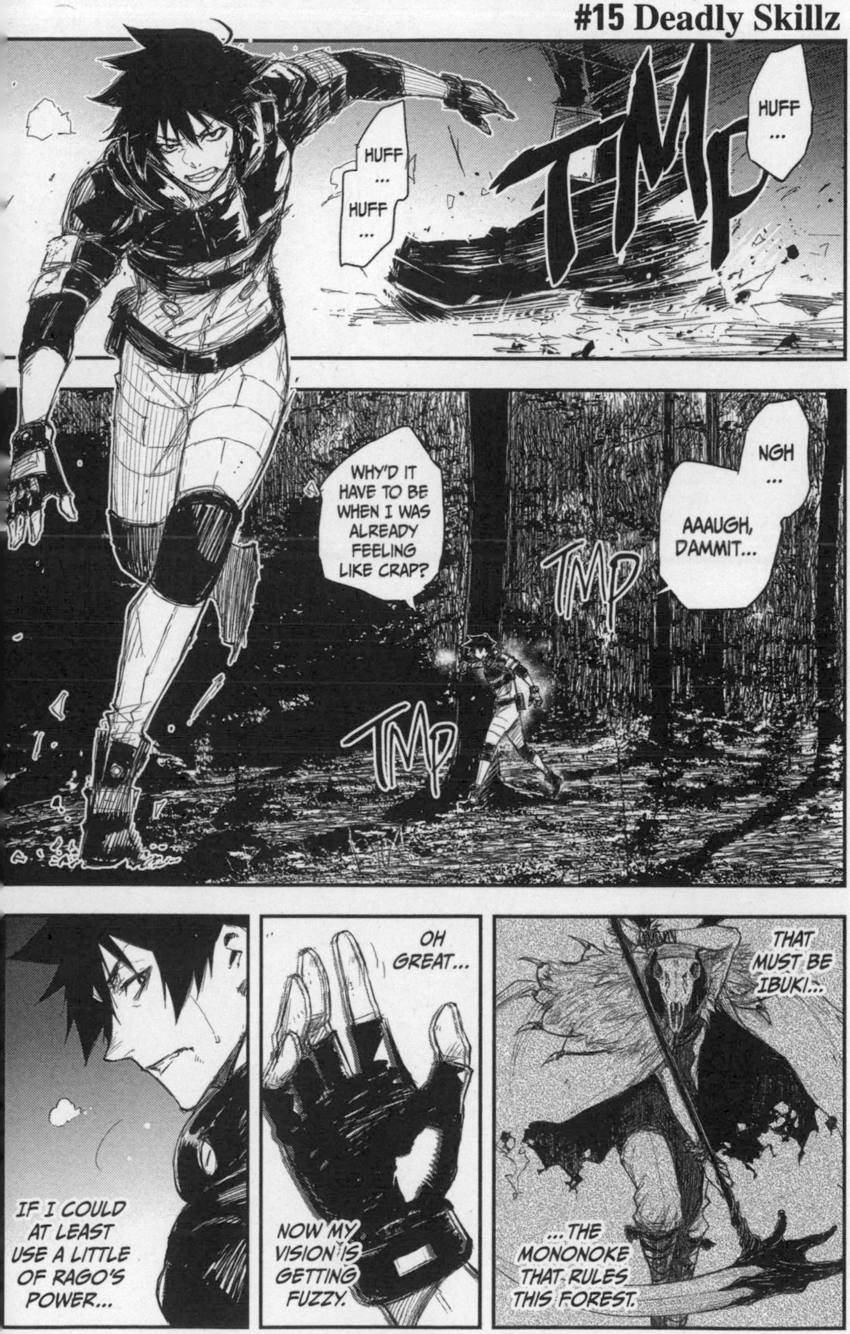
HUFF ...
TMP
HUFF ... HUFF ...
NGH ... AAAUGH, DAMMIT...
TMP
WHY'D IT HAVE TO BE WHEN I WAS ALREADY FEELING LIKE CRAP?
TMP
THAT MUST BE IBUKI...
...THE MONONOKE THAT RULES THIS FOREST.
OH GREAT...
NOW MY VISION IS GETTING FUZZY.
IF I COULD AT LEAST USE A LITTLE OF RAGO'S POWER...

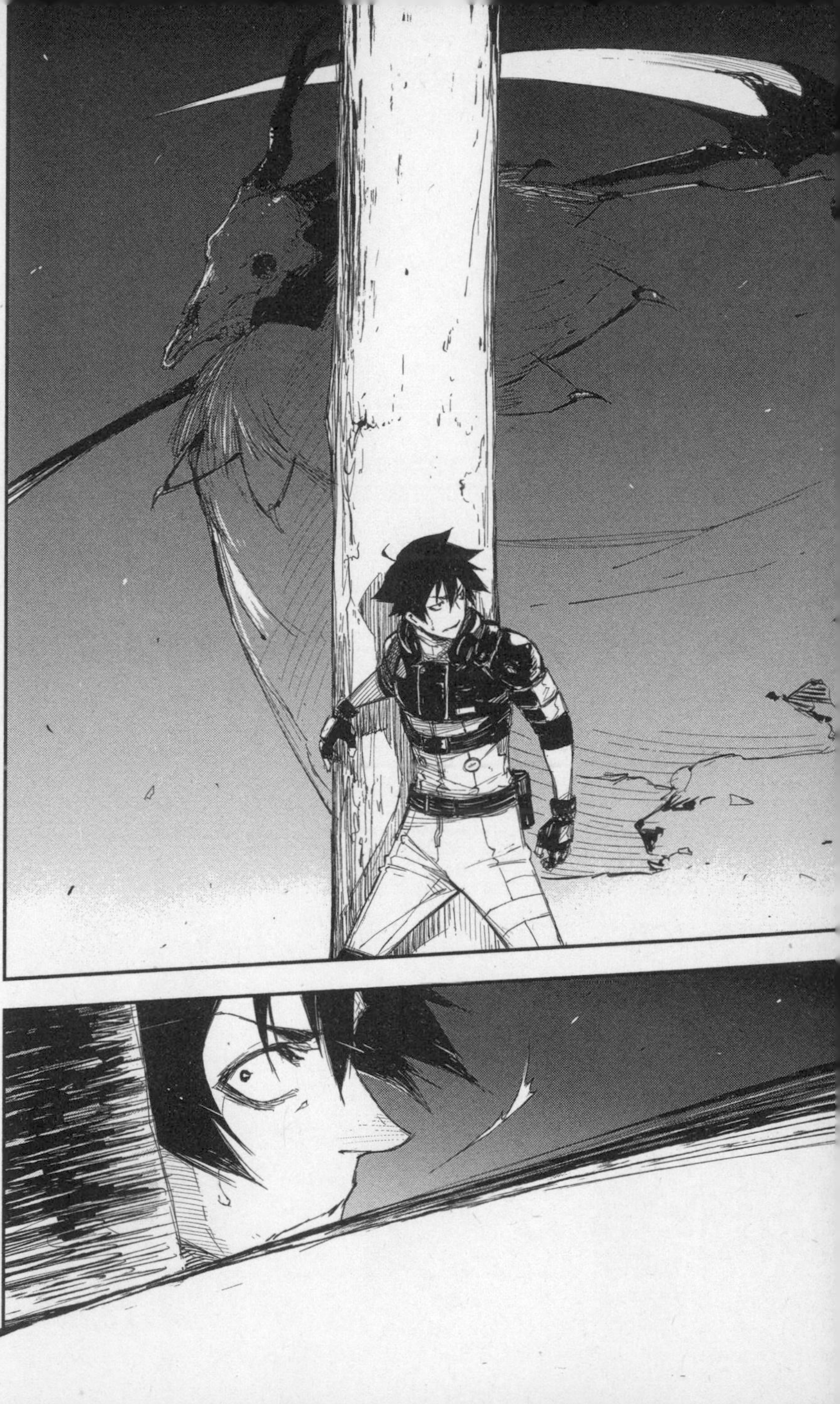

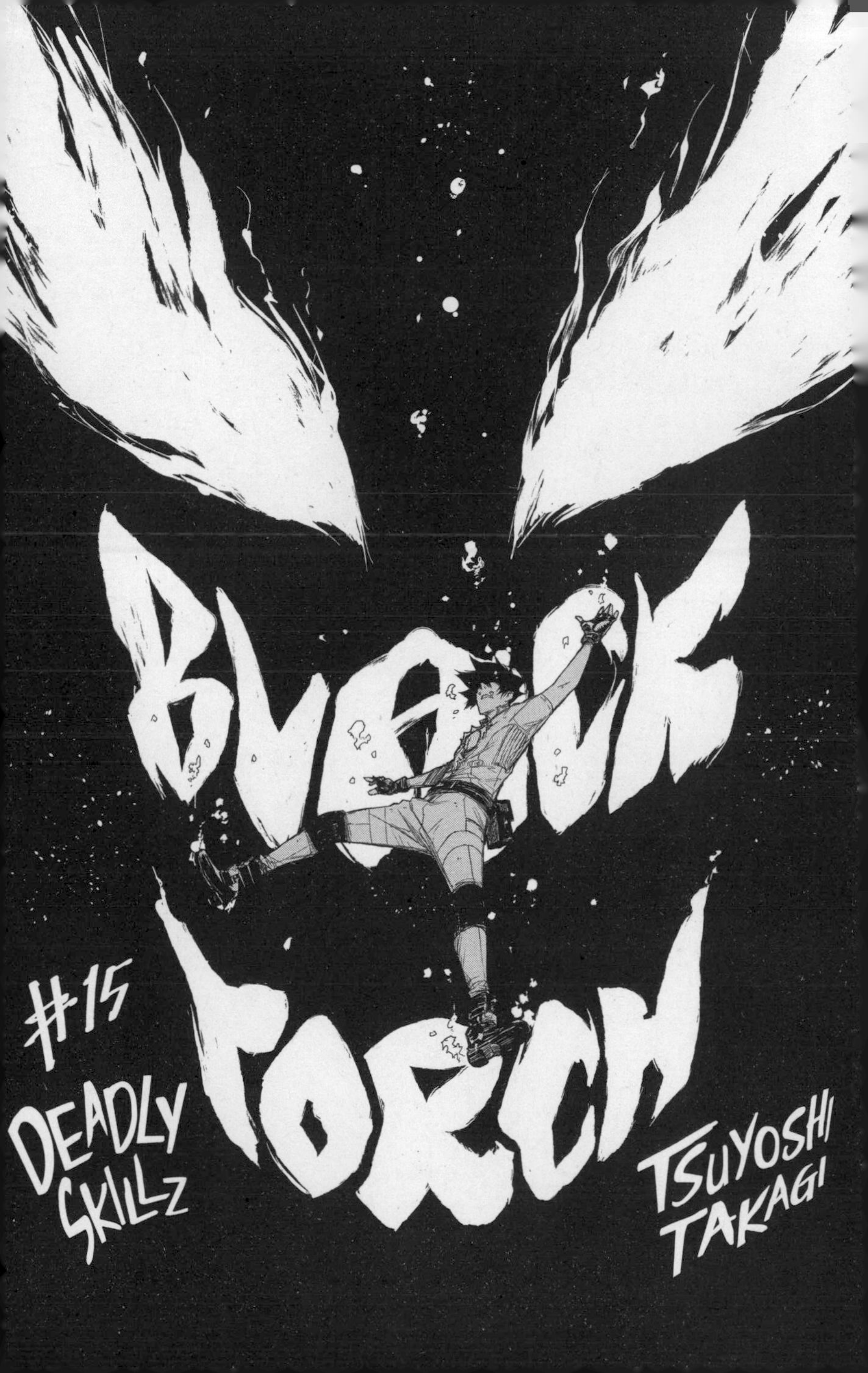
BLACK TORCH
#15
DEADLY SKILLZ
TSUYOSHI TAKAGI

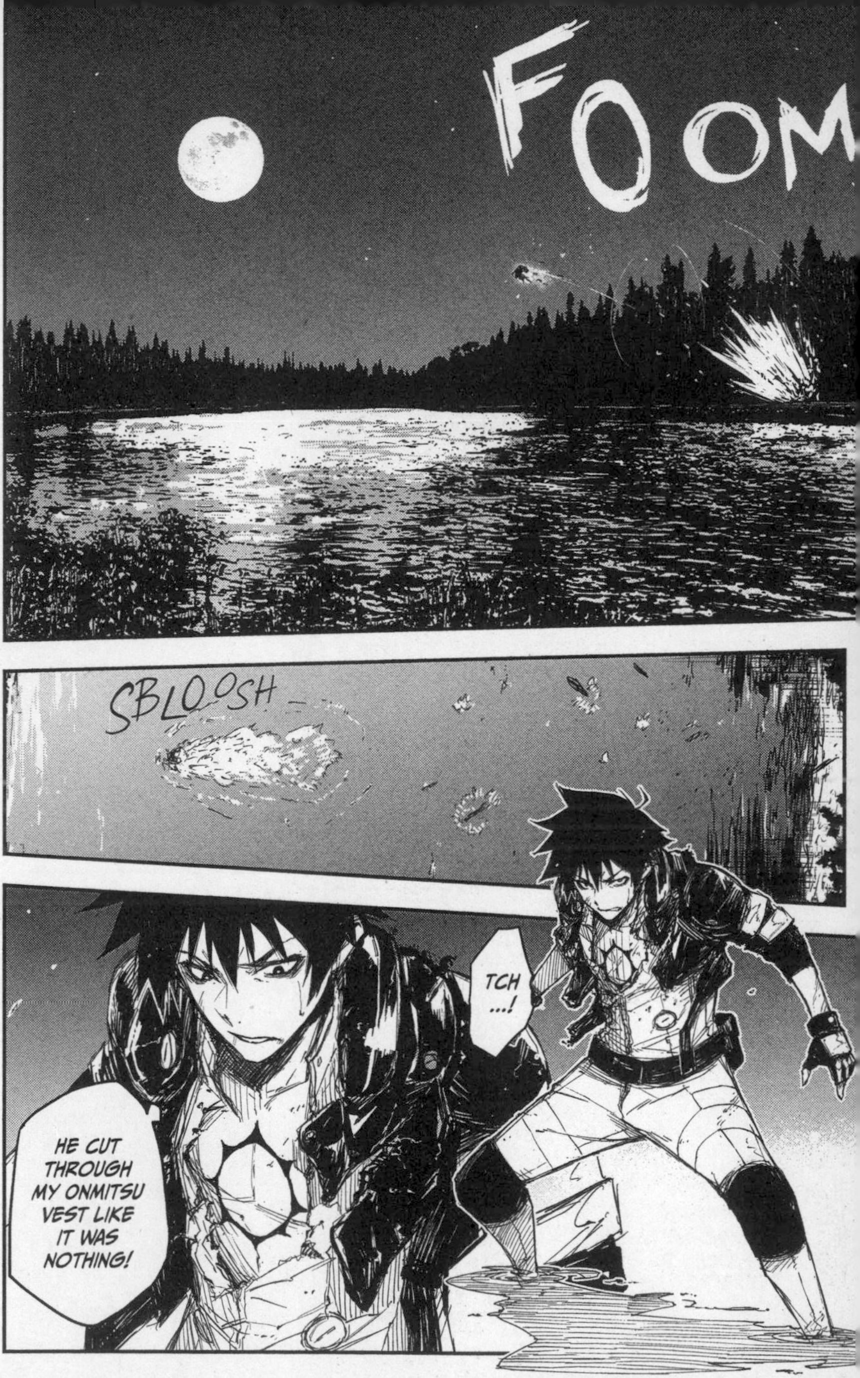
FOOM
SBLOOSH
TCH ...!
HE CUT THROUGH MY ONMITSU VEST LIKE IT WAS NOTHING!

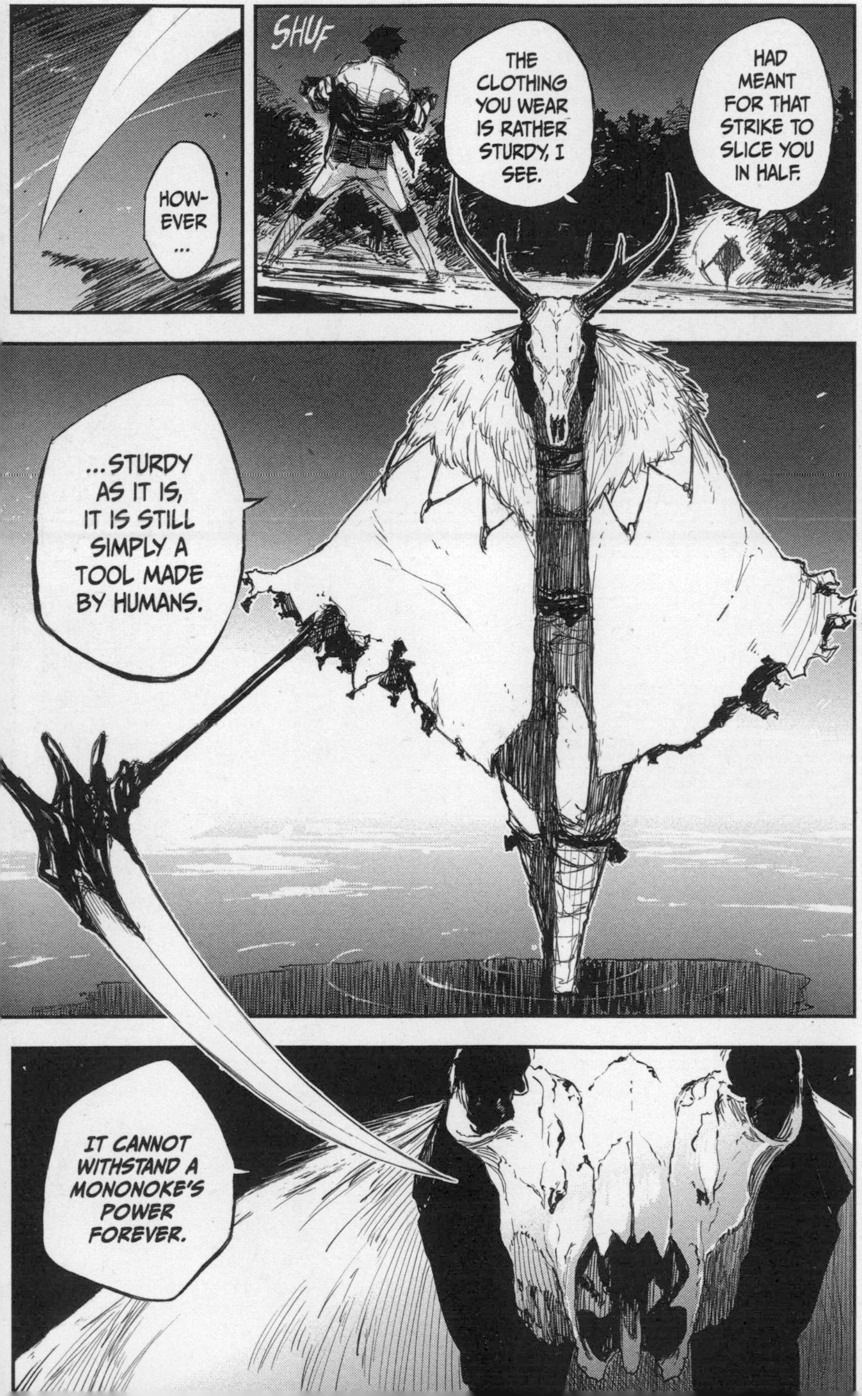
HAD MEANT FOR THAT STRIKE TO SLICE YOU IN HALF.
THE CLOTHING YOU WEAR IS RATHER STURDY, I SEE.
SHUF
HOW-EVER ...
...STURDY AS IT IS, IT IS STILL SIMPLY A TOOL MADE BY HUMANS.
IT CANNOT WITHSTAND A MONONOKE'S POWER FOREVER.

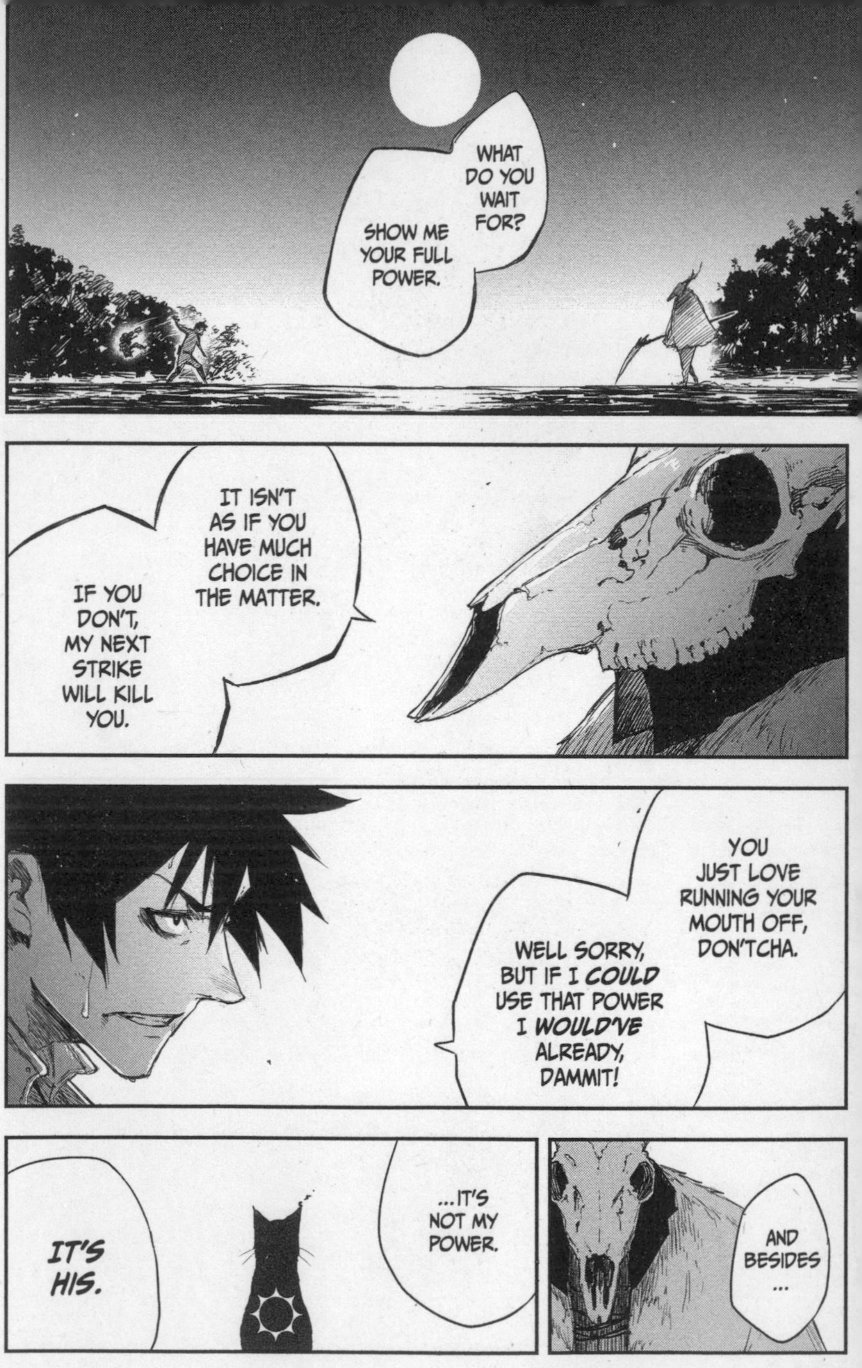
WHAT DO YOU WAIT FOR?
SHOW ME YOUR FULL POWER.
IT ISN'T AS IF YOU HAVE MUCH CHOICE IN THE MATTER.
IF YOU DON'T, MY NEXT STRIKE WILL KILL YOU.
YOU JUST LOVE RUNNING YOUR MOUTH OFF, DON'TCHA.
WELL SORRY, BUT IF I *COULD* USE THAT POWER I *WOULD'VE* ALREADY, DAMMIT!
AND BESIDES ...
...IT'S NOT MY POWER.
IT'S HIS.

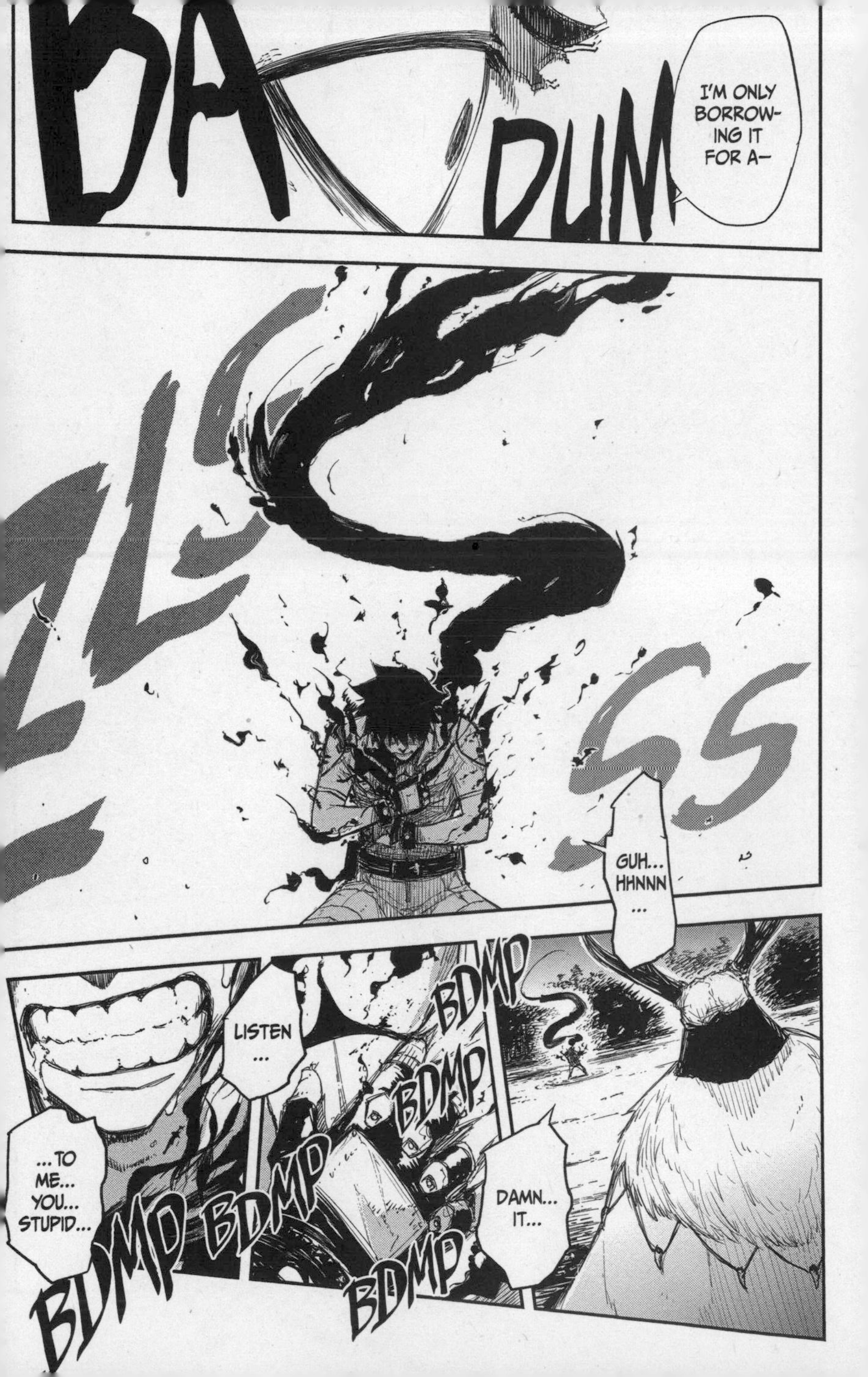
I'M ONLY BORROWING IT FOR A—
DA DUM
ZZSSS
GUH... HHNNN ...
DAMN... IT...
BDMP
BDMP
BDMP
LISTEN ...
BDMP
...TO ME... YOU... STUPID...
BDMP

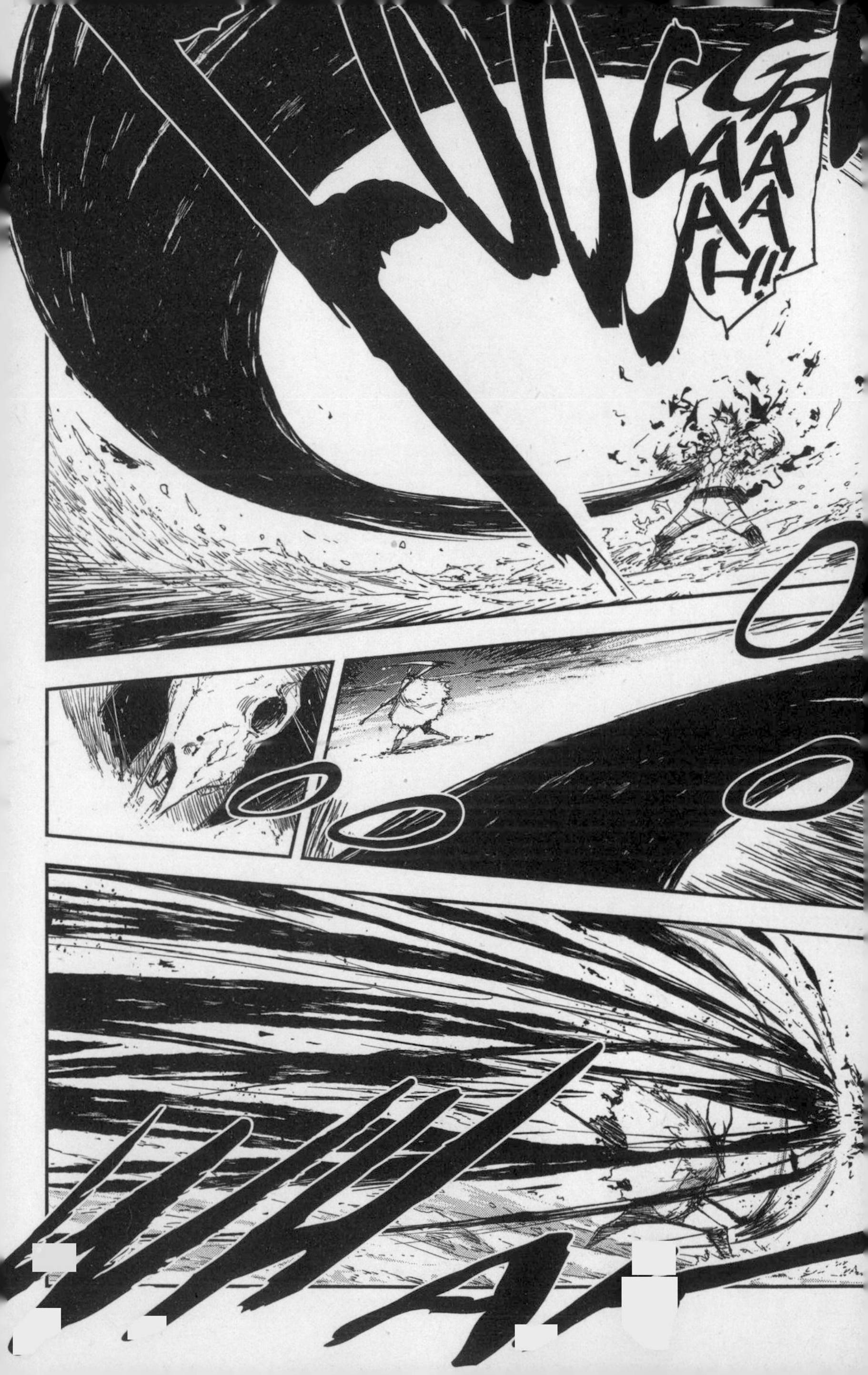
GRAAAAH!!

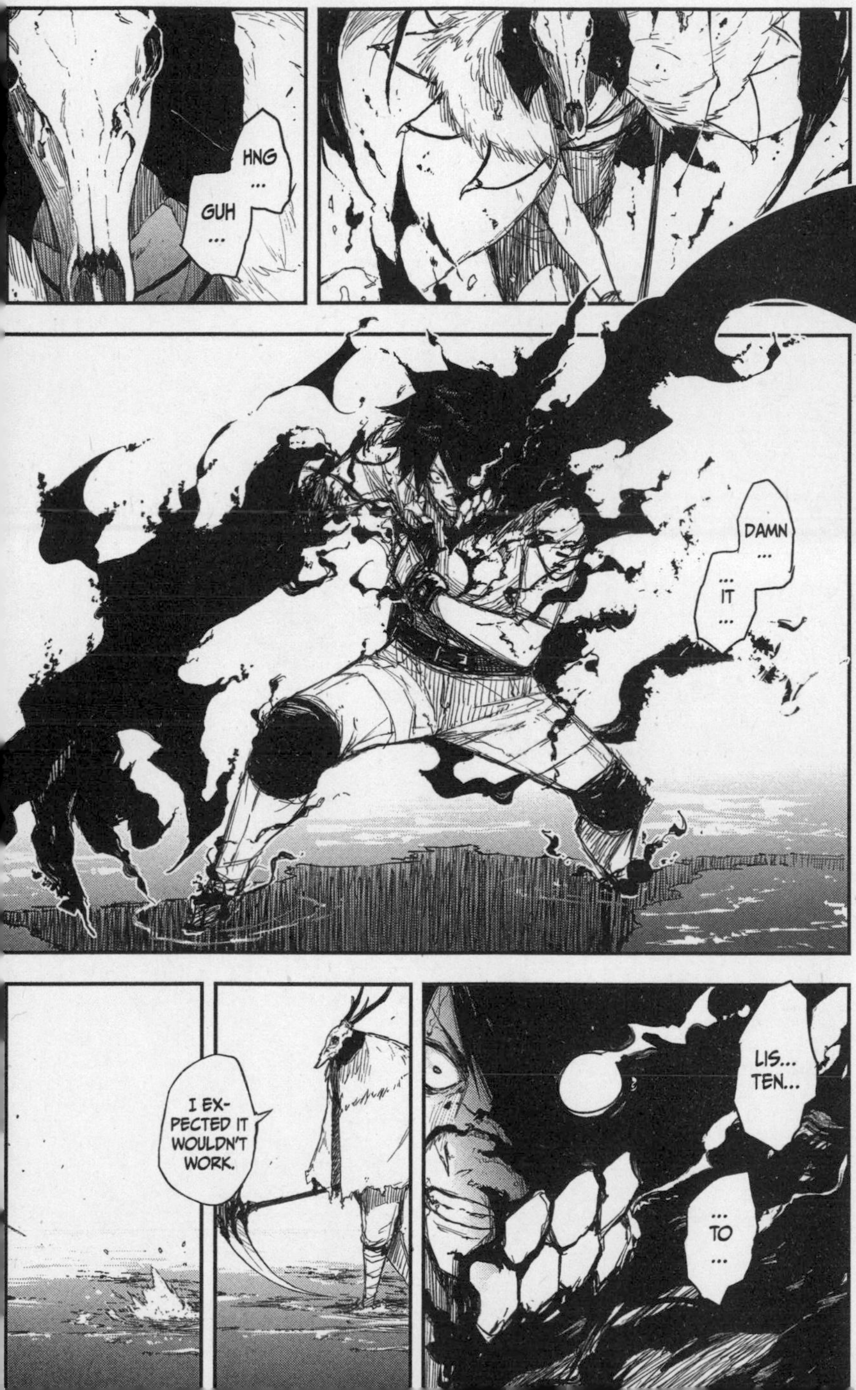
HNG ... GUH ...
DAMN ... ... IT ...
LIS... TEN...
... TO ...
I EX-PECTED IT WOULDN'T WORK.

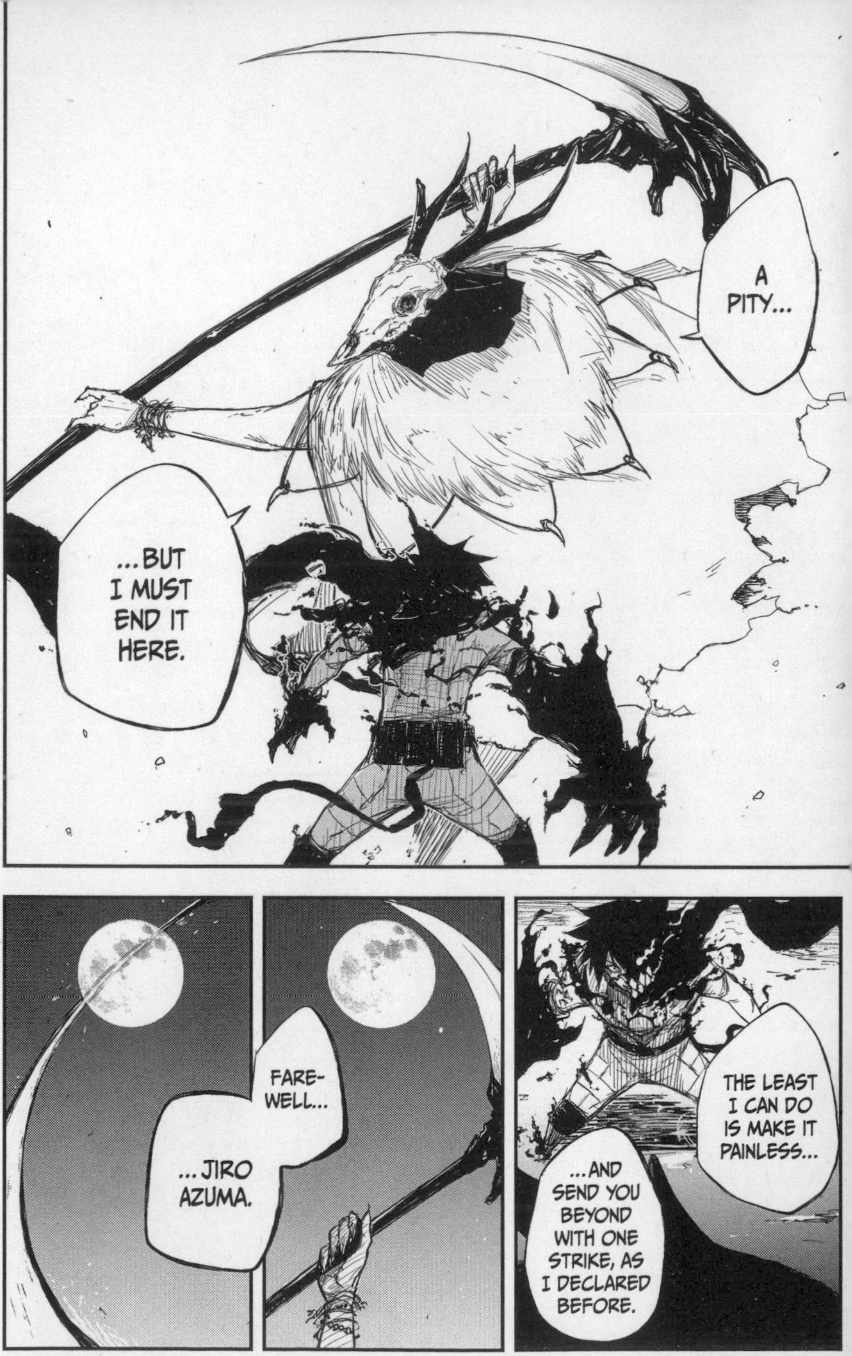
A PITY...
...BUT I MUST END IT HERE.
THE LEAST I CAN DO IS MAKE IT PAINLESS...
...AND SEND YOU BEYOND WITH ONE STRIKE, AS I DECLARED BEFORE.
FARE-WELL...
...JIRO AZUMA.

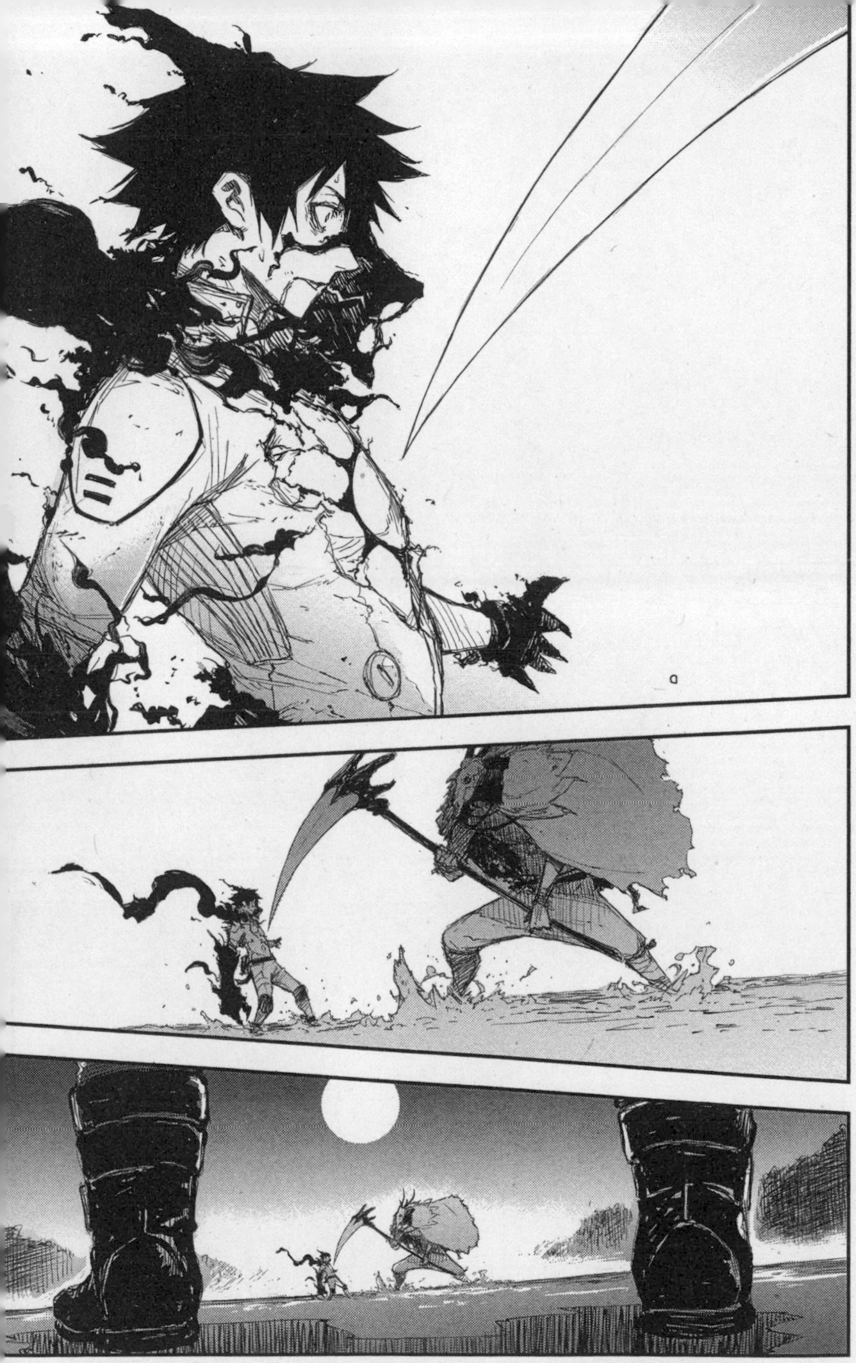

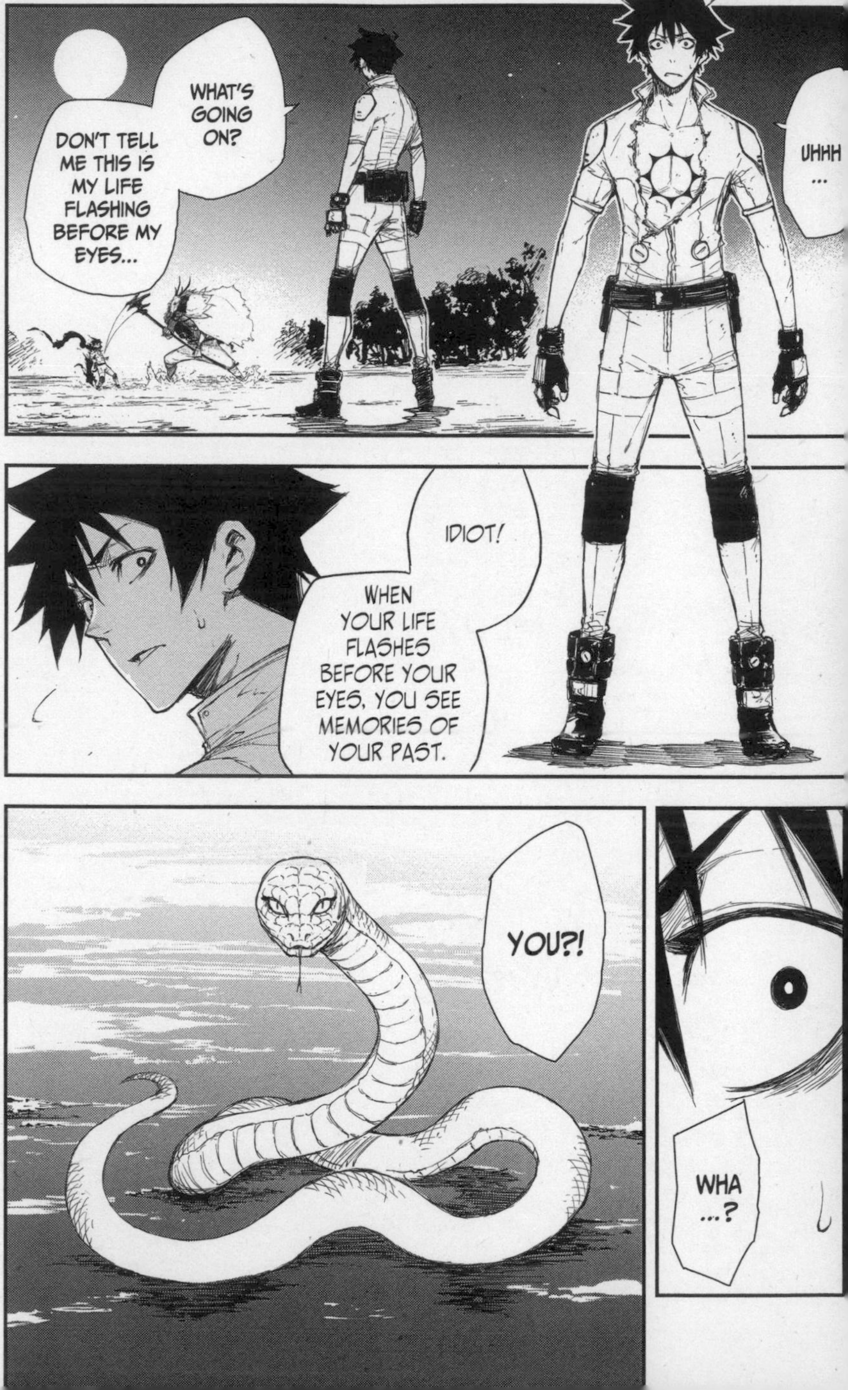
UHHH ...
WHAT'S GOING ON?
DON'T TELL ME THIS IS MY LIFE FLASHING BEFORE MY EYES...
IDIOT!
WHEN YOUR LIFE FLASHES BEFORE YOUR EYES, YOU SEE MEMORIES OF YOUR PAST.
WHA ...?
YOU?!

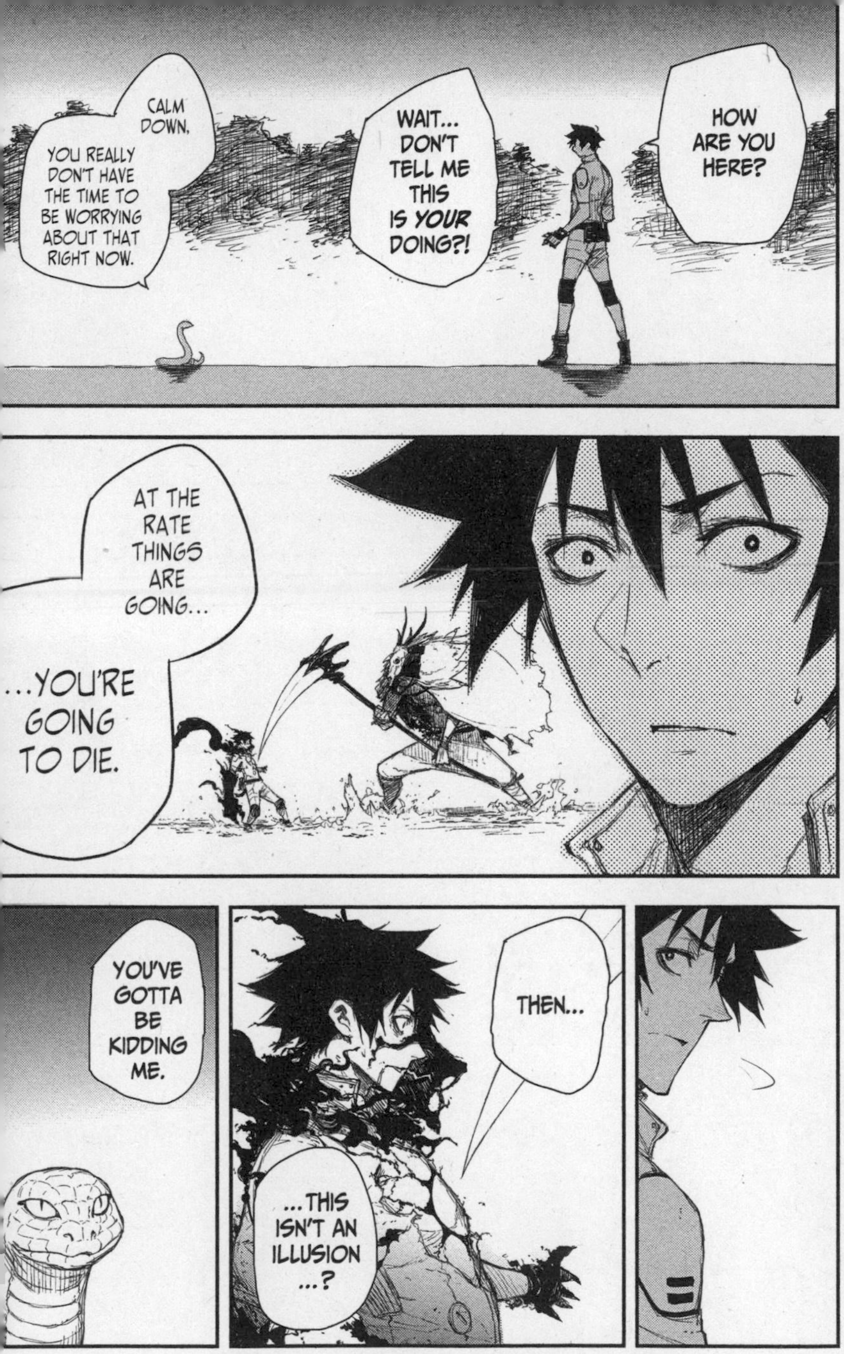
HOW ARE YOU HERE?
WAIT... DON'T TELL ME THIS IS *YOUR* DOING?!
CALM DOWN,
YOU REALLY DON'T HAVE THE TIME TO BE WORRYING ABOUT THAT RIGHT NOW.
AT THE RATE THINGS ARE GOING...
...YOU'RE GOING TO DIE.
THEN...
...THIS ISN'T AN ILLUSION ...?
YOU'VE GOTTA BE KIDDING ME.

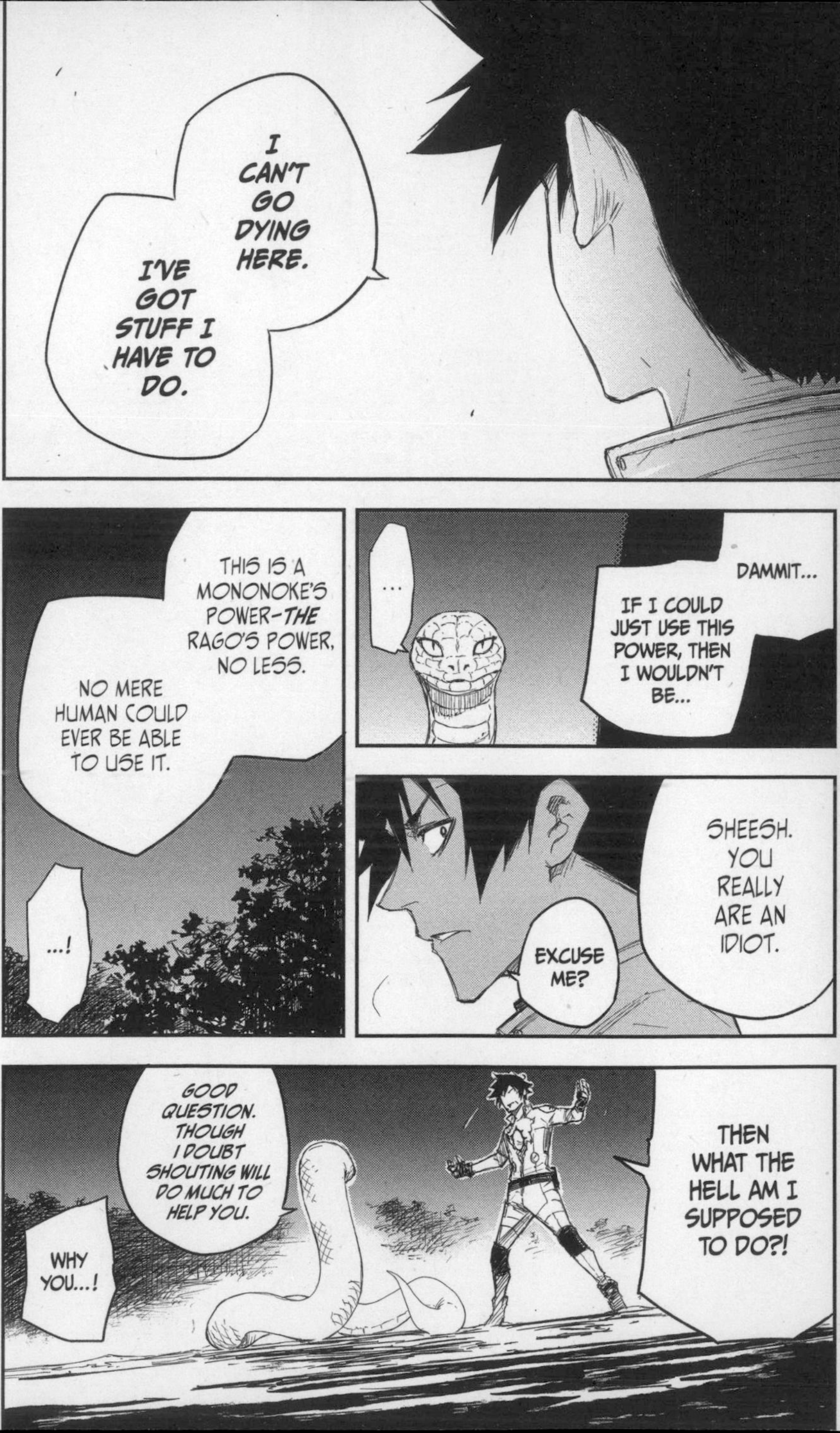
I CAN'T GO DYING HERE.
I'VE GOT STUFF I HAVE TO DO.
DAMMIT...
IF I COULD JUST USE THIS POWER, THEN I WOULDN'T BE...
...
SHEESH. YOU REALLY ARE AN IDIOT.
EXCUSE ME?
THIS IS A MONONOKE'S POWER—*THE* RAGO'S POWER, NO LESS.
NO MERE HUMAN COULD EVER BE ABLE TO USE IT.
...!
THEN WHAT THE HELL AM I SUPPOSED TO DO?!
GOOD QUESTION. THOUGH I DOUBT SHOUTING WILL DO MUCH TO HELP YOU.
WHY YOU...!

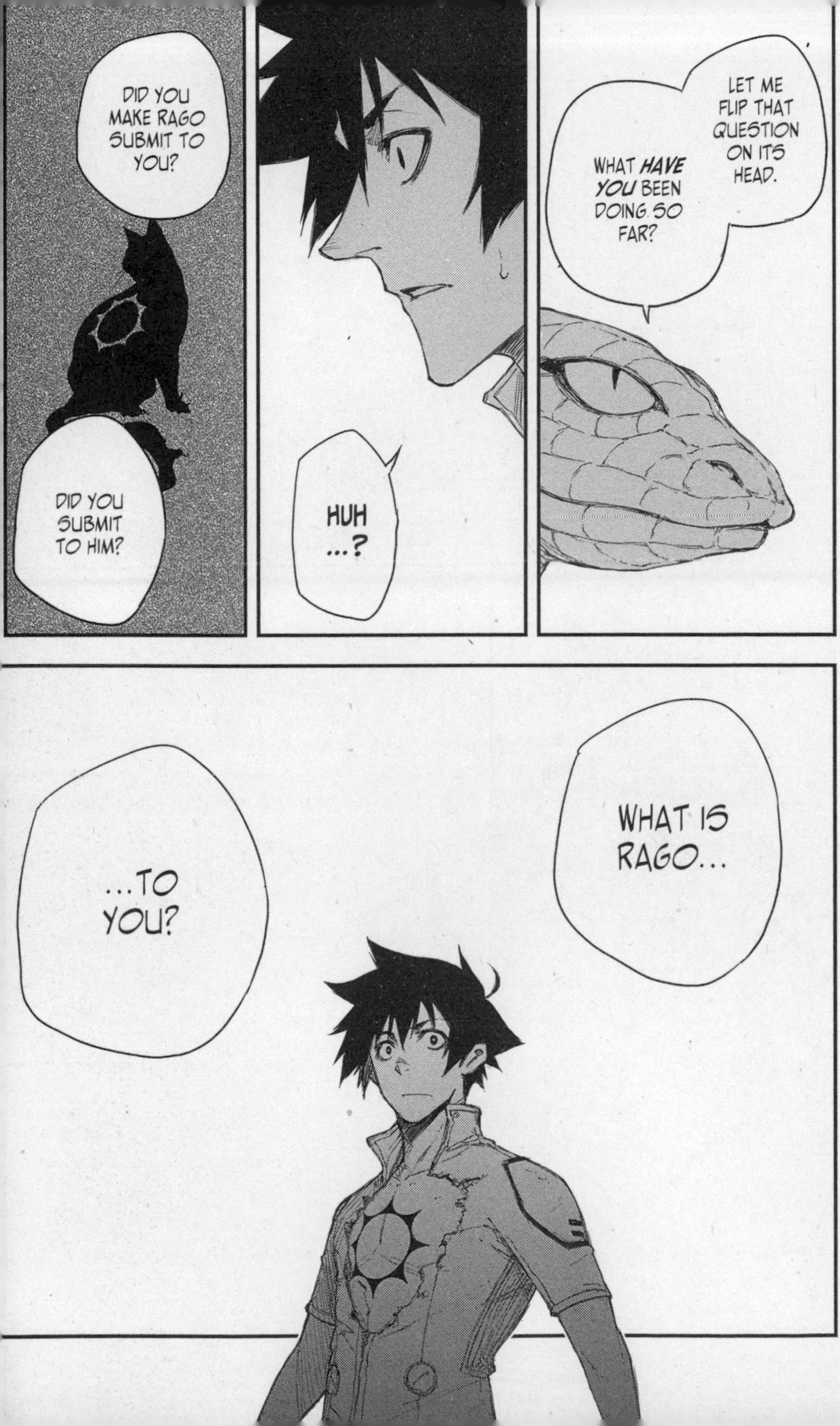
LET ME FLIP THAT QUESTION ON ITS HEAD.
WHAT HAVE YOU BEEN DOING SO FAR?
HUH ...?
DID YOU MAKE RAGO SUBMIT TO YOU?
DID YOU SUBMIT TO HIM?
WHAT IS RAGO...
...TO YOU?

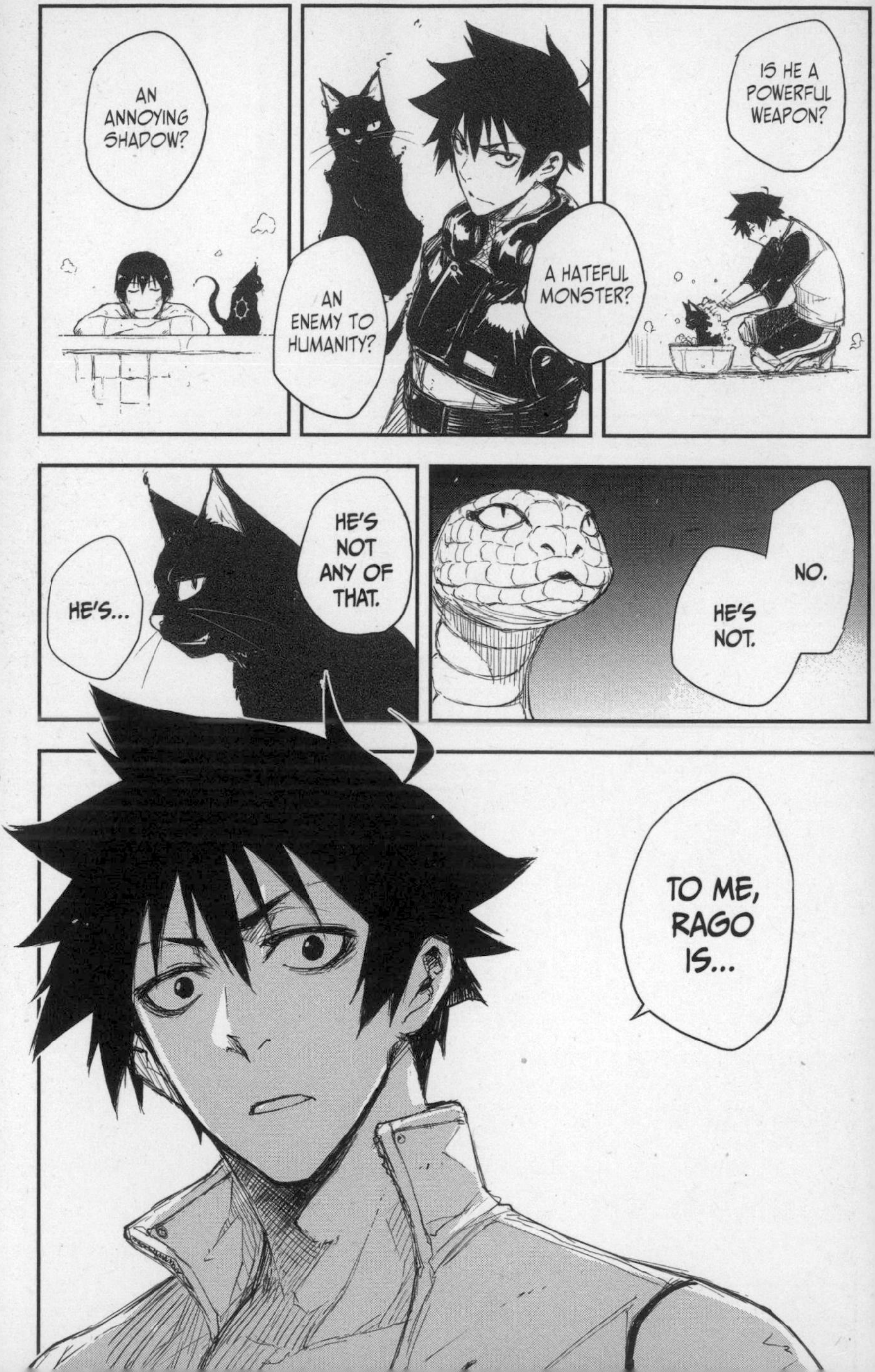
IS HE A POWERFUL WEAPON?
A HATEFUL MONSTER?
AN ENEMY TO HUMANITY?
AN ANNOYING SHADOW?
NO.
HE'S NOT.
HE'S NOT ANY OF THAT.
HE'S...
TO ME, RAGO IS...

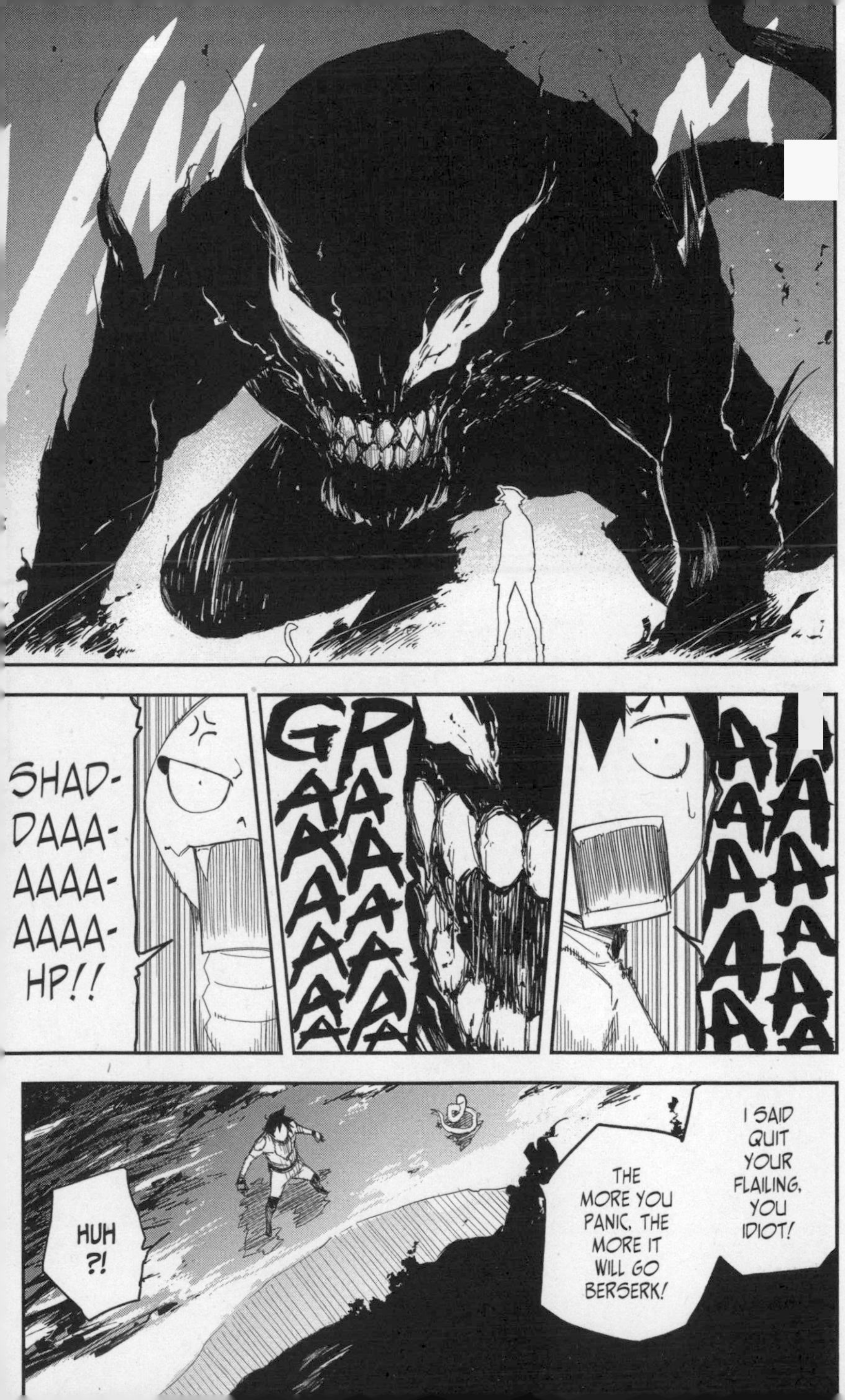
SHAD-DAAA-AAAA-AAAA-HP!!
I SAID QUIT YOUR FLAILING, YOU IDIOT!
THE MORE YOU PANIC, THE MORE IT WILL GO BERSERK!
HUH?!

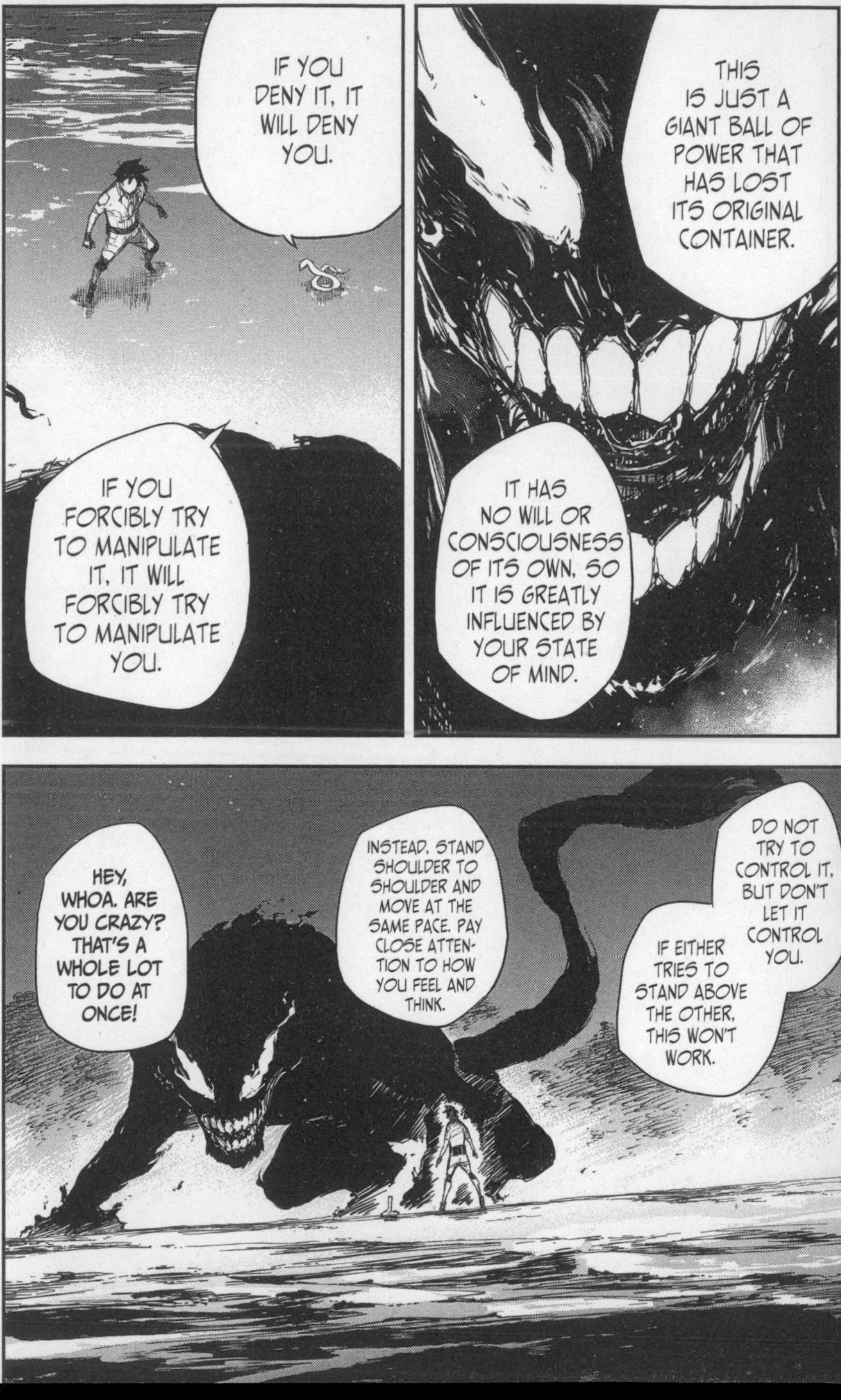
THIS IS JUST A GIANT BALL OF POWER THAT HAS LOST ITS ORIGINAL CONTAINER.
IT HAS NO WILL OR CONSCIOUSNESS OF ITS OWN, SO IT IS GREATLY INFLUENCED BY YOUR STATE OF MIND.
IF YOU DENY IT, IT WILL DENY YOU.
IF YOU FORCIBLY TRY TO MANIPULATE IT, IT WILL FORCIBLY TRY TO MANIPULATE YOU.
DO NOT TRY TO CONTROL IT, BUT DON'T LET IT CONTROL YOU.
IF EITHER TRIES TO STAND ABOVE THE OTHER, THIS WON'T WORK.
INSTEAD, STAND SHOULDER TO SHOULDER AND MOVE AT THE SAME PACE. PAY CLOSE ATTEN-TION TO HOW YOU FEEL AND THINK.
HEY, WHOA. ARE YOU CRAZY? THAT'S A WHOLE LOT TO DO AT ONCE!

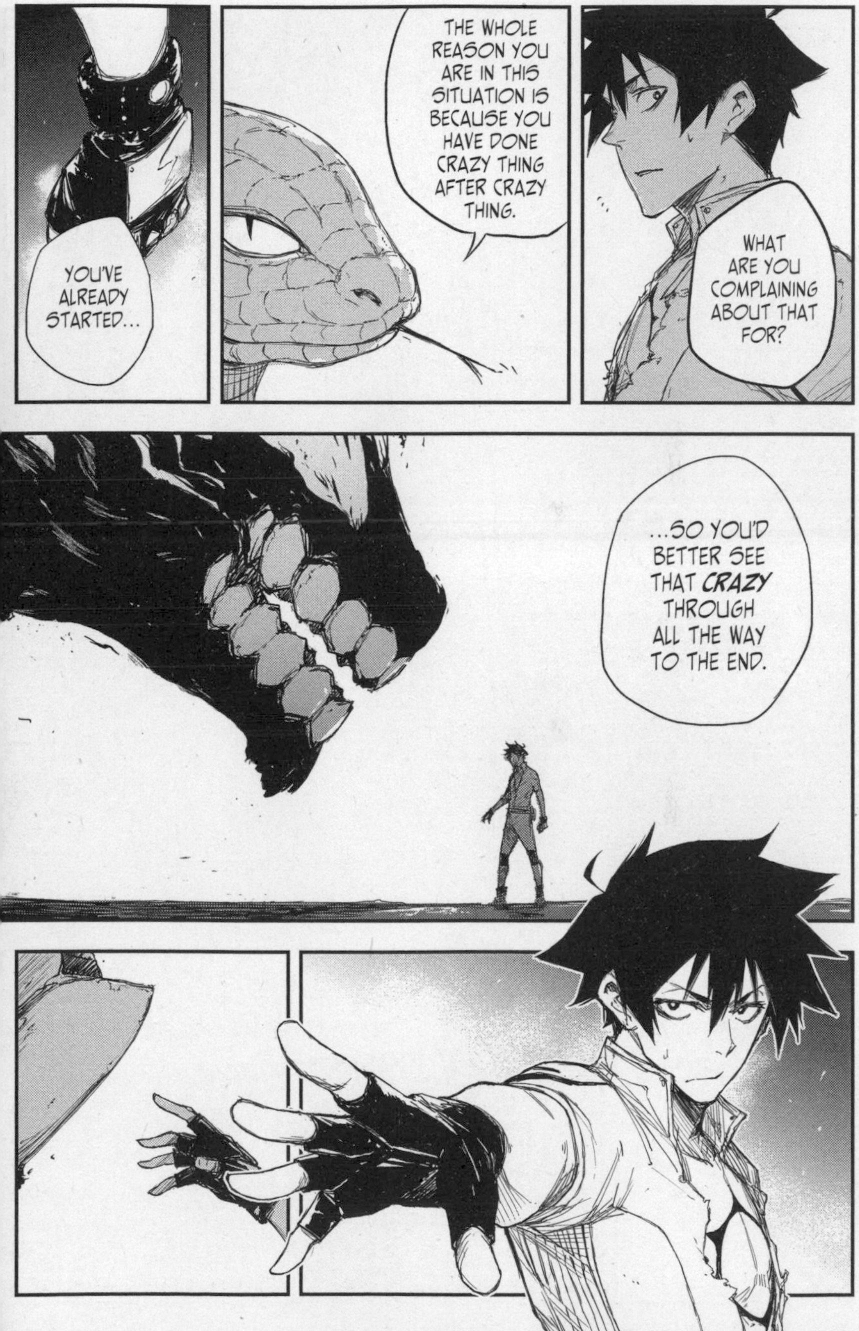
WHAT ARE YOU COMPLAINING ABOUT THAT FOR?
THE WHOLE REASON YOU ARE IN THIS SITUATION IS BECAUSE YOU HAVE DONE CRAZY THING AFTER CRAZY THING.
YOU'VE ALREADY STARTED...
...SO YOU'D BETTER SEE THAT ***CRAZY*** THROUGH ALL THE WAY TO THE END.

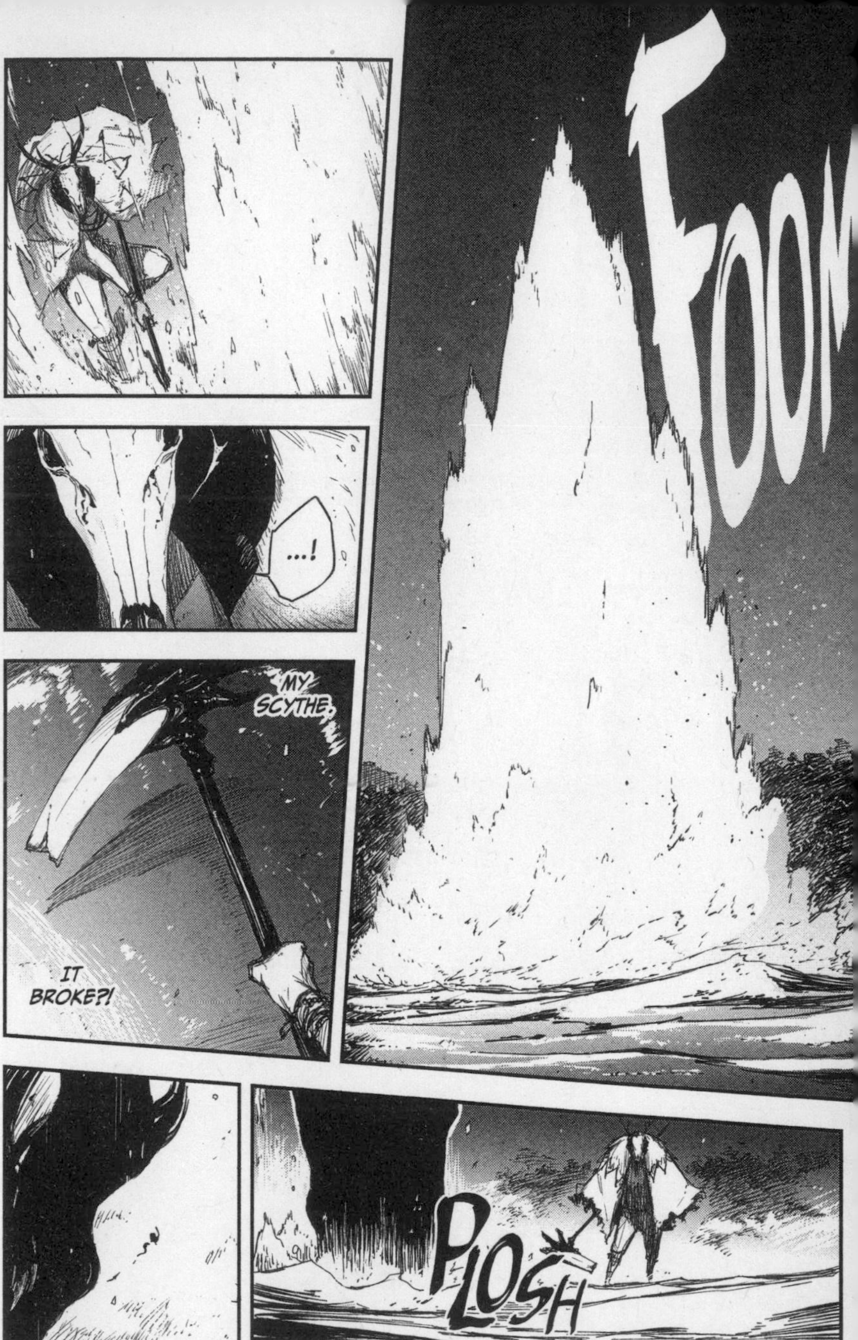
FOOM
...!
MY SCYTHE,
IT BROKE?!
PLOSH

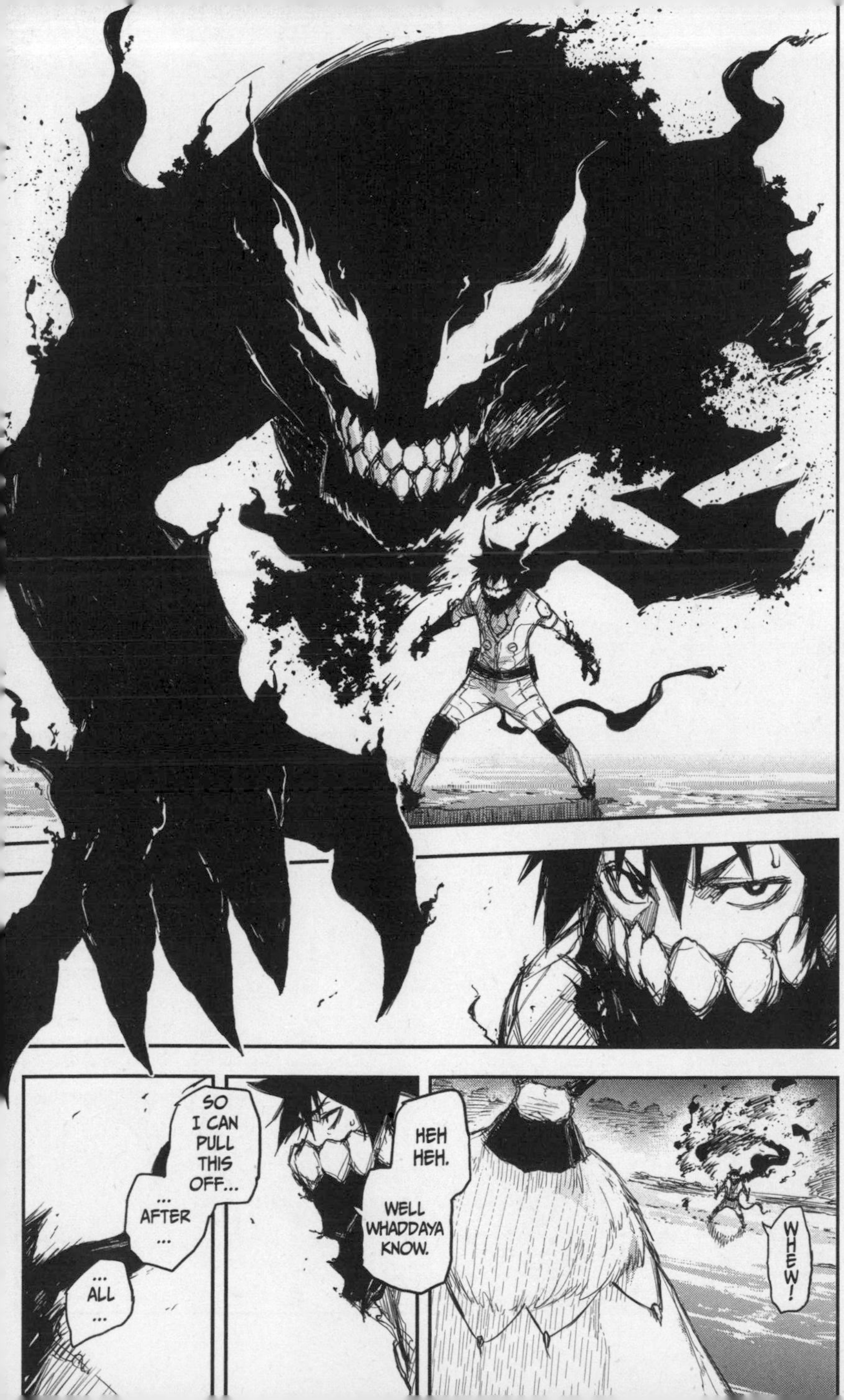
WHEW!
HEH HEH.
WELL WHADDAYA KNOW.
SO I CAN PULL THIS OFF...
...AFTER...
...ALL...

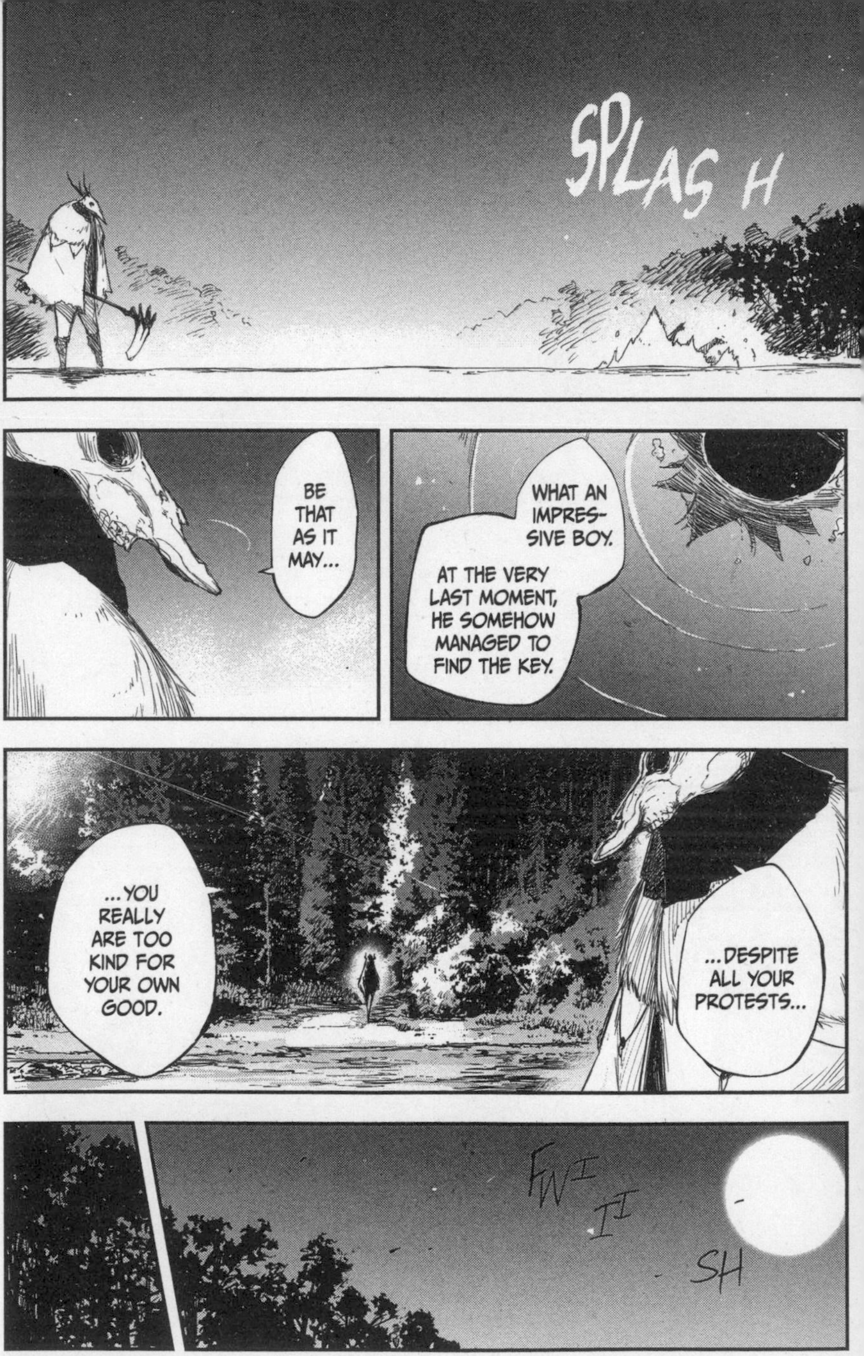
SPLASH
WHAT AN IMPRESSIVE BOY.
AT THE VERY LAST MOMENT, HE SOMEHOW MANAGED TO FIND THE KEY.
BE THAT AS IT MAY...
...DESPITE ALL YOUR PROTESTS...
...YOU REALLY ARE TOO KIND FOR YOUR OWN GOOD.
FWIISH

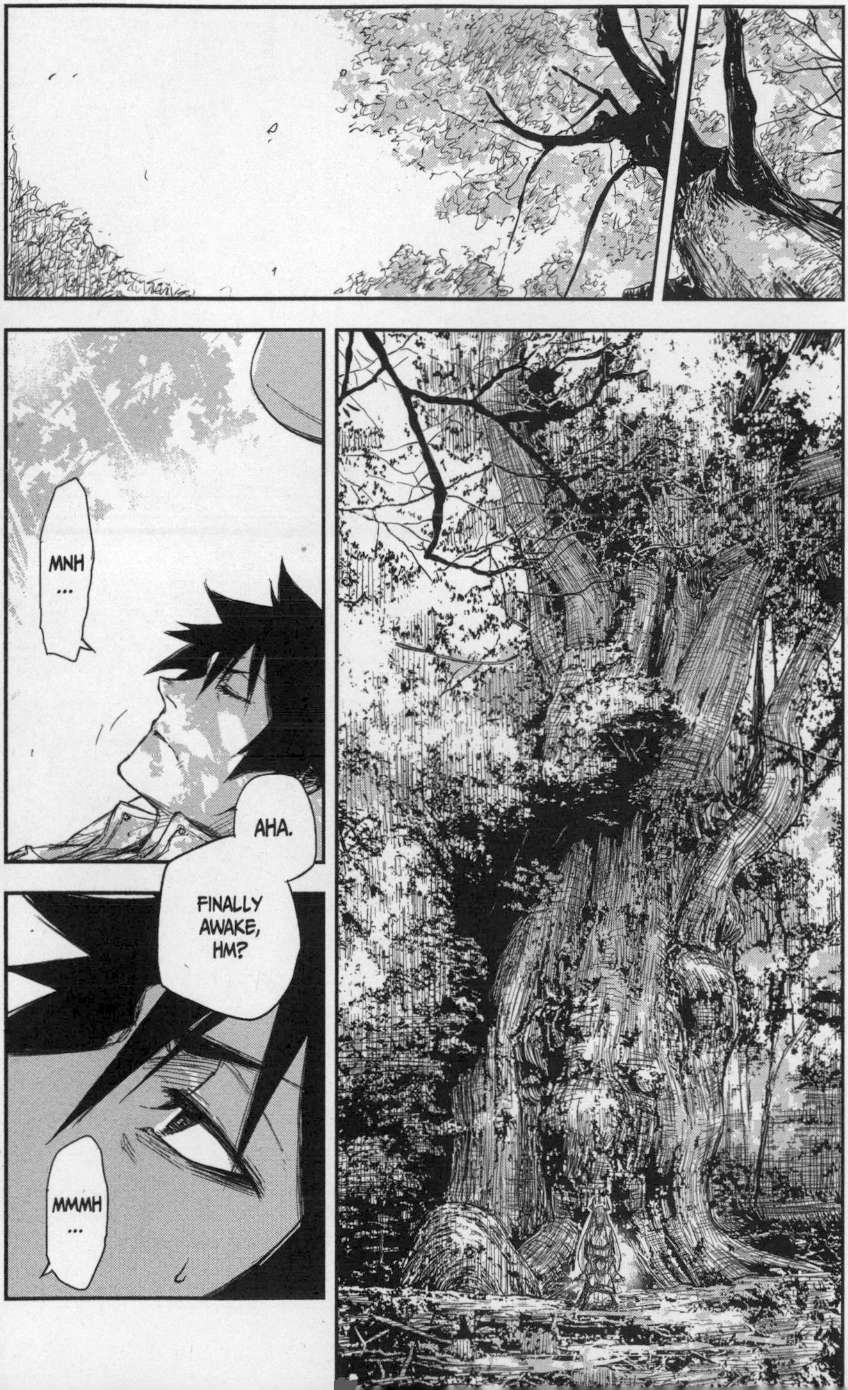
MNH ...
AHA.
FINALLY AWAKE, HM?
MMMH ...

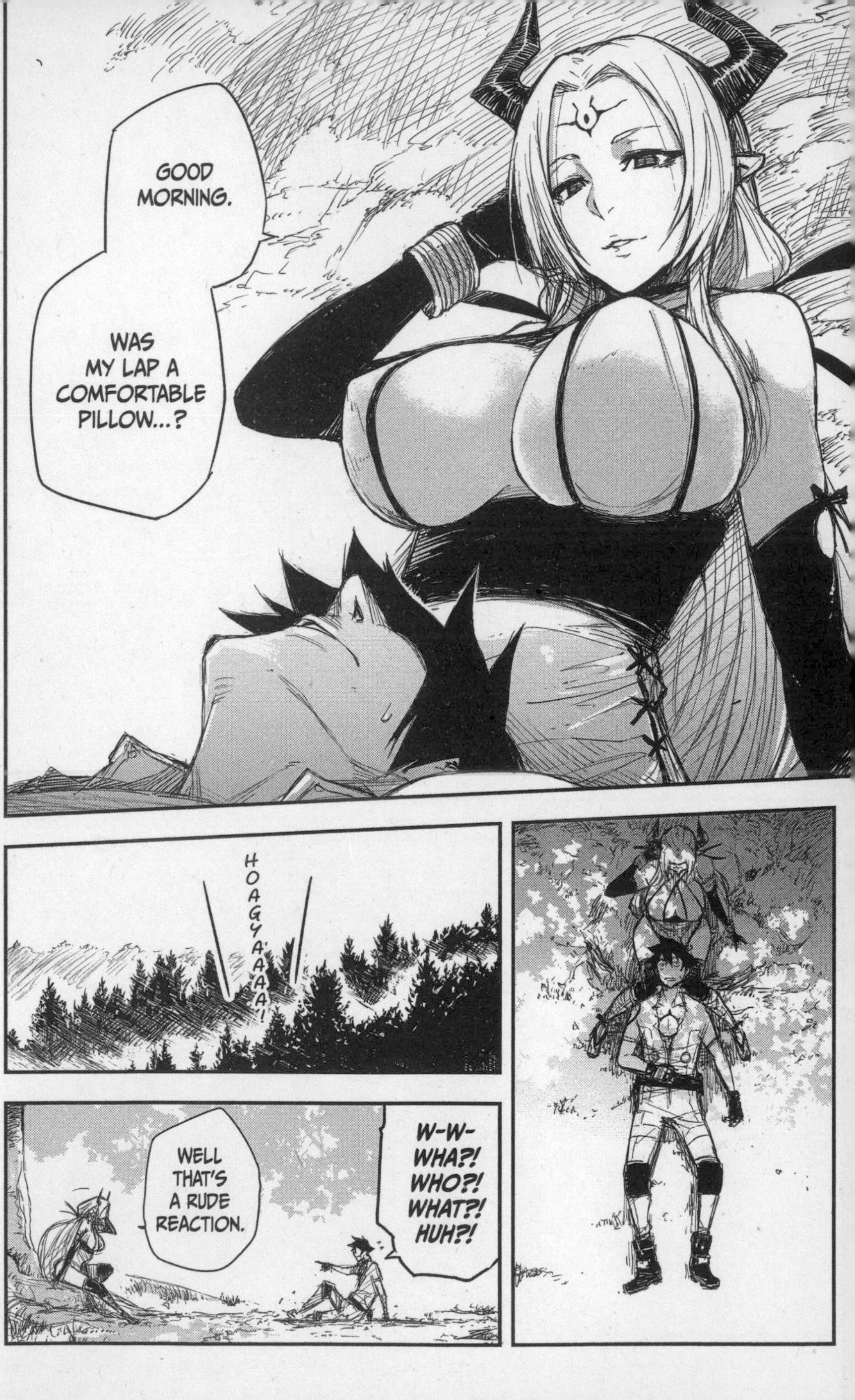
GOOD MORNING.
WAS MY LAP A COMFORTABLE PILLOW...?
HOAGYAAAA!
W-W-WHA?! WHO?! WHAT?! HUH?!
WELL THAT'S A RUDE REACTION.

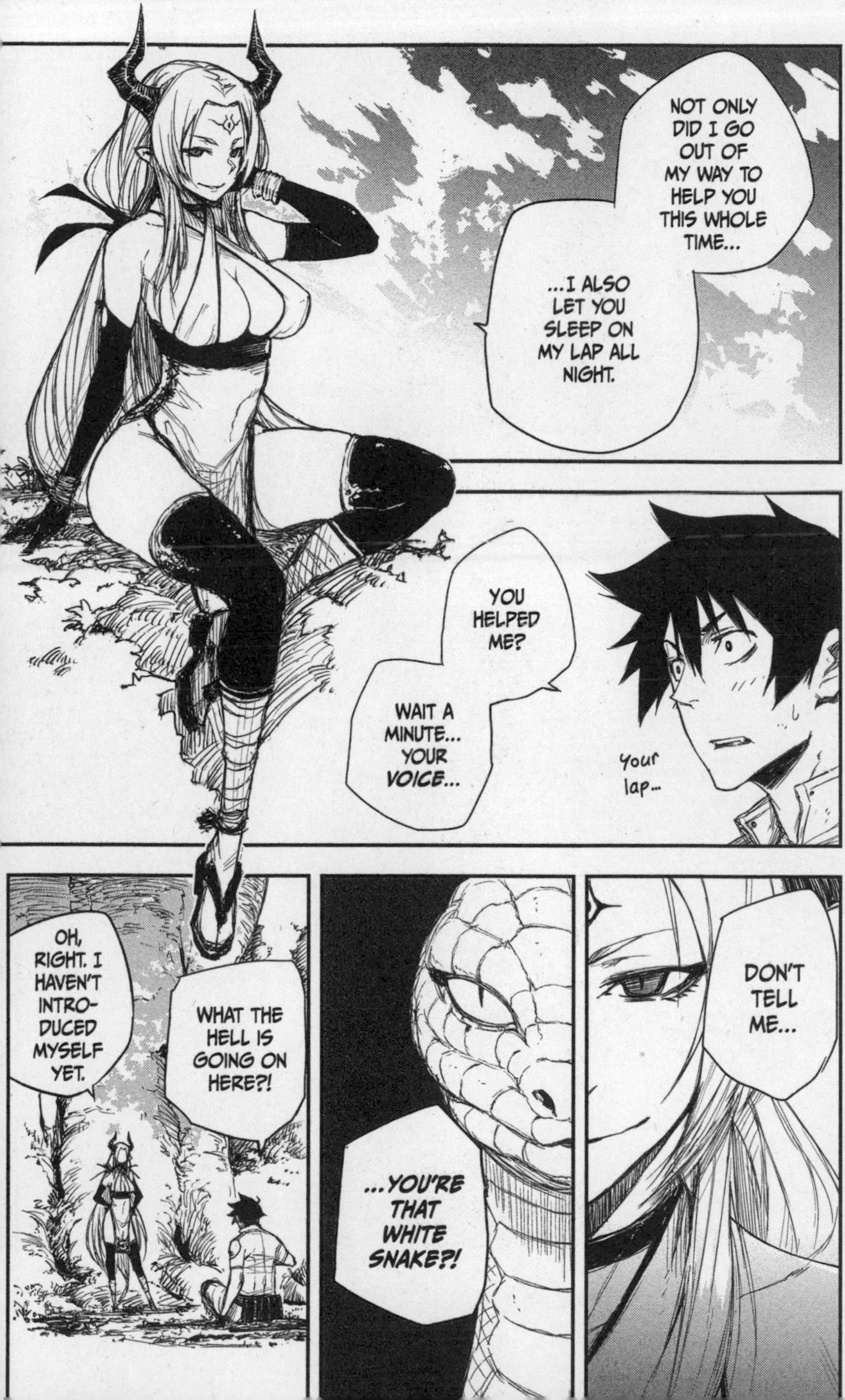
NOT ONLY DID I GO OUT OF MY WAY TO HELP YOU THIS WHOLE TIME...
...I ALSO LET YOU SLEEP ON MY LAP ALL NIGHT.
YOU HELPED ME?
Your lap...
WAIT A MINUTE... YOUR VOICE...
DON'T TELL ME...
...YOU'RE THAT WHITE SNAKE?!
WHAT THE HELL IS GOING ON HERE?!
OH, RIGHT. I HAVEN'T INTRODUCED MYSELF YET.

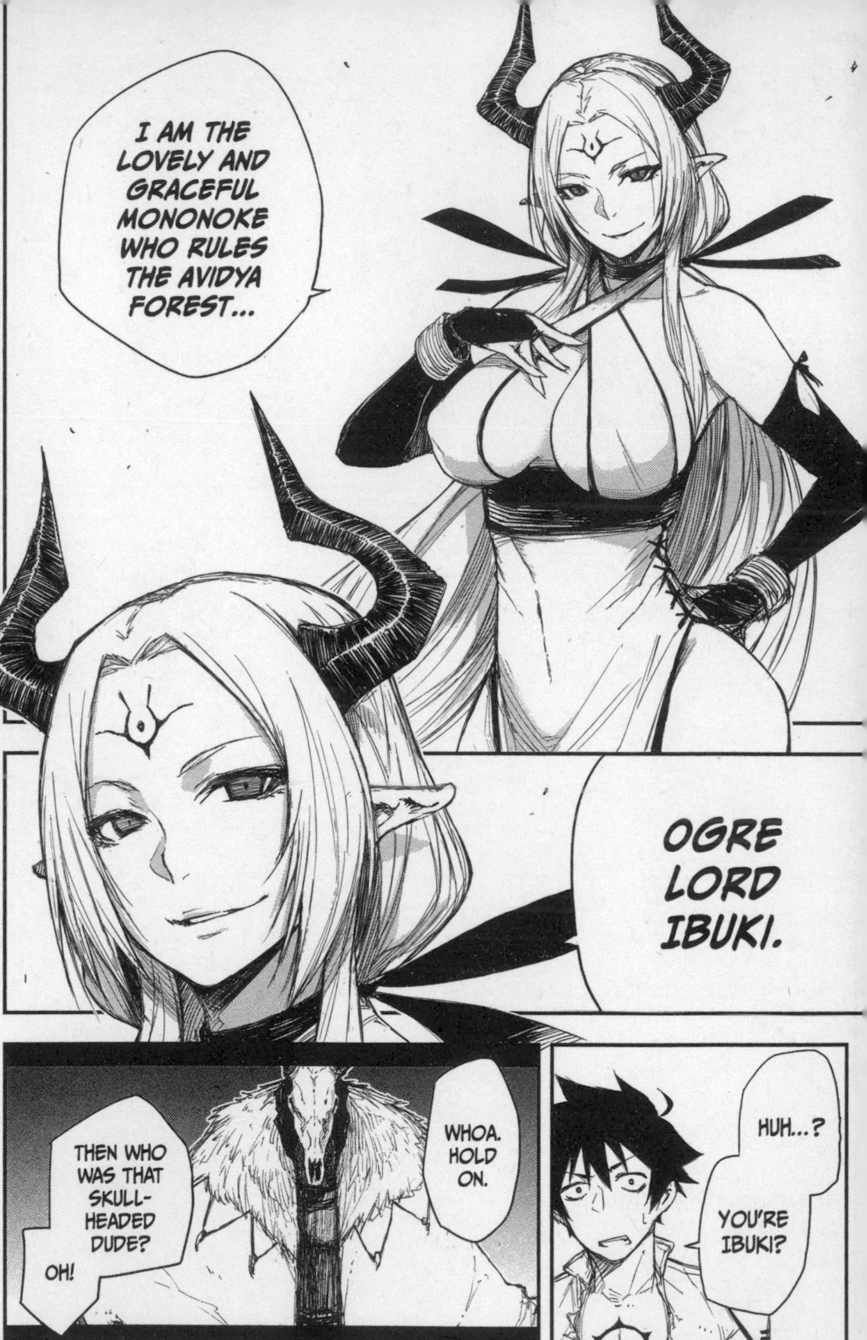
I AM THE LOVELY AND GRACEFUL MONONOKE WHO RULES THE AVIDYA FOREST...
OGRE LORD IBUKI.
HUH...?
YOU'RE IBUKI?
WHOA. HOLD ON.
THEN WHO WAS THAT SKULL-HEADED DUDE?
OH!

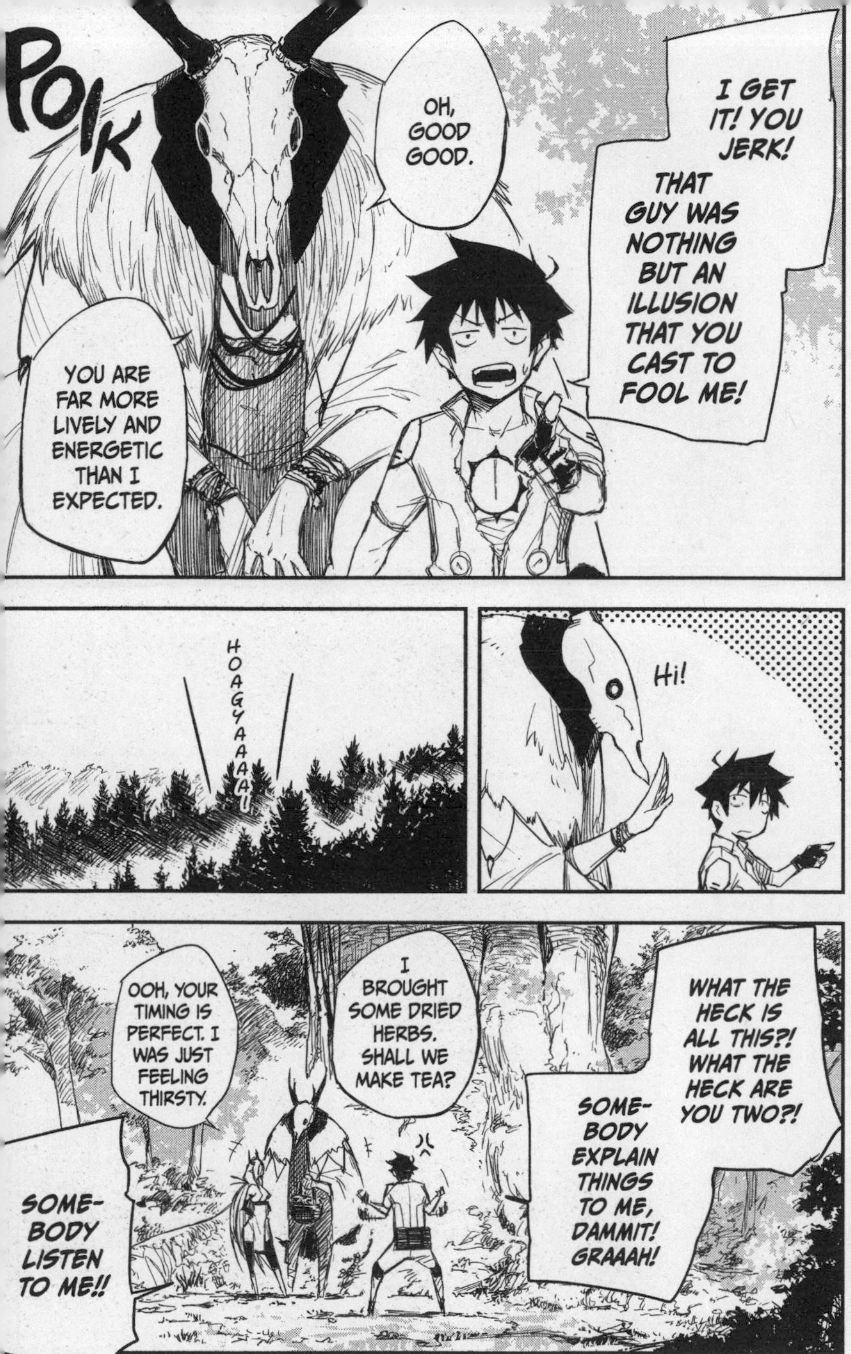
I GET IT! YOU JERK!
THAT GUY WAS NOTHING BUT AN ILLUSION THAT YOU CAST TO FOOL ME!
OH, GOOD GOOD.
POK
YOU ARE FAR MORE LIVELY AND ENERGETIC THAN I EXPECTED.
Hi!
HOAGYAAAAA!!
WHAT THE HECK IS ALL THIS?! WHAT THE HECK ARE YOU TWO?!
SOME-BODY EXPLAIN THINGS TO ME, DAMMIT! GRAAAH!
I BROUGHT SOME DRIED HERBS. SHALL WE MAKE TEA?
OOH, YOUR TIMING IS PERFECT. I WAS JUST FEELING THIRSTY.
SOME-BODY LISTEN TO ME!!

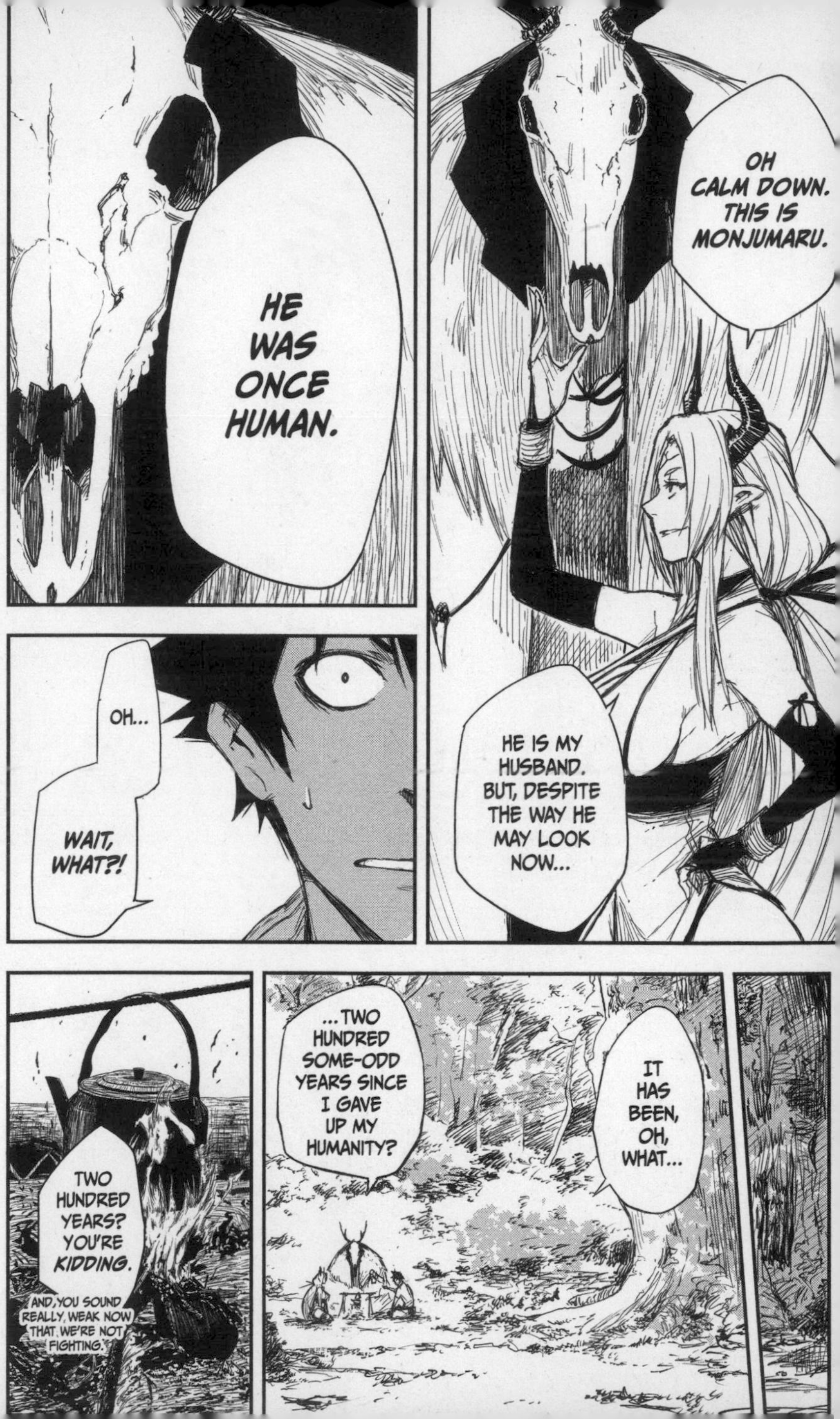
OH CALM DOWN. THIS IS MONJUMARU.
HE IS MY HUSBAND. BUT, DESPITE THE WAY HE MAY LOOK NOW...
HE WAS ONCE HUMAN.
OH...
WAIT, WHAT?!
IT HAS BEEN, OH, WHAT...
...TWO HUNDRED SOME-ODD YEARS SINCE I GAVE UP MY HUMANITY?
TWO HUNDRED YEARS? YOU'RE KIDDING.
AND YOU SOUND REALLY WEAK NOW THAT WE'RE NOT FIGHTING.

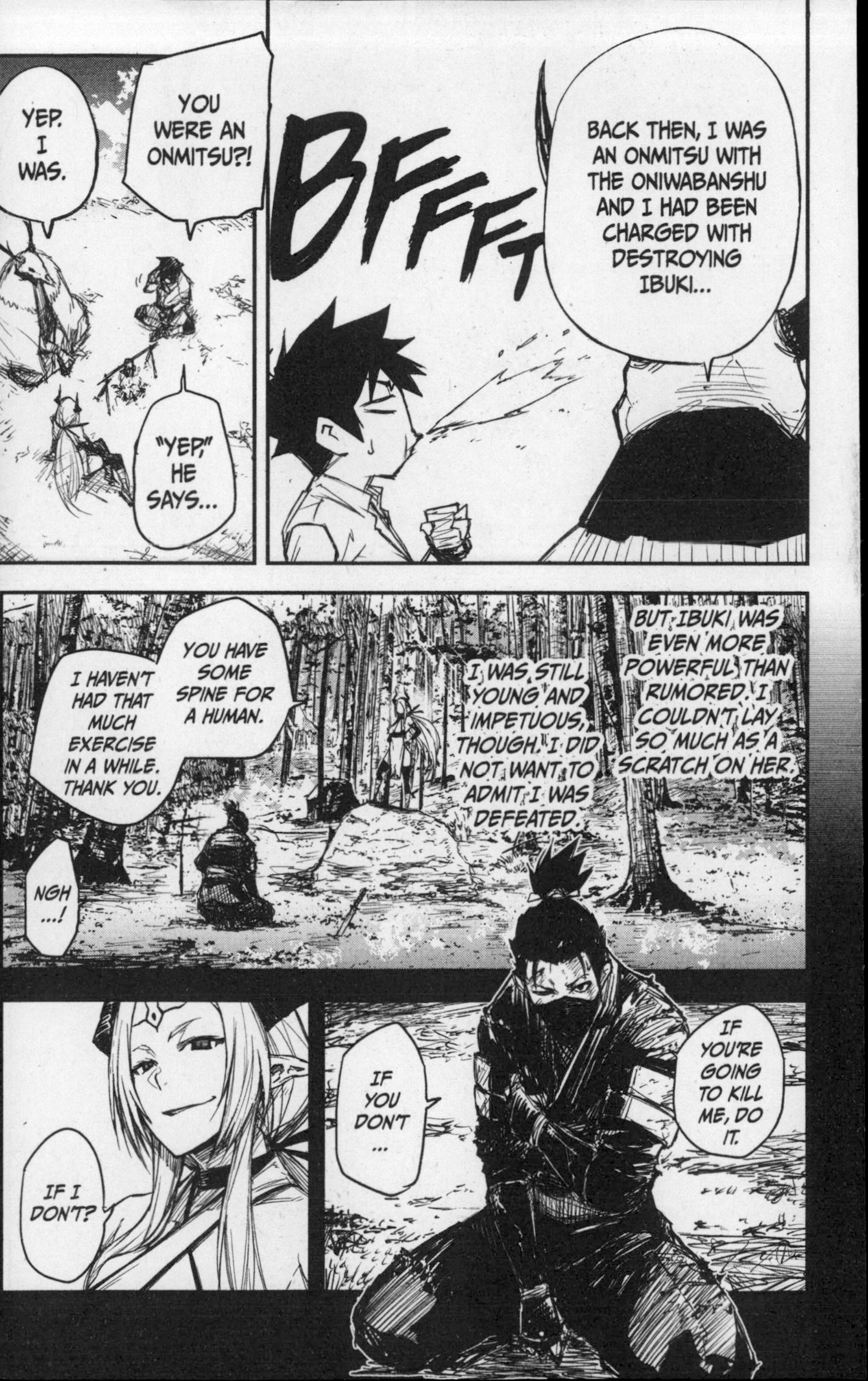
BACK THEN, I WAS AN ONMITSU WITH THE ONIWABANSHU AND I HAD BEEN CHARGED WITH DESTROYING IBUKI...
BFFFT
YOU WERE AN ONMITSU?!
YEP. I WAS.
"YEP," HE SAYS...
BUT IBUKI WAS EVEN MORE POWERFUL THAN RUMORED. I COULDN'T LAY SO MUCH AS A SCRATCH ON HER.
I WAS STILL YOUNG AND IMPETUOUS, THOUGH. I DID NOT WANT TO ADMIT I WAS DEFEATED.
YOU HAVE SOME SPINE FOR A HUMAN.
I HAVEN'T HAD THAT MUCH EXERCISE IN A WHILE. THANK YOU.
NGH ...!
IF YOU'RE GOING TO KILL ME, DO IT.
IF YOU DON'T ...
IF I DON'T?

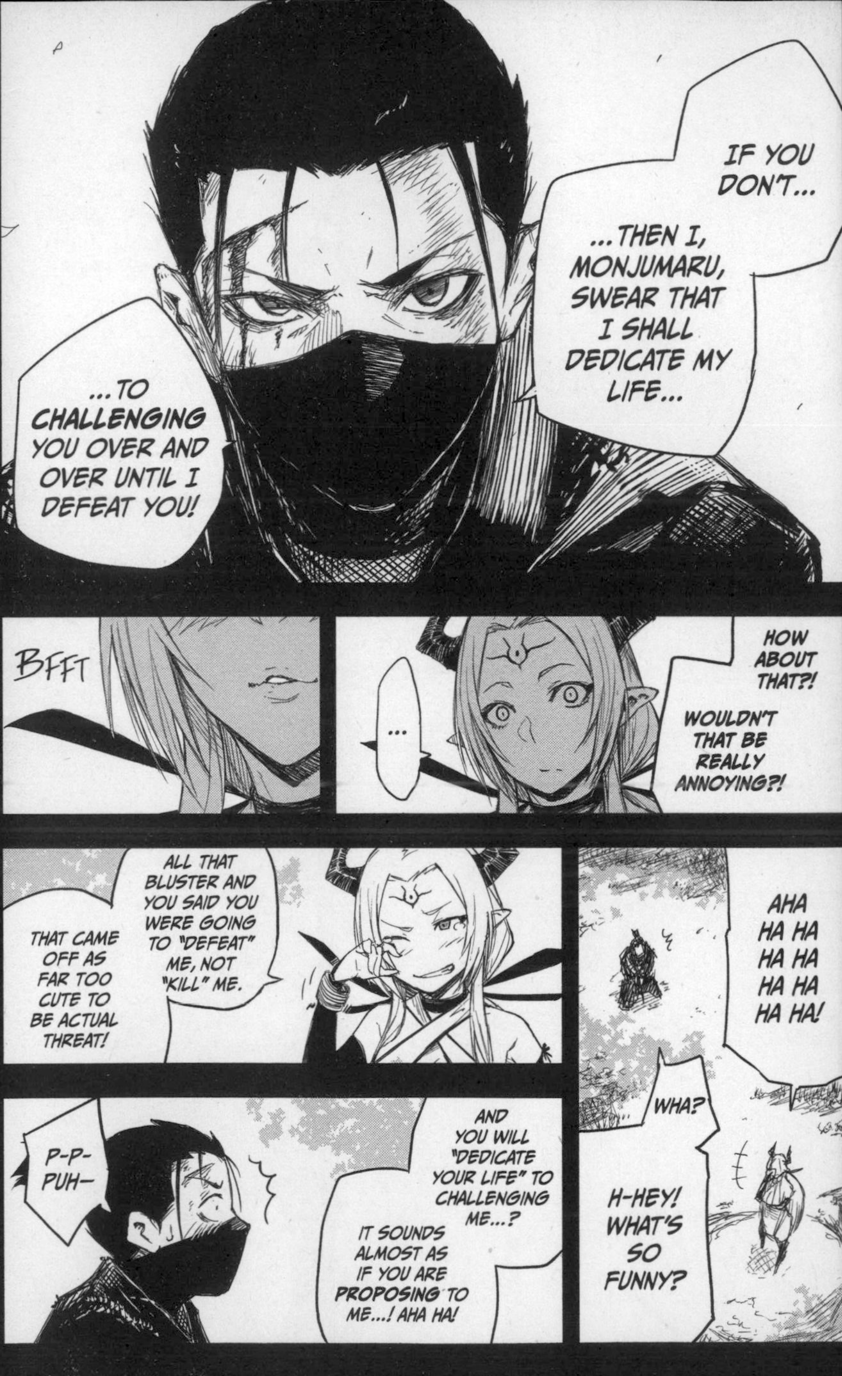
IF YOU DON'T...
...THEN I, MONJUMARU, SWEAR THAT I SHALL DEDICATE MY LIFE...
...TO CHALLENGING YOU OVER AND OVER UNTIL I DEFEAT YOU!
HOW ABOUT THAT?!
WOULDN'T THAT BE REALLY ANNOYING?!
...
BFFT
AHA HA HA HA HA HA HA HA HA!
WHA?
H-HEY! WHAT'S SO FUNNY?
ALL THAT BLUSTER AND YOU SAID YOU WERE GOING TO "DEFEAT" ME, NOT "KILL" ME.
THAT CAME OFF AS FAR TOO CUTE TO BE ACTUAL THREAT!
AND YOU WILL "DEDICATE YOUR LIFE" TO CHALLENGING ME...?
IT SOUNDS ALMOST AS IF YOU ARE PROPOSING TO ME...! AHA HA!
P-P-PUH—

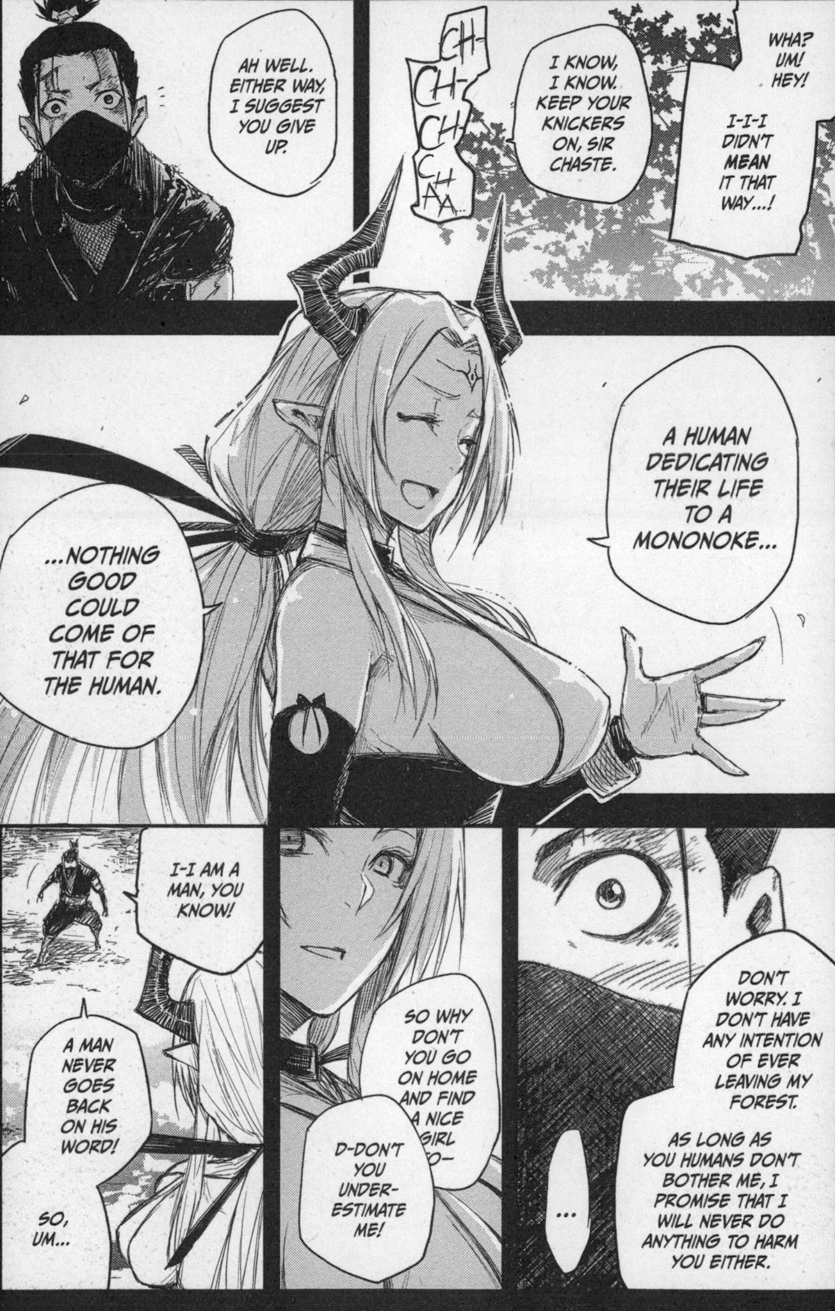
WHA? UM! HEY!
I-I-I DIDN'T MEAN IT THAT WAY...!
I KNOW, I KNOW. KEEP YOUR KNICKERS ON, SIR CHASTE.
CH-CH-CH-CHAA...
AH WELL. EITHER WAY, I SUGGEST YOU GIVE UP.
A HUMAN DEDICATING THEIR LIFE TO A MONONOKE...
...NOTHING GOOD COULD COME OF THAT FOR THE HUMAN.
DON'T WORRY. I DON'T HAVE ANY INTENTION OF EVER LEAVING MY FOREST.
AS LONG AS YOU HUMANS DON'T BOTHER ME, I PROMISE THAT I WILL NEVER DO ANYTHING TO HARM YOU EITHER.
...
SO WHY DON'T YOU GO ON HOME AND FIND A NICE GIRL TO—
D-DON'T YOU UNDER-ESTIMATE ME!
I-I AM A MAN, YOU KNOW!
A MAN NEVER GOES BACK ON HIS WORD!
SO, UM...

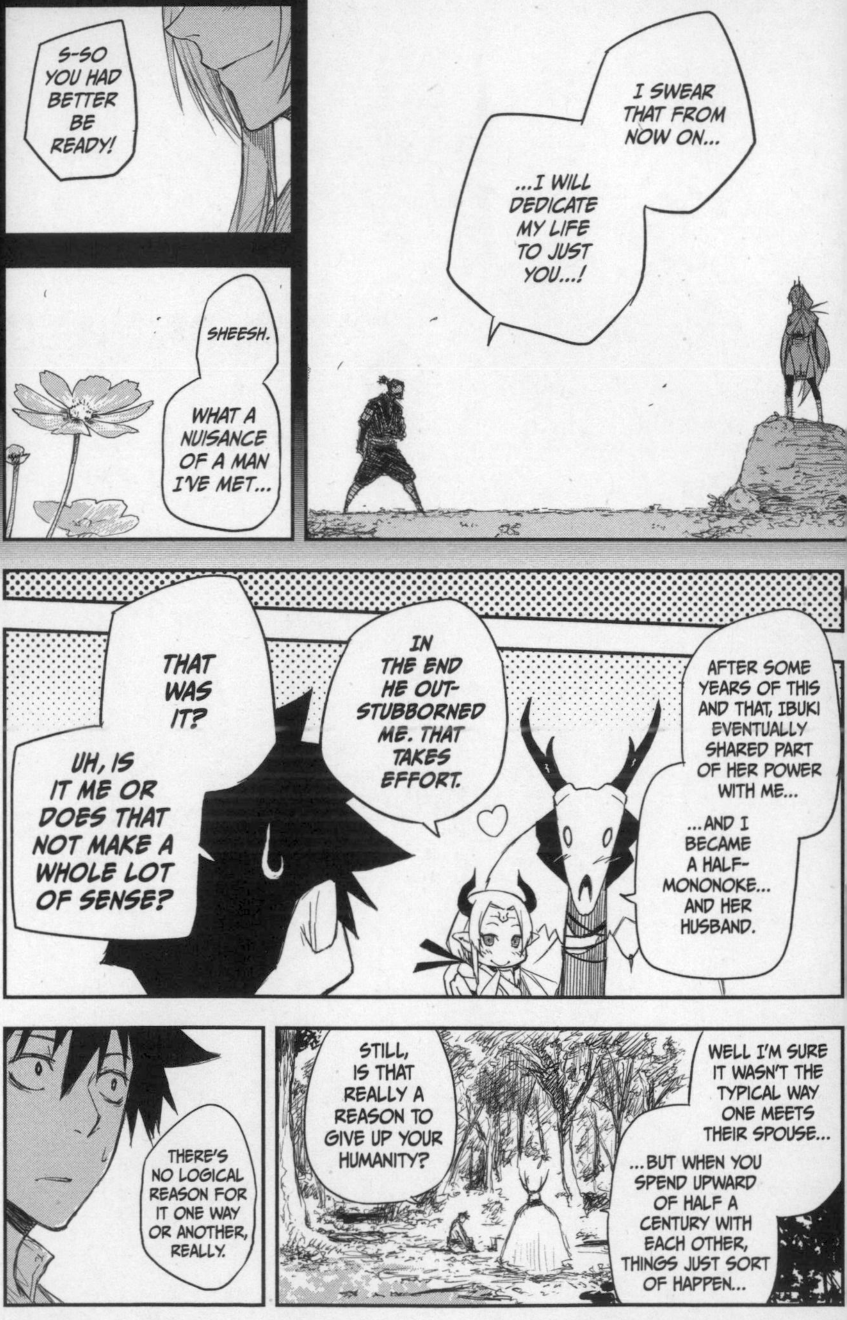
I SWEAR THAT FROM NOW ON...
...I WILL DEDICATE MY LIFE TO JUST YOU...!
S-SO YOU HAD BETTER BE READY!
SHEESH.
WHAT A NUISANCE OF A MAN I'VE MET...
AFTER SOME YEARS OF THIS AND THAT, IBUKI EVENTUALLY SHARED PART OF HER POWER WITH ME...
...AND I BECAME A HALF-MONONOKE... AND HER HUSBAND.
IN THE END HE OUT-STUBBORNED ME. THAT TAKES EFFORT.
THAT WAS IT?
UH, IS IT ME OR DOES THAT NOT MAKE A WHOLE LOT OF SENSE?
WELL I'M SURE IT WASN'T THE TYPICAL WAY ONE MEETS THEIR SPOUSE...
...BUT WHEN YOU SPEND UPWARD OF HALF A CENTURY WITH EACH OTHER, THINGS JUST SORT OF HAPPEN...
STILL, IS THAT REALLY A REASON TO GIVE UP YOUR HUMANITY?
THERE'S NO LOGICAL REASON FOR IT ONE WAY OR ANOTHER, REALLY.

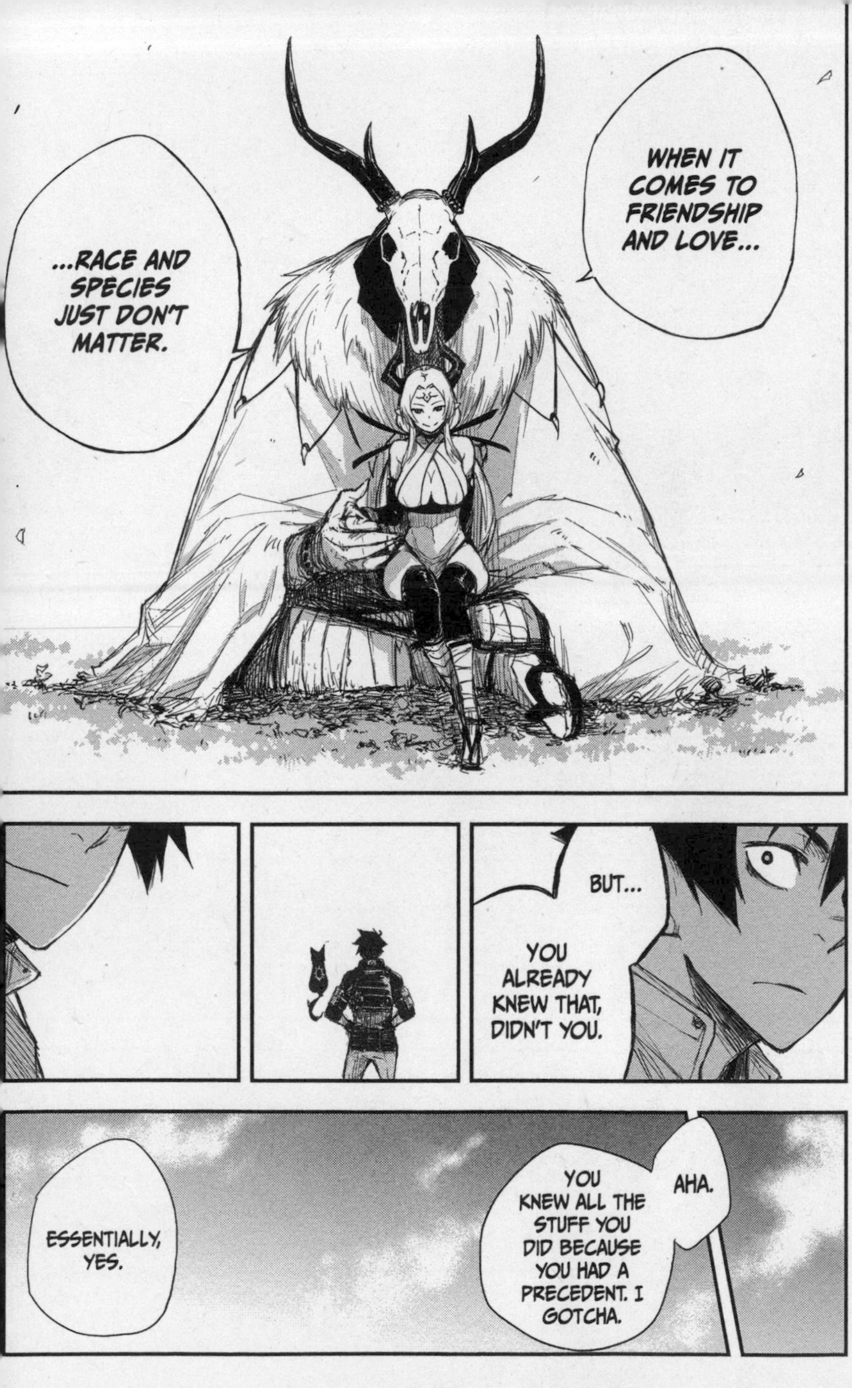
WHEN IT COMES TO FRIENDSHIP AND LOVE...
...RACE AND SPECIES JUST DON'T MATTER.
BUT...
YOU ALREADY KNEW THAT, DIDN'T YOU.
AHA.
YOU KNEW ALL THE STUFF YOU DID BECAUSE YOU HAD A PRECEDENT. I GOTCHA.
ESSENTIALLY, YES.

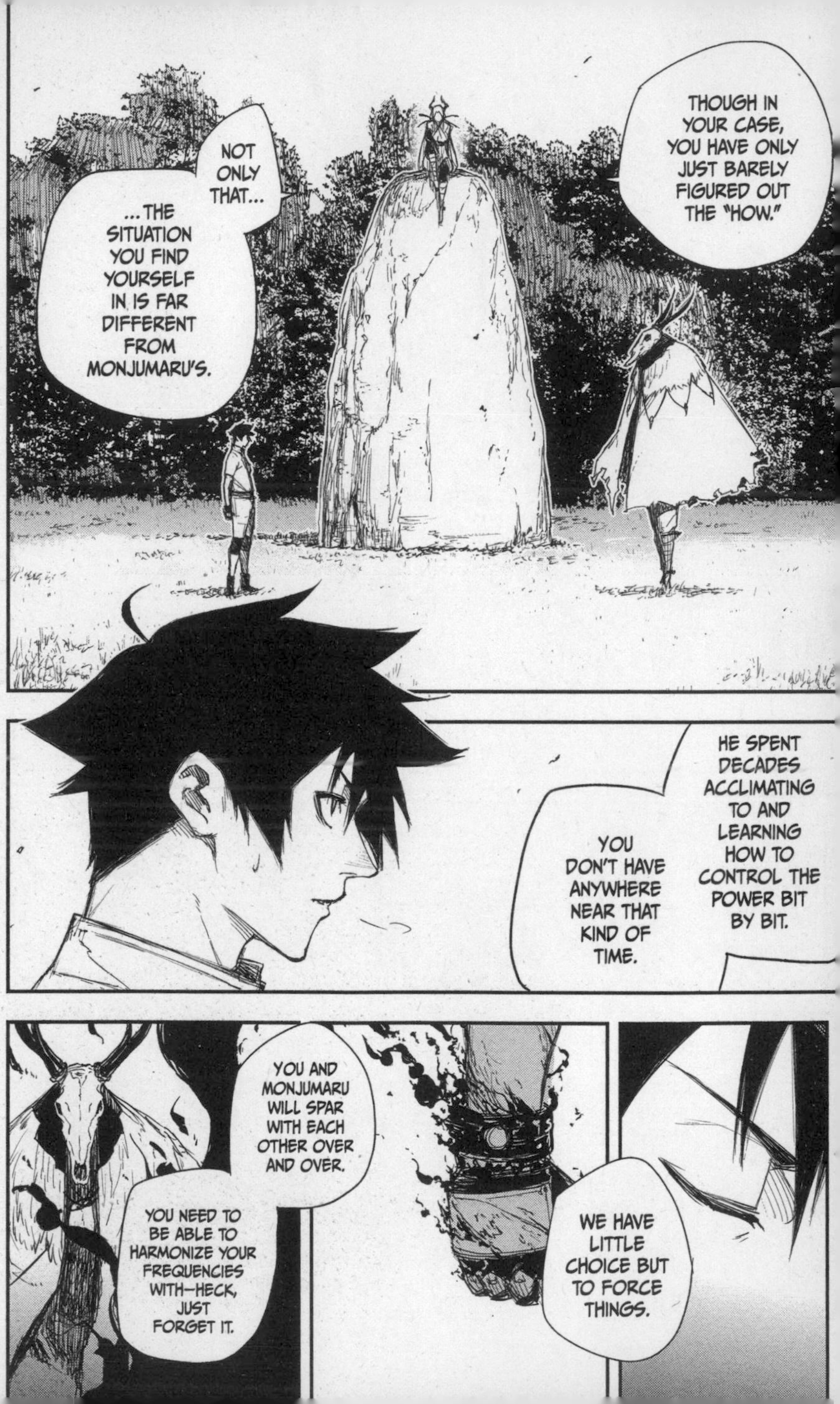
THOUGH IN YOUR CASE, YOU HAVE ONLY JUST BARELY FIGURED OUT THE "HOW."
NOT ONLY THAT...
...THE SITUATION YOU FIND YOURSELF IN IS FAR DIFFERENT FROM MONJUMARU'S.
HE SPENT DECADES ACCLIMATING TO AND LEARNING HOW TO CONTROL THE POWER BIT BY BIT.
YOU DON'T HAVE ANYWHERE NEAR THAT KIND OF TIME.
WE HAVE LITTLE CHOICE BUT TO FORCE THINGS.
YOU AND MONJUMARU WILL SPAR WITH EACH OTHER OVER AND OVER.
YOU NEED TO BE ABLE TO HARMONIZE YOUR FREQUENCIES WITH—HECK, JUST FORGET IT.

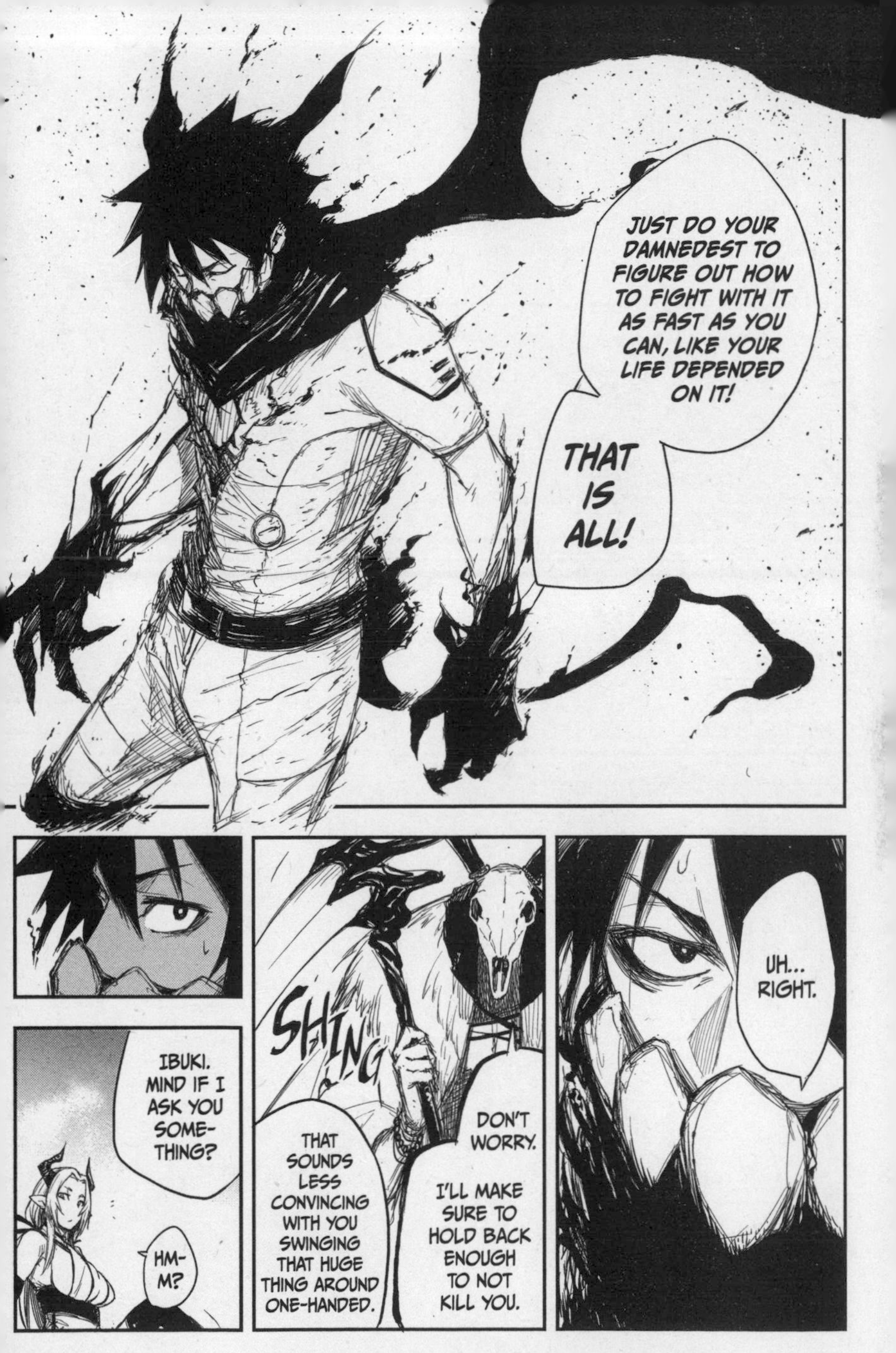
JUST DO YOUR DAMNEDEST TO FIGURE OUT HOW TO FIGHT WITH IT AS FAST AS YOU CAN, LIKE YOUR LIFE DEPENDED ON IT!
THAT IS ALL!
UH... RIGHT.
SHING
DON'T WORRY.
I'LL MAKE SURE TO HOLD BACK ENOUGH TO NOT KILL YOU.
THAT SOUNDS LESS CONVINCING WITH YOU SWINGING THAT HUGE THING AROUND ONE-HANDED.
IBUKI. MIND IF I ASK YOU SOMETHING?
HM-M?

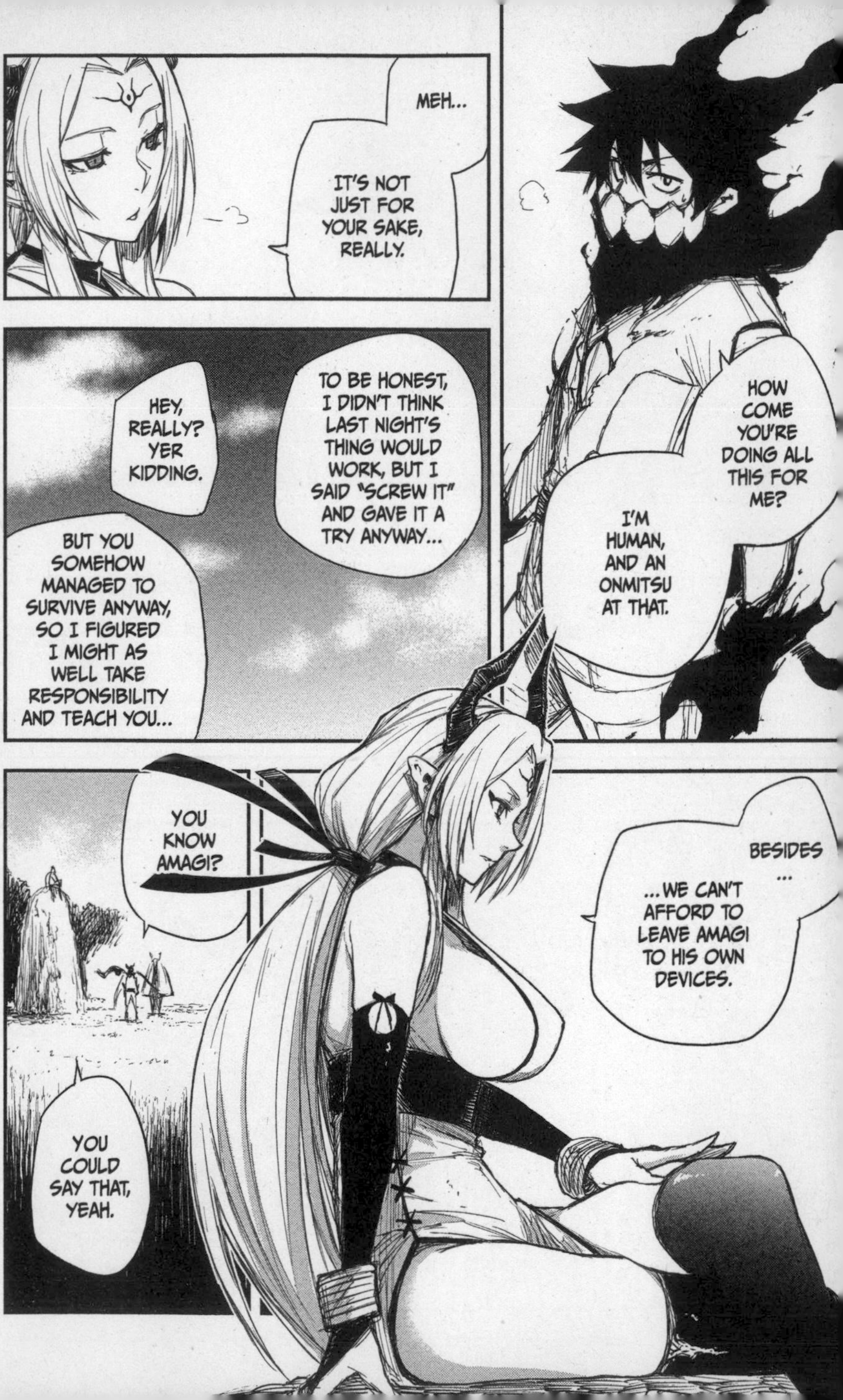
HOW COME YOU'RE DOING ALL THIS FOR ME?
I'M HUMAN, AND AN ONMITSU AT THAT.
MEH...
IT'S NOT JUST FOR YOUR SAKE, REALLY.
TO BE HONEST, I DIDN'T THINK LAST NIGHT'S THING WOULD WORK, BUT I SAID "SCREW IT" AND GAVE IT A TRY ANYWAY...
HEY, REALLY? YER KIDDING.
BUT YOU SOMEHOW MANAGED TO SURVIVE ANYWAY, SO I FIGURED I MIGHT AS WELL TAKE RESPONSIBILITY AND TEACH YOU...
BESIDES...
...WE CAN'T AFFORD TO LEAVE AMAGI TO HIS OWN DEVICES.
YOU KNOW AMAGI?
YOU COULD SAY THAT, YEAH.

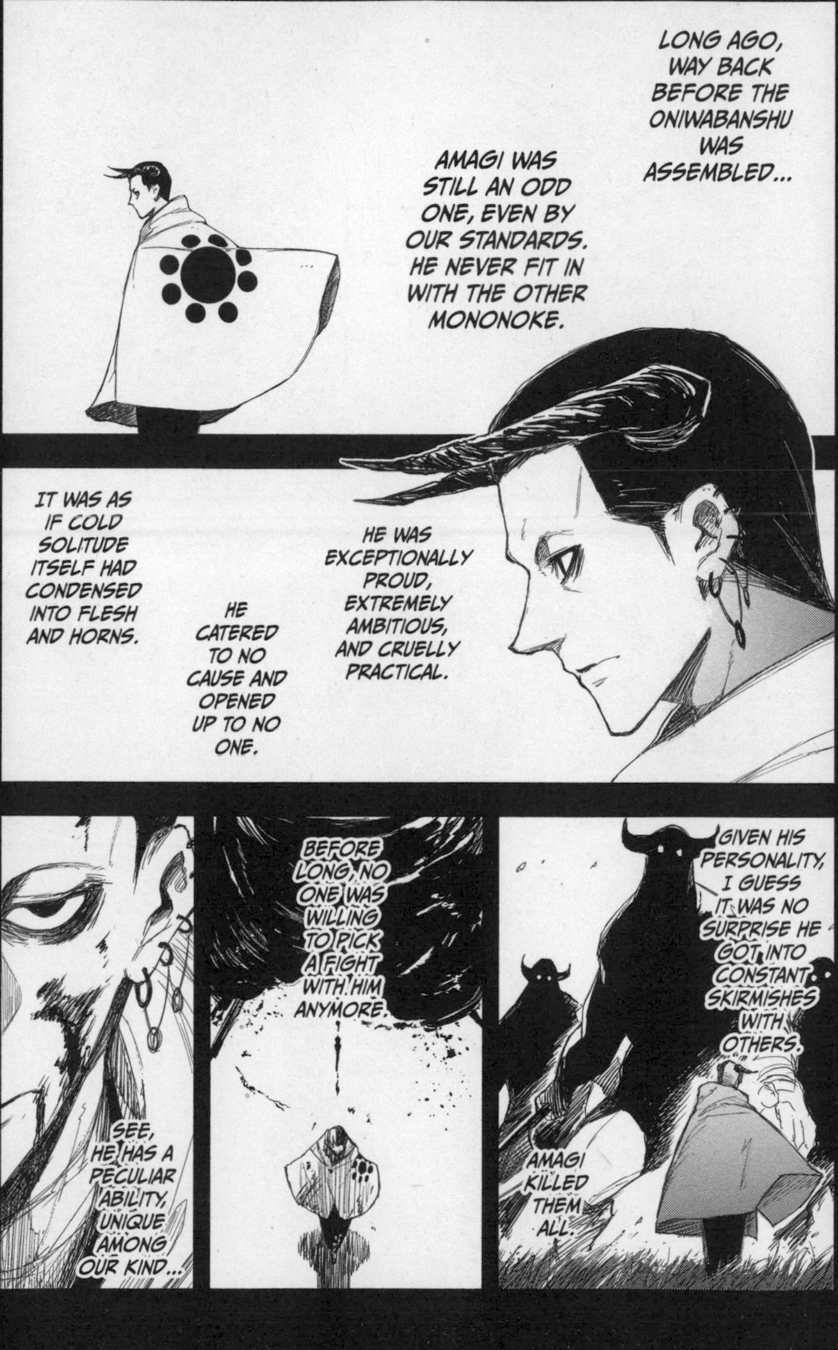

LONG AGO, WAY BACK BEFORE THE ONIWABANSHU WAS ASSEMBLED...
AMAGI WAS STILL AN ODD ONE, EVEN BY OUR STANDARDS. HE NEVER FIT IN WITH THE OTHER MONONOKE.
HE WAS EXCEPTIONALLY PROUD, EXTREMELY AMBITIOUS, AND CRUELLY PRACTICAL.
HE CATERED TO NO CAUSE AND OPENED UP TO NO ONE.
IT WAS AS IF COLD SOLITUDE ITSELF HAD CONDENSED INTO FLESH AND HORNS.
GIVEN HIS PERSONALITY, I GUESS IT WAS NO SURPRISE HE GOT INTO CONSTANT SKIRMISHES WITH OTHERS.
AMAGI KILLED THEM ALL.
BEFORE LONG, NO ONE WAS WILLING TO PICK A FIGHT WITH HIM ANYMORE.
SEE, HE HAS A PECULIAR ABILITY, UNIQUE AMONG OUR KIND...

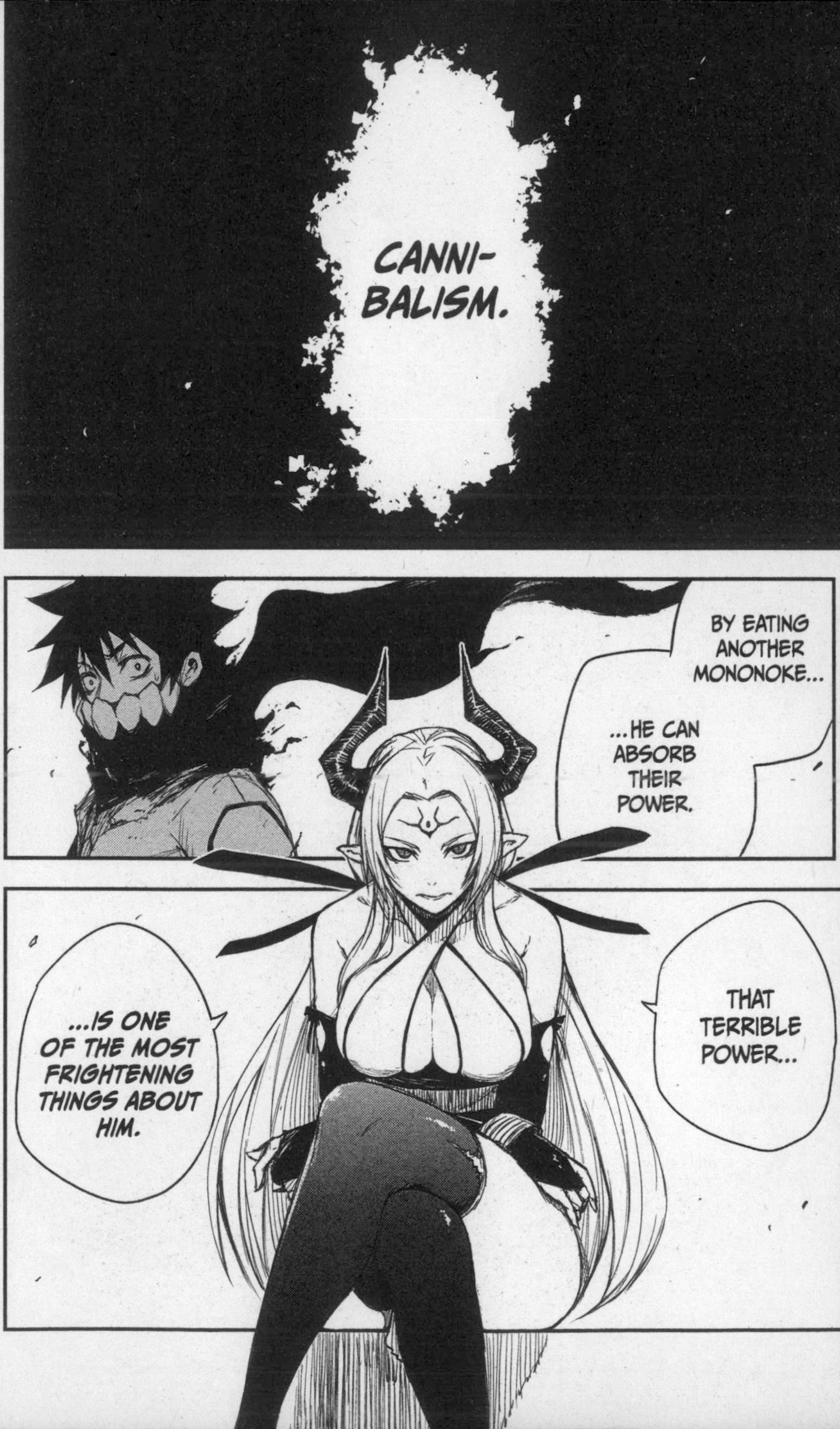
CANNI-
BALISM.
BY EATING ANOTHER MONONOKE...
...HE CAN ABSORB THEIR POWER.
THAT TERRIBLE POWER...
...IS ONE OF THE MOST FRIGHTENING THINGS ABOUT HIM.

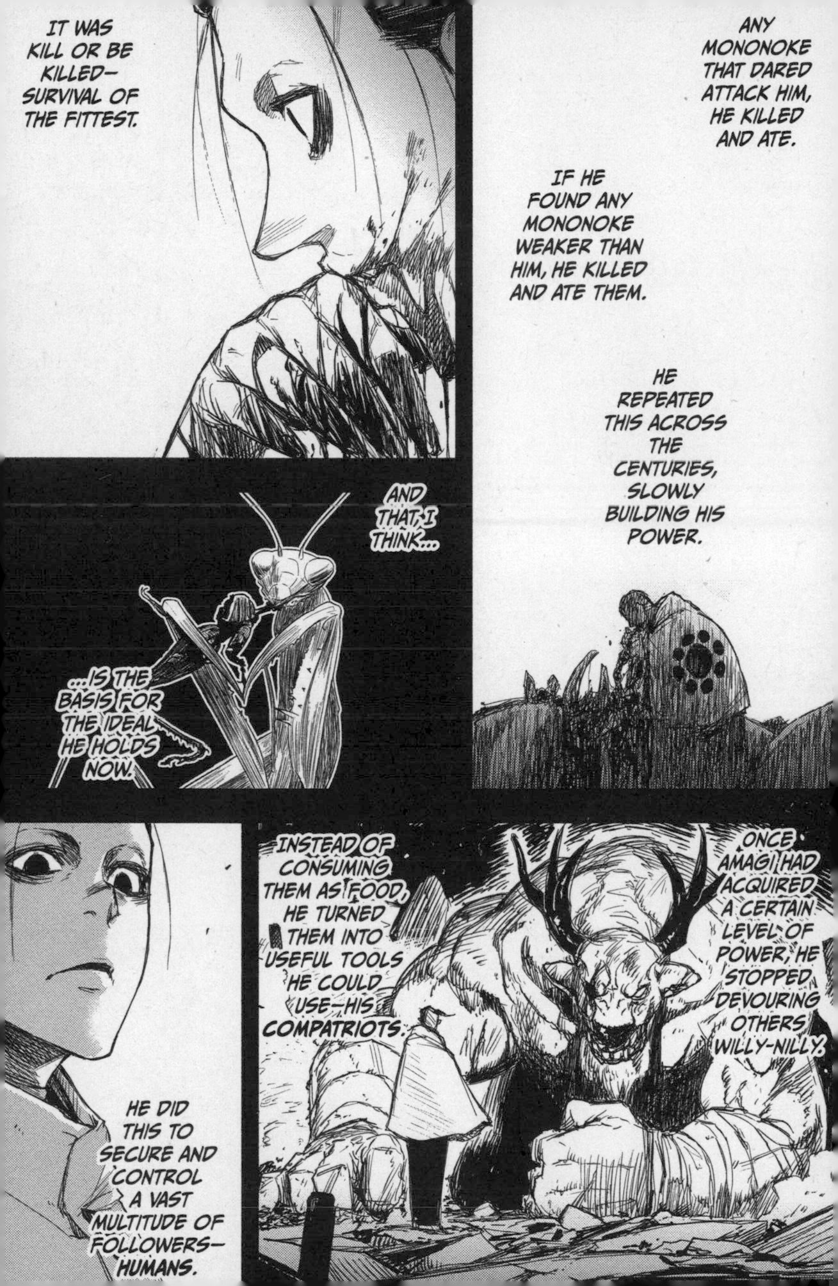
ANY MONONOKE THAT DARED ATTACK HIM, HE KILLED AND ATE.
IF HE FOUND ANY MONONOKE WEAKER THAN HIM, HE KILLED AND ATE THEM.
HE REPEATED THIS ACROSS THE CENTURIES, SLOWLY BUILDING HIS POWER.
IT WAS KILL OR BE KILLED— SURVIVAL OF THE FITTEST.
AND THAT, I THINK...
...IS THE BASIS FOR THE IDEAL HE HOLDS NOW.
ONCE AMAGI HAD ACQUIRED A CERTAIN LEVEL OF POWER, HE STOPPED DEVOURING OTHERS WILLY-NILLY.
INSTEAD OF CONSUMING THEM AS FOOD, HE TURNED THEM INTO USEFUL TOOLS HE COULD USE—HIS COMPATRIOTS.
HE DID THIS TO SECURE AND CONTROL A VAST MULTITUDE OF FOLLOWERS— HUMANS.

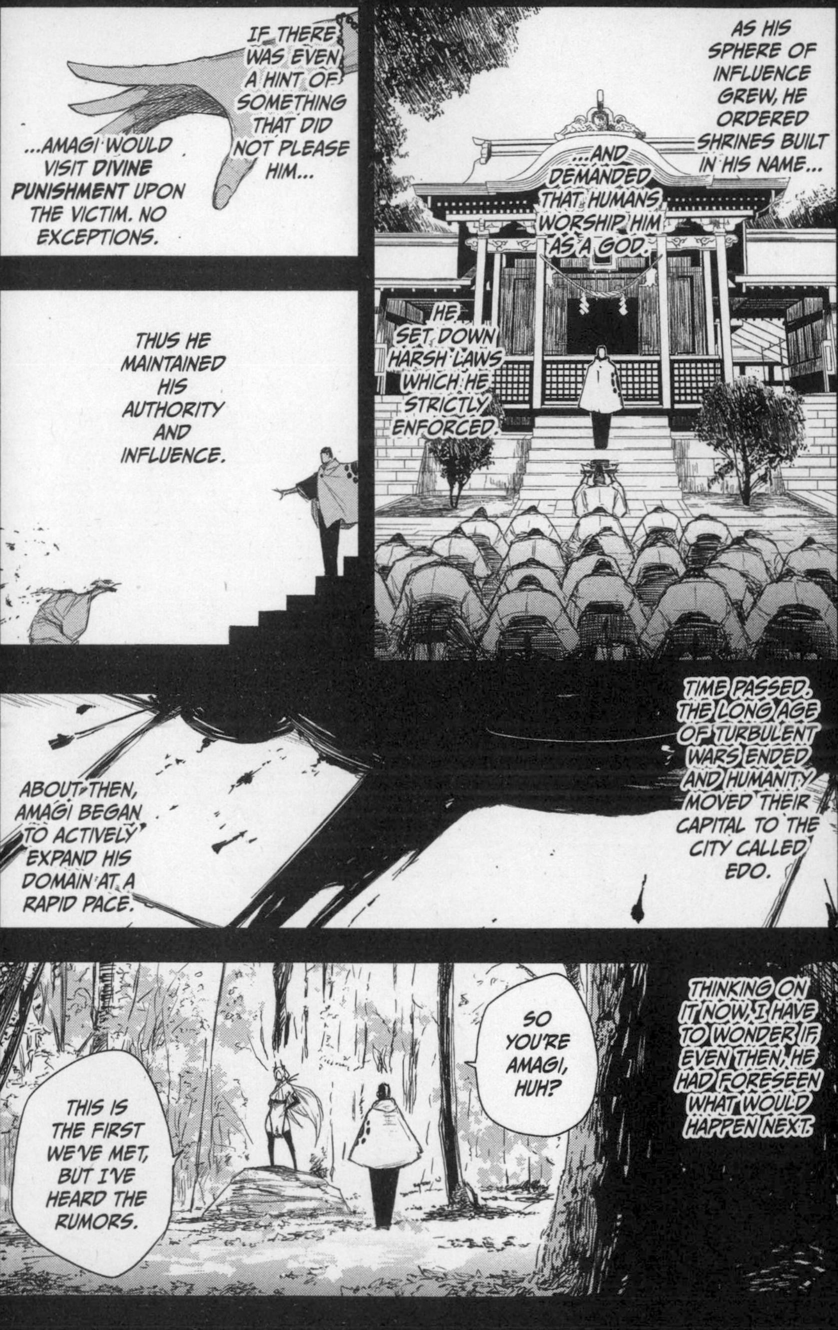
AS HIS SPHERE OF INFLUENCE GREW, HE ORDERED SHRINES BUILT IN HIS NAME...
...AND DEMANDED THAT HUMANS WORSHIP HIM AS A GOD.
HE SET DOWN HARSH LAWS WHICH HE STRICTLY ENFORCED.
IF THERE WAS EVEN A HINT OF SOMETHING THAT DID NOT PLEASE HIM...
...AMAGI WOULD VISIT DIVINE PUNISHMENT UPON THE VICTIM. NO EXCEPTIONS.
THUS HE MAINTAINED HIS AUTHORITY AND INFLUENCE.
TIME PASSED. THE LONG AGE OF TURBULENT WARS ENDED AND HUMANITY MOVED THEIR CAPITAL TO THE CITY CALLED EDO.
ABOUT THEN, AMAGI BEGAN TO ACTIVELY EXPAND HIS DOMAIN AT A RAPID PACE.
THINKING ON IT NOW, I HAVE TO WONDER IF, EVEN THEN, HE HAD FORESEEN WHAT WOULD HAPPEN NEXT.
SO YOU'RE AMAGI, HUH?
THIS IS THE FIRST WE'VE MET, BUT I'VE HEARD THE RUMORS.

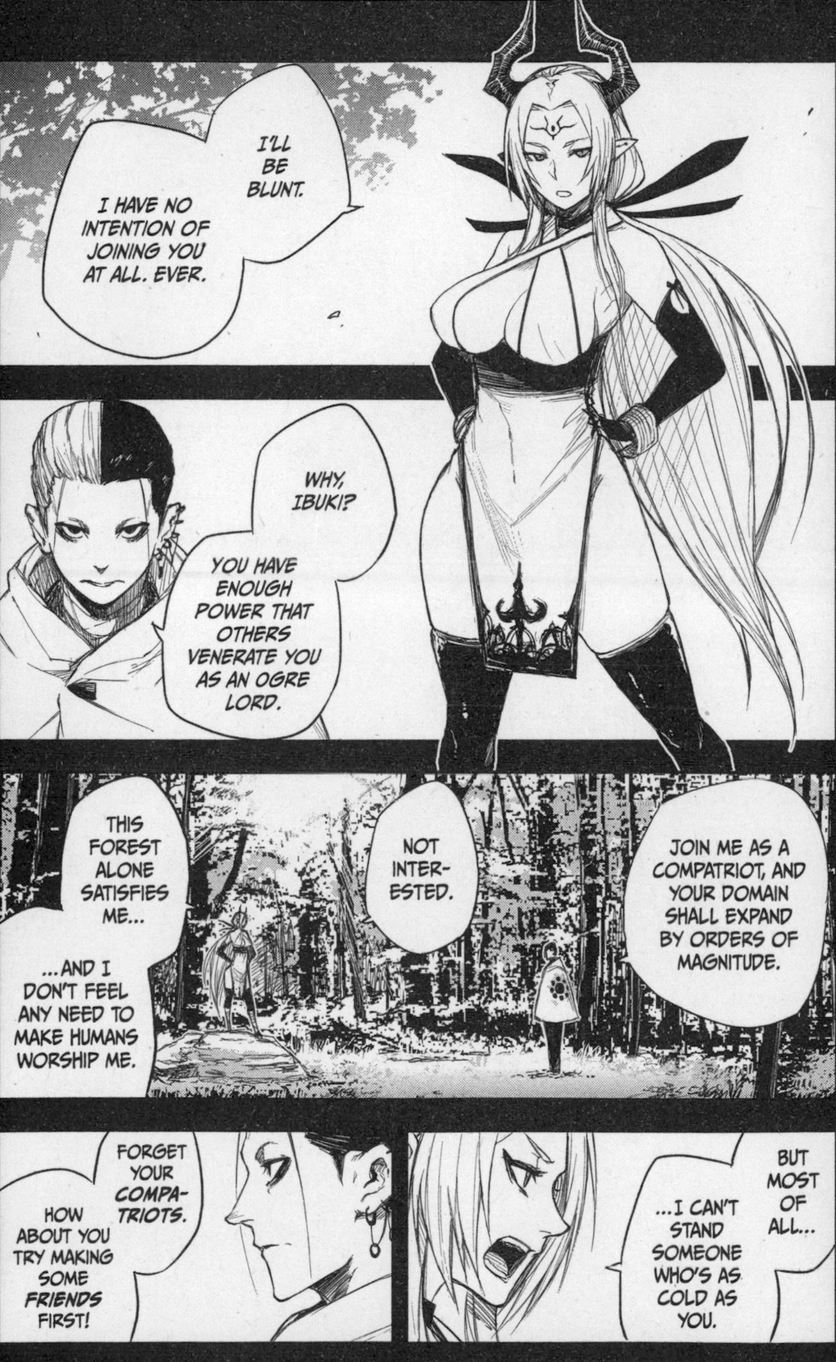
I'LL BE BLUNT.
I HAVE NO INTENTION OF JOINING YOU AT ALL. EVER.
WHY, IBUKI?
YOU HAVE ENOUGH POWER THAT OTHERS VENERATE YOU AS AN OGRE LORD.
JOIN ME AS A COMPATRIOT, AND YOUR DOMAIN SHALL EXPAND BY ORDERS OF MAGNITUDE.
NOT INTER-ESTED.
THIS FOREST ALONE SATISFIES ME...
...AND I DON'T FEEL ANY NEED TO MAKE HUMANS WORSHIP ME.
BUT MOST OF ALL...
...I CAN'T STAND SOMEONE WHO'S AS COLD AS YOU.
FORGET YOUR COMPA-TRIOTS.
HOW ABOUT YOU TRY MAKING SOME FRIENDS FIRST!

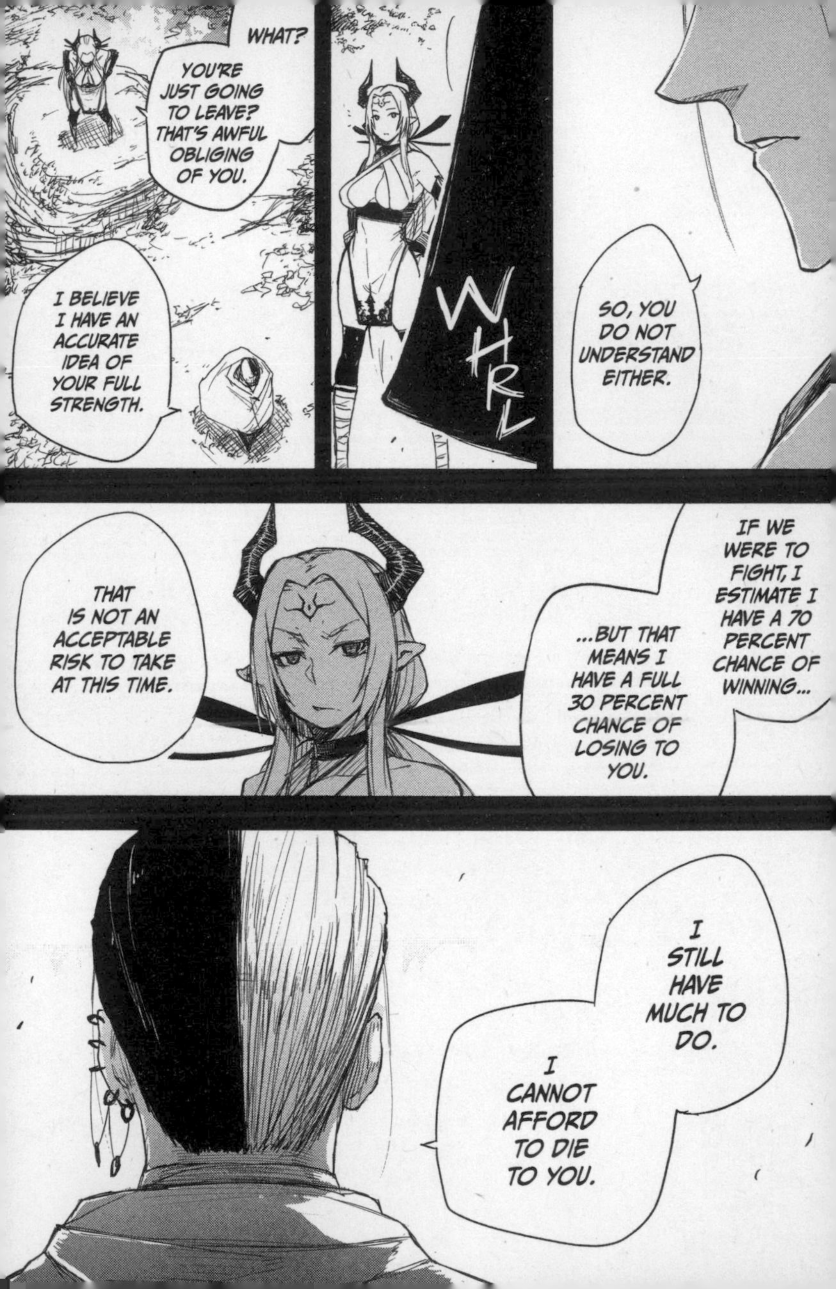
SO, YOU DO NOT UNDERSTAND EITHER.
WHRL
WHAT?
YOU'RE JUST GOING TO LEAVE? THAT'S AWFUL OBLIGING OF YOU.
I BELIEVE I HAVE AN ACCURATE IDEA OF YOUR FULL STRENGTH.
IF WE WERE TO FIGHT, I ESTIMATE I HAVE A 70 PERCENT CHANCE OF WINNING...
...BUT THAT MEANS I HAVE A FULL 30 PERCENT CHANCE OF LOSING TO YOU.
THAT IS NOT AN ACCEPTABLE RISK TO TAKE AT THIS TIME.
I STILL HAVE MUCH TO DO.
I CANNOT AFFORD TO DIE TO YOU.

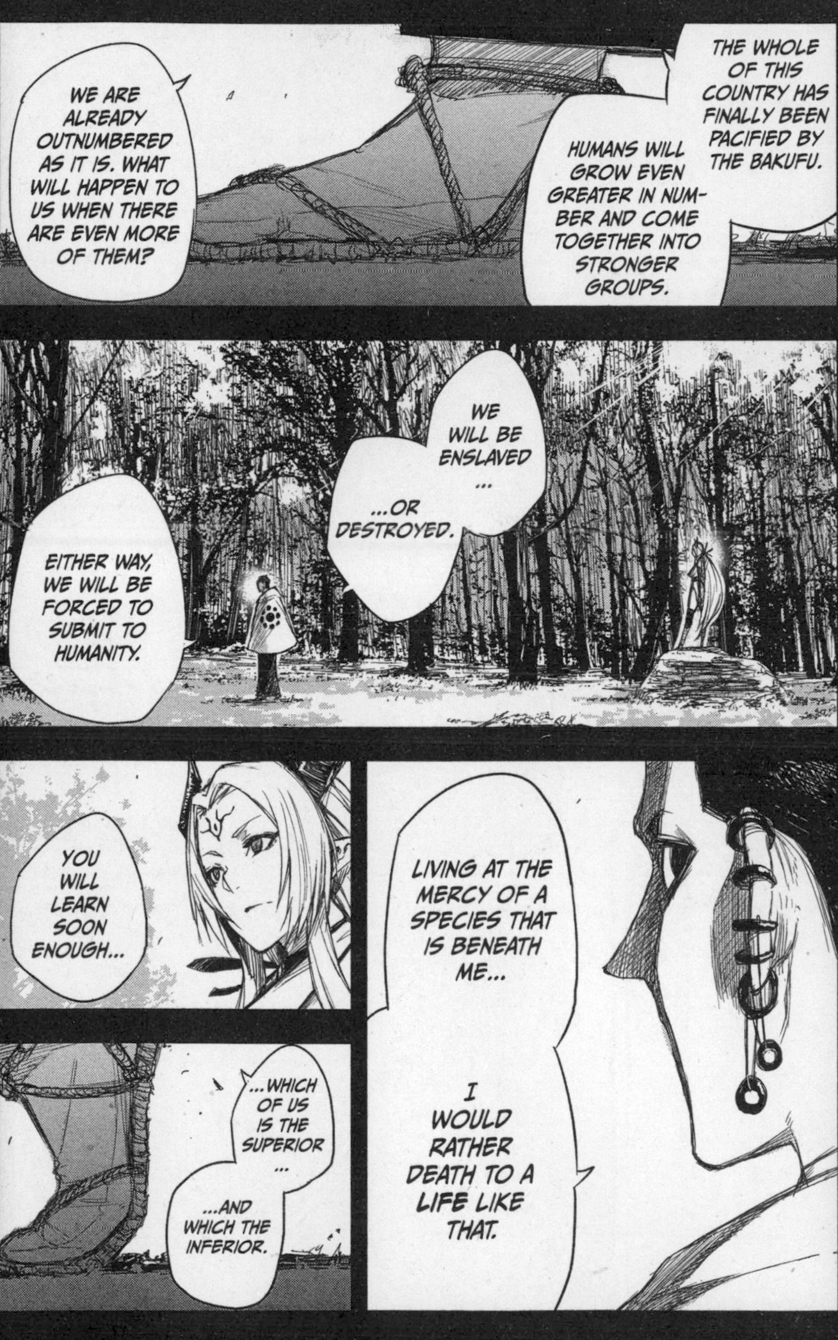
THE WHOLE OF THIS COUNTRY HAS FINALLY BEEN PACIFIED BY THE BAKUFU.
HUMANS WILL GROW EVEN GREATER IN NUMBER AND COME TOGETHER INTO STRONGER GROUPS.
WE ARE ALREADY OUTNUMBERED AS IT IS. WHAT WILL HAPPEN TO US WHEN THERE ARE EVEN MORE OF THEM?
WE WILL BE ENSLAVED ...
...OR DESTROYED.
EITHER WAY, WE WILL BE FORCED TO SUBMIT TO HUMANITY.
LIVING AT THE MERCY OF A SPECIES THAT IS BENEATH ME...
I WOULD RATHER DEATH TO A LIFE LIKE THAT.
YOU WILL LEARN SOON ENOUGH...
...WHICH OF US IS THE SUPERIOR ...
...AND WHICH THE INFERIOR.

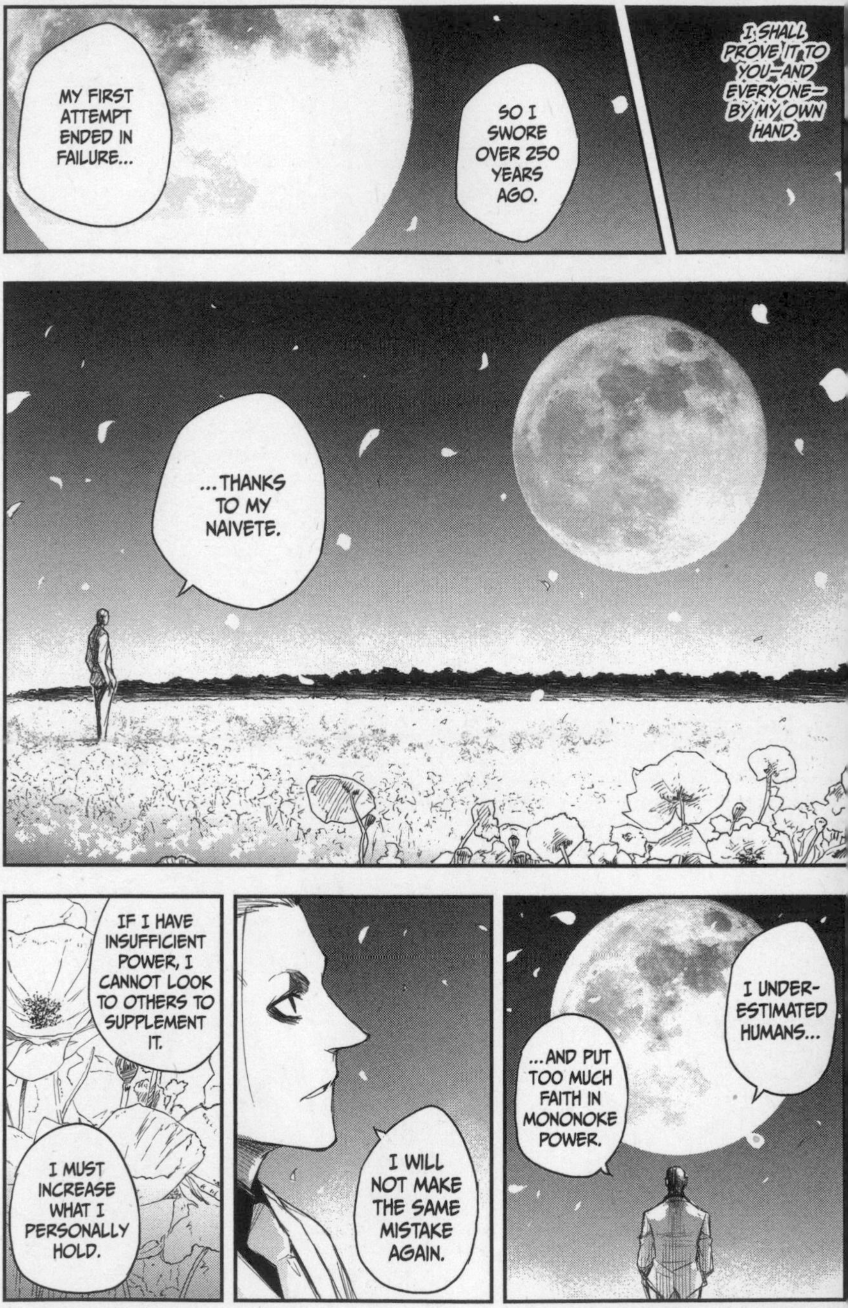
I SHALL PROVE IT TO YOU—AND EVERYONE—BY MY OWN HAND.
SO I SWORE OVER 250 YEARS AGO.
MY FIRST ATTEMPT ENDED IN FAILURE...
...THANKS TO MY NAIVETE.
I UNDER-ESTIMATED HUMANS...
...AND PUT TOO MUCH FAITH IN MONONOKE POWER.
I WILL NOT MAKE THE SAME MISTAKE AGAIN.
IF I HAVE INSUFFICIENT POWER, I CANNOT LOOK TO OTHERS TO SUPPLEMENT IT.
I MUST INCREASE WHAT I PERSONALLY HOLD.

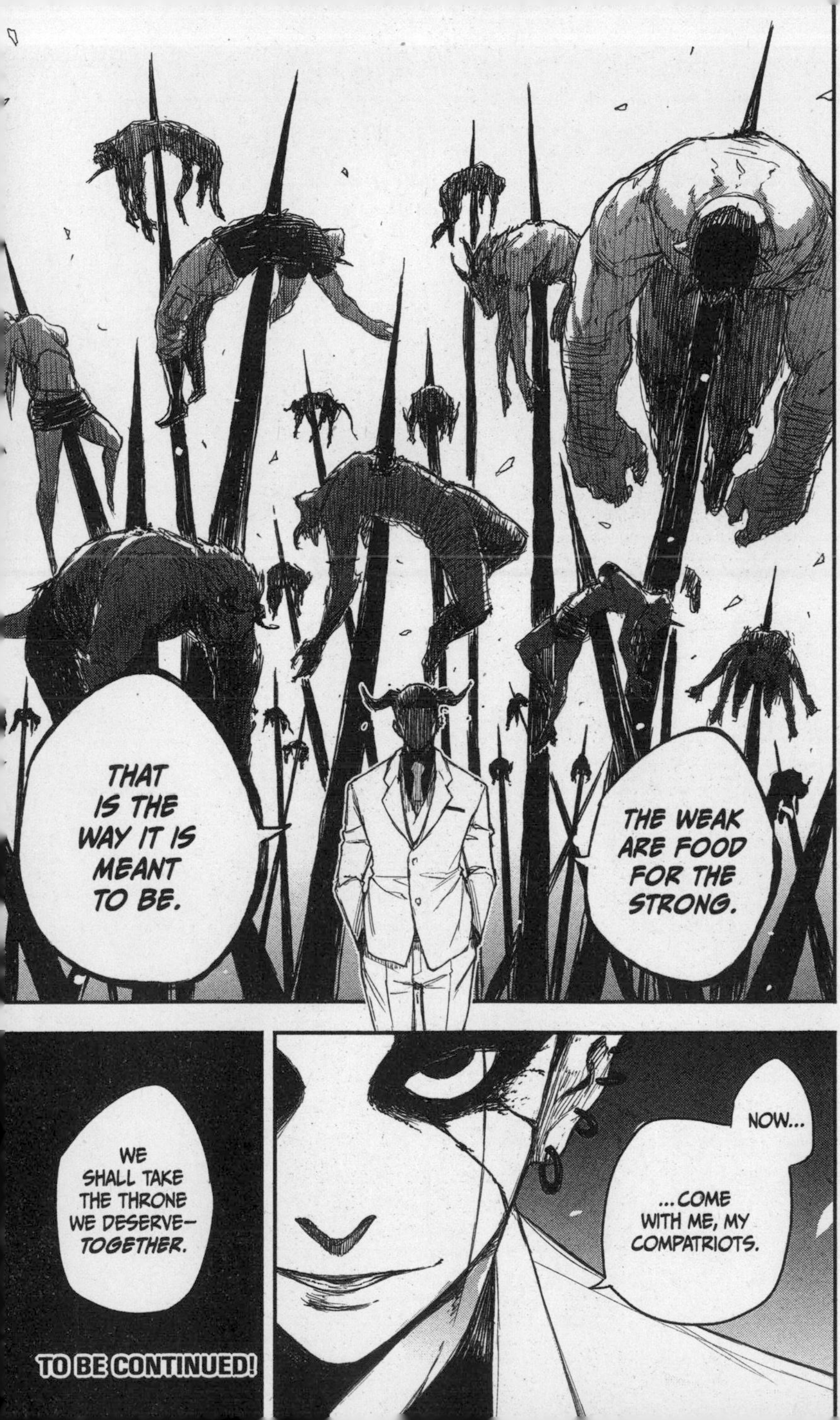
THE WEAK ARE FOOD FOR THE STRONG.
THAT IS THE WAY IT IS MEANT TO BE.
NOW...
...COME WITH ME, MY COMPATRIOTS.
WE SHALL TAKE THE THRONE WE DESERVE—TOGETHER.
TO BE CONTINUED!

REIJI'S HOSPITAL STAY

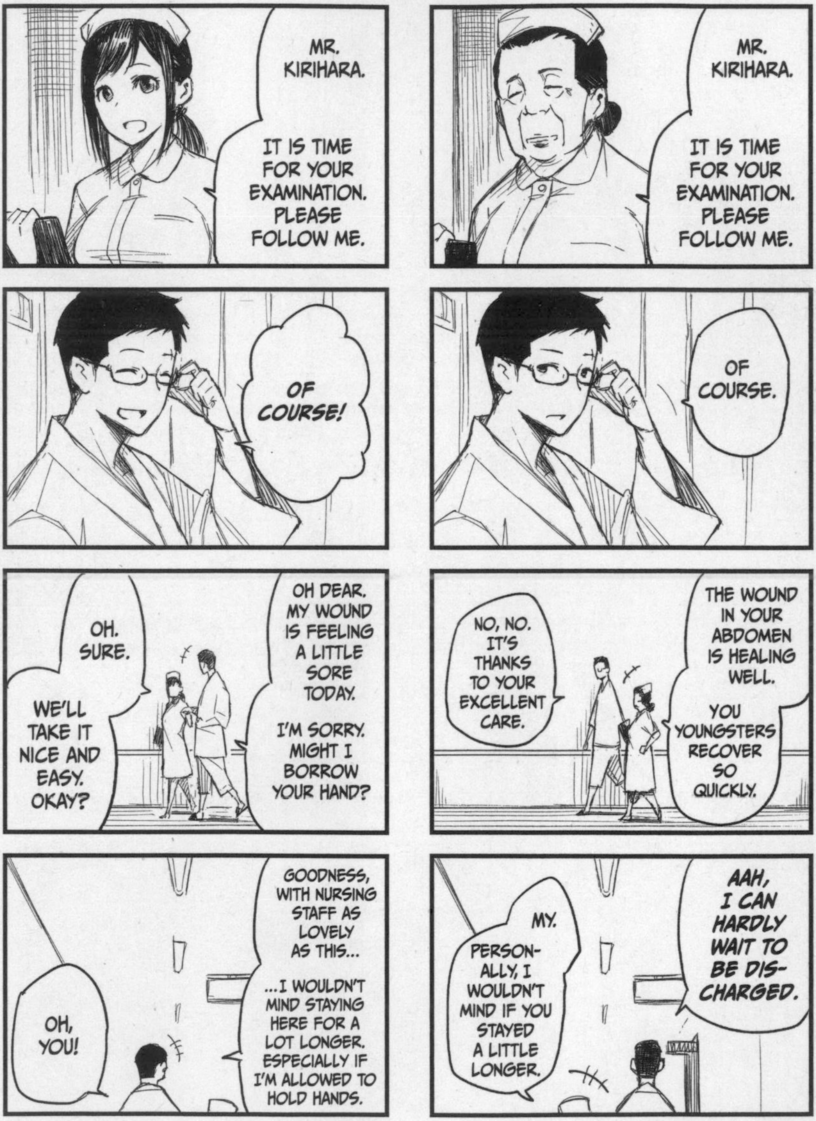

MR. KIRIHARA.
IT IS TIME FOR YOUR EXAMINATION. PLEASE FOLLOW ME.
OF COURSE.
THE WOUND IN YOUR ABDOMEN IS HEALING WELL.
YOU YOUNGSTERS RECOVER SO QUICKLY.
NO, NO. IT'S THANKS TO YOUR EXCELLENT CARE.
AAH, I CAN HARDLY WAIT TO BE DIS-CHARGED.
MY.
PERSON-ALLY, I WOULDN'T MIND IF YOU STAYED A LITTLE LONGER.
MR. KIRIHARA.
IT IS TIME FOR YOUR EXAMINATION. PLEASE FOLLOW ME.
OF COURSE!
OH DEAR. MY WOUND IS FEELING A LITTLE SORE TODAY.
I'M SORRY. MIGHT I BORROW YOUR HAND?
OH. SURE.
WE'LL TAKE IT NICE AND EASY. OKAY?
GOODNESS, WITH NURSING STAFF AS LOVELY AS THIS...
...I WOULDN'T MIND STAYING HERE FOR A LOT LONGER. ESPECIALLY IF I'M ALLOWED TO HOLD HANDS.
OH, YOU!

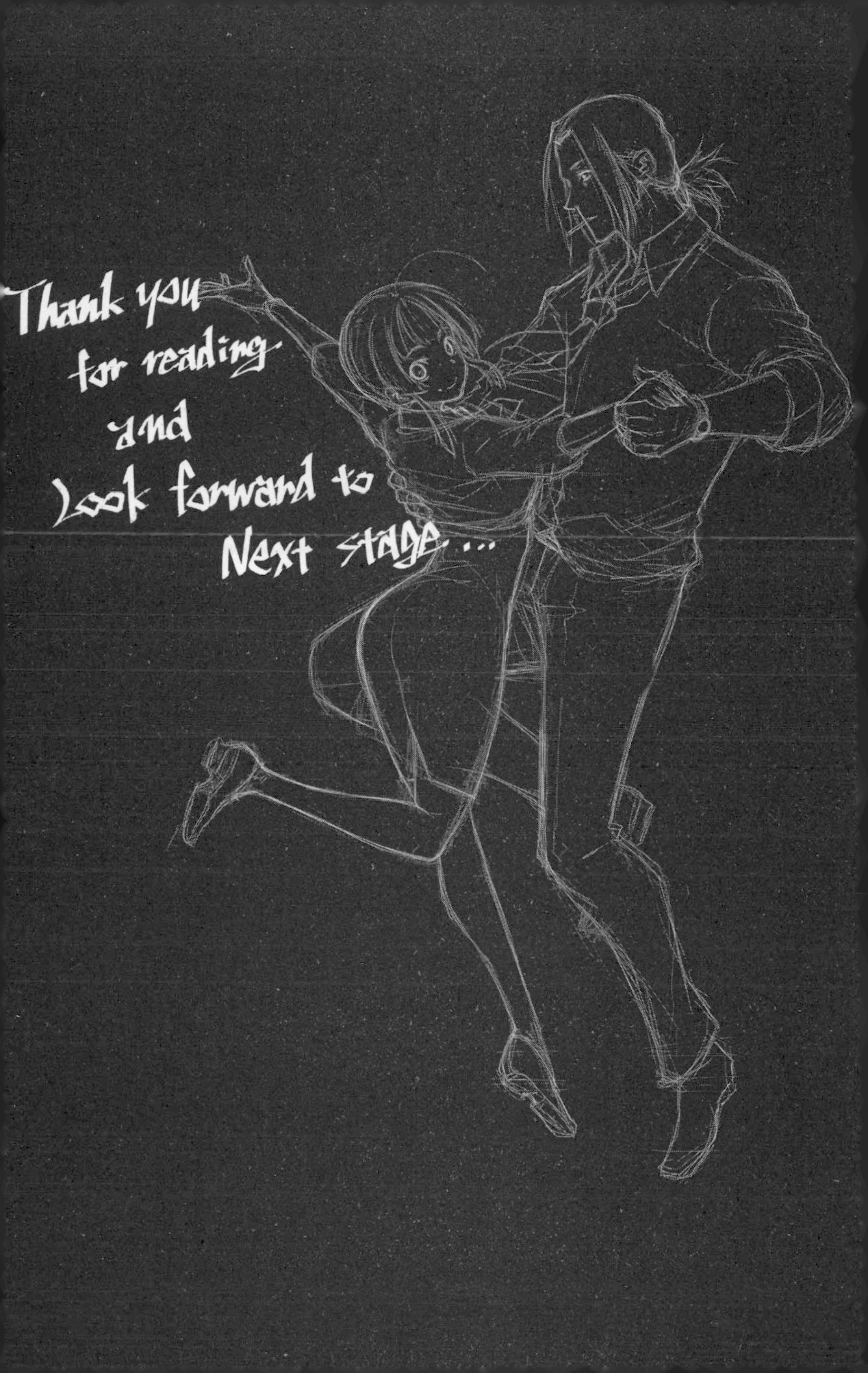
Thank you
for reading
and
Look forward to
Next stage...

POORLY WRITTEN AFTERWORD!

THANK YOU FOR MAKING YOUR WAY TO THE END OF THE BOOK! I'M TAKAKI.

WELL THEN, I THINK I'LL MAKE THE TOPIC OF THIS AFTERWORD THE CHARACTERS' NAMES.

TO BE HONEST, I DIDN'T REALLY MAKE THAT BIG A DEAL OUT OF NAMING THEM. THOUGH OF COURSE I DID HAVE A FEW REASONS FOR PICKING THE NAME "JIRO AZUMA" FOR THE MAIN CHARACTER. THERE'S FRENCH CARTOONIST "MOEBIUS" JEAN GIRAUD (WHICH SOUNDS LIKE "JIRO" IN JAPANESE), PROFESSOR JIRO UEDA FROM THE MOVIE *TRICK*, ACTOR JIRO SATO... AND MANY OTHERS.

BASICALLY, I JUST REALLY LIKE THE NAME JIRO, SO IT MADE COMPLETE SENSE TO ME TO NAME MY MAIN CHARACTER JIRO. I GOT HIS LAST NAME, AZUMA, FROM THE MAIN CHARACTER OF THE BEAT TAKESHI FILM, *VIOLENT COP*.

AS FOR ICHIKA AND REIJI—JIRO'S NAME HAS THE CHARACTER FOR "TWO," IN IT, SO I WAS LIKE "MEH, I'LL JUST USE 1 (ICHI) AND 0 (REI) FOR THEIR NAMES, I GUESS." ICHIKA. REIJI. I'M SORRY YOUR CREATOR IS SO LAZY.

AS FOR EVERYONE ELSE, I PICKED NAMES THAT JUST KINDA SEEMED TO FIT THEM WHILE STILL SOUNDING KINDA LIKE ACTUAL PEOPLE'S NAMES. A FRIEND OF MINE ONCE TOLD ME THAT "RAGO" AND "KISHIMOJIN" SOUNDED REALLY OUTLANDISH, BUT NEITHER IS A MADE-UP NAME. BOTH ARE ACTUAL NAMES USED IN REAL LIFE. (RAGO IS JAPANESE FOR THE HINDU DEITY RAHU, AND KISHIMOJIN IS THE JAPANESE FOR THE BUDDHIST DEITY HARITI.) I DID A LITTLE RESEARCH AND THERE IS ACTUALLY A FAMILY WITH KISHIMOJIN FOR A LAST NAME OUT THERE. THAT IS SO COOL.

ANYWAY, THAT'S HOW I CAME UP WITH ALL THE NAMES FOR THE CAST OF THIS SERIES. THOUGH TO ME, I KINDA FEEL LIKE THEY DON'T REALLY BECOME CHARACTERS UNTIL YOU READERS TAKE THE NAMES I'VE GIVEN THEM AND ATTACH THEM TO THE FACES I'VE DRAWN FOR THEM.

AND, AS ALWAYS, NOW THAT I'VE STARTED RAMBLING I THINK IT'S TIME I FINISHED UP.

I HOPE TO SEE YOU IN THE NEXT VOLUME!

Tsuyoshi Takaki

Photo shoot for cover illustration.

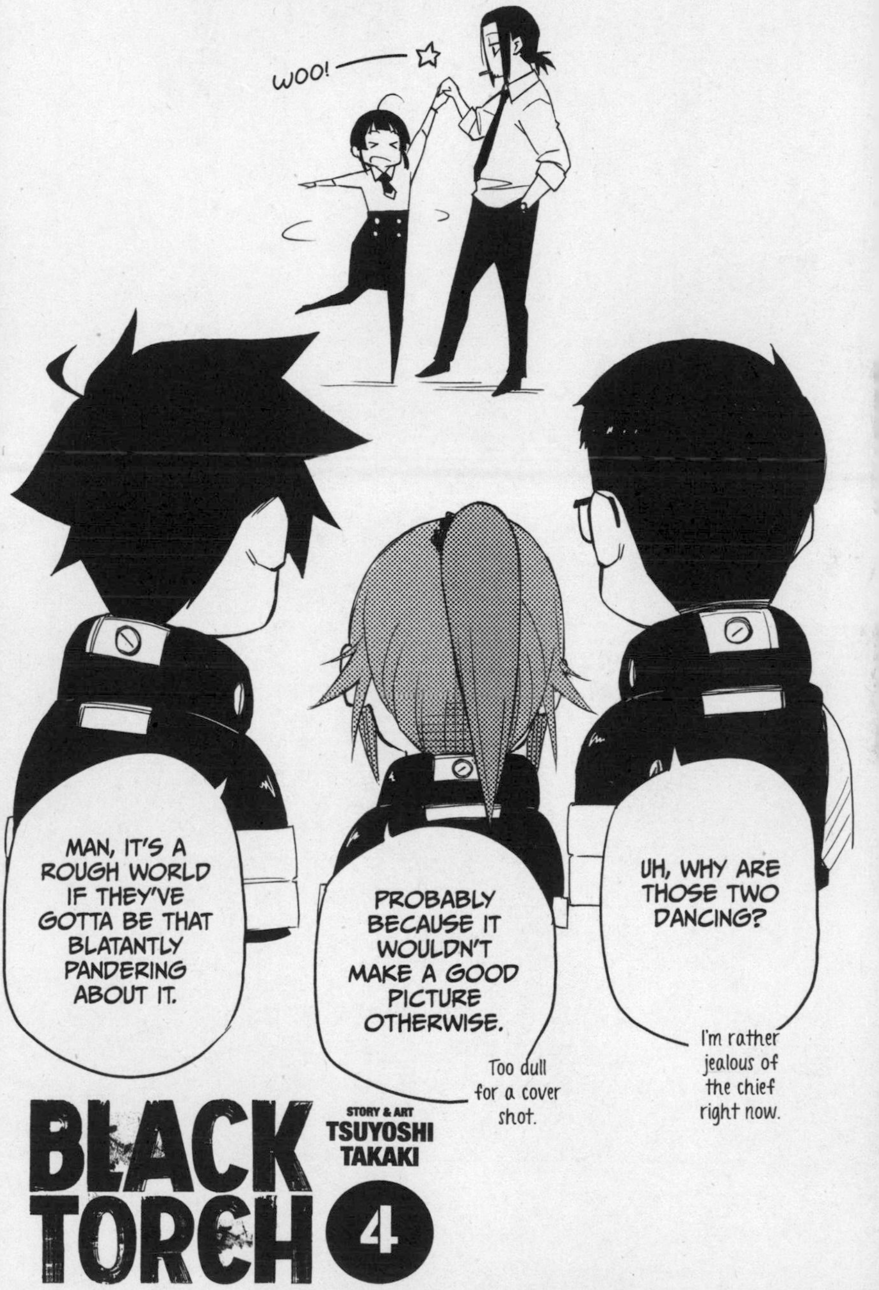
WOO!
UH, WHY ARE THOSE TWO DANCING?
I'm rather jealous of the chief right now.
PROBABLY BECAUSE IT WOULDN'T MAKE A GOOD PICTURE OTHERWISE.
Too dull for a cover shot.
MAN, IT'S A ROUGH WORLD IF THEY'VE GOTTA BE THAT BLATANTLY PANDERING ABOUT IT.

BLACK TORCH 4

STORY & ART
TSUYOSHI TAKAKI

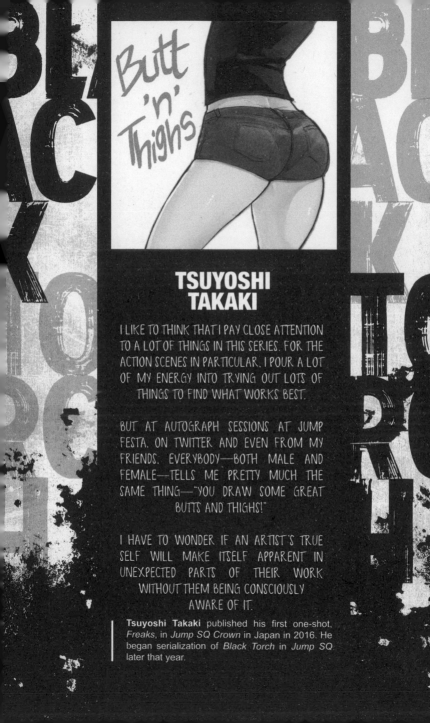

TSUYOSHI TAKAKI

I LIKE TO THINK THAT I PAY CLOSE ATTENTION TO A LOT OF THINGS IN THIS SERIES. FOR THE ACTION SCENES IN PARTICULAR, I POUR A LOT OF MY ENERGY INTO TRYING OUT LOTS OF THINGS TO FIND WHAT WORKS BEST.

BUT AT AUTOGRAPH SESSIONS AT JUMP FESTA, ON TWITTER AND EVEN FROM MY FRIENDS, EVERYBODY—BOTH MALE AND FEMALE—TELLS ME PRETTY MUCH THE SAME THING—"YOU DRAW SOME GREAT BUTTS AND THIGHS!"

I HAVE TO WONDER IF AN ARTIST'S TRUE SELF WILL MAKE ITSELF APPARENT IN UNEXPECTED PARTS OF THEIR WORK WITHOUT THEM BEING CONSCIOUSLY AWARE OF IT.

Tsuyoshi Takaki published his first one-shot, *Freaks*, in *Jump SQ Crown* in Japan in 2016. He began serialization of *Black Torch* in *Jump SQ* later that year.

BLACK TORCH

VOLUME 4

SHONEN JUMP Manga Edition

STORY AND ART BY **TSUYOSHI TAKAKI**

Translation/Adrienne Beck
Touch-Up Art & Lettering/Annaliese Christman
Design/Julian [JR] Robinson
Editor/Marlene First

BLACK TORCH © 2016 by Tsuyoshi Takaki
All rights reserved. First published in Japan in 2016 by
SHUEISHA Inc., Tokyo. English translation rights arranged by
SHUEISHA Inc.

The stories, characters and incidents mentioned in this
publication are entirely fictional.

Published by VIZ Media, LLC
P.O. Box 77010
San Francisco, CA 94107

Printed in the U.S.A.

10 9 8 7 6 5 4 3 2 1
First printing, May 2019

viz.com

shonenjump.com

Black ✦ Clover

STORY & ART BY YŪKI TABATA

Asta is a young boy who dreams of becoming the greatest mage in the kingdom. Only one problem—he can't use any magic! Luckily for Asta, he receives the incredibly rare five-leaf clover grimoire that gives him the power of anti-magic. Can someone who can't use magic really become the Wizard King? One thing's for sure—Asta will never give up!

www.viz.com

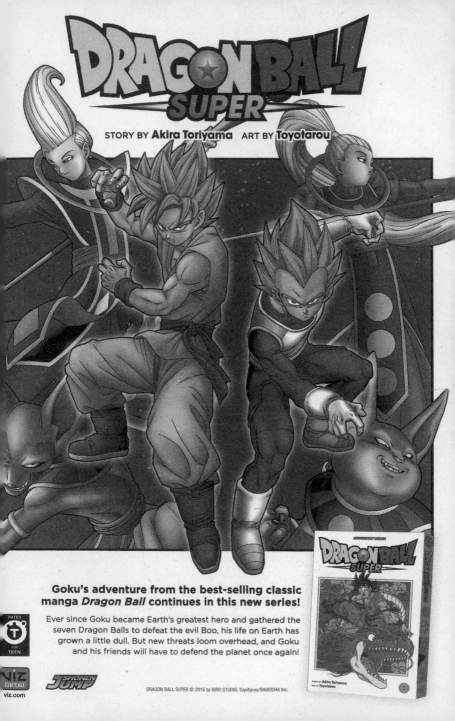

YOU ARE READING THE WRONG WAY

Black Torch reads from right to left, starting in the upper-right corner. Japanese is read from right to left, meaning that action, sound effects, and word-balloon order are completely reversed from English order.

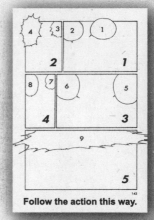

Follow the action this way.